Public Relations Writing

Public Relations Writing

THIRD EDITION

JAMES MAHONEY

OXFORD UNIVERSITY PRESS
AUSTRALIA & NEW ZEALAND

OXFORD
UNIVERSITY PRESS

Oxford University Press is a department of the University of Oxford.

It furthers the University's objective of excellence in research, scholarship, and education by publishing worldwide. Oxford is a registered trademark of Oxford University Press in the UK and in certain other countries.

Published in Australia by
Oxford University Press
253 Normanby Road, South Melbourne, Victoria 3205, Australia

© James Mahoney 2017

The moral rights of the author have been asserted.

First edition published 2008

Second edition published 2013

Third edition published 2017

All rights reserved. No part of this publication may be reproduced, stored in a retrieval system, or transmitted, in any form or by any means, without the prior permission in writing of Oxford University Press, or as expressly permitted by law, by licence, or under terms agreed with the appropriate reprographics rights organisation. Enquiries concerning reproduction outside the scope of the above should be sent to the Rights Department, Oxford University Press, at the address above.

You must not circulate this work in any other form and you must impose this same condition on any acquirer.

National Library of Australia Cataloguing-in-Publication entry

    Creator: Mahoney, James Scott, 1947- author.

    Title: Public relations writing / James Mahoney.

    Edition: 3rd edition

    ISBN: 9780190304652 (paperback)

    Notes: Includes bibliographical references and index.

    Subjects: Public relations–Australia.

    Written communication–Australia.

    Business communication–Australia.

    Interpersonal communication–Australia.

Reproduction and communication for educational purposes
The Australian *Copyright Act 1968* (the Act) allows a maximum of one chapter or 10% of the pages of this work, whichever is the greater, to be reproduced and/or communicated by any educational institution for its educational purposes provided that the educational institution (or the body that administers it) has given a remuneration notice to Copyright Agency Limited (CAL) under the Act.

For details of the CAL licence for educational institutions contact:

Copyright Agency Limited
Level 11, 66 Goulburn Street
Sydney NSW 2000
Telephone: (02) 9394 7600
Facsimile: (02) 9394 7601
Email: info@copyright.com.au
Edited by Liz Filleul
Text design by Jennai Lee Fai
Typeset by Newgen KnowledgeWorks Pvt. Ltd., Chennai, India
Indexed by Jeanne Rudd
Printed in China by Leo Paper Products Ltd.

Links to third party websites are provided by Oxford in good faith and for information only. Oxford disclaims any responsibility for the materials contained in any third party website referenced in this work.

FOREWORD TO THE THIRD EDITION

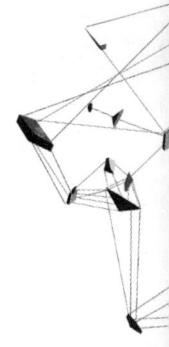

Imagine this. You are about to employ a new public relations graduate. She understands all of the latest technologies. She is a whiz at research. She is on a first name basis with every journo in town. She understands the most modern methods of evaluation, and her organisational skills are second to none. But then you find out she has a gap in her skill set—she can't write. Would you still give her a job?

When James Mahoney first said he was writing a book about writing for public relations, a collective sigh of relief was heard from senior PR professionals. What used to be the most treasured talent of the PR practitioner is now often relegated to the bottom of the list when the modern professional tallies all of the skills required to perform their craft.

Now in its third edition, *Public Relations Writing* continues to focus on one of our profession's most important essentials – the ability to write clearly, simply and in a way that imparts meaning to the audience.

James is a passionate advocate of the art of writing. Not the beautifully crafted writing of our literary masters or the verbose offerings of some of our community leaders, but the artistry of writers who send a message with their words. Clear, precise, active and ethical. Simplicity is the key.

What I particularly like about this text is that it applies this skill across the full range of writing tasks required by the modern public relations practitioner. Whether you need to write a strategy or a blog, a speech or a media release, you will find the answers here.

Oh, and would I employ that graduate who can't write? At the very least I would make sure she studied this book first.

Tracy Jones
Life Fellow and former National President
Public Relations Institute of Australia

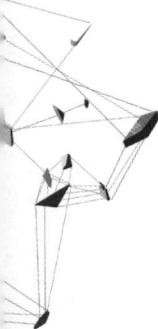

CONTENTS

Tables and figures	xi
Using this book	xii
Acknowledgments	xvii
Public relations toolkit	xviii

1 INTRODUCTION — 1

About public relations jobs — 3
Public relations activities have a clear, strategic purpose — 7
Clear, effective writing and the importance of grammar, spelling and style — 9
An introduction to public relations terminology — 13
Planning the details — 15
Tip sheet: The importance of language — *18*

2 CONTEXTS FOR PUBLIC RELATIONS — 22

Public relations as a strategic function — 22
Public relations and environmental scanning — 23
Listening to target publics — 25
Identifying and analysing issues — 26
Keeping on track — 29
Linking public relations to corporate strategic plans — 30
Contribution to organisational decision-making — 32
Linking public relations to a strategic business plan — 33
Public relations and management — 33
Building relationships with senior executives — 35
Building, maintaining and enhancing relationships with target publics — 36
Theory in practice — 38
Tip sheet: Matching theory to pathways and public relations tools — *43*

CONTENTS

3 RESEARCH AND PLANNING FOR PUBLIC RELATIONS — 47

About public relations strategy — 47
Research for public relations — 49
Identifying communication issues and needs — 55
How writing a situation analysis helps to set the context for the plan — 56
Writing a situation analysis — 58
Tip sheet: Multicultural communication — *63*

4 PUBLIC RELATIONS GOALS AND OBJECTIVES — 66

A public relations matrix — 66
Public relations consultants — 68
Meaningful goals and objectives — 69
What are goals? — 69
What are objectives? — 70
Matching goals and objectives — 71
Setting goals that reflect issues and communication needs — 71
Writing measurable objectives that pursue goals — 72
Target publics — 73
Why 'general public' doesn't work — 75
Journalists and the news media as target publics — 76
Tip sheet: How theories can inform practice — *80*

5 DEVELOPING AND WRITING MESSAGES — 87

The importance of messages — 87
Messages need to be relevant — 88
A caution about messages — 89
Messages, communication pathways and tools — 90
How many messages? — 90
Informative messages — 91
Persuasive messages — 92
Matching messages to goals and objectives — 95
Are messages relevant to selected target publics? — 96
Establishing appropriate communication pathways — 98
Identifying effective tools to deliver messages to target publics — 100

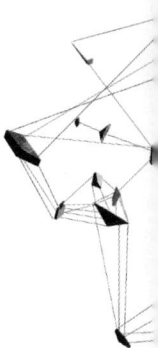

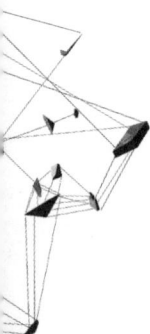

CONTENTS

6 WRITING AND PLACING A MEDIA RELEASE — 107

About journalists — **107**
The Fourth Estate — **108**
Journalists as target publics — **109**
What happens to your media release after you've distributed it? — 110
Competition for news space — 111
The daily choice — 112
What is a media release? — **112**
What is a media kit? — 114
Understanding news — 115
Finding news: What news frames will make my release work? — 116
Writing a media release — 120
Using a template and 'Five Ws and H' — 121
The inverted pyramid — **122**
The news lead — 123
Which journalists will be interested in your release? — 128
Barriers to getting your media release published — 130
Tip sheet: Writing a media release — *134*
Tip sheet: Working with the news media — *136*

7 WRITING FOR SOCIAL MEDIA AND THE WEB — 146

Flexible tools — **146**
Using the internet — **150**
Reading material published on the internet — **150**
Standing out — **151**
Writing to an objective — **151**
Remember your readers — **153**
Concise, accurate copy — **153**
Headings — 154
Link material to other sources — 154
Using lists — 155
Using graphics, podcasts and videos — 155
Stick to the template — 155
Public relations and blogs — **156**
The power of email — **156**
Will I or won't I? — 157
Choosing the right tone — 157

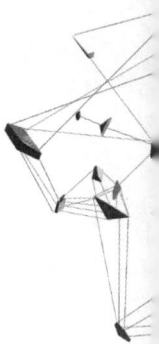

Precision and clarity always work	158
Treat recipients with respect	158
How important am I?	158
Attachments	158
Proofread	159
Privacy	159
Did social media kill PR?	**159**
Tip sheet: Social media usage	*165*
Tip sheet: Writing a video script	*174*

8 INTERPERSONAL COMMUNICATION 177

Blame the ancients	**177**
Speeches as a public relations tool	**178**
Planning a speech	**180**
Preparing a speech outline	182
Writing a speech draft	184
Preparing your speaker	187
After the speech	187
Presentations	**187**
Planning and writing a presentation	188
Exhibitions and trade shows	**188**

9 BEYOND THE MASS NEWS MEDIA 192

Building a matrix of PR tools	**192**
Deciding what tools for which task	**193**
About annual reports	**194**
Planning and writing brochures	**195**
Writing a backgrounder	197
Writing fact sheets	198
Writing talking points	199
Compiling a media kit	**200**
Newspaper features	**203**

10 COMMUNICATION WITHIN ORGANISATIONS 210

Principles of employee communication	**210**
Knowing the game plan	**211**

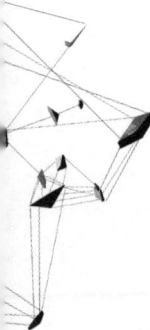

Preparing an employee communication plan	**213**
Staff newsletters	215
Meetings with employees	216
Email	218
Employee communication during change	**221**
Report writing	222
Writing a memo	222
Writing a file note	223
Writing a submission	223

11 GETTING THE JOB DONE — 229

Flying by the seat of your pants	**229**
Project management	**230**
Using timelines	231
Writing a budget	232
Consultants' fees	234
Working with consultants	236
Briefing designers	237

12 WRITING A PUBLIC RELATIONS EVALUATION PLAN — 243

Why evaluate?	**243**
How is public relations evaluated?	**244**
Making an evaluation work	247
Writing an evaluation plan	250
Evaluating the public relations impact on organisational credibility	252
Evaluating response capability	**253**
Measuring the financial impact of public relations	**253**
Building a program evaluation	254

A Reflection	259
Glossary	261
References	267
Index	273

TABLES AND FIGURES

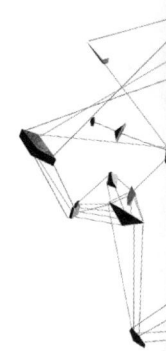

TABLES

Table 3.1	The elements of a public relations strategic plan	48
Table 4.1	Matrix of a corporate public relations program	67
Table 4.2	Hallahan's five classifications of target publics	75
Table 6.1	Definitions of some public relations tools for the news media	114

FIGURES

Figure 2.1	A basic organisational structure	34
Figure 2.2	Target public classification	40
Figure 4.1	Formula for writing objectives	72
Figure 5.1	Formula for writing a persuasive message	94
Figure 6.1	The inverted pyramid	122
Figure 12.1	Evaluating organisational credibility	252
Figure 12.2	Evaluating response capability	253

USING THIS BOOK

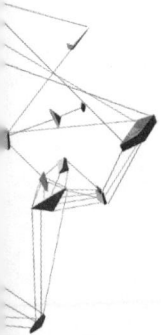

Clear, precise, active language is good for democracy and for society. Active language incites activity. It helps to establish trust between the governors and the governed and the managers and the managed. Honesty and good intentions and deceit and incompetence are more easily recognised.

Don Watson, 2003

What a strange way to begin a book about public relations writing. Watson's quote, from his book *Death Sentence: The Decay of Public Language*, doesn't deal with public relations at all. Yet that quote encapsulates what good public relations writing should be: clear, concise, inspiring, informative, active and ethical language. Beginning practitioners must write that way if they are to work successfully in contemporary public relations. Potential employers expect nothing less than highly competent professional writing from new and not-so-new employees, and often complain that public relations graduates do not know how to write. This is an important criticism to remember because journalism students (who one day you'll need to convince to use your material) begin to write news stories from the first week of their university studies. They know what 'news' is and they practise their craft of recognising and writing it daily. If you take nothing else away from this book, remember clear, precise, active and ethical.

So how might you use *Public Relations Writing* to develop those skills? This is a book about 'doing' public relations by using the different writing approaches needed for specific public relations tools. That approach is based on evidence that students learn best from experiential, or active, learning.

The book deals with public relations as an ethical and professional element of strategic organisational management. It encourages students to regard themselves as beginning practitioners who need to understand the social, economic, political and multicultural contexts in which they work. The book deals with writing from a professional practice perspective but refers where appropriate to relevant communication theories. It includes advice to help plan, write and implement communication pathways and public relations tools.

Also included are practical exercises for professional skills development that are rewarding, challenging, realistic and, sometimes, fun.

Academics will find readings, tutorial exercises and themes for lectures that can be adapted for public relations practice classes, especially units dedicated to public relations writing.

The chapter structure

Each chapter typically includes:

- a brief outline of the direction of the chapter
- *practice points* that highlight practical information
- *activities* to engage students in practical tasks related to points discussed in the text

- *practice notes* that expand on specific aspects of professional practice. This third edition has a new practice note that gives a media release writing and distribution checklist.
- *a thought on theory* panels that discuss communication theories relevant to the topic
- an end-of-chapter *summary*
- a *reflection* designed to help students to think through issues related to the chapter's topic; some deal with ethics
- a *practice task* involving writing exercises related to the primary focus of the chapter.

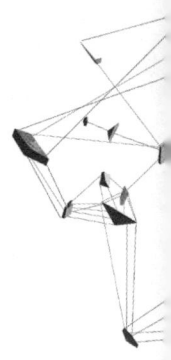

This book is grounded in the view that all public relations activity flows from a strategic plan that supports an organisation's business goals, so the chapter structure loosely follows the traditional outline of a public relations strategy. This approach recognises that effective writing is just as much about planning and evaluation as it is about e-newsletters, speechmaking, podcasting, media releases, report writing, displays, and planned, targeted tweeting. Rapid and continuing advances in the use of electronic technologies and gadgets for communication mean that for beginning practitioners, using today's 'new media' is second nature, but, like older practitioners have had to do, will also mean that maybe in in twelve months or less they'll need to learn new skills.

There is a seriously fundamental point here: technology and gadgets are fascinating and powerful tools, but they are just that, and successful professional public relations practice relies on far more than tweeting, blogging and Facebook posting. Professional practice needs people who can effectively use all this technology, but they need to do it within the context of a strategic plan while adhering to the fundamental principle—the central theme of the book—that clear, concise and accurate writing is essential for all public relations tools. That principle applies whether messages are sent via the net, SMS, a corporate video, social media applications, or a stock-standard hard-copy media release. Learning to use the technology is not the purpose of this book; learning to write for that technology is.

Tip sheets

Tip sheets—a traditional public relations tool used to alert journalists to possible news stories—have been included on topics like: the importance of language; multicultural communication; writing a media release; social media writing tips; working with the news media; and writing a video script. There's a tip sheet that links some major theories underpinning public relations with professional practice. Another matches theory to communication pathways and public relations tools. The tip sheet on writing a media release uses a real example produced as part of a student exercise that has been marked up to demonstrate how the public relations writing principles discussed in this book were applied. The media release format used in this book is in the classic style of journalists writing news stories. Examples of other media release formats are available online at Oxford Ascend.

International examples

Cases and examples from Canada, New Zealand, Hong Kong, South Africa, Thailand and the United States have been included to demonstrate how public relations writing and practice is applied in

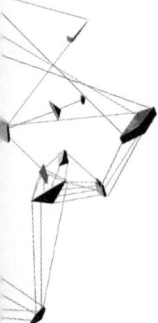

diverse contexts. Some chapter exercises in the book use these international examples, but the situations they describe are not necessarily real. The point of them is to show that public relations principles are universal and are used to address issues in many contexts. Thus, for example, the issues posed for the Hong Kong Metro exercise may also affect a practitioner in New York, London, Paris, Sydney or Auckland—or locally, maybe in the context of a bus network.

Understanding context and strategy

The first five chapters deal with what practitioners do, why they do it and how this is linked to an organisation's business goals. These chapters outline professional terminology and discuss the basic concepts behind strategic public relations planning, and the importance of understanding the social, economic, political and cultural environments in which practitioners work. This, then, is context: understanding that an organisation is part of the wider world in which business competition is not the only factor to be considered in planning and implementing public relations activities.

Chapter 1: Introduction

This introductory chapter deals with:

- public relations as an integral element of an organisation's business strategy
- the need for public relations activities to have a clear purpose and to be part of a strategic plan
- clear, effective writing as an essential skill for practitioners
- public relations terminology and the importance of grammar, spelling and style.

Chapter 2: Contexts for Public Relations

This chapter discusses the contextual frameworks for professional practice by considering:

- public relations as a strategic management tool
- relationships with senior managers and target publics
- environmental scanning
- legal and ethical frameworks.

Chapter 3: Research and Planning for Public Relations

The role of research in public relations strategic planning is covered by considering questions such as:

- the importance of strategic planning to public relations practice
- the role of research in public relations planning
- how to identify communication issues facing an organisation
- how to write a situation analysis.

Chapter 4: Public Relations Goals and Objectives

This chapter deals with key aspects of strategic public relations planning, such as:

- how to write communication goals and objectives
- the importance of identifying target publics for a public relations program.

Chapter 5: Developing and Writing Messages

This chapter covers crucial steps in strategic planning such as:

- developing and writing informative and persuasive messages
- matching messages to target publics, goals and objectives
- establishing appropriate communication pathways
- identifying effective public relations tools to deliver messages to target publics.

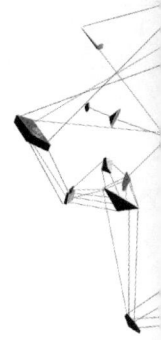

Writing for professional practice

Chapters 6–12 deal with the day-to-day writing tasks of professional practice.

Chapter 6: Writing and Placing a Media Release

This chapter recognises that writing for the mass media is still a required skill for public relations practitioners. It examines:

- why it is important to be clear about what you mean by the term *media*
- what media tools are, and how they are used
- the news process
- how to identify 'news'
- how to write and distribute a media release.

Chapter 7: Writing for Social Media and the Web

The goal of this chapter is to help you to understand how public relations *tools* can be adapted, or written specifically, for web and social media applications. It examines:

- how to adapt your writing to the needs of social media
- the importance of public relations tools that use web and social media applications.

Chapter 8: Interpersonal Communication

This chapter focuses on:

- the basic principles of writing a speech
- the roles of informative and persuasive communication in interpersonal communication
- how presentations are used to advance clients' messages.

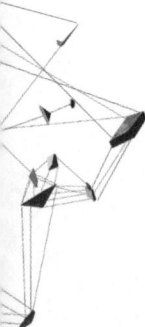

Chapter 9: Beyond the Mass News Media

This chapter explores the breadth of public relations practice, beyond media relations and tactical social media use. It will help you to:

- recognise the breadth of material that public relations writers produce
- understand the need to adapt your writing style to different formats
- appreciate how public relations tools are linked together to implement communication pathways.

Chapter 10: Communication within Organisations

This chapter covers the essential role of in-house public relations staff and external consultants in employee communication by examining:

- how communication pathways are used in employee communication
- the tools used to communicate with employees
- internal report writing.

Chapter 11: Getting the Job Done

Practitioners need to work with other specialists to implement public relations projects. This chapter deals with:

- project management
- building knowledge of production processes
- writing a brief for contractors.

Chapter 12: Writing a Public Relations Evaluation Plan

This brief final chapter stresses the importance of evaluating public relations activity against agreed goals and objectives. The way a PR strategy will be evaluated needs to be written into a strategy document, so this chapter addresses questions such as:

- Why evaluate?
- Were goals and objectives actually achieved?
- Did the messages, pathways and tools work?
- What can be done better next time?

The Toolkit

The resources provided in the toolkit at the beginning of this book are used in the *activities* and *practice tasks* as examples of the tools practitioners use to research and plan for public relations strategy and to write and implement tools. Additional resources are available online at Oxford Ascend.

ACKNOWLEDGMENTS

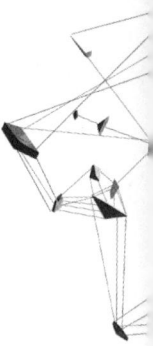

An Australian fan once asked the Irish-American larrikin and author Malachy McCourt to explain the title of his memoir *A Monk Swimming*, as the book didn't seem to be about either monks or swimming. McCourt replied that 'a monk swimming' was how, as a kid in Ireland, he had always heard the words 'amongst women' in the 'Ave Maria'. There was nothing more to the title than a writer's clever use of a misheard phrase. McCourt's issue with the clarity of a prayerful chant became a subconscious gauge for a major theme of this book: the need for clear, precise and accurate writing in public relations. So, too, did the work of the Australian wordsmith Don Watson, who uses words as they are meant to be used and will not relent in his campaign to convince us to do the same. I am thankful to have had opportunities to hear and read their insights.

Karen Hildebrandt at Oxford University Press commissioned this third edition, but took on new responsibilities before the revision started. Karen has always encouraged this work. Shari Serjeant was a wonderfully supportive replacement who enthusiastically agreed to the additional tip sheets and other alterations to the book. Liz Filleul has been a magical editor. Liz's eagle eyes found inconsistencies in the text and, like the work of a good newspaper sub-editor, her subsequent changes were subtle and sensitive. I am grateful to Alex Chambers for co-ordinating the editing and production processes.

Textbooks are for students. I have been enormously heartened by the positive feedback on the earlier editions given by the beginning practitioners who have studied with me at the University of Canberra. That some use the book in their professional practice is a special form of positive feedback, indicating that they still find it useful in coming to grips with writing in a range of public relations contexts. And it is pleasing that others, whom I have not taught but who have used the book at university, have commented favourably on it, too. I have also appreciated the support of academic colleagues at other universities who continue to prescribe this book for their public relations classes. Many senior colleagues from professional practice have provided insights, comments and ideas for this third edition, and I thank them for their continued interest. I am delighted that Tracy Jones, one of Australia's leading public relations practitioners, has written the Foreword for this edition.

None of this would have happened without a supportive family. Thanks for that, especially my wife, Dr Janine Mahoney, who, as always, encourages these endeavours.

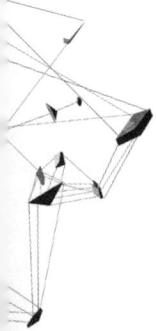

PUBLIC RELATIONS TOOLKIT

Introducing the toolkit

Successful and effective public relations work involves planning the logistics of a strategy as much as what you need to write. Thinking through, and writing down, the steps you need to follow to organise a special event, or to produce a webcast, means that you won't forget any important part of the process. Planning what you need to write in a media release means that you will include all the important points your client wants to make. Similarly, formative and summative research that you need for a situation analysis, or for an evaluation, needs to be scheduled so that it is conducted at the appropriate time, and you'll need some kind of technique for interpreting the results so that you can assess how they impact on your organisation.

Fortunately, there are some simple tools for planning all these things. Some of these tools are included in this kit to help you with some of the basic tasks in public relations planning and writing that are discussed in this book. The tools will help you to:

- analyse research to write strategic goals and objectives
- set out the steps you need to take to plan and implement an event
- develop the main points for a media release
- plan a speech
- write a video script.

> ### ■ PRACTICE NOTE USING THE TOOLKIT
>
> Many of the professional practice activities throughout the book refer to the tools that have been included in this toolkit.
>
> You can easily set these tools up using your word-processing software's table-formatting application. When you do that, each cell of the table will automatically expand as you add in new information. You can prepare a Gantt chart with your spreadsheet software.
>
> If you search the internet, you can find planning tools for time management, problem solving and decision-making, and detailed project planning software. These additional tools include formats for a 'force-field analysis' that enable you to identify the forces that help or hinder change proposals, or for a PEST analysis to identify the political, economic, socio-cultural and technological aspects of your market, or factors that impact on your organisation. Some electronic diary programs that you can use on your computer, or on your smartphone or tablet, also include applications that help with planning. So, too, do some paper-based diary systems.
>
> The media release and speech-planning worksheets in the toolkit are based on professional practice experience and the work of many other public relations scholars.

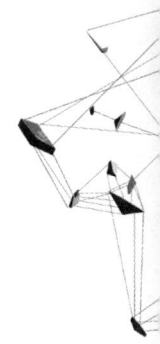

Time management

All practitioners are busy. The way they manage their time at work is vital for completing assignments on time and within budget. Good planning includes managing your work time effectively.

It is a good idea, then, to link your planning process with your diary. By doing that, you can block out the times you need to spend on writing, planning, in meetings with clients and colleagues, or making phone calls. Use the 'Task' or 'To Do List' function of your electronic or hard-copy diary to record the jobs you need to do each day. That might mean an entry like 'Prepare next week's work-in-progress agenda' or 'Write boss's speech outline'. That way you can keep track of what you need to do each day. If you use a laptop computer, smartphone or tablet—or all of them—upload copies of the planning tools you have prepared for each of your projects so that you have access to them when you travel, but make sure you always have access to the latest version on all your devices and regularly synchronise. And back up.

Timesheets

If you work in a public relations consultancy, you'll probably need to fill out a timesheet each day so that the company can invoice clients for the time you spend on their projects. Consultancies have their own timesheet formats, and you'll be briefed on these when you join the firm.

The planning worksheets

The planning worksheets in the toolkit for media releases and speeches are easy to use. Just answer the basic questions about your release or speech to help you cover all the points that should be included.

Adapt the worksheets for other purposes, like writing a backgrounder, fact sheet or brochure, or planning the text for a display or a podcast.

Strengths, weaknesses, opportunities and threats (SWOT) analysis

A SWOT analysis is a simple analytical tool that helps you to review formative research findings so that you can write a situation analysis, and goals and objectives, for a public relations strategy.

- *Strengths* are characteristics of the organisation that can help it to achieve its goals.
- *Weaknesses* are characteristics of the organisation that might harm its ability to achieve its goals.
- *Opportunities* are external conditions that will assist the organisation to achieve its goals.
- *Threats* are external conditions that could prevent the organisation from achieving its goals.

By setting out a SWOT analysis in a table, you can compare your assessments in each of the quadrants and work out, for example, which strengths you might use to overcome a possible market threat.

To use this tool, think about your organisation's strengths and weaknesses from an internal perspective, and opportunities and threats as external factors that will help or hinder what you are trying to do.

Ask realistic questions that will help you to set out the strengths, or good points, of your organisation (or its point of view on an issue) as well as the areas in which it could improve—its weaknesses. Do the same thing to identify external opportunities (perhaps an emerging market) and the things that may prevent you from doing what you plan—the weaknesses.

Write the answers down in a concise way in the relevant quadrants of the SWOT tool. You can then write goals that build on strengths, or minimise threats, or pursue opportunities, or deal with weaknesses.

Sometimes you might regard opportunities and threats as internal factors. For example, an organisation undergoing structural change might see that as an opportunity or, if the change process is generating industrial relations problems, as a weakness. As in many aspects of public relations, it is a good idea to be flexible in the way you use a SWOT analysis tool.

SWOT analysis tool

STRENGTHS	WEAKNESSES
OPPORTUNITIES	THREATS

Issues matrix

An issues matrix is a simple tool that can help you to work out the importance of issues that your organisation faces, and to identify those you need to focus on in strategic public relations planning. The matrix helps you to classify issues by the *impact* that they would have on your organisation, and by the *probability* that they will happen.

Generally, these classifications work in the following way.

Probability

- A *high-probability* issue is one that is happening now, or could happen in the next six months.
- A *medium-probability* issue is one that could happen between six months and a year from now.
- A *low-probability* issue is one that could happen in twelve months or later.

Impact

- A *high-impact* issue is one that is already having, or will have if it were to occur, a major effect on the organisation's operations or policies. That is, a high-impact issue is one that will disrupt operations, cause the organisation to make a major change to its policies, or result in some kind of crisis.
- A *medium-impact* issue is one that may have a significant effect on the organisation's operations or policies.
- A *low-impact* issue is one that will not have a significant impact on what the organisation does, but about which the organisation needs to be aware.

To identify the issues for your matrix, use the outcomes of your formal and informal research to make a list of up to thirty issues (there may not, of course, be that many—and there may be more) that your organisation either faces or could face in the next two years. Work with your team and other people in the organisation to classify them by *impact* and *probability*. Record the issues in the sections of the matrix that match your impact and probability classifications. Your organisation will mostly be focused on the issues that you enter into the sections that are highlighted by the light-grey shading.

For most organisations, an explosion in a manufacturing facility would be a *high-impact, low-probability* issue, but one that they should at least consider. The national bodies of professional sporting codes might classify 'players caught taking recreational drugs' as a *high-impact, medium-probability* issue. That classification would mean the code believes it is likely a player will be caught in the next six months, and that this would cause embarrassment. Most of the time, a 'change of government' would be a *low-probability, low-impact* issue years out from an election. Closer to the election, that classification could change depending on whether opinion polls suggest a change of government at the election is likely and how a new government's policies might affect the organisation.

It is a good idea to write a briefing note about each issue you include in the matrix so that you have the background, facts you might need, a discussion about the impact it might have on your organisation, and contact details for people who are experts in an easily accessible file.

By regularly reviewing the issues in your matrix and their classifications, and your briefing notes—say every six months—it is possible to keep an up-to-date assessment of the issues you need to address now, think about for possible future action, and be aware of over the longer term. You should be flexible and change impact and probability classifications if needed so that you always have an up-to-date assessment of the issues you face.

Issues management matrix

		IMPACT		
		HIGH	MEDIUM	LOW
PROBABILITY	HIGH			
	MEDIUM			
	LOW			

PUBLIC RELATIONS TOOLKIT

Using a project checklist

Checklists are important planning tools that help you to keep track of everything that needs to be done to implement a public relations project. Sometimes, public relations teams use a Gantt chart (see the example on this page) to show this information. A Gantt chart is a graphic illustration of the information in a checklist and shows the timeline in which individual activities need to be completed. Project management software can be especially helpful when you need a 'critical path' for activities. A critical path is a timeline of the activities needed—sometimes before other parts of the process can be started—to complete a project. Computer software automatically sets out the critical path.

Gantt chart

Task	Resp.	Day 1 2 3 4 5 6 7	1 2 3 4 5 6 7	1 2 3 4 5 6 7	1 2 3 4 5 6 7
	Day	1 2 3 4 5 6 7	1 2 3 4 5 6 7	1 2 3 4 5 6 7	1 2 3 4 5 6 7
	Week	1	2	3	4
	Month	January			

PUBLIC RELATIONS TOOLKIT   xxiii

Project checklist

To use the checklist, write the detailed tasks you need to do to plan (book a room, launch the website, get approval for the display concept, submit the boss's speech for approval, for example), implement (update the Facebook page, greet people as they arrive, hand out media kits) and evaluate an activity, in each row of the wide column. Add in details of the resources you need (chairs for a media conference) to make the activity happen. Then use the smaller columns to indicate who is responsible for each task, and the dates on which that task should begin and end (allocating a realistic amount of time for each task). Enter the date each task is completed in the last column of the checklist.

When you fill out the evaluation section of a checklist, make sure that you indicate how you will actually measure the success of the activity you are planning.

Checklists can be used as agendas for work-in-progress meetings because they provide a lot of detailed information about who is doing what and when. A quick review of tasks and progress in achieving them makes planning and implementation easier.

1. Planning

Task	Responsibility (initials)	Start date	Due date	Date completed

2. Resources

Task	Responsibility (initials)	Start date	Due date	Date completed

3. Implementation

Task	Responsibility (initials)	Start date	Due date	Date completed

PUBLIC RELATIONS TOOLKIT

Task	Responsibility (initials)	Start date	Due date	Date completed

4. Evaluation

Task	Responsibility (initials)	Start date	Due date	Date completed

Meeting minutes

Below is an example of minutes from a client meeting that sets out what was discussed, what action will be taken, who is responsible for that action, and the time frame in which action should be taken. Most public relations consultancies use something like this so that they can keep track of decisions about their clients' projects. Consultancies also have special formats for recording discussions at initial meetings with clients so that they can effectively plan strategies.

Public relations meeting minutes

Date:	7 March 2020
Location:	Ideal Widgets' Head Office
Time:	9 a.m,
Attendees:	John Lacy, Sally Richards, Rob Huang, Petra Hatharasinghe

Item	Topic	Responsibility	Due
1	**Facebook page** Needs to be developed for May/June launch. Material completed and approved end May.	PH	May/June
2	**GWI releases** Great Widget Ideas media release completed and approved, waiting for distribution approval.	RH/JL/PH	June
3	**National survey** The draft release to be on hold until after the survey is completed and then updated with results of May distribution.	SR/JL	May

Item	Topic	Responsibility	Due
4	**Brand activation campaign** Brand activation release developed and on hold pending Fred Jones interview with *The Daily News* (publish links on Facebook page and website—see 'Interviews' below).	PH/RH; SR will coordinate links	JL to call Simon Canning to suggest an interview
5	**Widget choices** Media release to be prepared for approval for Ideal Widgets. Release prepared and approved; awaiting distribution approval.	PH	Early June
6	**Marketing Magazine** PH discussed with *Marketing Magazine* whether they are interested in running an article on in-store effectiveness.	PH	June
7	**Inside Retailing** RH and PH to develop article on trends in store, along with in-store labelling.	RH/PH	June

8	**Other**
	Interviews
	Business owners (weekend papers, feature sections):
	1. *Daily News*
	   Simon Canning is interested in interview with Fred Jones on company and in-store marketing and the direction the company has taken in getting consumers to buy products in store.
	2. *The National Herald*
	   Feature writer Alex Thomas is interested in interview with Fred on company and in-store marketing trends, moving from brand awareness to sales and consumer surveys.
		RH/PH/SR	Now on hold pending *National Herald* interview; Fred's interview with AT set up; SR to call on 1 June to confirm time

	Projects **Integrated marketing** RH to develop story on integrated marketing in line with advertising trends and last week's *B&T* article. **Industry seminars** Investigate industry seminar and possible speaking engagements for Ideal.		Paul Martin happy to do interviews on new widget technology as well; SR to identify online news sites for opportunities

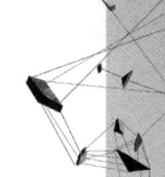

Item	Topic	Responsibility	Due
9	**Releases distributed:** 1 Uses program engages shoppers in store 2 Ideal expands marketing team (new appointments) **Releases to be distributed:** 1 Great Widget Ideas launch 2 Widget choices 3 Brand activation		March March

Media release planning worksheet

Remember: use news frames to identify media release topics. Write media releases in the inverted pyramid style. Use '5Ws and H' (see p. 121) to plan what you need to say.

1. Planning questions

a. What is the specific focus of this release? (For example, what is the news frame?)	
b. Who are the target publics for this release? Where do the target publics get their news and information? Which reporters work for those news sources—and which of them specialises in covering our industry?	
c. What public relations objective will this release support? (For example, what is the organisation's purpose for issuing this release? Is it to increase sales of a product? Is it to position the company as a leader in the field? Is it to show concern for the environment?)	
d. What do you want to achieve with the media release? Is the objective to inform, to change attitudes and behaviour, or to increase attendance at an event?	
e. What themes should this media release highlight?	

2. Outline for your media release

Heading	
Lead paragraph: succinctly summarise the most important point of your story—the news frame or frames. Use the inverted pyramid and '5Ws and H'.	
Main idea for paragraph 2: *the most important facts; attribution (Who is saying all this?); less essential information.*	

Main idea for paragraph 3: *essential background material; names of key characters or sources; a second important element; names of secondary characters or sources.*	
Main idea for paragraph 4: *elaboration on material in paragraph 2.* Can you use a direct quote? Remember the punctuation requirements for a direct quote.	
Main idea for paragraph 5	
Main idea for paragraph 6	

Speech planning worksheet

1 Format

Introduction

- *Get attention*: tell people why they should listen.
- *Establish rapport*: create a bond with your audience, and show them what you have in common.
- *Preview*: tell people what they are going to hear.

Body/discussion

- *List main points*: arrange main points logically, usually in order of importance.
- *Support with data*: provide evidence to support each main point.

Conclusion

- *Review*: summarise the key points the audience has heard.
- *Memorable statement*: create a desired frame of mind that will stay with the audience.
- *Call for action*: encourage the audience to act in a certain way, if that is appropriate, needed or applicable.

2 Detailed planning

Preliminary questions

1. What are the expectations of this audience:
   a. towards me?
   b. towards my topic?
   c. towards this specific situation? (Are there any extenuating circumstances that should be covered?)
2. How do I expect the audience to be affected by my speech or presentation?
   a. Will the general purpose of my speech or presentation be to inform, persuade, reinforce certain ideas or entertain?
   b. What is the specific point I want the audience to remember, or the call for action I want to leave with them? (For example, complete this sentence during your speech planning: After this speech or presentation, the audience will …)

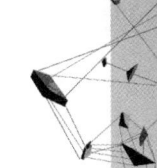

The body of the speech

3. Will my speech or presentation be arranged (tick appropriate box):
   - ☐ chronologically?
   - ☐ spatially?
   - ☐ topically?
   - ☐ by cause and effect?
   - ☐ by problem and solution?
4. The structure I have chosen is best because …
5. What are the three or four main points suggested by the structure I have chosen?
   - Main point 1:
   - Main point 2:
   - Main point 3:
   - Main point 4:
6. How will I support the main points? Will I use statistics, examples, analogies, case studies, direct quotations?
   - Main point 1 will be supported by …
   - Main point 2 will be supported by …
   - Main point 3 will be supported by …
   - Main point 4 will be supported by …
7. How should I adapt my language and word choice to suit audience expectations?
   a. To what extent should I use jargon and buzz words?
   b. To what extent should I be conscious of defining certain words?
8. How should I use visual aids?
   a. What should be visualised?
   b. Why should it be visualised?
   c. How should it be visualised?
9. How should I introduce the speech or presentation?
   a. Why should my audience listen to this message?
   b. How will my audience benefit from listening to me?
   c. How can I make my audience want to listen?
   d. The audience should listen to me because …

Conclusion

10. How should I conclude the speech?
    a. How do I relate the conclusion to the main points I have covered?
    b. In conclusion …

Video script template

Tip: Set up a word-processing document like this using a two-column table. Match up the Video and Audio information side-by-side. Type the script, and who reads it, in the Audio column (see the Tip Sheet on page 174). Each column will expand as you type. In the Video column, type in the visuals, titles, graphics and supers you want to accompany the script.

Video title:

Writer:

Date:

VIDEO	AUDIO

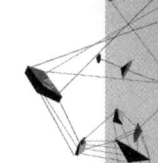

INTRODUCTION 1

Public relations is planned communication: there is a reason for everything practitioners write. Even the strategic public relations plan that identifies the goals and objectives an organisation wants to achieve when it communicates with target publics, and the ways in which it will deliver its messages, must be written clearly, accurately and concisely. This chapter will:

+ discuss the importance of clear, concise writing in public relations
+ demonstrate how writing is involved in every public relations activity
+ illustrate the links between public relations activities and an organisation's business plan
+ introduce some specific public relations terms
+ discuss planning tools.

Public relations practitioners write a lot. An ability to do that clearly and concisely for a wide range of public relations applications is a skill that all practitioners need. At the end of your studies, the principles and theories that underpin public relations **practice** will be clear. You will have developed critical thinking skills to help you work through **issues** to find effective solutions for client communication opportunities—after all, university teaches us to think critically, even if we don't recognise it at the time. So, in your first job you'll be expected to know that public relations tasks are always implemented in the context of an overarching plan that provides a strategic framework for everything that you do. But writing clearly, concisely and accurately will be the most highly valued skill you'll take into a job. You will get better at it the more you **practise** writing.

This book will help you to learn about the importance of writing in all aspects of public relations practice. Clear, concise and accurate written material helps organisations to communicate effectively with the people who are important to them. Good writing is also required when you prepare a public relations plan. None of us ever stops learning and improving our public relations practice. Your personal development as a **practitioner** will depend not only on what you discover in this book and on what else you explore at university; it will also come from practising public relations, learning from senior practitioners, reading widely and identifying trends.

practice: a noun that describes the professional work of public relations people.

issue: an internal or external factor that has an impact on the organisation's ability to pursue its business.

practise: a verb that describes the action of doing public relations work.

practitioner: a professional who does public relations work.

When you undertake an internship, or work experience, as part of your studies, you'll begin to understand how public relations is an exciting and creative profession and how much of professional practice is about change. That understanding will increase as you work full time and become a more experienced practitioner, for public relations is a profession that deals with why and how organisations and individuals build and maintain relationships with people that matter to them. Public relations is not only about promoting corporations or celebrities. Practitioners can work on issues that are important to society, say for an organisation that helps homeless young people, or issues of international significance like raising money to help combat AIDS and other diseases in disadvantaged countries. At other times practitioners work on projects of specific local interest only. Practitioners can be involved in politics, often by helping organisations to have their views heard in the clamour of public discourse, but also as partisans working for politicians or industry associations.

A THOUGHT ON THEORY: A DEFINITION AND THOUGHTS ABOUT BOUNDARY SPANNING

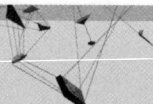

Public relations is concerned with building relationships between organisations and the people who are important to them. In 2011–12, the Public Relations Society of America led an international crowdsourcing campaign and public vote to develop a definition of public relations. That initiative resulted in the definition, 'Public relations is a strategic communication process that builds mutually beneficial relationships between organisations and their publics'. The Public Relations Institute of Australia (PRIA) has a similar definition: 'The deliberate, planned and sustained effort to establish and maintain mutual understanding between an organisation (or individual) and its (or their) publics'.

These two professional association definitions include four important words: strategic, deliberate, planned, and sustained. That is, nothing in PR is, or should be, undertaken just for the sake of it. The PRIA website (<www.pria.com.au>) provides a sense of what that might be so. It notes,

> What is significant is that public relations people are pivotal to the communication process between an organisation/individual and their publics. They must understand the needs of an organisation and they must be attuned to the needs of the publics.
>
> It is the job of public relations practitioners—whether they are individuals, in-house employees or in consultancies—to fully understand the communication process and to develop strategies, which ensure that any form of communication is clear, honest and unambiguous so that the messages are easily understood by the respective target audiences.

The PRIA website says that in the context of the information era, which has brought about a massive change in the communication process, public relations could easily be described as the management function that evaluates public attitudes, shows how an organisation or individual's policies and procedures are consistent with the public interest, and plans and executes a program of action to earn public understanding and acceptance. These two descriptions of public relations lead us to the notion of boundary spanning.

Marianne Sison (2012) describes boundary spanning as an important concept within systems theory. This theory holds that organisations are systems operating as part of a bigger system—their environment—and that to survive they need to adapt to what is happening in that environment. For example, in the twenty-first century, climate change and carbon emissions are significant issues in many manufacturing businesses' external environments. Regulations to reduce carbon emissions, or indeed to tax them, are being introduced in many countries. Manufacturers are required to change their practices as a result, or in a systems theory context, to adapt to what is happening in their environment. Sison says that how much organisations adapt depends on whether their own systems are 'open' or 'closed'. An organisation that has an 'open system' approach recognises that to be successful it must interact with the world around it. Because public relations staff identify external issues that are important to the organisation, they are boundary spanning. Sison says this role of interpreting events and issues in the outside world for the organisation, and of presenting the organisation's views to its publics, largely characterises what public relations people do. Boundary spanners are then 'knowledgeable, articulate, responsive to change, and sensitive to the preferences of the external organisation with which they are dealing' (Sison, 2012, p. 63).

ABOUT PUBLIC RELATIONS JOBS

Public relations people work for a wide range of organisations and situations. Most are employed by companies, industry associations, not-for-profit organisations, government agencies and local councils, or in public relations consultancies. Some work with politicians and celebrities, advising them on how to use the mass news media. Some find jobs in journalism. The most common jobs have titles like these:

+ public relations officer
+ public affairs officer
+ stakeholder relations manager
+ webpage coordinator
+ media adviser
+ media relations officer

public relations: the deliberate, planned and sustained effort to establish and maintain mutual understanding between an organisation (or individual) and its (or their) publics.

- communications coordinator
- crisis manager
- lobbyist
- investor relations manager
- internal communications coordinator
- issues analyst
- publications manager
- publisher
- events manager
- marketing coordinator
- market researcher
- copywriter
- speechwriter.

This list demonstrates the breadth and diversity of public relations, challenging the common view that the profession is focused only on the mass news media, or on using social media applications. The profession involves many more activities, some of them highly skilled strategic tasks, than these tactical and technical activities. Whatever a practitioner's job title, daily work tasks are varied, and often one person has responsibilities in a number of areas. Tasks include:

- researching issues that may have an impact on an organisation and writing material that will help to manage those issues
- preparing strategic plans that help an organisation achieve its communication goals
- writing media releases, backgrounders, fact sheets, and question and answer sheets
- planning and managing an organisation's website—and writing material for it
- initiating and managing the organisation's social media applications and activity
- setting up media conferences
- arranging one-on-one interviews for clients with individual **journalists** in the press or in radio or television
- organising displays and exhibitions
- writing **leaflets**, booklets and newsletters and other materials that implement a public relations plan and support sales and marketing efforts
- writing speeches and presentations for senior executives
- organising meetings for clients with target publics
- arranging events to, for example, recognise a staff member's long service, celebrate an organisation's anniversary or specific milestone, or **launch** a new product
- managing an organisation's philanthropic sponsorships.

Some practitioners work as private **consultants**—that is, in companies that comprise teams of public relations specialists, much like accountancy and legal firms. Consultants are paid fees to provide skilled advice and practical public relations help to other organisations that may not have their own in-house practitioners, or to support in-house activities. Opportunities in consultancies include

journalist: a professional who works in the news media. Not all journalists are reporters; some are editors and sub-editors.

leaflet: a small publication of several pages.

launch: an event, or action, that marks the beginning of a project.

consultant: an external public relations practitioner engaged by the organisation to work on a specific project or to provide advice.

specialising in promoting new products, helping organisations in times of crisis, communicating with employees, or engaging in financial public relations, which might include promoting a company about to list on the stock exchange or to make a major new share offer. Some consultancies have practitioners who are experts in helping companies to build relationships with governments at all levels (in private enterprise companies this specialisation is often called government or corporate relations). A major task for people who work in these areas is to identify, analyse and manage the social, political and economic factors that impact on an organisation's ability to pursue its business interests. Practitioners in government departments work on programs that tell war veterans, for example, about changes to their pension rights, or help farmers understand how a looming locust plague will affect their crops, or provide information about aviation safety, or health benefits, or education. Universities employ practitioners to produce material that tells students about courses they can take. Most medium to large businesses employ public relations staff to develop and manage programs that reach out to their **target publics**. These programs might link the company to the communities that surround its manufacturing plants, provide regular information—including annual reports and quarterly financial statements—to shareholders, deal with questions from the media about the company's activities, manage philanthropic activity, manage communication with employees, involve the business in trade exhibitions, or manage writing speeches for senior executives. Senior consultants and managers of government and private company public relations staff also counsel senior management on strategic matters. In this counselling role, practitioners may not actually produce anything, but their advice—based on their expertise in public relations practice and boundary spanning, and on their knowledge of politics and how our society works—provides valuable information for strategic decision-making.

target public (or often 'public'): the people to whom public relations messages are directed.

Job advertisements illustrate the varied work tasks of public relations practitioners. For example, one of Australia's largest public relations consultancies advertised for two senior practitioners. One, to be known as a 'Group Director', would be responsible for designing and overseeing 'innovative communication strategies' for the consultancy's clients in the health-care industry. Applicants for the other position—the Director, Corporate & Finance—would need to have 'strong relationships with key business journalists, advisers and commentators'. When eBay advertised for an Australian Public Relations Manager, the job description told potential applicants that they would 'manage reputation, particularly with respect to trust and safety, taking a proactive approach to issues management and media and public education'. These examples reflect our earlier definitions of *public relations* and *boundary spanning*. They also demonstrate the importance of strategy, and of building and maintaining relationships in public relations practice.

Local, state and national government agencies regularly tell their current and potential clients about the services they provide through newspaper advertisements. These advertisements demonstrate public relations theory and practice at work: they are applications of the 'public information' model (J. Grunig, 2001). In most cases, an agency's public relations team also promotes its services to potential clients through the news media. Public relations staff research client attitudes for feedback about whether the services actually meet client needs.

> ### PRACTICE POINT
>
> Many organisations seek the opinions of their target publics in relation to their plans. Sometimes this is done via a webpage feedback link; at other times the organisation sets up direct consultations with people who might be affected by the plans. This happened in Australia in 2011–12, when the federal government agency responsible for managing the water resources of two important rivers, the Murray and the Darling, sought community responses to a new environmental plan. Consultation involved first distributing the plan using a range of public relations tools, and then engaging in a series of community meetings across a number of states. The community consultation meetings were often hostile because the plan involved reducing the amount of water that would be available to farmers. Yet the process illustrated *two-way communication* at work (Grunig, 2001).
>
> In most countries, government agencies use public relations and advertising tools to tell citizens about their rights and responsibilities: pay your taxes now; vote next week; the new health benefits scheme will meet the cost of your spectacles; find out more information at this website. These campaigns are not designed to engage in a dialogue with target publics and are examples of the *public information model* described by James Grunig and Todd Hunt (see Grunig, 2001).

ethics: '*1* the science of morals in human conduct. *2 a* moral principles; rules of conduct. *2 b* a set of these (medical ethics)' (*Australian Concise Oxford Dictionary*, 6th edn).

Whatever their speciality, whatever the industry they work in, whatever their responsibilities, practitioners must be aware of, and observe, **ethical** standards. In everything that we do, we are responsible for our personal behaviour. We are bound not only by the many laws that deal with how companies should work, copyright and libel, workplace health and safety, equal opportunity, and broadcasting, but also by the standards of behaviour required by our employer, and our professional ethical code. In addition to telling the truth practitioners must be careful not to deceive people by omitting relevant information.

> ### ■ PRACTICE NOTE PUBLIC RELATIONS ETHICS
>
> Professions in most countries have associations that promote the profession, represent the interests of practitioners and establish ethical frameworks within which people practise. Doctors, lawyers, accountants, psychologists, physiotherapists, engineers, plumbers and electricians all have associations for these purposes. Maintaining ethical standards of practice is essential for all professions. Associations that represent public relations practitioners recognise the responsibility that their members owe to the community and to their clients and employers. While not all practitioners are members of these associations (often called 'institutes'), those who are accept that they must abide by professional codes of ethics (sometimes also called 'codes of practice') and that they can be penalised if they do not.

> Codes of ethics outline the principles that govern how practitioners should work if they are to do so fairly and honestly. Some are statements of principles; some are sets of strict rules. All are about ensuring high standards of practice. For example, such codes generally talk about practitioners
>
> + being fair and honest with their employers, clients and prospective clients, fellow workers, public officials, the communications media, the public and fellow members
> + not doing things that are likely to discredit themselves, their employers or clients, or their professional organisation
> + not using incorrect or misleading information—and making sure they do not mislead inadvertently
> + protecting confidential information about present and former employers' and clients' business affairs, technical methods or processes, except if ordered by a court to do otherwise
> + making sure that they are not compromised by conflicting interests
> + ensuring that they do not intentionally harm the professional reputation or practice of another member.

In some countries, codes of ethics are applied to practice through initiatives designed to educate members about how they should work ethically, rather than through a punitive regime. Nevertheless, complaints against members are formally investigated, and in some countries members can be penalised for unethical practice if complaints are upheld. Penalties for breaching a code can include cancellation of membership. Sometimes investigations of complaints result in practice notes that explain how the code should be interpreted and how members should observe the code.

PUBLIC RELATIONS ACTIVITIES HAVE A CLEAR, STRATEGIC PURPOSE

Every public relations activity has a clear purpose from the simplest logistical planning for a doorstop media **interview**, through to projects to address low community awareness of the importance of a healthy diet and regular exercise in preventing diabetes. Nothing is implemented without a reason. These reasons are set out in public relations **strategies** or plans. We'll look at strategic plans and what goes into them in more detail later, but we need to consider some basic information about them here because they are vital to what we do as practitioners.

Senior practitioners, most often the managers of public relations teams, are responsible for planning what, how and why their organisations communicate with their target publics. Sometimes this is done with the help of an external consultant. This senior practitioner role reflects their status as the most experienced members of an organisation's public relations teams and their regular, sometimes daily, interactions with top management. An organisation's most senior managers

interview: an event at which a journalist asks someone questions, usually on a one-to-one basis.

strategy: what organisations and individuals do to achieve goals, usually over the long term. Like many terms used in business and other areas, strategy is a military term.

dominant coalition: the most senior group of decision-makers in an organisation. Membership of a dominant coalition can vary according to the issue being addressed, or a particular operational focus.

message: information given to target publics to create awareness, or build credibility, or persuade them to take action that is favourable to the organisation. Messages can be informative or persuasive.

public relations strategic plan: a plan setting out how an organisation will achieve its communication goals and objectives.

(often described as the **dominant coalition** because they are the most influential people in the organisation) want to know how public relations activities can enhance business performance, and they therefore want those activities to be prepared in a strategic context.

Strategic plans should be prepared for an individual project, like the launch of a new product, or to establish a cohesive and integrated framework for all the components of the organisation's continuing public relations activities, or to help the organisation to deal with the particular social, political, economic and environmental issues it faces.

For example, when a manufacturer launches a new product—perhaps a new mobile phone with new integrated and flexible social media apps—its public relations staff, or their external consultants, will prepare a strategic plan to make sure that potential customers, retailers and the relevant news media are aware of the new product. This strategic plan might include a special event to launch the phone, a program of visits to retailers to explain its features, an information kit for government regulators, and a media kit that includes a media release and technical information for specialist journalists who write about telecommunications. Perhaps there'll be a series of shopping centre stands in major cities to demonstrate the apps, and there will almost certainly be Facebook and Twitter posts. Importantly, the plan will outline why the manufacturer is doing these public relations activities, what needs to achieved, who the target publics are, the **messages** that need to be communicated and how these messages will be delivered. It will also outline the people, funds and equipment needed to make the plan work and set out how success will be measured. This plan will support the efforts of the sales and marketing team. Detailed planning like this will ensure that the whole process of publicising the new phone and its apps, and convincing people to buy it, will be integrated so that goals, objectives and messages are consistent. This approach will also make sure that everyone involved in communicating messages about the phone knows what they have to do, when they have to do it and to whom their messages are directed.

Your university probably has a public relations plan that reflects the institution's goals and objectives in research and teaching. The PR team will manage a series of annual projects designed to tell staff and students and a range of people outside the university about its teaching programs, about successful students, and about the research achievements of lecturers. Some projects will be conducted in cooperation with other parts of the university. A program might include:

+ the annual open day
+ providing information to the media
+ managing the website
+ the university's newsletters
+ linking the institution with the community by hosting the local Tournament of Minds competition
+ a monthly literary lunch
+ a quarterly meeting between senior academic staff and local business leaders
+ regular contact with the university's graduates.

Each part of that program should have its own **public relations strategic plan** with direct links to a plan for the whole public relations department. This plan will outline why the university conducts public relations activities, the messages it wants to send to target publics, how it will deliver them and how it will measure success. From time to time the university will need to implement a specific one-off public relations project—perhaps participating in a special event in your city that celebrates the achievements of local young people, or maybe managing a crisis. If the project is that special event celebrating young people, the public relations staff, or perhaps a consultant from a local agency, will write a strategic plan for a display the university has decided to contribute to the event. Just like the strategy outlined above, that plan will set out what the university wants to achieve with the display, the messages it wants to send to people, how it will present those messages, and how it will measure the display's success. The strategy will in turn be integrated with the university's marketing plan. The overarching goal will be to attract students and funding for research. For a crisis the PR team will use a strategy already written setting out who the university needs to talk to, how to deal with students and their families, staff, the local community and neighbours, the authorities, and the news media. Messages will be developed at the time of the crisis.

Public relations strategic plans have clear and vital links to an organisation's business strategy. All successful organisations have plans that set out what they want their business to achieve and how they'll go about pursuing goals and objectives. These strategic business plans include a great deal of financial information, and they are used to guide all parts of the organisation in planning their activities and how, for example, they'll achieve production and sales targets and manage risks. If a company wants to be the best widget (look up the definition!) maker, the strategic business plan will set out how it will do that, what its production and sales targets are, where its potential market is, the staff skills it needs in order to build the widgets and ensure quality, and the cost and pricing structures that will make it viable. The company's public relations plan will reflect and support those goals and objectives by listing activities designed to establish and maintain positive relationships with a range of people, including staff, who are important to the company's success.

Clear, effective writing and the importance of grammar, spelling and style

In the spring of 2006, the previously unknown private papers of Australia's first Nobel Prize Laureate for Literature, the late Patrick White, came to light when they were bought by the National Library of Australia. White was one of Australia's most distinguished writers, and his private papers included drafts of his novels (including a previously unknown one), diaries and other material. They were unknown because White had denied he had kept any papers, even to his biographer, the Sydney writer David Marr, but they were found and kept by White's literary agent after he died. Among them was a 1983 report White had written for the Australian Broadcasting Commission's Standing Committee on Spoken English. White's report was published in November 2006 by the *Sydney Morning Herald*'s weekly *Spectrum* magazine ('Overheard by the vivisector', 11–12 November 2006, p. 18). White was one of a panel that had been asked to report on how ABC announcers used spoken English. He described the experience as 'a depressing few weeks' of listening for 'faults of pronunciation, grammar and vocabulary'. His report criticised announcers who 'maul a language to which one is devoted', but White listed some criticisms that apply to written as well as spoken English: 'A few of my personal hates: "prior to" when "before" is much more elegant. "Commence" for "begin". "One more time" for "once more". It always mystifies me why we have to say "take out" when "win" is such a neat, clean word (bowing to the Americans?). The most odious of all: "presently" and "currently" for the unequivocal NOW.' Imagine how White would have reacted to the modern phrase 'a crisis situation' when 'a crisis' is enough.

Richard Stanton, a former senior public relations practitioner, journalist and academic, begins the discussion about the importance of clear writing in his book *Media Relations* (2007) with a question: 'Why do we have to bother with grammar?' Stanton answers his question by arguing that correct use of grammar is important 'because we are required to present our message in a highly readable, clearly understandable fashion … As in the structure of a news story, a news release requires that we convey meaning clearly and with structure. So the well-constructed sentence becomes our best friend' (p. 78). Although commenting about the written word in a much more serious format than a news release, the Sydney author and lawyer Roy Williams described great writing as a medium that 'fosters understanding among human beings' (*Review, The Weekend Australian*, 28–29 October 2006, p. 8). That's a powerful idea, expressed even more powerfully in Williams's observation that the Chinese author Gao Xingjian (whose book of essays Williams was reviewing) had managed, even in the translation, to articulate 'so many of my private thoughts'.

In their different ways, White, Stanton and Williams are making the point that words, and the way we put them together to produce sentences, matter. Words are like bullets, and their specific meanings make the points we want to convey in our written and oral communication. Grammar and syntax are the rules or conventions we follow when we put words together into sentences so that what we are trying to say makes sense to others. Understanding how to use words in this way is important for public relations practitioners. So, too, is recognising that the ubiquitous short forms and dodgy sentences used on social media are not appropriate for serious business communication. Our task is to deliver **informative** and **persuasive** messages on behalf of our internal or external clients through a range of public relations tools—the things that our target publics actually see. We should write those words in logically constructed sentences that are clear and concise and that do not waste words. The famous public relations practitioner, teacher and author, Fraser Seitel, says that writing is *the* (his emphasis) fundamental public relations skill (2011, p. 11), but he notes that the sad fact is that 'public relations people, by and large, are horrible writers' (p. 329). It need not be so.

informative communication: a message delivery strategy that utilises tools that only provide information.

persuasive communication: a message delivery strategy that uses tools designed to persuade people to a particular point of view or to take action.

> **PRACTICE NOTE** THE POWER OF WORDS
>
> A senior newspaper sub-editor had an aversion to the use of *very*, as in 'very big', because he argued that it was wasteful and synonyms could make the point anyway. The sub-editor cut the word from copy and found another to express the ideas journalists were trying to convey. Thus a 'very big building' became a 'large building' or even an 'edifice'.

> A public relations student wrote this 29-word sentence in an assignment:
>
>> I work in the Workers' Compensation section which is charged with the duty of administering the Workers' Compensation Act 1951 and takes over 10 000 calls in any given year.
>
> It is a valid sentence that provides a lot of information about the student's part-time workplace. But for our purposes it can be shortened to seventeen words and still provide that information:
>
>> My section, Workers' Compensation, administers the Workers' Compensation Act 1951 and takes over 10 000 calls a year.
>
> If the first *Workers' Compensation* and the two commas are cut from the sentence, it still makes sense and provides the same information.
>
> Cutting words from a sentence may help to make your point concisely, but does that result in accuracy? Read the sentence again and think about the use of *over*. In this case, would *more than* be a more accurate choice? The definitions of *over* and *more* in the *Australian Concise Oxford Dictionary*, 6th edition, suggest 'more than' would be the accurate way to qualify the number of telephone calls the Workers' Compensation section receives each year.
>
> Another public relations student wrote the following as the lead paragraph of a media release required for an assignment:
>
>> The Australian Red Cross Blood Service is announcing the launch of a new community relations project ...
>
> That information could have been expressed more succinctly this way:
>
>> The Australian Red Cross Blood Service has launched a new community relations project ...
>
> or
>
>> A new community relations project to ...
>
> Another example comes from an answer given in a third-year PR exam:
>
>> Messages can be delivered in a variety of different ways.
>
> This is what is called a tautology: when two words are used to do a job that one word was capable of doing on its own. It should have been expressed as either 'a variety of ways' or 'in different ways'.
>
> The point is that we shouldn't waste words in public relations (or any) writing; we should use them clearly and precisely.

Everything we write as practitioners is destined to be consumed by others, often by journalists who are taught from early in their careers to write succinctly and accurately. They are bombarded daily with **media releases** from hopeful public relations people and they must select those that deliver real news. A muddled media release full of spelling and grammatical errors that is not 'news'

media release: the supply of information on issues and events to the media, usually in written form (see Stanton, 2007).

won't get the media coverage for which it was produced because it won't get past a busy journalist's initial sifting process. That is the simple, but most important, lesson about writing for the news media that many, even senior, public relations people do not grasp. Perhaps more importantly, our written work in reports and publications, on websites and in displays is produced for people to whom our clients want to direct specific messages. If they cannot understand what we are saying, or do not recognise the sentence construction we are using, then our ability to deliver information, or to make a point, has failed. The text published on a company's website needs to be written in a style that is factual and concise if it is to convey important information about the company.

One of Australia's most acclaimed wordsmiths, Don Watson, speechwriter for former Prime Minister Paul Keating (and his biographer), has complained about the way in which politicians, public servants and managers use words. Of all the people who should write and speak clearly and use words like bullets, politicians are the worst at it. And sometimes, public relations people, who write their speeches and media releases, are to blame. On the first page of his book *Watson's Dictionary of Weasel Words, Contemporary Clichés, Cant and Management Jargon* (2005), Watson says politicians have 'sucked the meaning out of words; and the result is just … melancholy. They are shells of words: words from which life has gone, facsimiles, frauds, corpses' (Watson, 2005, p. 1). He is writing about the almost uncanny ability of politicians, public servants and management types to use buzzwords, jargon and complicated sentences when simple words and sentences make the point more clearly. The people who use these words, especially politicians, says Watson, 'imitate the emptiness of management jargon to weasel their way past our better instincts' (Watson, 2005, p. 10).

Public relations practitioners also need to avoid clichés, inappropriate jargon and management-speak. In his earlier book *Death Sentence: The Decay of Public Language* (2003), Watson issues a warning to journalists that applies with equal force to public relations practitioners. Journalists, he says, must 'choose their own words carefully and skilfully and insist that others do the same. The proper relationship of journalists to the public language is that of unrelenting critics' (p. 5).

Most organisations have their own specific rules in relation to preferred spellings (one *g* in *wagon* instead of two, for example), how reports and correspondence should be set out on a page, email language and, sometimes, which typefaces must be used in publications, in advertising, on the web and in email. These 'style guides' are formal documents approved by senior management. In public relations contexts, style guides include rules for writing a media release. Some media release rules differ from the approach that you'll learn from this book. In government departments, for example, it is often more important to begin a release with the title and name of the relevant minister than it is to start with the main news point. On the other hand, you can generally be more creative when you are writing for a company or a not-for-profit organisation. Nevertheless, it is vital that you are aware of the style guide of the organisation in which you work and that you follow that style.

None of this is to suggest that creativity in writing is not an important skill for public relations practice. It is, but creativity also requires accurate grammar and spelling, clear sentence construction and precision of meaning. Mastering these rules enhances your creativity.

So, we must insist on clarity and simplicity in what we write for others and for ourselves. Don't use four words when one will do—but always choose the accurate word; avoid jargon and clichés;

use a dictionary if you are unsure of spelling; buy a thesaurus (or use an online one—provided it will give you the correct context of words for your country's English usage) to find synonyms and antonyms (look those words up in your dictionary if you've not heard of them); and make sure your computer's word-processing program is set to appropriate version of English for your country. Above all, proofread what you write—and proofread again.

> **PRACTICE POINT**
>
> Many people have problems using apostrophes. To find out how to use them correctly, look up the definition of *apostrophe* in your dictionary, or use your search engine to find out, or just visit the Apostrophe Protection Society at <www.apostrophe.org.uk>.

An introduction to public relations terminology

All professions have their own ways of recording what they do. Doctors, for example, keep detailed notes on hospital patients' blood pressure, temperature, medication and other details. Scientists meticulously record the aims, methodology and results of their research in a consistent and internationally recognised format so that their experiments can be easily replicated by other researchers. Teachers prepare outlines of what will be studied in a particular subject, what students should know at the end of the course, and what students will do in individual lessons.

Professions also use specific words to describe the steps in their planning and implementation processes for projects, or to record information. One way to describe these words is 'jargon'. People who use jargon are often accused of speaking gibberish, or talking in an unintelligent way or of debasing language (look up the definition of *jargon* in your dictionary), especially if they are not in the relevant profession. Used in the correct context, jargon can be acceptable, but all public relations writing needs to be sensitive to the audience.

'Terminology' is another way of describing these collections of words. *The Australian Concise Oxford Dictionary*, 6th edition, defines *terminology* as 'the system of terms used in a particular subject'.

Public relations has its own 'system of terms'. Practitioners use the terms in their daily work because they are integral to professional life. We need to know them and to understand the contexts in which they are used. In Chapter 3 we'll see examples of how these terms are used in strategic public relations planning. For now, let's look briefly at some of the key terms practitioners use.

Target public: This is the correct public relations term for the people at whom we direct activities and messages. People who work in advertising use the term 'target audience', and those in marketing use 'target market'. Each activity can have one or more target publics, and identifying target publics accurately is perhaps the most important step in planning a public relations program. In the mobile phone example we looked at earlier in this chapter, a target public might be 'people aged 18–24'. Later we'll look at different categories of target publics.

analysis: a detailed examination of something. In public relations, analysis involves examining the internal and external environments that impact on the organisation, or examining research results.

reputation: what is said about a person (or organisation) or their behaviour; how others regard a person (or organisation).

relationship: a connection or association between people or organisations.

task: something that needs to be done to implement a plan.

Situation analysis: Usually the first part of a public relations strategic plan, this is where practitioners analyse the communication issues and opportunities an organisation faces, and assess the results of formal and informal research. It is in this part of a public relations plan that a practitioner analyses the organisation as well as the external environment in which it operates. An effective situation **analysis** will help practitioners to identify goals, objectives and target publics so they can develop effective messages, determine communication pathways and public relations tools, and prepare budgets and timelines for implementing the plan. In our new mobile phone example, the situation analysis would discuss issues like the market for this gadget, its special features, who potential buyers might be (our target publics), the results of research about what interests them (music or text messaging or environmental protection), how the company can reach those buyers and how the law might apply to the new phone.

Goal: A public relations goal is a broad statement of what the organisation hopes to achieve. Public relations goals reflect an organisation's business strategy and deal with **reputation**, **relationships** or **tasks**. While we'll look more closely at writing goals in Chapter 3, a goal for our mobile phone manufacturer might be to 'build and maintain a positive relationship with 18–24-year-old customers'.

Objective: A public relations objective is a precise and measurable statement of what an organisation needs to do in order to achieve a goal. Each goal should have more than one objective, each a step towards achieving the goal. Objectives express exactly what needs to be achieved in a defined timeframe. They deal with raising *awareness*, building *acceptance* or convincing publics to take *action* in support of the organisation. An example would be 'to generate a 25 per cent increase in awareness among 18- to 24-year-olds about the environmentally friendly manufacturing process for our mobile phones in the next six months'. The key requirement for objectives is that they can be measured—and that's important when we reach the end of a public relations program and need to evaluate how well it worked. To evaluate success in achieving the objective above, a practitioner would assess whether the public relations activity achieved a 25 per cent increase in awareness in the six months.

Message: Messages are the information given to target publics to create *awareness* about a client's product, or its views about an issue. Messages are also written to build *credibility*, and to persuade a target public to take *action* that supports a client's interests. Messages can be *informative* or *persuasive*. To use our mobile phone example, a message might be that 'Our Australian factory is powered by solar energy'—a message that would help to build credibility for the company.

Communication pathway: Often called 'message delivery strategy'. In this book, communication pathway is used because it is a simpler way of describing how a message will travel from an organisation to its target publics. Communication pathways, then, define the *methods* an organisation will use to reach its target publics. For example, a pathway might be to 'use interpersonal communication to deliver our positive environmental messages to 18- to 24-year-olds'. Interpersonal communication means talking directly with, or writing personally to, target publics rather than trying to reach them via a media release or a brochure.

Tools: A public relations tool is an **output**. These are the activities that a target public sees, or experiences, like websites, tweets, blogs, Facebook posts, displays, publications, meetings, media releases and special events. One tool to implement the communication pathway outlined above might be a blog on which engineers working for the new mobile phone manufacturer can talk directly with 18- to 24-year-olds about how solar power is used in their factory. Sometimes, public relations, or communication, tools are described as 'tactics', but we're using 'tool' because it is a simpler concept that actually describes the products we produce.

It helps to think of communication pathways as *how* messages will be delivered and tools as *what* you will use to deliver them. Think of pathways as snail mail and tools as the letters inside envelopes. We'll look at this in more detail later.

output: a measurement of the frequency with which a program's public relations tools were used.

Planning the details

Most people write 'to do lists' when they plan parties, their weekly workloads or their holidays. When they are getting ready for a 21st birthday party, for instance, they write down the things they need to do, to buy, to book and to set up, and the people they want to invite. When planning their working week, they list the things they need to do to achieve their project objectives: phone people, attend meetings, write reports, book a hire car or visit the library to research a topic. When you go on holidays, you write a list of the clothes and other things you need to pack, what you need to do to get to your holiday location, and the places you want to visit and which flight to book. Some people write to do lists in their diaries each evening before they leave the office so that they have a planned program for the next working day. Each task in the list is given a priority, and those with a high priority are pursued before those with lesser importance. Planning in detail like this means that we do not forget important steps in organising our personal work or other tasks, that we meet deadlines that have been set for us, and that we can check progress so that problems and barriers can be sorted out before they affect the outcomes we want to achieve.

Detailed planning is an important element in effective public relations. This involves working out what we want to say in speeches and media releases, tweets and on Facebook, the company blog, website and emails to staff, preparing **timelines** for implementing public relations tools, and compiling **checklists** that record what needs to be done from the planning stage of a project until its success is evaluated, when each step starts and ends, and who is responsible for what. Planning includes budgeting for the resources that will be needed: people, finance and technology.

timeline: a graphic representation or typed list of the length of time taken to complete a task.

checklist: a planning tool that identifies the tasks that need to be undertaken to implement a project.

Many public relations organisations have templates to help staff in this planning. In later chapters, we'll look at using templates for planning media releases and speeches so that we can identify goals and objectives, the target public and the messages we need to deliver. We'll also look at a simple checklist that you can use to plan your public relations assignments.

So now you are ready for the next step in your adventure. In Chapter 2 we'll look at the importance of context in planning and implementing public relations activities, how PR is a strategic management function, and how we need to consider the world around us when we are planning and implementing our plans, as well as the legal and ethical frameworks that govern what we do.

SUMMARY

In this chapter, we've introduced public relations and looked at:

+ the role of clear and concise writing in everyday public relations activities
+ jobs that practitioners do, and how these reflect the theories that underpin public relations practice
+ some of the terms that we'll use during our studies and future careers
+ the importance of detailed planning
+ how public relations strategies link to an organisation's business plan.

In later chapters these ideas will be further explained and you'll have the opportunity to apply the concepts to specific situations by working on some practical cases. For now, you might like to write a list of the points in this chapter that have helped you to understand more about what public relations people do.

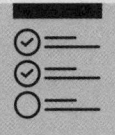

ACTIVITIES

Compare Codes of Ethics

Some examples of public relations codes of ethics can be found on the websites of the following organisations:

- Canadian Public Relations Society: www.cprs.ca/aboutus/code_ethic.aspx
- Chartered Institute of Public Relations, United Kingdom: www.cipr.co.uk/content/about-us/about-cipr/code-conduct
- Public Relations Institute of Australia: www.pria.com.au/member-centre/code-of-ethics
- Public Relations Institute of New Zealand: www.prinz.org.nz/Site/About/ethics_code.aspx
- Public Relations Society of America: www.prsa.org/AboutPRSA/Ethics/
- Public Relations Institute of South Africa: http://prisa.co.za/documents/Code%20of%20Ethics/Prisa%20code%20of%20ethics%20%20professional%20standards.pdf
- The international association for these organisations, the Global Alliance: http://www.globalalliancepr.org/code-of-ethics/

Visit these websites to read the codes of ethics or practice. Note the similarities and differences in relation to how each organisation structures its code and expresses its ethical standards. Why might such differences exist? (Answering this might take you on a journey of discovery about how best to express and implement codes of ethics in the twenty-first century.) What are the major themes reflected in the codes? Are the principles on which the codes are based different? Where and how? Which code most clearly expresses ethical principles? Why?

Practice task

Try your hand at writing clearly and concisely. Choose a topic that interests you and write no more than 300 words about it. Maybe you'll want to write about your last holiday, tell some of your family's history, write about your pet dog, critique your favourite movie, praise the best football team in the world or say why you'd love to fly to the moon.

When you've finished your piece, share it with another public relations student. Read each other's work and make suggestions about how your work could be improved. What is the main message each of you tried to give readers? Could some of the things you have written be expressed more clearly, or more concisely, or more accurately? Could the spelling and punctuation be improved?

TIP SHEET: THE IMPORTANCE OF LANGUAGE

Humans use languages to communicate with each other. A language is what the *Australian Concise Oxford Dictionary* describes as the 'faculty of speech'. But *language* has other meanings, including 'a style of expression' and 'the use of words'. These seem like trite points, but we often forget that 'a style of expression' is also the grammar, or system and structure, of a language. Grammar, then, sets out the rules we use to construct sentences that are spoken or read. And when we use words, they must be spelt accurately, and used in the correct context.

English is a complicated language, even if it is your first language. Yet we cannot avoid the fact that applying the rules for writing sentences, spelling correctly, and punctuating accurately (an apostrophe, for example, does not indicate a plural) is the most basic requirement for a public relations practitioner. Applying the rules does not stop you from writing creatively, but it does demonstrate to anyone who reads your material that you are professional.

Often, senior professionals criticise public relations graduates for their alleged inability to write. A lot of that criticism is because some graduates don't spell correctly, or don't follow the conventions of grammar—faults that can easily be avoided by using a dictionary or thesaurus, understanding sentence construction, and proofreading. Imagine the howls of derision from journalists who receive media releases full of grammatical and spelling errors, and think about how such carelessness would damage your professional reputation, especially with your boss.

AN OLDIE BUT STILL A GOODIE

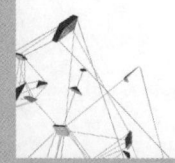

For many years, the classic reference for the rules of English grammar was a dictionary-like publication, *Fowler's Modern English Usage* (Oxford University Press), first published in 1926. Battered and dusty copies of 'Fowler' remain in public relations offices, newsrooms and other places where people care about English expression. The preface of the reissued first edition (2009) describes it as 'the most famous book on its subject ever written'. Even though English usage is dynamic, and the author, H.W. Fowler, might be outraged by modern practice, it is still a valuable reference. It will, for example, provide a page and a half of discussion about split infinitives; definitions of when to, and when not to, use words like *practise*, *stationary* and *geographic*. It has tracts on correct punctuation, using double possessives, English versus American expression and spelling, and French words and phrases commonly used in English. It even has a section on spelling, listing common words that often cause difficulty.

Access to Fowler, or a similar reference, a good dictionary and a thesaurus (for synonyms and antonyms—look those words up too)—either online or in hard copy, is essential for a practitioner, and no one should ever feel awkward about consulting them.

WRITING WHAT YOU ACTUALLY MEAN TO SAY

Journalists can also be caught out with errors in English expression. Perhaps journalists' published errors are more serious because the news publishing process has so many in-built checks. The following example shows one glaring error of expression and punctuation. It appeared in a feature story about a Rugby League footballer in England who suffered a heart attack after a game. The story, about his recovery and return to playing, was published in the sports section of an Australian weekly newspaper because the player was an Australian. After reporting on the player's ambulance trip to hospital, the story reads:

> Dosed up on morphine in the operating theatre, the Leeds doctors immediately performed a coronary angioplasty to blast away a clot in [the player's] heart.
>
> ('Road to recovery', *The Sunday Telegraph*, 16 December 2012, p. 57)

Read literally, the article conveys the impression that the doctors were dosed up on morphine when the reporter actually means the player. But it is an example of another common problem in writing: 'reversing into sentences' (Morris & Goldsworthy, 2012). That is, it would have been better for the journalist to have divided the 'paragraph' (see Chapter 6) into two sentences. One could have said the player was given morphine and then taken to the operating theatre; the other could have dealt with what the doctors did.

Here's a rather bold example of how punctuation can change a meaning. Consider the sentence:

> A woman without her man is nothing.

Enraged at that thought? And so you should be. But punctuate the sentence and the meaning can change:

> A woman: without her, man is nothing.

The lesson is that the rules of grammar and punctuation exist to help us write clearly and accurately, so that we always express ourselves in the ways we intend to be read and understood.

PRACTICE MAKES PERFECT

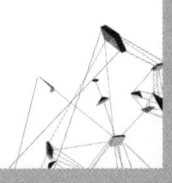

This is an old cliché, but a still relevant one. You won't write accurately unless you practise writing. You cannot learn how to write a news lead for a media release, for example, on your first try. Learn and understand the principles, and practise regularly. An employer will expect you to be able to write a useable media release almost from day one of your job, and you'll need the same skills when you do an internship.

Read widely, especially serious newspapers and news websites, and analyse how the material you peruse is constructed, how words are actually used, to understand the style and spellings used by the publication. Read newspaper features by senior writers and newspaper editorials (also known as 'leaders', the columns in which the editor expresses the paper's views about politics, the economy, social issues, foreign affairs or even a whimsy).

Read articles on the websites of *The Times* (<www.thetimes.co.uk>), *The New York Times* (<www.nytimes.com>), *The South China Morning Post* (<www.scmp.com>), *The Age* (<www.theage.com.au>) and other major publications to see how news is reported, the issues they are interested in, and how their senior writers express themselves. Explore the *Arts & Letters Daily* website (<www.aldaily.com>), especially the links to recent essays and the work of various columnists.

DON'T WASTE WORDS

Words have specific meanings, and they need to be used correctly. For example, Fowler discusses the different meanings and uses of *stationary* and *stationery*, observing that each must be used accurately in the correct context. English is tricky on matters like this as there are so many words that sound the same but are spelt differently and mean different things, such as *to*, *two* and *too*. Be careful to use words in their correct context and for their correct meaning. Turn your computer's language and spelling settings to those for your country.

It is also a good idea to build your vocabulary by finding synonyms for commonly used words. After all, variety is good. One quick way to help build your vocabulary is do one of those word puzzles in which you are given a set of letters and have to find as many words of four or more letters in the jumble as you can. An easy way to work on synonyms is to do a regular crossword. Here are some examples of how answers to crossword clues can build your knowledge of synonyms.

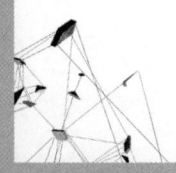

Clue	Answer
reserved	reticent
trite	hackneyed
look narrowly	peer
give consent	accede
apprehend	arrest
notion	idea
tribe	clan
method	system
extremities	ends
dogma	tenet
halts	stops
naïve	artless
trap	snare
at hand	near

But always be aware of the jocular crossword compiler who'll try to confuse with a clue like 'listeners'. *Audience*, the obvious response, won't fit the available space, but *ears* will.

IN SUMMARY

Learning to write messages and public relations tools appropriately for specific publics relies on applying professional principles (especially, in our case, news frames and the inverted pyramid, as discussed in Chapter 6) to the foundations of correct English grammar, punctuation and spelling. And practice. Sometimes it is difficult to move away from deeply ingrained high school or university essay-writing approaches, which you should continue to use when appropriate. But professional public relations writing, especially when applied to writing media releases, is far easier when you work on understanding the principles set out in Chapter 6. There's a kind of golden rule: write simply, accurately and concisely, and follow the principles of news framing and the inverted pyramid. It really works.

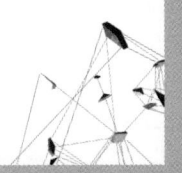

2 CONTEXTS FOR PUBLIC RELATIONS

After reading this chapter you will understand how public relations practitioners need to be aware of the social, political, economic and cultural environments in which they work, and how what they plan and write is linked to an organisation's strategic goals. The chapter deals with:

+ public relations as a strategic function
+ building and maintaining relations with senior management and an organisation's target publics
+ the legal and ethical frameworks in which public relations practitioners work.

PUBLIC RELATIONS AS A STRATEGIC FUNCTION

Niccolò Machiavelli gets a bad rap these days. Machiavelli was a sixteenth-century diplomat, public servant and philosopher in the city-state of Florence, now one of the major cities of modern Italy. His treatise on statecraft, *The Prince*, was written for the Medicis, the family that ruled Florence. *The Prince* provided practical advice about how rulers (princes) should govern and keep control of their states. Today Machiavelli's advice is often regarded as a harsh and cynical approach to governing. The pejorative term *Machiavellian* is used against people who are regarded as behaving in a devious way.

So, what's a sixteenth-century political philosopher doing in a 21st-century book about public relations? Much of Machiavelli's advice to the Medici rulers of Florence is relevant in the modern world. For example, *The Prince* includes a lesson about 'How far human affairs are governed by fortune, and how fortune can be opposed'. By 'fortune', he means luck, or a person's destiny. Machiavelli writes that a prince 'who adapts his policy to the times prospers, and … the one whose policy clashes with the demands of the times does not'. Machiavelli is suggesting that rulers who understand what is happening in their society are generally more successful than those who do not.

Public relations practitioners also need to be aware of 'the demands of the times' and how they impact on their clients or employers. Being able to identify and interpret important issues and trends in the world around us so that we understand the **context** in which effective public relations

context: 'the circumstances relevant to something under consideration *(must be seen in context)*' so that something that is *out of context* is 'without the surrounding words or circumstances and so not fully understandable' (*Australian Concise Oxford Dictionary*, 6th edn).

can work is an essential skill for a practitioner. Joep Cornelissen describes context as a 'complex commercial, economic, political, technological, social and cultural world' (2005, p. 105).

When a practitioner can explain the issues at play in an organisation's external environment (that is, the world around it, the issues in that 'world'), why those issues are important, and how they can be effectively addressed by public relations action, they also demonstrate professional knowledge and earn respect from senior management. They are then regularly included in top level organisational discussions about strategic directions, sought out for their advice on how to handle issues, and asked by clients or organisational managers for help to solve communication issues. Working like this is an important strategic function, one that enhances your value as an employee, and one that shows you are capable of doing far more than technical tactical activities.

Let's look at how public relations practitioners can identify and understand what is happening in the world around them so that they can better develop programs to meet the business and communication goals of their clients, or of the organisation for which they work. Practitioners need to do this kind of thinking before they plan communication tools and start to write them.

PUBLIC RELATIONS AND ENVIRONMENTAL SCANNING

Roy Vaughn and Steve Cody (2007), experienced American practitioners, have written about this role on the Public Relations Society of America's website. They describe public relations as a kind of barometer that measures external and internal pressures on organisations and that translates the impacts of cultural, societal, generational and political shifts on those organisations. To be effective, they say, practitioners, especially senior people who advise and counsel organisational leaders, need to spend more time pursuing information on these trends and objectively analyse what they mean. Vaughn and Cody say that it is impossible for practitioners to identify every element of global change. Nevertheless, they argue that practitioners will be able to lead more of the important discussions in their organisations and with clients if they are measuring these shifts in society.

One way of understanding the complexities of context is to imagine that you are approaching our world from space. Once you identify Earth, you can recognise the environment in which it exists. As you come closer to Earth, you can see that nothing much is ever still. People are going about their lives; transport and communication systems link them; sport is being played; products are made and sold; wars are fought; some parts of the globe are calm; and the weather is doing, well, what the weather does. Modern technology has facilitated almost instantaneous connections between people, making business easier, faster, more cost effective, giving us access to more and more information in formats that would amaze people from earlier generations. Technology has generally improved our lifestyles, health and access to entertainment choices. It has changed transport, the way we study, and how we build and maintain relationships, connect with others, watch sport, make decisions, choose our leisure pursuits and manage our health. And then there's today's news media that provides instant live coverage of wars, celebrity weddings, important international meetings, politics in most countries, natural disasters, share prices and sports action from the other side of the world. Our world is a pretty busy place. All this is the complex context in which our world works.

■ PRACTICE NOTE ENVIRONMENTAL SCANNING

The task of interpreting the complex and changing world for clients is known as 'boundary spanning', which is possible after a practitioner engages in effective 'environmental scanning'. This kind of strategic analysis identifies changes in the environment in which an organisation operates and how they will affect the organisation and its activities (Cornelissen, 2005). James Grunig and colleagues found in their research that the 'most excellent' public relations departments participated in organisational strategic management by scanning social, political and institutional environments to bring an external perspective to strategic decision-making (Grunig, 2006). Robert Dilenschneider, one of the world's leading practitioners, has said that chief executives want practitioners who can help them project what the future marketplace will look like from consumer, regulatory, political, cultural and social perspectives (Dilenschneider, 1989). The management scholars David Bach and David Allen (2010) have provided a context for understanding these points. They have written about how social, political and economic issues play out in an organisation's 'non-market environment'. It is in this environment that governments, regulators, activists, citizens and non-government organisations participate in debates about issues, debates that are reported and analysed by the mass news media. Examples of issue debates are those about climate change, tax policy, law and order, education, health care, same-sex marriage, agricultural policy, refugees and immigration, unemployment, housing loan interest rates, and military equipment purchases. Bach and Allen argue that chief executives need to be aware of debates about issues that affect their organisations because they impact on their organisations' market environment—the place where they do business with suppliers and customers, and compete for market share. Environmental scanning also includes making sure that you are aware of the issues that occur inside the organisation. These are the issues that concern employees and managers.

Environmental scanning and analysis is as important as the work of financial experts who provide companies with analyses of how they will be affected by changes in oil prices, or the cost of raw materials, labour, electricity or taxes. Public relations professionals write reports interpreting issues, events and changes in politics, society and culture to explain what these mean for organisations. Sometimes these analyses include predictions about future changes and how they might impact on the organisation. Practitioners who specialise in this forecasting work are known as 'futurists'.

So, practitioners who understand the internal and external environments in which their clients and organisations work develop and implement effective public relations programs; those who do not are less successful. The eminent Australian practitioners Candy Tymson, Peter Lazar and

Richard Lazar (2006) point out that public relations plays a strategic role in identifying, responding to and creating trends. They describe public relations as a 'communication driver' that creates awareness, educates and influences public opinion, promotes and protects reputations, guides organisations to communicate change, and helps them to re-examine the values and ethics of their operations. That's a serious responsibility and one that reflects just how 'the times' influence the ability of an organisation to communicate effectively with its target publics.

LISTENING TO TARGET PUBLICS

In trying to understand how an organisation interacts with the broader society, identifies the views of target publics and begins a dialogue with them about issues, public relations practitioners become a two-way conduit between an organisation and its publics, a vital element in symmetrical communication.

> ### PRACTICE POINT
>
> They might be modest little punctuation marks and, as the *Style Manual for Authors, Editors and Printers* (2002) describes them, the smallest break in the continuity of a sentence, but commas can be literary terrorists. Misplace a comma when you are writing, and what you intended to say may not be what you said. Thus, *He was not run over, mercifully* means something else altogether if the comma goes missing.
>
> Despite this tendency to unexpectedly cause us grief when we write, commas can be useful. In the sentence above, the comma has been used to avoid ambiguity. They can also improve clarity (for example, by breaking up a series of nouns or adjectives), to link clauses and phrases and to show that words have been omitted. Sometimes people use more commas than they need to; sometimes they don't use enough. In modern writing, the decision to use a comma or not is often a personal choice, provided that the choice doesn't lead to an unintended meaning.
>
> Use your search engine to investigate commas and how to use them.

An example of context being important for writing messages that resonate with target publics is the way in which municipal councils, sporting clubs and other recreational facilities deal with water restrictions imposed during Australia's frequent droughts. Many erect signs that advise that the water they use on playing fields or in parks and gardens is recycled, or from a nearby river, rather than from the reticulated local water supply. Others use signs to say that they are observing local water restrictions. This simple communication tool reflects community concern about the use—and waste—of water. It says to target publics, 'We're using an appropriate alternative to the town water supply.'

IDENTIFYING AND ANALYSING ISSUES

The Australian expert Tony Jaques points out that not every issue is strategic, but that 'all issue management should be strategic in its approach and implementation' (2009a, p. 21). That is important advice for both beginning and experienced practitioners because it means we should be continually identifying and assessing the issues that will face our clients in the mid and long terms, not just restrict our environmental scanning to those that are happening 'now'.

Perhaps more than any other group, politicians try to identify the issues that the community believes are important. Sometimes, because of the focus politicians put on an issue, they are able to generate sufficient media interest to make it a matter of community concern. Politicians who oppose the government try to do this all the time, which is why in election years, especially, they raise questions about 'law and order', the natural environment, public transport, education, or failures in the health system. All this is done to suggest that the government is not doing its job properly, and the topics oppositions choose to pursue are often determined by what opinion polls tell them. Politicians also keep a watchful eye on opinion polls that measure voting intentions and which party leader is most favoured. Polling companies usually include questions about voting intention in all their regular surveying, and the results are published in the major newspapers, often becoming news stories in their own right. Political parties, of course, have their own opinion polling contractors, who research a wide range of issues in significant depth. These opinion poll results are important to politicians as they develop, or modify, policies to attract voters. Opinion poll results about poor approval ratings for leaders have been used by people in all political parties to argue that their leaders should be changed. Alan Ramsey, a former senior political commentator for *The Sydney Morning Herald*, wrote about politicians' addiction to opinion polls: 'Every political leader you ever heard likes to pretend opinion polls don't matter, that the "only poll that matters is the one on election day". They're lying, obviously' (*Sydney Morning Herald*, 3–4 February 2007). Ramsey wrote that politicians cannot ever afford to ignore the polls, whatever the message the results give. 'The opinion polls are a politician's very life force,' Ramsey wrote. And he observed that the party that wins on election day is the one that fine tunes its campaign strategy month to month, week to week, 'even day to day'. This is true of politicians in every democracy. For example, in the 2016 US Presidential election opinion polls appeared almost every day reporting which candidate was ahead in which states; some predicted how many Electoral College votes the two candidates had at various stages of the campaign.

Public relations practitioners are also alert to the information that the opinion polls provide because it is useful in the **desk research** that is part of **environmental scanning**. Where they have a budget for it, practitioners also hire polling companies to research community attitudes to issues that are important to their organisations or clients. From time to time, the polling companies themselves ask people about issues that concern them. For example, once or twice a year, major polling companies around the world publish the results of their survey of community attitudes

desk research: research that practitioners can do from existing published sources like reports, historical data, the media, official files, and websites.

environmental scanning: a process of identifying, analysing and interpreting internal and external social, political and economic factors that impact on an organisation's ability to pursue its business.

to a wide range of issues, and this data often indicates which issues are of most importance to citizens (or, to be more accurate, respondents to the polls). Research findings like this can often, later, be accessed from the polling companies' websites free of charge. More detailed reports that include in-depth analyses are also commercially available from the polling companies. All this data, whether we pay for detailed reports or just scan the publicly available material, can be used as part of environmental scanning.

Research for public relations need not be expensive because there is a lot you can do yourself from your desk. For example, Fred Volkmann, the former vice-chancellor for public affairs at Washington University in St Louis, shows how inexpensive and simple desk research can be using publicly available information about issues that concern people. Volkmann says this can be gleaned from the news media, organisations' reports and other published material, such as official government papers. He also says that in many cases public relations staff can use readily available database and spreadsheet applications to do their own inexpensive research and analysis. Doing this kind of simple desk research, Volkmann's team found that many alumni did not like stick-on mailing labels on letters sent to them (especially if they were crooked) and that many often rubbed the signatures on official letters to determine whether they were written with a pen or printed during the production process (they disliked the latter approach, especially if the signature was printed in a coloured ink).

Water management, global warming and the environment are mainstream issues in the politics of most countries. In Australia, one of the driest continents on earth and with its population concentrated around the coastline, politicians are acutely aware of community concern about the effect of frequent droughts, especially on agriculture and the river system, especially in the eastern states. The need for better management of Australia's water resources led to the appointment in 2007 of a Cabinet-level federal minister for the environment and water and a $10 billion program to realign state and federal responsibilities in this area, with a special focus on the Murray–Darling River catchment. The Murray–Darling is Australia's biggest river system and feeds major agricultural areas. By 2012 the issues of water conservation, allocations of water to irrigators, and improving river flows had not been resolved, and political, economic and social issues continued to dominate debates about the river system. In 2016, after the federal election, the Minister for Agriculture took on responsibility for water policy. As long-term issues like these remain part of Australian political discourse, public relations practitioners working for, say, agricultural companies and public sector agencies will analyse the impact of government policies and legislation related to global warming, the environment and water management on their organisations. They'll write strategies to make target publics aware of the initiatives their organisations take to minimise the impact of their operations on the environment and diminishing water supplies. Many companies have sections of their websites that deal with policies on environmental protection and sustainable development (see, for example, BHP Billiton's approach to these issues at <http://www.bhpbilliton.com/community/environmental-sustainability>). These sites reflect acceptance of community concerns about these issues.

A THOUGHT ON THEORY: HOW THEORIES HELP IN PRACTICE

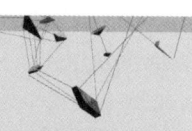

Much of the time we spend studying public relations at university is taken up with understanding the theoretical background to what we do in practice. By understanding how, for example, people process information, we are able to work out how to write and deliver effective messages to target publics that are important to our clients. As Dan Lattimore and colleagues have noted, theory explains or predicts the way things work or happen (Lattimore et al., 2004).

Cornelissen argues the need for practitioners to inform their work with theory and research. He says that those who do this (professionals he describes as 'reflective practitioners') are better able to work out how to adapt to changing circumstances rather than relying on intuition and trial and error. In his book *Corporate Communications: Theory and Practice* (2005), Cornelissen writes that theory is a resource to help practitioners continuously question and revise their views, and make sense of their situation and experiences. He says that practitioners who use this critical and reflective ability are not only proficient in the technical aspects of their jobs, but are also more sophisticated in interpreting the broader economic, social and political contexts of their practice and in understanding the kind of society their work is reproducing or changing.

Cornelissen has long been interested in the ways in which practitioners use theories developed by academics. In an article published in 2000, he discusses three models by which theories and concepts are translated into practice. He describes the *instrumental* use of theory as a traditional, problem-solving approach whereby academic theory and research provide rational solutions to managerial problems in a direct and instrumental way. In the *conceptual* model, abstract academic knowledge is applied to practical cases by means of generalisations, concepts and ideas. The third model, the *translation* model, treats theory and practice as 'intertwined mutually influential entities in the generation of knowledge'. Cornelissen explains that the *translation* model recognises that scientific knowledge is hardly ever used unchanged in a practical setting. In other words, practitioners 'transform' and interpret research outcomes within the context of professional understanding.

The team that Grunig led to investigate excellence in public relations included a practitioner who provided an understanding of how the theories they were examining worked in practice (Grunig, 2006).

Cornelissen argues that as pragmatic professionals, public relations practitioners will adopt ideas from the 'rich pool of academic theory', where these are relevant to their practice. Almost every journal article and textbook that you will read will have examples of theories that are relevant to public relations. This is because understanding theory makes the practice of public relations more effective. As Lattimore and colleagues suggest, you will need to build a set of theories to help your professional practice. You also might find that when you start work your office already uses a theoretical base for its activities, even though this might not be explicitly stated.

FURTHER READING

For further reflections on theory, see Bach and Allen (2010, pp. 41–8); Cornelissen (2000, pp. 315–26; 2005, esp. chs 1 and 4); Grunig (2006, pp. 151–76); Jaques (2009a, pp. 19–33; 2014) and Lattimore et al. (2004, esp. ch. 3).

KEEPING ON TRACK

Trying to understand the times and what they mean for an organisation is not something that happens only once or twice a year. It is a continuing task, perhaps even a responsibility. It involves knowing about the political system and its key players, having some understanding of how the economy works, and showing some interest in the news of the day. How might you react if you were asked to prepare a program for a newly appointed managing director to visit the key officials in the state government department responsible for your industry if you didn't know about the role of public servants in advising politicians? If you were not aware that the media were reporting expectations of a larger than normal crowd at the footy grand final, how could you advise your client, a private bus company that runs services to the ground, about how to use that news as a way of publicising the company's plans for the game?

The importance of context has been stressed by Professor Anne Gregory, who notes that organisations do not exist in isolation and that history is littered with examples of companies that failed to spot changing industry trends quickly enough and adapt to them (Gregory, 2009a, p. 20). Those companies suffered a loss of market share, financial collapse, or bad publicity because of the way they treated their workforce. Gregory says that given the critical role of public relations in building goodwill between organisations and their publics, practitioners should carefully consider both the external and internal contexts in which they operate.

PRACTICE POINT

As practitioners we should have enquiring minds, be alert to what is happening in the world around us, and read, watch, listen to or click on news and current affairs—maybe all of those. The daily news is living history. What is reported in the news often leads to public relations activity because news can create opportunities for your organisation, or clients, to contribute to debates on current issues, or it can provide a context for other PR activity like a product launch. For example, issues being reported in the news provide opportunities for a university's public relations staff to promote its academics as specialist commentators. News producers are always looking for people to comment on current events and issues, which is why you read, see or hear experts from every sector of the economy in or on 'the news'.

Now is a good time to start some environmental scanning about the world around you. Read your city's daily newspaper every day—online or in hard copy; regularly watch a serious television current affairs show; bookmark one or two news sites on your web browser and visit them regularly; set up a news feed to your mobile phone or tablet. Read a biography about an important person; read a book about history; seek out the opinion pieces in the weekend newspaper in which experts comment on the issues that concerned your city, your state or the nation in the past week; read some of the large number of weekly, fortnightly and monthly news magazines available at your local newsagency. You could even take a break from the recorded music on your phone or tablet and download a podcast about an important issue from a radio current affairs program. Doing some or all of this will help you to start understanding the times in which you will work. You won't find it boring or a waste of time; you might even find it fascinating. You will find that if you keep at it, being aware of the world beyond your social media applications will give you an understanding of current events that will make you highly employable as someone who can work out how your clients or organisation can use the news to promote them.

LINKING PUBLIC RELATIONS TO CORPORATE STRATEGIC PLANS

In Chapter 1, we touched on the need to link public relations plans to an organisation's strategic business plan. And the previous section has discussed the need for practitioners to be aware of the world around them by engaging in environmental scanning when they counsel senior managers and write public relations plans. Here we'll look at how all this comes together to ensure that the work of the public relations department, or consultant, reflects the business directions of an organisation.

The definition of public relations discussed earlier described it as a practice that establishes and maintains mutual understanding between an organisation and its publics. Scholars and practitioners have used the ideas in definitions like this to explain how organisations in many industries (for example, telecommunications, mining, manufacturing, agriculture, fitness and education) and government agencies (state, federal and local) use public relations. They all regard public relations as closely allied with the work of senior management.

At the start of their book, Scott Cutlip and his colleagues (2006) describe public relations as a management art and science, and as an organisational management function. They argue that public relations is inescapably tied, by nature and necessity, to top management, a relationship in which public relations staff provide counsel and communication support. The eminent US scholar Robert Heath (2001) also sees public relations as a management function that seeks to achieve what he describes as mutually beneficial relationships between organisations and their publics through the use of rhetoric. Fraser Seitel describes public relations as the 'management interpreter' that helps organisations to accurately and candidly communicate ideas about management decisions and policy rationales (Seitel, 2011, pp. 38–9). Seitel says that in the twenty-first century, public relations, no matter how it's defined, is an 'essential element' for organisations (p. 48). The British scholar Emma Wood notes that a key dimension of corporate communication—a sectoral specialty of public relations—is its relationship to overall organisational strategy (Wood, 2009, p. 551). Wood says that linking the two is vital in ensuring communication is taken seriously by the highest levels of management. This link between an organisation's strategic corporate plan and public relations strategy means senior practitioners often advise top management about dealing with communication issues that impact on the organisation's ability to go about its business. This is often called strategic counselling (see Mahoney, 2017, ch. 13, for a discussion of this role). In this strategic advisory role, senior practitioners need an understanding of management, negotiation skills and communication theory (Macnamara, 2012, pp. 253–5) so that they can provide advice in a well-informed, but detached, way (Mahoney, 2013). Joy Chia describes this as promoting integrity by taking an objective, well-researched view of an organisation's activities so that a practitioner can 'advise and be valuable to management' (Chia, 2009, p. 48). Working in this way is not easy, especially when management must be advised on options for handling bad news that might impact on an organisation's reputation, credibility and corporate social responsibilities, or on an emerging issue the organisation has never before had to confront (Mahoney, 2013).

Thinking about what an organisation does, includes the notion of its **business**. That word, *business*, is used in its broadest sense in public relations. People in our profession are not only employed by corporations. They also work in not-for-profit organisations, industry associations, charities, service clubs, aid organisations, politics, sporting clubs, celebrity promotion, and commercial business and industry. In these work contexts, *business* does not only have the commercial meaning of making and selling products, of earning and, sometimes, losing money; it also means a person's occupation or the things that concern or interest them. It is in this sense that charities, not-for-profit organisations, government agencies and so on engage in *business*. Their interests are in providing services for others. Of course, all organisations need money to finance what they do, and they must be aware of and contain the costs of pursuing their interests. Charities, for example, raise funds to finance their activities, often to fund research into disease or to support families in need, and they report annually on how they spent those funds. Most make a point of explaining how much of the funds they raise is spent on the causes they support, and how little goes to administrative expenses. It is also vital for a charity to be aware of community attitudes about donating funds to particular causes. A charity might research which socio-economic groups donate more to charities supporting medical research on childhood diseases than to those providing clothing to homeless people in winter. By understanding these elements of the context in which it operates, a charity can develop effective plans for fund-raising, to promote its good works, and to show how it will spend the money it raises.

business: usually what organisations do; a series of things that an organisation, or an individual, needs to deal with.

> **PRACTICE POINT**
>
> Whenever there is a major natural disaster like earthquakes, bushfires, devastating storms, or floods, national and international aid agencies rush to help in the recovery and relief efforts. Most agencies require large amounts of money to do this work. Other groups, such as the international organisation Médecins Sans Frontières (MSF)—which sends volunteer doctors and other medical staff to places affected by natural disasters—seek donations to support specifically targeted relief efforts. When MSF reaches its financial targets for specific aid projects, it says so publicly and asks people still willing to donate to select another of its projects to support. In this way, the organisation shows that it spends donated funds responsibly.
>
> Visit the website of a large aid organisation that you know and investigate its latest annual report (usually in the publications section of the 'Media Centre') to find out how the agency explains its expenditure on disaster relief or other forms of humanitarian aid.

CONTRIBUTION TO ORGANISATIONAL DECISION-MAKING

Public relations professionals believe that their skills in interpreting the times and counselling clients on ways to respond to them provide a unique set of strategic management tools. These tools, effectively used, qualify them for what many describe as 'a seat at the management table', where they are able to participate in high-level discussions about corporate strategy, business planning and performance, and communication opportunities.

In his book on strategic communication planning, the Australian practitioner Kim Harrison (2011) identifies what it takes to be a good public relations consultant. Harrison's points also apply to practitioners working 'in-house'. Harrison says that being good at counselling clients and implementing public relations activities requires an uncommon combination of skills and attributes. These can be summarised as:

+ creativity and business acumen
+ being quick thinking, street-smart, media savvy and abreast of current affairs and newsmakers
+ understanding how business works—especially your own and the client's
+ making a lot of contacts in the profession, the industry and the news media
+ being a strategist and an opportunist
+ working ethically and being loyal to clients, but having the courage to confront clients where necessary.

Harrison is suggesting that good practitioners understand not only the context in which their clients operate, but also how organisations work and are managed. Good management is about leadership and guiding an organisation to achieve its objectives in a constantly changing environment, but in responding to, or driving, change, good managers need to communicate effectively with shareholders, external authorities, staff, customers and suppliers (Tymson, Lazar & Lazar, 2006). Once the business direction and strategy have been decided, every decision and action will involve a cause and effect, and result in an outcome. Much of this will be determined by how well decisions are communicated and understood (Tymson, Lazar & Lazar, 2006). This is the idea that underpins the link between a public relations plan and the organisation's strategic plan. But how is that link made?

LINKING PUBLIC RELATIONS TO A STRATEGIC BUSINESS PLAN

Let's look first, briefly, at formal organisational structures to identify the ways in which the public relations team works in organisations to counsel senior executives and to implement communication plans.

Companies, clubs, schools, sporting associations and other organisations have formal functional structures—systems that enable work to be carried out, instructions to be communicated and business to be managed as efficiently as possible and in an orderly way. Most organisational structures are hierarchical—that is, with different levels of management, each with its own degree of authority over the area for which it is responsible. For large organisations, management structures can be quite complicated, and there is continuing scholarly debate about which model is the best fit for what type of organisation. A simple management structure is shown in Figure 2.1. At the top of the structure, the Board of Directors is legally responsible for everything the organisation does and sets the major strategic business directions. A chief executive officer (CEO, also known as a managing director, or president in North America and often in Asia) is responsible for overall, day-to-day management of the organisation in line with the board's policies. At the next level, the CEO is assisted by general managers, who are responsible for different aspects of the organisation's business. A number of managers at the next level are responsible for specific work teams.

Public relations and management

There is no standard 'reporting point' for the public relations team. Often the public relations manager reports to the CEO, the executive who most practitioners believe should, in any case, be most directly involved in their work. Sometimes the public relations manager reports to a general manager, often the executive responsible for marketing. Grunig and his colleagues found in their excellence study that if public relations was subordinated to marketing or another management function (say 'operations'), it lost its unique role in strategic management (Grunig, 2006). In many organisations, no matter who the public relations team reports to, the public relations manager has direct access to the CEO and general managers, the group often known as the 'dominant coalition'— or, colloquially, as the C-Suite. Membership of the dominant coalition is not static, since it can vary according to the issues being addressed or for a particular operational focus.

When the board agrees on a strategic business plan, everyone in the organisation needs to know about it, as do some external target publics like shareholders, the stock exchange, customers, suppliers and financial journalists.

Figure 2.1 A basic organisational structure

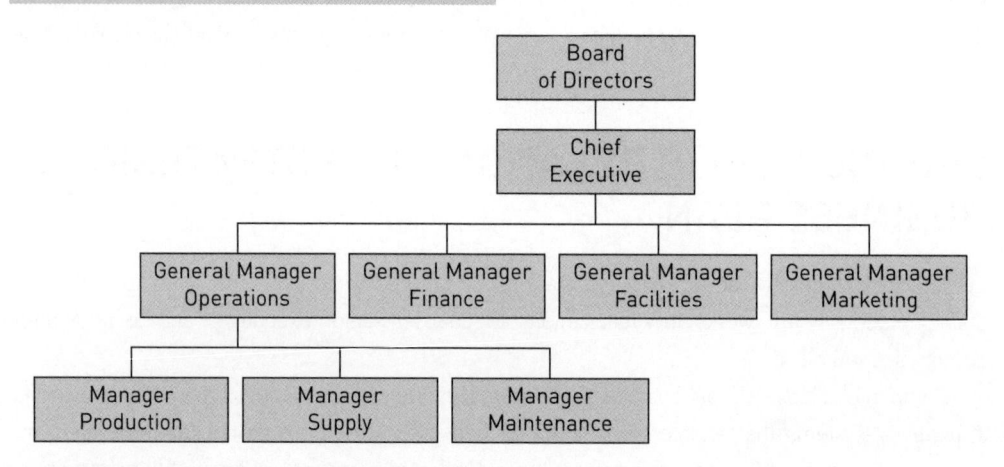

```
                    Board
                 of Directors
                      |
                    Chief
                  Executive
   _____|_____
   |            |             |           |
General      General       General     General
Manager      Manager       Manager     Manager
Operations   Finance       Facilities  Marketing
   |
   |_____|_____|
   |          |          |
Manager    Manager    Manager
Production Supply     Maintenance
```

Thus the communication goals, objectives, communication pathways and tools that we discussed briefly in Chapter 1 are written to reflect the business directions in which the organisation is heading. As its fundamental starting point, the plan for the organisation's regular public relations activities should indicate that it is designed to help achieve the organisation's strategic business goals. For example, if the fictitious company Ideal Widgets Pty Ltd decides on a new strategic business goal to produce the safest widgets on the market, the public relations plan should reflect that. So, the public relations team will write:

+ a communication *objective* aimed at increasing knowledge of the safety benefits of Ideal's widgets among customers by, say, 50 per cent over six months
+ communication *messages* that include references to the fact that the widgets exceed required safety standards and cost less than competitors' products
+ a *communication pathway* indicating how the messages will be delivered to *target publics*
+ an outline of the public relations *tools* that will implement the strategy, using the appropriate communication pathway.

We'll look more closely at this kind of strategic planning later in the book.

Wood notes that the link between communication activities and the strategic business plan is often regarded as vital if the highest levels of management are to take communication seriously. Writing about the role of corporate communication directors (senior public relations people), she argues that when they are able to contribute at a high organisational level, these communication professionals 'must be able to help determine the *organisational* goals rather than merely being confined to setting *communication* goals' (Wood, 2009, p. 552, her emphasis).

Dilenschneider has been more direct, telling an international public relations conference in Australia in 1988 that CEOs want public relations people who, among a list of eight attributes, help them make money, and tie strategic communication planning to business objectives (Dilenschneider,

1989). While Dilenschneider was talking decades ago, his views are still valid today, and contemporary public relations scholarship (such as Grunig's excellence study) includes research on topics related to what he had to say.

Building relationships with senior executives

Public relations practitioners and scholars argue strongly for public relations input into the development of strategic management plans. John Allert and Clara Zawawi, for instance, write that a practitioner's input into the design of the strategic business plan influences how well it is understood by the organisation's publics. If the strategy cannot be understood and accepted by publics, they write, it will be an unworkable document (Johnston & Zawawi, 2004).

To achieve that input, public relations managers must build relationships with executives at all levels of the organisation and be able to advise them about how they can communicate with their staff and external publics. This is an important function, whether the manager reports directly to the CEO or to someone else. Building these special, privileged relationships (Mahoney, 2013 & 2017), and making sure that others in the public relations team have similar cross-functional working relationships, is vital to the success of public relations. Good relationships provide opportunities for identifying activities, interesting people, and research and development discoveries that can be used to promote the organisation. They also ensure access to people at all levels, often when it is needed urgently, and they generate requests for advice on communication opportunities. Lynette McDonald and Aparna Hebbani (2011) note that these relationships determine whether practitioners are viewed as skilled technicians or strategic counsellors. The fact that public relations practitioners at all levels can build these relationships is a privilege that not all other professionals enjoy, and it is one we must respect, not only for the access it provides but also for the trust it generates. Often senior practitioners are given confidential information, hear the private as well as public thoughts of the CEO, and have authority to do and say things that other, sometimes more senior, employees do not enjoy.

PRACTICE POINT

In the web article cited earlier in this chapter, Vaughn and Cody (2007) note that the need for outstanding writing may be the one constant in the public relations profession. 'If you can write well, you can think well,' they say. They observe that basic writing skills in relation to spelling, punctuation and grammar have slipped in today's busy world as a result of 'tech-induced shorthand'. By this they mean the way in which the curt, sometimes non-grammatical, styles we use to write email and text messages have impacted on other forms of writing. Vaughn and Cody stress the importance of writing as a core public relations competency and urge practitioners to 'take steps to make sure your own writing stays crisp, and be the constant voice for quality writing in your organisations or for those you counsel'.

These relationships, and the trust associated with them, are crucial when senior practitioners counsel senior executives on a particular course of action—say, in a crisis. They are equally crucial in the day-to-day decision-making of the organisation when senior practitioners are working at a strategic level. Good working relationships ensure that public relations is valued. Grunig and his team have helped us to understand why this would be so. They discovered that involvement in strategic management is the critical characteristic of excellent public relations but that unless it is 'empowered to be heard', public relations has little effect on organisations (Grunig, 2006). Our profession won't be heard, and thus empowered, if we have not built effective relationships and demonstrated that we are capable of contributing at the management table by linking strategic communication to business strategy. That approach applies even if the practitioner is only occasionally privy to the management team's discussions.

Building, maintaining and enhancing relationships with target publics

It is axiomatic that effective, 'excellent' public relations requires that organisations build and maintain relationships with target publics, especially if we accept the definition presented in Chapter 1. Practice that pursues Grunig and colleagues' symmetrical model recognises the need for dialogue with target publics and accepts that policy might change as a result. Heath's notion of public relations as a rhetorical practice also recognises that there is a relationship between an organisation and its publics. Heath (2001) says that as rhetoric (which he describes as strategic), public relations enables organisations and their publics to develop mutually meaningful and influential relationships.

> **PRACTICE NOTE** LEGAL AND ETHICAL FRAMEWORKS
>
> State and national legal codes have implications for the practice of public relations. Specific state and federal laws deal with practitioners' personal responsibilities and help them to decide what they can do and how they can do it. Other laws are concerned with how organisations are set up and managed. Others protect our rights, those of clients, those with whom we work, and those about whom we might write a comment in a media release or other publication. Even more laws deal with the rights of consumers, set frameworks for resolving disputes and govern the media. In many countries, government agencies are pondering complex questions about how to legislate rights and responsibilities related to social media.
>
> Rhona Breit, a lawyer and Australian journalism lecturer, describes this as a complex and diverse legal environment (in Johnston & Zawawi, 2009, pp. 78–107). This system includes laws that:
>
> + protect people's reputations (the law of defamation)

- set out how companies (including public relations consultancies) must be set up and managed, and how they should report their annual financial performance (the national corporations law)
- govern financial transactions (banking and so on)
- require fair trading (the federal *Competition and Consumer Act 2010*)
- require contracts for services to be in written form
- cover how practitioners can use the internet for electronic transactions and to distribute information
- provide people with copyright for their work and products, and protect rights to intellectual property (that is, the ownership of ideas)
- deal with professional and personal liability.

Practitioners are, of course, also required to observe all of the legal code, not just those laws that relate to their practice. Australian lawyer Anny Slater warns that the legal code has many traps for unwary practitioners, who need to be aware that they could be liable not only for their own actions, but also for those of their employees, their agents (people who represent them) and their clients if they condone them (Slater, 2006). Slater warns that we should consider the possible consequences of our actions before we act. It is always useful to ask a lawyer for advice if you are concerned about a course of action.

Most workplaces have access to legal counsel when there is a need for advice about the implications of a planned activity. Many large organisations employ permanent legal staff. Others retain an external legal firm to provide advice.

Intertwined with this legal framework is a matrix of personal ethics, our profession's formal code of ethics, and formal organisational codes of conduct. This matrix of ethics guides not only the way in which we practise public relations, but also how we behave at work and relate to others. A former president of the Public Relations Institute of Australia, Lelde McCoy (2009), reminds us that as ethics is important to both organisational excellence and public relations, practitioners should be in the forefront of the movement for ethical conduct. This is another example of public relations practitioners being involved in strategic management, in this case by fulfilling a role that McCoy describes as the 'corporate conscience' (p. 119).

Corporate behaviour has become a major issue in recent years as public companies in all parts of the world have collapsed, executives have been jailed, workers have lost their jobs, and shareholders have lost their investments as a result of misconduct by directors, chief executives and other managers. Yet whatever role senior practitioners might play as the 'corporate conscience' in advising the dominant coalition, there is a requirement for each of us to work in an ethical way. Harrison (2011) reminds us that a core role of public relations is advocacy on behalf of a client or employer, provided it is ethical practice (p. 10).

> This is a legitimate role, and both McCoy (2009) and Harrison (2006) outline mechanisms by which we can decide whether planned actions are ethical. McCoy's eight steps are as follows:
>
> 1. Objectively evaluate the specific issue, client or organisation before determining whether it merits public relations advocacy. This involves recognising any moral dimensions to the task or problems and identifying the parties who will be affected by their decisions and their obligations to each.
> 2. Respect publics as individuals with rights to adequate information to make informed choices.
> 3. Consider their cultural values and beliefs.
> 4. Tell stakeholders about the reasons behind decisions.
> 5. Clearly identify all communication on behalf of the client/organisation as originating from that source.
> 6. Act truthfully, without evasion or deception.
> 7. Know the law and public policies.
> 8. Know yourself and your core principles and ensure they are reflected in your behaviour.

Theory in practice

All the theories and models that scholars use to understand and explain how public relations works depend on the idea that there is a relationship between an organisation and its publics. Despite academic arguments about which model or theory—or even definition—best describes how the profession works, most of them can work in tandem. A mix of several theories can be used in a campaign. For example, one stage of a public relations campaign for a local government agency responsible for roads might effectively apply the *public information* model to let drivers know about changes to the traffic flow while street repairs are done; in another stage, the agency could effectively use the *two-way symmetrical* model to seek drivers' views about future traffic-flow plans and how driving around the city could be improved. It is not, of course, that practitioners sit around the office trying to work out which theory will be useful in a given situation, or that they even discuss 'theory'. In reality, most probably don't want to ever hear about 'theory' in work chat. But their knowledge of theoretical concepts helps them to make valuable practice decisions even if theory is never mentioned – except perhaps as an example of the way a planned pathway and public relations tools work together when they make a presentation to a client. The important point is that every organisation wants to **inform** its publics about its business and products or services, and to **persuade** them to look on them favourably. An organisation is unlikely to achieve a favourable result if it does not attempt to build a relationship of some kind with its publics.

The chart in Figure 2.2 is a simple method for classifying target publics according to the way in which they relate to an organisation. Some provide an **input**; others receive an *output;* another group *services* the organisation; a fourth *governs* the way in which it operates. Some publics can be included in more than one category. For example, employees are in the *input* segment because they provide their skills; they are in the *output* segment because they are paid by the organisation. The tax agency *governs* an organisation because it administers the taxation law, and an electricity authority *services* a manufacturing company because it provides power. Customers receive an *output* when they buy products. Not all target publics are shown in the chart, and you can probably identify and list more for each segment. The importance of this simple classification of target publics is that it helps to work out the basis on which relationships are formed (remember the definition of public relations?). That means you can identify common issues between your organisation and its target publics and what you need to do to maintain the relationship … in good shape, of course.

When you consider the different ways in which each target public relates to the organisation, the need to build and maintain special relationships with each one becomes apparent. If Ideal Widgets Pty Ltd has a poor relationship with the utility company that provides electricity to the production plant, the supplier may not be totally enthusiastic about providing assistance during an expansion of the plant. And a failure to build a relationship with the local community near the plant doesn't help Ideal Widgets when residents protest about increased traffic in their suburb as a result of the expansion. An effective strategic public relations plan for Ideal Widgets would include *objectives*, *communication pathways* and *tools* for building and maintaining these relationships, and carefully written *messages* that take account of the special relationship each target public has with the company. In line with the earlier discussion about 'the world around us', Ideal's public relations team would have previously identified the possibility of community concern at increased traffic in the suburb as part of its environmental scanning.

Here is a task that will help you to understand this point: a factory in an outer city location would list the local transport providers as suppliers—for employees to get to and from work (rail, bus, roads), and for the delivery of the materials to make products and for the despatch of those products to customers. Now, think about the issues that might affect the relationship between the factory and its transport suppliers: what would damage the relationship; what would keep it strong; who would be important in this; who else among other target publics (and classifications) might be affected? When you have finished this task, you'll have taken a significant step in issues identification and strategic planning.

inform: in a public relations context, to clarify, instruct, or demonstrate a point.

persuade: in a public relations context, to convince a target public to adopt a point of view or to take a particular action.

input: the formative research used to write a situation analysis.

Figure 2.2 Target public classification

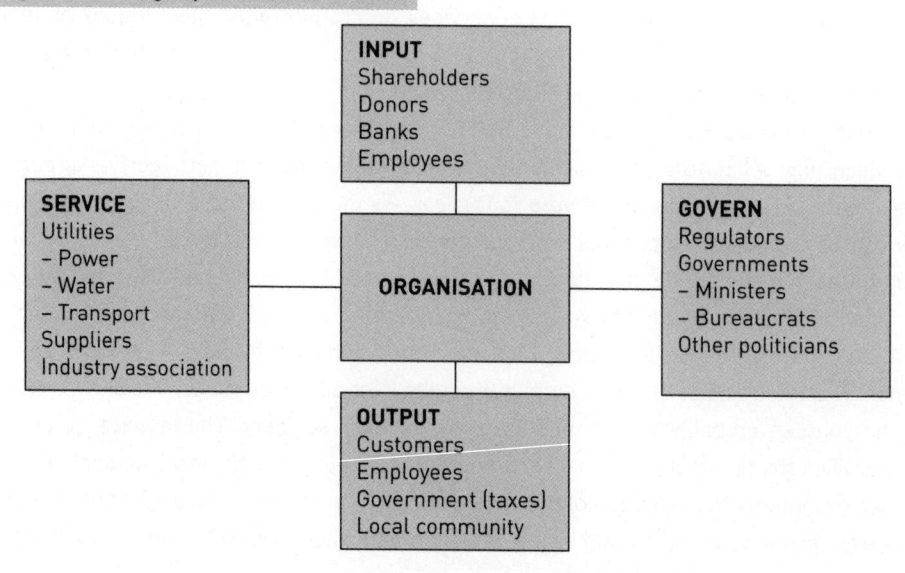

```
                    INPUT
                    Shareholders
                    Donors
                    Banks
                    Employees

SERVICE
Utilities
– Power                                     GOVERN
– Water          ORGANISATION               Regulators
– Transport                                 Governments
Suppliers                                   – Ministers
Industry association                        – Bureaucrats
                                            Other politicians

                    OUTPUT
                    Customers
                    Employees
                    Government (taxes)
                    Local community
```

> ### PRACTICE POINT
>
> Many senior public relations practitioners express concern about how modern language has become sloppy and often blame the use of smart technology and its associated jargon, buzzwords and clichés. It is our responsibility as professional communicators trying to deliver important information to target publics that we write simply and avoid corrupted public language, jargon, buzzwords and clichés. Leave that style of writing to advertising copywriters.

SUMMARY

In this chapter we've looked at:
+ why public relations practitioners need to be aware of the social, political, economic and cultural environments in which they work
+ the importance of environmental scanning
+ how public relations is used as a strategic management tool
+ building and maintaining relations with senior management and an organisation's target publics
+ the legal and ethical frameworks in which public relations practitioners work.

REFLECTION

As part of your **reflection** about this chapter, assume that you work in the public relations team of Ideal Widgets. The team has written a special public relations plan for the plant expansion, and you have been tasked with implementing a controlled media communication pathway to reach a section of your local community that mostly comprises elderly retired people. The communication, or public relations, tool for which you are responsible is a leaflet (yes, they are still used and they are still important PR tools) that will be mailed to all the houses in the area where the retirees live. Your team knows from its environmental scanning that the retirees are concerned about increased traffic in their area as a result of Ideal's proposed plant expansion. You also know that other, non-retired people who live in the area are not as concerned about the traffic but want assurances that the roads around the local primary school will not become more dangerous. The text you write for the leaflet must explain the expansion and include specific messages that reassure the retirees that they will not be adversely affected. On the bus to work you listen to a podcast of the previous night's radio current affairs program in which a local activist claims that the expansion will mean road closures and traffic redirections that will increase risks for older residents walking in the area.

Reread the code of ethics for your country's professional public relations institute to work out how it would help you approach this writing task. What steps might you take to satisfy yourself that the information you have about the expansion, and its impact on the local traffic, is accurate?

reflection: thinking about information you have read, or your experiences, to analyse what you have learnt.

1. Finding Out

Try your hand at some environmental scanning.

In your city's daily newspaper (the hard copy, or from its website), identify an article that reports on an issue that concerns people. It might be a local issue about parking, or an issue about levels of crime, or the availability of places at university.

Practice task

Make a list of the main points in the article. Then use your web browser to investigate how other newspapers, radio and television (their sites are easily located), and relevant blogs have reported the issue. Research the issue via one of the databases available in your university library or use your internet search engine. Try to answer these questions:

- How long has the issue concerned people?
- Why are they concerned?
- Who is saying what about the issue?
- What interests do they represent?
- What organisations might be affected by the issue, and in what ways?

2. Starting to write

Having reflected on the ethical considerations of your writing task, and having decided—on the basis of information you have been given by the general manager responsible for the expansion—that you have no ethical problem, you now need to write the leaflet (see above). You need to plan your approach before starting to write, so:

- identify the target publics who should receive the leaflet
- list five dot points that you will use as headings to help you to prepare the text.

Write no more than fifty words explaining how the leaflet would demonstrate that Ideal Widgets is open to community suggestions about the plant expansion and its potential impact on local traffic. Make sure you mention how the leaflet could be published on Ideal Widgets' website.

TIP SHEET: MATCHING THEORY TO PATHWAYS AND PUBLIC RELATIONS TOOLS

In the first two chapters we looked at examples of theoretical concepts that can inform professional public relations practice. This tip sheet shows theory-based factors you should think about before you start to write material for your clients.

The two tables below set out how two specific theoretical concepts can inform the selection of communication pathways and public relations tools (see the 'An introduction to public relations terminology' section of Chapter 1) to reach target publics effectively. Together, the tables illustrate that professional public relations practice is multi-dimensional in the way it uses a mix of communication pathways and tools to deliver messages to target publics to inform, generate dialogue, and/or to persuade people to take action on an issue. That is why a strategic public relations plan needs careful planning to ensure the best possible chance of success.

Table 1 lists factors you need to think about when choosing communication pathways and tools. That is, before you start to write, you'll need to consider: how many people need to receive your messages (*reach*); how much information or argument you need to include (*richness*); how and when your messages will be distributed and how you can try to ensure the content is actually delivered to target publics (*control*); how many times you need to send messages (*repetition*); and what resources will be needed (*efficiency*). The table lists examples (you could list many more) of pathways and tools that match these factors.

Table 1 Factors that determine communication pathways and tools

Factor: need to consider	Potential communication	
	Pathways	Tools
Reach: Number of people to receive messages	Uncontrolled media	Media releases Media conference Fact sheet Q and A sheet Backgrounder One-on-one journalist briefings Email
	Interactive media	Social media applications where appropriate

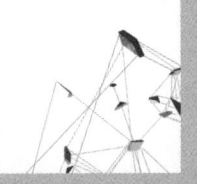

Factor: need to consider	Potential communication	
	Pathways	Tools
Richness: The amount of information or argument needed to support messages	Controlled media	Own publications Website Blog Speech Podcast Display Email and attachment
Control: Of content, timing and distribution of messages	Controlled media	Own publications Website Email and attachment Social media applications
	Special events	Sponsor event/group Display Speech
	Interactive media	Social media applications Website Email dialogue
	Sponsorship	Sponsor community group Sports team sponsorship Sponsor art exhibition Sponsor fun run/walk
Repetition: Frequency of message delivery or how many times publics will hear messages	Blend of pathways	Mix tactics to pathways Consider using Grunig's models (see below)—all, or some, to ensure messages are repeated through different pathways and tools. You will need to consider timing implications for implementing tools in you planning.
Efficiency: Best use of available resources	Uncontrolled media	Media release—potentially wide reach for the message at low cost
	Interpersonal media	Face-to-face meetings for a small target public group
	Controlled media	Using your own website, emails, publications, and direct mail means you can reach a specific public.

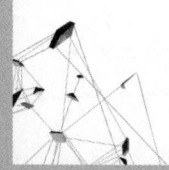

CHAPTER 2: CONTEXTS FOR PUBLIC RELATIONS

Table 2 suggests another way of thinking about what you need to do before you start writing. It relates pathways and tools to the framework proposed by James Grunig and Todd Hunt (1984) to describe how public relations is practised. Their four-model framework can be used to work out communication pathways and tools for specific tasks: only issuing a media release (*press agentry*); providing target publics with straightforward information (*public information*); making an argument without seeking to build relationships (*asymmetrical communication*); and sincerely attempting to build equal relationships by engaging in dialogues about issues with target publics (*two-way symmetrical communication*).

Table 2 shows examples of how this might work. Remember that the multi-dimensional nature of public relations means that the four models are not mutually exclusive—all four can be used for different aspects of a single campaign and they are synergistic. Exactly how the models can help you depends on the goals and objectives you are trying to achieve and the complexity of the issues with which you are dealing, as well as the factors set out in Table 1. Are you, for example, engaged in an informative campaign supporting the launch of a new smartphone research app for university students, or a persuasive campaign to convince people to donate to a charity funding research into cures for cancers suffered by kids? Which of the factors in Table 1 would you need to consider in each example when you match pathways and tools using the Grunig and Hunt models?

Table 2 Communication pathways and tools using Grunig's and Hunt's four models

Model	Potential communication	
	Pathways	Tools
Press agentry	Uncontrolled media	Media releases Media conferences Interviews by journalists Fact sheets Backgrounders Q and A sheets Email
Public Information	Uncontrolled media	Media releases Interviews by journalists Fact sheets Publications Email
	Interactive media	Website—feedback mechanism Social media applications
	Controlled media	Publications Website

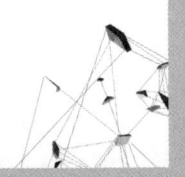

Model	Potential communication	
	Pathways	Tools
Asymmetrical (or one-way) Communication	Uncontrolled media	Media releases Media interviews Q and A sheets
	Special event	Static shopping mall display
	Sponsorship	Sponsor local community centre Sponsor the national ballet
	Controlled media	The organisation's own publications Website
Symmetrical (or two-way) Communication	Interpersonal media	Face-to-face meetings/talks Community meetings Staff at displays for dialogue Email and snail mail Interactive media Social media applications Email Special events Community meetings Staff at town hall display Open house site visits

Given the range of public relations tools practitioners can use, you could list many more in each category. But as communication between an organisation and its publics becomes more symmetrical (or two-way) it enables dialogue. An example is the role of humble email. In press agentry, public information, and asymmetrical communication, email is a one-way tool with no expectation that anyone will respond to it. Of course, good organisational media relations practice would mean that if a journalist did respond to your email with a question you would reply as soon as possible with an answer. When communication is truly two-way and initiates a dialogue, email is a handy device for interaction between and organisation and its target publics. Table 2 also illustrates how using the mass media is essentially one-way communication practice. That is not to say that news reporting of your information won't start a dialogue. But campaigns that rely solely on an uncontrolled media communication pathway may not be as effective as they could be.

Adapted from Mahoney, 2017, pp. 201–3

RESEARCH AND PLANNING FOR PUBLIC RELATIONS

3

This chapter introduces the basic concepts of public relations research and strategic planning. After reading the chapter, you should understand:

+ the importance of strategic planning to public relations practice
+ the role of research in public relations planning
+ how to identify the communication issues facing an organisation
+ how to write a situation analysis.

ABOUT PUBLIC RELATIONS STRATEGY

Few people go on holiday without planning where and when they'll go, how they'll get there, and what they'll do while they are away. Their travel agent will prepare an itinerary that gives details of the dates they'll travel, transport times, accommodation details and the associated costs. If they do not use a travel agent, they'll have worked these details out for themselves, perhaps by studying a road map so that they know how to drive to their destination and to plan rest stops, or by consulting an airline or train timetable. Tourist guides for their holiday destination will help them to work out the attractions they'll visit, tours they'll go on and which are the best local beaches. All this planning helps people to budget for what they'll need to spend while they are on holiday.

A public relations strategic plan does the same thing for professional practice. It is about maximising opportunities and minimising problems. A strategic plan tells us where we need to start, how to get to our destination and how we'll know that we have arrived, by identifying:

+ opportunities for the organisation to tell its story—or address problems it might face, especially in a crisis
+ specific goals and objectives
+ messages for target publics.

A strategic plan also identifies how messages will be delivered, the tools that will be used to do that, and the budget and other resources that will be needed, and it includes timelines and checklists for getting everything done. The plan will also explain how success, or failure, will be measured.

Anne Gregory (2009b) tells us that planning won't make a poorly conceived program successful in achieving its objectives, but it will make it more likely that the program will be well conceived.

Table 3.1 sets out the classic elements of a public relations strategic plan. A strategic plan will also include an executive summary, outlining the important points in the detailed plan. (For a detailed discussion of the elements of a public relations strategy, see Mahoney, 2017, ch. 4.)

Table 3.1 The elements of a public relations strategic plan

Situation analysis	The analysis of a detailed examination of the communication issues and opportunities facing an organisation. The emphasis is on *analysis*; that is explaining why issues are important, and what they mean to an organisation, not just listing them. A situation analysis is based on formative research. It is in this part of a public relations strategy, or plan, that a practitioner writes about the organisation and its internal and external environments, and identifies and explains issues that the public relations plan will address. A well-researched and written situation analysis will determine how successful the strategy will be.
Goals	Broad statements of what the public relations strategy is designed to do. Public relations goals reflect an organisation's business strategy and deal with reputation, relationships or tasks. A plan can have one or more goals. See the example in Chapter 1.
Objectives	These are precise and measurable steps setting out what is needed to achieve a goal. Objectives express exactly what needs to be achieved in a defined time frame. They deal with raising awareness, or building acceptance or convincing publics to take action in support of the organisation. Each goal can have one or more objectives, but there must be more objectives than goals. Use verbs (for example, raise, build, generate, increase, maintain, improve—sometimes even reduce, negate, minimise) when you write objectives. Make sure your objectives state what change (perhaps a percentage) you want to achieve, and the time by which you anticipate that happening. See the discussion of objectives in Chapter 1 for an example.
Messages	These provide information to a target public about a client's product or views on an issue. They help to build credibility, or to persuade a target public to take some action that will support the client's interests. Messages can be informative or persuasive. Formative research will help to identify gaps in knowledge among specific target publics and therefore messages that might be needed to increase their awareness.
Target publics	These are the people with whom the organisation builds relationships. They are those to whom we direct messages to raise awareness, generate acceptance and promote action. Formative research for a public relations plan will help you to identify your client's target publics. Target publics share issues with the organisation, often depending on the situation they and the organisation face.

Communication pathways	Sometimes described as 'message delivery strategies', these explain how messages will be delivered to target publics. They identify how a practitioner will *reach* target publics; they are not the tools or activities that will be used. For example, a program of face-to-face meetings with target publics would be described as an 'interpersonal communication' pathway.
Communication tools	Tools are public relations activities, or 'products' that implement communication pathways. They are what a target public sees or experiences: tweets, email, displays, publications, meetings, media releases, websites, blogs, podcasts, videos, hard copy and electronic posters, letters and special events. Each pathway can be implemented by using several tools tailored for individual target publics.
Implementation	This describes the financial, human and technological resources needed to implement the plan. This includes a timeline for when things need to be done, and a checklist of actions and responsibilities. See Chapter 10 for samples of checklists and timelines.
Evaluation	This explains how you will measure the success of the plan. Among the basic questions for an evaluation are: Did we achieve our goals and objectives? Did the target publics take the action we sought? Were the pathways and tools appropriate for the target publics? Was the plan completed on time and within budget? In each case, ask: If not, why not? Can we do it better next time? What stopped us from achieving our goals and objectives? An evaluation should compare outcomes with objectives.

Before practitioners write strategic plans, they need to find out as much as they can about the communication issues (sometimes, crises) that their client faces.

Research for public relations

In the first two chapters, we saw how a strategic public relations plan links to, and supports, an organisation's overall business strategy. We looked at the need to identify and understand the context in which our client organisation operates, and the communication issues that it faces.

What do we know; what do we need to find out; how might we do it?

Finding out about the organisation—what it does, its business environment, its plans for the future, how its internal systems work, the communication issues it faces—is the starting point for a strategic plan. This is known as **formative research**. The research you conduct at the end of a campaign to work out whether you achieved your goals and objectives—an evaluation— is known as **summative research**.

Formative research will help you to identify goals, objectives, messages and target publics. It will be important for determining communication pathways and tools, and it will set a benchmark against which you can measure your success.

Effective public relations practitioners are continually researching, even if they are not engaged in a formal process. Through their daily reading, watching and listening to news and public affairs

formative research: formal or informal research that is conducted before a public relations plan is written and that is used to inform the situation analysis.

summative research: formal or informal research conducted at the end of a campaign to assess effectiveness.

and their consultation with others inside and outside the organisation about current or emerging issues and communication opportunities they are engaged in *environmental scanning*. One Australian practitioner who specialises in agricultural public relations strategy and practice makes sure she monitors all the relevant Twitter and Facebook accounts of companies, industry associations, spokespeople, newspapers, journalists and politicians who are involved in agricultural policy and politics. With her consistent reading of newspapers and watching of agricultural news programs, this monitoring enables her to keep up-to-date with the industry and catch journalists' calls for help in chasing stories. That is an example of consistent and regular environmental scanning.

Formal research

quantitative research: research that reports results as numbers.

qualitative research: research that is concerned with finding out people's attitudes and opinions.

Formal **quantitative** or **qualitative research** enables a practitioner to identify levels of awareness and acceptance of a client's organisation or products. It can identify issues that need to be addressed by a public relations program. Research of this kind can be commissioned through commercial market research companies. The information it provides helps practitioners to write public relations goals, objectives and messages, and to identify target publics. Qualitative research findings often assist practitioners to work out communication pathways and tools. Most importantly, formative research can be used to set a benchmark against which you can measure the success of your public relations program. To do that, a practitioner would repeat the formative research after the program and measure changes to awareness and acceptance.

It is not always possible for a client to allocate money for formative and summative research of this kind, because it can be expensive. However, if the costs can be included in the project budget, the research will contribute significantly to the plan's strategic effectiveness. Often, especially in large companies, research for public relations purposes is funded as part of a broader marketing budget.

Desk research

evaluation: the process of reviewing whether a public relations plan achieved its goals and objectives.

Not all research need be expensive. Effective research is still possible if you do not have a budget to engage a market research company. In many cases 'desk research', which you, or other members of your team, can do from existing material, official reports, historical data, the media and the organisation's files, will produce valuable information for planning and **evaluation**. Searches of websites relevant to the organisation, or of organisations that study public issues, can also yield important, useful information for a situation analysis.

> ### PRACTICE POINT
>
> Practitioners do not always need to pay for research. Often they can access a wide range of publicly available research information. If a practitioner needs special research—and this is often a requirement of public relations campaigns—then commercial market research companies can be paid to undertake it.

Using the library

Libraries, among the first institutions to recognise the importance of electronic storage and management of information, are a primary resource of research data. The catalogues of the national, state and university libraries can be accessed electronically. From an electronic search of a library's catalogue, you could, for example, find out what international experts have written about the contribution that solar power could make to future energy generation. A visit to your state library will enable you to search back copies of newspapers to find out how the media covered the development of solar energy. Other major sources of research information are the libraries of national and state parliaments, which publish online research reports on a wide range of domestic and international social, economic and political issues.

If you live in Australia, for example, you could use the website of the Australian Bureau of Statistics (ABS), which conducts a five-yearly census, to search for data that shows that by 2051 Sydney and Melbourne will still be the two most populous cities in Australia, with 5.6 million and 5.0 million people respectively. Think about how demographic data available from sources like these can be useful in planning public relations activities.

Annual reports as a research source

A good first step in formative research is to review the organisation's latest **annual report**. Annual reports deal with the organisation's performance for the latest financial year. For most Australian organisations, the **financial year** runs from 1 July of one year until 30 June in the following year, although some organisations use the calendar year as their financial reporting year.

Annual reports are an opportunity for companies to provide more information about their activities than can be covered in the formal, legally required financial statements. That is why most annual reports include sections from the board of directors and the chief executive officer that review performance during the past year, set out plans for the future and comment on issues that the organisation has faced in the last year, or could confront in the coming year. Many annual reports also include information about staff, the company's research and development achievements, new operational facilities, and other initiatives taken during the year. Publishing information about how the organisation has performed on social and community issues and environmental concerns, as well as financial data, is known as 'triple bottom line' reporting. When they report performance in this way, organisations are attempting to show that they are not just interested in financial outcomes.

An annual report will reveal important and detailed information about the organisation's financial position, its operations and business interests, past performance and plans for the future—all vital to helping practitioners understand their client's business and its communication needs. Public relations staff are usually heavily involved in producing annual reports, so these reports are also great resources for assessing how senior practitioners present important information about organisations.

annual report: an official publication that deals with the organisation's performance for the previous twelve months, usually the financial year.

financial year: the twelve months for which a company reports its annual financial performance.

> **PRACTICE NOTE** FINANCIAL REPORTING
>
> For most organisations, especially companies, annual reports are a legal requirement, and they must follow formal accounting standards to report in detail how the organisation used its finances. A formal, legal annual report comprises tables giving details of the organisation's annual financial accounts, the explanatory notes attached to them and an accompanying statement by the board of directors. Annual reports must be given to all shareholders and be lodged with various government agencies. Companies whose shares are traded on the stock exchange must provide their annual report to the exchange.
>
> Public relations practitioners are usually responsible for producing an organisation's annual report. This involves planning, researching and writing the text (except for the financial statements, which are usually prepared by the finance and accounting teams). Practitioners manage the design (and printing and distribution when hard copies are required) of annual reports, as well as posting the report on the organisation's website. Detailed checklists and timelines—including deadlines for research, writing, photography, design, typesetting, senior management approvals at all stages, and printing and distribution—are important in this process. This often hectic assignment requires good interpersonal communication skills, because practitioners must work cooperatively with people at all levels of the organisation, and with external contractors, to get the annual report produced and distributed.
>
> In Australasia there are awards for annual reports judged the best in their sector of the economy (see <http://www.arawards.com.au>). The winners in these awards are exemplars of what is required to produce a top-quality annual report.

Access to market and political research

All the major market research companies conduct regular surveys—often called omnibus surveys—that ask questions for their clients on a range of consumer-related trends and social issues. Most of these surveys regularly research state and federal voting trends to find out which political party is likely to win an election, who is most favoured as prime minister and how citizens feel about current issues. In some countries, opinion poll companies specialise in this political intelligence gathering. The results of these opinion polls are published in major newspapers and magazines and are reported online and in news programs. During elections, the results of opinion polls become stories in their own right, often becoming the main story on nightly television news bulletins. A political leader's standing 'in the polls' is sometimes used as an excuse for members of their party to vote them out and to elect someone else, as has happened in Australian state and federal politics several times.

All these surveys generate important demographic information about respondents, which the market research companies' clients analyse to help them understand attitudes towards their products, or opinions on social issues, or voting intentions. For example, the Public Relations Manager of Ideal Widgets Pty Ltd could pay to have questions included in a regular omnibus survey to find out what people think about the company's safe new widget. From the results, Ideal Widgets might find that single, female respondents living in your city aged 20–25 years, in full-time work and earning $45 000–$50 000 a year, and intending to vote for the Greens at the next election know nothing about widgets. You might like to think about what that might mean for Ideal's communication efforts in your city.

> ## PRACTICE POINT
>
> By exploring the websites of the major market research companies, you can find information that is useful for public relations planning, especially for identifying issues and market trends. All these companies use their websites to publish reports on their research. Papers written by experts about their market and opinion research findings can also be accessed on these sites. The World Advertising Research Centre (<**www.warc.com**>) is also a good resource for case studies and research data, as are the websites of banks, industry associations (lobbies), government agencies and private 'think tanks'.

Media monitoring

The public relations departments of most private enterprise and government organisations pay an external **media monitoring** agency to provide a daily online summary of how the media have reported their business. This commercial service can include access to a full copy of a newspaper story, or an actual copy or transcript of a radio or television report. The summary also provides demographic information about the readers of newspapers in which a story appeared, or about the listeners and viewers of radio and television programs, and if the organisation pays for it, an analysis of all this information.

Daily media monitoring is not just important for finding out whether your media release was published or broadcast. It is also invaluable for monitoring issues that affect your organisation and for tracking who might be reading or listening to the public debates about them. It also helps you to work out how and when you might participate in those debates and where you might target a media release.

Another media source of opinion and comment on public affairs are weekly specialist programs on radio and television. These programs cover the arts, science, business, religion, ethics, history, the law, health, social commentary, politics and philosophy, and most material they broadcast can be downloaded as podcasts, or viewed on your tablet computer.

media monitoring: the regular scanning of the print and electronic media for articles of interest to the organisation. Most organisations contract a commercial media monitoring agency to do this work.

Universities as research resources

Another research resource are the hundreds of academics at universities. Most academics make themselves available to the mass news media for expert comment about the issues of the day in their fields of expertise. Universities list these experts in the 'for media' sections of their websites, and one commercial organisation offers an online service that helps people to locate academic and other experts (visit <**www.expertguide.com.au**> to see how this works). For example, academics regularly comment to reporters (or write their own articles) about tensions in the Middle East, trade policy, national politics, health issues, the economic outlook, legal and constitutional matters, crime, education, and science.

Researchers working in scientific research can be important sources of expert advice. In Australia, for example, scientists at the Commonwealth Scientific and Industrial Research Organisation (CSIRO) can provide expert information on issues related to science. Most universities have world-leading academics who can be engaged as consultants. Sometimes academics will provide advice free of charge, and they are often willing to address conferences and seminars on the areas of their expertise. Universities also use their official websites to publish research results and other background material quoting their academics' views on issues and research outcomes. One example of this is the website for the Massachusetts Institute of Technology—one of the world's top universities—which changes the major story and associated image on its home page every week. (Visit <**www.mit.edu**> to explore how MIT covers important research outcomes and makes information available to the news media.) This is a valuable example of how an organisation's public relations team can use its website to promote news and information.

An innovative approach to accessing informed, plain-English analysis of current issues by academics is the website *The Conversation* (<**www.theconversation.edu.au**>), which was established to provide 'an independent source of analysis, commentary and news from the university and research sector—written by acknowledged experts and delivered directly to the public' (<**theconversation.edu.au/who_we_are**>). The website is a joint venture between a number of universities, has more than 4000 contributors and is read worldwide.

Think tanks

think tank: an organisation that employs specialists to research and comment on important public issues.

Most countries have privately funded institutions that employ specialists to research and comment on important public issues. These institutions are colloquially known as policy '**think tanks**' because their specialists ponder problems and propose solutions to them. One Australian 'think tank' is the Lowy Institute, which specialises in ideas about Australia's role in the world. The Centre for Strategic Studies: New Zealand is an international and military affairs research institute. One of the world's most famous think tanks is the Brookings Institution, a private, non-profit organisation devoted to independent research and proposing innovative policy solutions. Some of the people who contribute to the work of think tanks, many of them eminent academics, are regular commentators in the mass news media, either through newspaper articles or appearances on radio and television. The think tanks publish reports, newsletters and journals, and conduct seminars about their work that can include information that practitioners might need to consider in their strategic planning. All claim to be 'independently funded', but it may be important for practitioners to decide whether individual think tanks have a particular social or political leaning.

The internet

The growth of the internet as a communication tool has provided the world with a wonderful research resource. The internet's search engines can connect us to such a diverse range of resources that it sometimes seems to be an overwhelming task to select those that are most relevant to what we need. Nevertheless, the 'net' can connect us to research and opinions that are important to our work. We can also improve our professional practice by regularly visiting websites that are designed to support practitioners, like the PRIA site (<**www.pria.com.au**>), the US site (<**www.prsa.org**>), New Zealand's (<**www.prinz.org.nz**>), and Britain's (<**www.cipr.co.uk**>).

> **PRACTICE POINT**
>
> When you search websites during your formative research, look for links like 'Newsroom', 'Press Room', 'For Media' or 'Journalists' to access the organisation's media releases. The media-release files, and archives, provide current information, as well as background to the issues the organisation is facing.

Identifying communication issues and needs

Formal research helps practitioners to determine awareness and acceptance of their client's business and products. Survey questions can be written to test for these. Statistics from a quantitative survey can provide information about the lack of awareness of Ideal Widgets' new product among young women in your city. A lack of awareness of a company, product or particular aspect of a public issue among a specific demographic category should cause a practitioner to investigate more deeply, especially if the demographic group is a vital target public. Qualitative surveying, perhaps using focus groups, can help to explain why people hold certain views. It may be that young females in your city don't know about the new widget because women don't use widgets anyway. Or it may be that none of the women in the group were exposed to the company's messages about widget safety, despite the fact that they are used by everyone every day. In the latter case, Ideal would have identified a communication issue—lack of awareness about its product among people in a specific target public—and it could write a public relations campaign to address this.

Information generated by formal research is important in identifying gaps in awareness and acceptance among target publics that may prevent them from taking positive action that supports an organisation's goals and objectives.

formal research: either qualitative or quantitative research that is normally commissioned through an external commercial market research company.

How writing a situation analysis helps to set the context for the plan

situation analysis: the first part of a public relations plan in which a practitioner analyses the communication issues facing an organisation and assesses the results of formal and informal research.

As the first section of a public relations plan, a **situation analysis** sets the scene by describing what needs to be done. It identifies the public relations issue for which the plan is being prepared and summarises your research.

> **PRACTICE POINT**
>
> To analyse something means to make a detailed examination of it. So, if the local pre-school asks you to help it raise funds, you'll need to examine why it doesn't already attract funds from the community. You'll do that by asking questions like: What has the pre-school done before to raise funds? Have people given reasons for not donating in the past? Where do the pre-school kids live: nearby? or do they travel? What kind of socio-economic profile does the local neighbourhood have? (Perhaps people who live there can't afford to donate.) Do people know about the pre-school? With answers to questions like these, and others that you might think of as you do your research, you'll be able to work out what the problem really is. Is it a question of people not even knowing that the pre-school exists (awareness)? Or do they not understand its role (acceptance)? Or do they think it is fully funded by the government and therefore does not need extra money (action—or, in this case, inaction)?

Writing a situation analysis requires you to express the main points accurately and succinctly. This is an important point, demonstrating that good writing skills are crucial to almost every aspect of public relations. For a situation analysis, you would be demonstrating your writing skills at the planning stage of a public relations project, even before you wrote a media release, or a blog post, or contributed something to the client's website.

A situation analysis is written as prose, with accurate paragraph and sentence construction. You can use subheadings and, where appropriate, bullet points to make the text easily accessible. The length of a situation analysis depends on the issue or opportunity you are dealing with. Some situation analyses are quite brief, especially those that deal with crises. Others, written for a major campaign or to explain the context for an organisation's overarching public relations strategy, need to be detailed because they are covering a range of issues and opportunities. Whatever the immediate context for the plan, the situation analysis should be written so that those who need to approve your plan understand the proposal and why you've suggested those activities.

A situation analysis should:

+ summarise the communication issue or opportunity the plan is being written to address
+ establish the environment in which the organisation works and what this means for the communication issue or opportunity you are dealing with

+ outline the findings of formal and/or informal research
+ provide information about the organisation and the target publics you have identified
+ summarise what you want the plan to achieve.

The situation analysis below shows one way of doing this, based on an explanation of the situation that the practitioners were addressing, the issues they needed to think about and their preliminary research findings.

> **PRACTICE NOTE** A SITUATION ANALYSIS
>
> In February 2011, the New Zealand city of Christchurch was devastated by an earthquake that killed 185 people and destroyed hundreds of homes and other buildings. Just ten weeks after the earthquake, the Christchurch City Council launched the Share an Idea initiative to generate community input into the development of the draft plan to rebuild Christchurch's central city.
>
> The following situation analysis describes the issues that the council's public relations team faced in implementing this project. Note how it describes the situation, summarises issues that need to be addressed, and outlines research used to plan what Christchurch City Council might do.
>
> ### Background
>
> The 22 February 2011 earthquake ripped through Christchurch, killing 185 people, destroying homes, communities, much of the city's heritage and the central city. The level of destruction saw the central city placed within a cordon—the heart of which still remains inaccessible to the public.
>
> Under the *Canterbury Earthquake Recovery Act 2011* (CERA), the Christchurch City Council was given nine months to develop the draft Central City Plan to rebuild the central city following the earthquake—a plan of this nature would normally take at least three years to develop.
>
> The Act of Parliament set out that the work was to be done in partnership with CERA, Environment Canterbury and Te Runanga o Ngai Tahu. Just as critical was involving the community to share their ideas in the four months council had to produce the draft for formal consultation.
>
> ### Preliminary research
>
> As this project arose from a natural disaster, there was limited time to plan— only five weeks from instigation to launch. There was early recognition that the success of the plan was reliant on getting wide input from all levels of our community. It was also recognised that as many of our community were

still traumatised by the event, suffering personal loss (homes, jobs and loved ones) and living with disruption and continual aftershocks, engagement with the community needed to be easy, inviting and a rewarding experience. Asking people to put their personal circumstances aside and focus on the central city was always going to be a challenge.

Local government is often criticised for lack of consultation and we knew the short time frame could make attempts to consult appear insincere. We knew individuals needed to control how, when and to what extent they interacted with Share an Idea, but most importantly, our community needed to know that their ideas had the power to influence the future of their city.

As a start to the project, council reviewed its existing strategies relating to the revitalisation of the central city—the Public Space Public Life report, a City for People Action Plan, Central City Revitalisation Strategy and Central City South Masterplan. This ensured there were strong links with this work, which council had already been working on with the community for almost a decade.

We also looked at international examples of how other cities had included their communities in taking ownership of the rebuild or revitalisation of their city, in particular how they managed the conversations and used the ideas.

Key directions from existing council strategies were used to start the conversation, our community being asked four simple questions:

+ How do you want to move about the central city?
+ What public spaces and activities do you want to see in the central city?
+ What type of businesses do you think are appropriate for the central city?
+ What do you think is needed to attract people back to live, work and play in the central city?

Throughout the six weeks, the ideas shared by our community through the expo, at the workshops and online were used to help define the emerging themes, develop new questions and drill down for a more detailed response from our community.

Edited extract from a 2012 Highly Commended Public Relations Institute of New Zealand annual awards entry by Christchurch City Council's Jan McCarthy, Michael Flatman and Ray Tye. Published with the permission of the authors.

Writing a situation analysis

To win the Public Relations Institute of Australia (ACT) Student Challenge, University of Canberra graduates Stephanie Lyons and Isabelle Herlt wrote a seven-page situation analysis for a strategy they developed for Heart Support-Australia (HS-A). The nationwide voluntary organisation assists people who have, or are likely to develop, cardiovascular disease. The situation analysis dealt with a challenge that faced HS-A and that it had identified: despite being the only organisation of its kind in Australia, and having operated for twenty years, it was relatively unknown outside the health sector. In their situation analysis, Stephanie and Isabelle wrote that to get more funding, HS-A needed to raise awareness about what it does, especially in the communities surrounding its branches. They conducted a **SWOT analysis** based on their research. This enabled them to identify, and discuss, strengths, weaknesses, opportunities and threats for HS-A, from which they developed goals and objectives and identified target publics. As part of their planning, they conducted three research studies, each of which examined a separate aspect of HS-A's communication with its target publics. One used the NewsBank database to examine all newspaper coverage of HS-A for the previous twelve months. A second used the transcript archives of the ABC Backyard local radio website to determine the prominence of cardiac health as a topic of local radio broadcasts. The third used literature review techniques in an internal communication study that examined all HS-A newsletters to determine whether they clearly communicated vital head office messages.

By using inexpensive (but no doubt time-consuming) formative research, Stephanie and Isabelle wrote a detailed situation analysis that explained HS-A's communication challenges and identified ways they could be addressed.

SWOT analysis: an analytical tool that helps to classify an organisation's strengths, weaknesses, opportunities and threats from formative research findings.

SUMMARY

This chapter introduced you to the importance of research in developing public relations plans to identify client communication needs. We also looked at the ways in which practitioners can access information that helps them to undertake research for strategic planning. We used this background to discuss how to write a situation analysis, the first part of a strategic public relations plan.

In the following chapters, we'll explore other elements of strategic planning: setting goals and objectives, identifying target publics, developing and writing messages, communication pathways and tools, and applying public relations writing to practical contexts.

REFLECTION

Imagine that you have been employed as a public relations consultant to SIDS and Kids, the organisation that promotes the annual Red Nose Day to raise awareness about the need for research into sudden infant death syndrome and other early childhood diseases. SIDS and Kids competes with all other community organisations for recognition and donations. It faces competition from a plethora of coloured ribbon and flower days and doorknock appeals for donations. What desk research could you do to find out how much money people donate to charities and other good causes, such as special relief funds for people affected by natural disasters? What does that information tell you about the causes to which people prefer to donate money? What information would you need in order to identify messages that SIDS and Kids could use to attract donations?

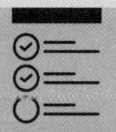

ACTIVITIES

1. Write a Research Summary

Assume you are a public relations officer for a company that has been making shoes for ninety-nine years. To celebrate its 100th year of operations next year, the company has decided to make a pair of slippers, free of charge, for every person in the country aged 100 years and over. You have been asked to find out how many people are actually 100 or older and the states they live in so that the company can plan the production of the slippers and a public relations plan to (a) locate each person and (b) promote what it is doing. Search the website of the national census organisation to identify how many people are aged 100 and over. Write no more than 100 words summarising what you find out.

2. Using Annual Reports as Information Sources

To understand how annual reports can help you to find out a lot of detailed information, go to the website of your bank and look for, and read, its annual report. Analyse how it reports to shareholders on its involvement with the community. Choose a major manufacturing company and read its annual report to discover how the company reported its achievements. Look at the graphic design that has been used to display the information in the report. Then select a state or national government agency and look for its annual report on its website. Are there any differences in the way in which the three organisations report? Work out from each annual report who the organisation's important target publics are. What issues are important to the organisation?

3. Legal Requirements for Annual Reports

A reasonable knowledge of the legal requirements for annual reports is important—and essential for practitioners who specialise in financial public relations. To find out about the legal requirements for annual reports, explore the website of the government agency that manages the laws relating to how companies and other organisations must operate. (Identifying that agency is a useful research task in itself.) You could also go to the stock exchange's website to find out the rules that govern the share market, ensuring the interests of people who buy and sell shares are protected.

4. Write a Brief Situation Analysis

Scan the finance pages of your local daily newspaper to identify a company that is 'in the news'. Write a summary of what the news stories are reporting about the company. Look up the company's website and search for its latest annual report (this will normally be for a financial year). Read the annual report and identify the issues that you believe the company faces. Search the internet for other information about the issues that you have identified. When you have completed this desk research, write a 500-word report that summarises the context in which the company works and the communication issues you think the company faces, and why those issues are important to the company. Include a bullet-point list of the target publics you think the company should focus on in a public relations strategy. Share your situation analysis with someone else and discuss what each of you has done.

Practice task

You are a public relations officer for Cool Musik, a new record company that has contracted the finalists in the last four years of a national television talent quest for rock music, Stars in the Making. Cool Musik's first album, featuring 18-year-old singer Ima Chanteuse, is to be released in three months. Ima is very popular with teenagers. After the launch of the album, Ima and her backing group, the High Notes, will tour capital cities and make personal appearances at major music stores. Ima will be in each city for two days only. You have been asked to prepare a public relations plan for the launch of Ima's album and her national tour.

Choose *one* of the following tasks:

1. Undertake desk research to identify:
   a. record stores in two major cities at which Ima could meet her fans. How many stores should Ima visit in each of those cities?
   b. at least three radio stations in one capital that you could approach to suggest on-air interviews for Ima. What time of the day would be best for Ima to be interviewed to ensure that her fans hear what she has to say?
2. Scan your capital city's major daily newspaper and make a list of the names and titles of the journalists who have written stories in that day's edition. To which of these journalists, if any, would you send a media release about Cool Musik's first album? If you can't find an appropriate journalist from the list you have made, go to the newspaper's website and try to identify the journalist who would be most interested in the release. Does the journalist you select have a special title? Use desk research techniques to identify appropriate journalists from two television stations in your capital city to whom you should send your release.

Another practice task on this topic appears at the end of Chapter 4, so keep your notes.

TIP SHEET: MULTICULTURAL COMMUNICATION

Given what we know about public relations planning, it is a fairly safe assumption that practice deals with 'difference'. That is, no two target publics share the same demographic characteristics, nor do they access information in the same way or need the same level of information. Often the differences relate to generations. For example, while many seniors use smartphones and social media applications, most probably do not use these tools to the extent that Gen Y does. The two generations share the same citizenship, but they don't necessarily share the same interests, political views, hobbies, lifestyles and ways of communicating with friends, families, employers, and the agencies and community organisations that support them. It could be argued, then, that seniors and Gen Y belong to different **cultures**—and understanding that difference, and what it means for public relations planning and writing, is another example of the importance of context in decisions about how an organisation should communicate with target publics.

György Szondi (2009) argues that culture and communication influence each other, especially if the latter is about symmetry. In that discussion, Szondi is writing about national cultures and how practitioners deal with differences when they work in an international context. In other words, practitioners need to be aware that messages, communication pathways and tools that might work in middle-class Western societies will not automatically be successful in, say, Thailand. Cultural differences explain why. Mohan Dutta and colleagues (2012) have argued powerfully for a culture-centred approach to public relations practice and scholarship.

culture: 'the customs, civilisation and achievements of a particular time or people' (*Australian Concise Oxford Dictionary*). Some people, perhaps migrants, suffer 'culture shock' when they experience an unfamiliar culture or way of life. *Multiculturalism* means the existence of many culturally distinct groups in a society.

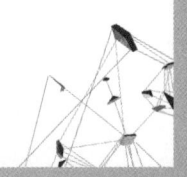

MULTICULTURAL COMMUNITIES

Almost every Western nation has experienced positive changes to its culture as a result of great waves of international migration, especially after the Second World War. The United States prides itself on its cohesive mix of people from different ethnic backgrounds, drawn from the many immigrant groups who have been arriving almost from the nation's inception. Australia had a similar experience after the Second World War. Displaced people and migrants from Greece, Italy and the former Yugoslavia saw Australia as a country of opportunity where they could rebuild their lives.

The make-up of multicultural populations and the migrations of refugees fleeing war and famine in the early part of the twenty-first century require practitioners to think more deeply about planning and writing public relations tools designed for diverse cultures. Marianne

Sison (2009a) has raised important questions that can help in that planning and writing. Sison notes that global public relations audiences comprise people of multicultural backgrounds. That means practitioners should ask some serious questions about multicultural publics in strategy development:

+ How do existing target public segmentation models account for cultural variability?
+ Whose cultural values predominate among multicultural audiences?

WRITING FOR MULTICULTURAL PUBLICS

Much public relations writing is undertaken at a basic level without answering Sison's questions. This basic approach involves translating material into a series of publications that reflect the predominant languages of the largest migrant groups. It is, of course, important to translate material, because not everyone is fluent in, say, English and may lack the literary skills to understand written English. Citizens from all ethnic backgrounds have rights and responsibilities, so there is an equity requirement to make sure they are properly advised about them. A common solution to this communication challenge is to provide translations of messages for printed and web-based material, and for radio, television and press advertising; to select appropriate communication channels to deliver them; and to employ people fluent in other languages to work in enquiry offices. Unfortunately, this simplistic response often becomes a last-minute activity, factored into the program because a policy requires it to be done. But is it effective, and is there another way?

Different cultures use words in different ways, react differently to authority, gender and social circumstances, support family members in different ways, and differ in the ways in which they go about business. Multiculturalism is not just about allowing people to speak their native language, or to live and worship in culturally appropriate ways; nor is it about enjoying the impact of African, Asian and Arabic cooking on the traditional local diet. It involves respecting that diversity, and for public relations practitioners, it also means planning and writing in an appropriate way.

In a discussion about culture and global public relations, Robert Wakefield (2010) raises two important points that apply equally for decisions about intercultural communication planning. He argues that practitioners should build strategies that do not lose sight of local publics and potential local issues, and that they should seek intercultural understanding. While these points are made in an international practice context, they recognise that publics in different cultures are concerned about different issues and that practitioners need to understand this.

Sison's (2009a) research found that cultural factors in twelve Australian award-winning public relations strategies designed to change behaviour were limited to representations of race and language. While these factors are important in attempting to get messages understood, Sison argues that strategic decisions should first be based on research into the community's cultural perspectives. Only one of the strategies (to promote the health benefits of a new cycle path) acknowledged cultural diversity, but the research component did not investigate what the diverse ethnic communities in the relevant community thought about bicycles as alternative means of public transport. The evaluation of this communication project (which was generally highly successful) did not provide comparisons between the overall outcome and those for ethnic communities. On a strategy designed to convince 18–26-year-old women to ask their doctors about a free cervical cancer immunisation (also generally rated successful), Sison argues that the research should have sought answers to questions like: How do different ethnic communities view vaccinations for women? What would be the religious and ethical considerations among young women from different communities, or second-generation families, regarding vaccination? How might these issues be addressed in the campaign? What are the cultural implications of using 'influencers' for health-related issues?

CULTURAL DIVERSITY

The importance of Sison's research is that it shows that cultural diversity should be a significant factor in all aspects of strategic communication planning. Based on their research, Arlette Bouzon and Joëlle Devillard (2009) argue that cultural communication is an essential business function. To plan and implement intercultural communication, practitioners need to, as Sison (2009a) puts it, acknowledge cultural variables beyond the descriptive factors of race, religion, language and values.

From a professional practice perspective, this isn't easy, but it is an extension of the need for stakeholder segmentation into relevant target public groups, for appropriate messages and for communication pathways to recognise cultural difference. Maybe effective intercultural communication needs separate and specific strategic planning. It certainly needs deeper consideration of message content, writing styles and delivery mechanisms that are culturally appropriate.

Based on 'Time Out: On intercultural communication',
in Mahoney, 2013, pp. 125–8

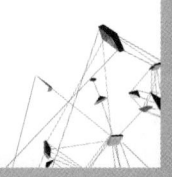

4 PUBLIC RELATIONS GOALS AND OBJECTIVES

This chapter examines public relations goals, objectives and target publics. The chapter will reinforce your appreciation of the public relations contexts in which your writing will be used. At the end of the chapter, you will understand:

+ how to write communication goals and objectives
+ the importance of identifying target publics for a public relations program.

A PUBLIC RELATIONS MATRIX

The public relations teams in most organisations work on more than one activity, many of which occur regularly. These activities are usually set out in a public relations strategy—a major research and *writing* task for practitioners. Writing a strategy requires the same basic skills as preparing any other aspect of public relations (accurate and precise use of words, and correct grammar), but, importantly, needs an understanding of how goals and objectives should be expressed to ensure the strategy's success, and to make sure it can be properly evaluated.

A top-level public relations strategy that includes all the regular PR activities should reflect an organisation's business plan and discuss the context in which public relations is conducted. This plan will also describe corporate goals and objectives, set out the key messages the organisation wants to convey to target publics, and outline how it will go about doing that. This guides planning for specific ongoing public relations activities, each of which will have specific goals, objectives, messages, target publics, communication pathways and tools.

All strategic public relations plans must include budgets, implementation timelines, and details about how success will be evaluated, and it is common for them to be revised annually.

Table 4.1 sets out the regular activities that might comprise an annual corporate public relations plan.

CHAPTER 4: PUBLIC RELATIONS GOALS AND OBJECTIVES

Table 4.1 Matrix of a corporate public relations program

Program	Public Relations Department			
Component	Community relations	Media office	Internal communication	Publications
Activity	Factory open day	Media releases	Staff newsletter	Graphic design
	Shopping mall display	Fact sheets	Staff intranet	Corporate brochures
	Community meetings	Social media	Social media	Annual report
	Local council liaison	Backgrounders	Christmas party	Website design
	Community hotline	Media briefings	Staff awards scheme	Design of social media tools
	Complaints	Media conferences		
	Special events	Media site tours		
	Site tours	Issues management		
		Crisis communication		
		Website		

Think of the chart as a **matrix** that shows examples of all the regular, planned things that the public relations team might do throughout a year. This public relations office 'program' would have goals and objectives that are directly linked to the organisation's overall strategy. The top level of the matrix is a corporate public relations *program*. This is divided at a second level into broad programs or *components* that are designed to, for example, build, maintain and enhance relationships with the local community, manage communication with investors, inform the media about the organisation, communicate with staff, and design and produce publications. Specific regular *activities* (we know them as public relations *tools*)—for example, displays, special events, open days, using social media applications, media releases, annual reports, the staff Christmas party and fact sheets—are related to the various *components* to complete the matrix. Often the media office supports the work of, for example, the community relations office, just as elements of the *program* from time to time support sales and marketing initiatives.

Of course, not all public relations programs are exactly like this. How a *program* is structured depends on the size of the organisation, the responsibilities of the PR team and how many regular things it has to do each year. The second level of the matrix reflects what might happen in a large team and can be usefully structured to give one or more people responsibilities for specific *components*. For example, a public relations office might comprise one team tasked to implement the *activities* in the media office; another group responsible for internal communication; and a third to run events and other initiatives in community relations.

matrix: a grid that shows in a graphic form how the parts of something—in this case, activities in a public relations plan—fit together.

The matrix is a visual demonstration that the professional things a public relations office does involve more than just dealing with the news media. While media relations is an important specialisation of public relations, it is not the only focus of the profession. Nor is using social media. A well thought out public relations strategy uses effective goals and objectives to reach target publics using a range of coordinated communication pathways and tools. In this way, a properly planned and effectively implemented strategy is a practical illustration of public relations definitions that describe it as a way of building, maintaining and enhancing relationships with people who are important to organisations. To do that a practitioner should use all the appropriate tools so that target publics can be reached in a number of ways.

Sometimes special plans are needed for a specific opportunity—for example, the launch of a new product. A special plan like this will reflect the organisation's overall communication goals and objectives, and messages, but those messages would be rephrased to reflect the purpose of the specific plan. Organisations also prepare special plans that set out how they will communicate with external and internal publics during a crisis. Crisis communication is a specialist public relations function.

PUBLIC RELATIONS CONSULTANTS

Not all strategic public relations activity is carried out by in-house teams. Hundreds of large and small *consultancies* or *agencies* provide public relations services to companies and other organisations, for a commercial fee. The *consultants* who work in these firms are highly skilled professionals who often specialise in particular areas of public relations practice, such as social media strategy, crisis communication or event management. Many consultancies have links with large international firms, which of course benefit their local clients. Sometimes public relations consultants are asked to review in-house plans, or to write and implement new strategic plans. This happens when the organisation does not have the in-house expertise to write a special plan, or if it needs additional specialists to help out with an ongoing project. Many organisations engage consultants to run their whole public relations program and to assist them when they face a crisis. It is also common for organisations to retain public relations consultants to provide high level strategic communication advice to senior managers.

> ### ■ PRACTICE NOTE LINKING PLANNING TO EVALUATION
> Planning strategic public relations as a matrix has an advantage: evaluation can be more effective. If each element of the matrix has its own goals and correctly written objectives that are consistent with the overall strategic goals and objectives, there will be clear links between the program, component and activities levels. That means that the success of the corporate program—the public relations department in Table 4.1—will be an outcome of the success of the components. The success of each component depends on the success of its activities. So a successful program

outcome (sPo) is the sum of successful component outcomes (sCo), which in turn are the sum of its successful activity outcomes (sAo). That's a bit like a maths formula:

$$sPo = sum(sCo_1 + sCo_2 + sCo_3), \text{ where } sCo = sum(sAo_1 + sAo_2 + sAo_3)$$

It looks a bit complicated, but in practice it works like the following example. At the end of each year the Manager of Public Affairs at Ideal Widgets Pty Ltd needs to report on how the corporate public relations program performed. The manager will ask questions like: Did we achieve the goals and objectives written for everything we did? Did each activity end the year within budget? What stopped us from achieving our goals and objectives? The manager will know that the success of the internal communication team (a component in the chart) can be determined by weighing up the positive and perhaps negative assessments of the outcomes of the various goals and objectives for the staff newsletter, intranet, Christmas party and awards scheme. In this way, the manager is measuring the success of Ideal Widgets' public relations program in a meaningful way. There are many ways to measure the success of goals and objectives—but more about that later.

Whatever the task, either writing a major corporate public relations plan, or a plan for an annual activity like an open day at a navy base, strategic plans include the elements outlined in Table 3.1 in Chapter 3.

MEANINGFUL GOALS AND OBJECTIVES

Writing goals and objectives that clearly set out what you want to achieve in a strategic public relations plan is critical. Much like highway signposts, they show you the way. A highway signpost that uses an arrow with the words 'Katoomba' conveys the broad message that if you follow this highway you'll get to Katoomba. That's like a public relations **goal**. A signpost that reads, 'Katoomba 100 km. Turn left 5 km' is like an **objective**: it is more detailed and it is measurable.

What are goals?

Goals deal with *reputation*, *relationships* or *tasks*. A public relations plan usually has more than one goal, and they define the broad parameters of what the plan is trying to do. Goals reflect the organisation's business strategy. You'll have identified what that is from discussions with your client and from your research, perhaps a review of the annual report.

For example, High Style Fashions, a company planning to produce women's clothing at a busy inner-city location, wants to ensure that people who live nearby, or who work in offices or other businesses in the same street, understand that trucks will deliver supplies and take finished clothes away at all times of the day. They'll need a public relations plan to address that. In this plan:

+ a *relationship* goal might be 'to promote a better appreciation of High Style Fashions' relationships with our neighbours'

goal: a broad statement of what the organisation hopes to achieve and which reflects the organisation's business strategy. Goals deal with reputation, relationships or tasks.

objective: a precise and measurable statement of what the organisation needs to do in order to achieve a goal. Objectives deal with changes: raising awareness, building acceptance and convincing publics to take action that is favourable to the organisation.

- a *reputation* goal might be 'to reinforce High Style Fashions' standing as a valued member of the local community'
- a *task* goal might be 'to increase local residents' attendance at High Fashions' annual open day'.

Because goals are broad statements, finding out whether they have been reached comes from measuring the success of the precise objectives.

What are objectives?

Think of objectives as steps towards meeting a goal. Each goal should have specific objectives to make sure the goal is achieved. Objectives support goals and must be measurable (see below).

Clear, precise and measurable objectives achieve **outcomes** by indicating the changes an organisation wants to achieve over time. Writing objectives to achieve outcomes means that we want to do more than produce a media release, build a display, post to Instagram or publish a newsletter. It means that we want to change something. That is why objectives are about building *awareness*, generating *acceptance* and persuading target publics to take *action*. The American public relations academic Ronald Smith (2009) says that awareness objectives deal with information and knowledge; acceptance objectives focus on how people react to information; and action objectives address a 'hoped-for response to information and feelings'. Outcome objectives do not say what communication pathways and tools will be used—pathways and tools have their own section in a strategy.

Some objectives can deal with producing things as opposed to bringing about a change ('Update the website weekly during the campaign', for example). These are process or output objectives. They can, of course, be measured in an evaluation ('We did update the website weekly'), but they are about doing things. In an evaluation, measuring output objectives gives an indication of work done not of changed attitudes, or of people taking action.

Objectives to generate *awareness* or *acceptance* or *action* are not mutually exclusive: you can write objectives directed at each of these in one public relations plan—and you should use a combination of *informative* and *persuasive* (or *motivational*) objectives. Informative objectives are about giving target publics information that is important to them, such as building awareness of something. Persuasive objectives try to convince people to take some kind of action.

For example, if a broad communication goal is 'to enhance our organisation's reputation', then objectives would help to achieve this by:

- building *awareness* of our corporate social responsibility activities
- generating *understanding* of the importance of those activities to local communities
- convincing target publics to take *action* by supporting those activities.

Of course, writing specific, clear, precise and measurable objectives to do this is a little more complicated than that, as we'll see in the next sections.

outcome: a measurement that shows whether a public changed its knowledge, attitudes and behaviours as a result of a public relations campaign. Achieving outcomes is the most important part of a public relations plan.

Matching goals and objectives

In June 2005, MasterFoods Australia New Zealand engaged the Melbourne-based public relations **consultancy** Socom to help it manage communication during the crisis that followed an extortion attempt, in which a person threatened to poison Mars and Snickers bars in the Australian state of New South Wales. Socom won a PRIA Golden Target Award for its campaign, which had the following goal and simple but precise objectives:

consultancy: a business that provides public relations services, sometimes also known as an agency.

Goal
Recall all Mars® and Snickers® products quickly and safely in NSW whilst protecting the reputation of MasterFoods.

Objectives
1. Protect public safety.
2. Ensure 90 per cent of the key messages are contained in the media coverage.
3. Return the products to shelf when it is safe, with at least 80% public support.
4. Return product sales to normal levels within four weeks of return.

Reflect on how the goal in this example deals with the company's business strategy and how the objectives are written to achieve the goal. Writing goals and objectives with this simplicity and clarity demonstrates how easily the success of a campaign can be measured because they say exactly what the client and the communication team want to achieve. They also reflect the client's concern with broader issues like public safety, not just its business interests.

Setting goals that reflect issues and communication needs

In the situation analysis for the MasterFoods crisis communication plan, the public relations consultants wrote that the challenge was to 'inform the public, manage the communications and maintain the trust of industry, consumers and employees in the company'. The snack food manufacturer needed to quickly gain control of a situation that had been instigated by the extortionist, because the need for safe and undamaged products was paramount.

Responding to this crisis was a huge logistical exercise: it involved contacting more than 40 000 retail outlets across the state and removing three million products from sale, while maintaining the trust and confidence of the community.

The brief goal written for this plan reflects our definition: it was a broad, general statement that addressed *reputation*, *relationships* and a specific *task*.

Writing measurable objectives that pursue goals

Dennis Wilcox and Glen Cameron (2012, p. 151), US academics who write about strategic public relations planning, suggest that you can test whether an objective is appropriate by asking:

+ Does it really address the situation?
+ Is it realistic and achievable?
+ Can success be measured in meaningful terms?

The objectives of the MasterFoods plan could all be measured. Public safety was protected because the products were taken off shop shelves and the community was told why this happened. No one got sick. The key messages were included in all of the communication that the company had with the media. The products went back on shop shelves as soon as possible after the crisis was resolved.

The objectives section in Table 3.1 reminds us to use verbs and to state the changes that need to happen when writing objectives. Writing objectives in this way ensures that they can be evaluated. A formula for writing objectives is shown in Figure 4.1.

Figure 4.1 Formula for writing objectives

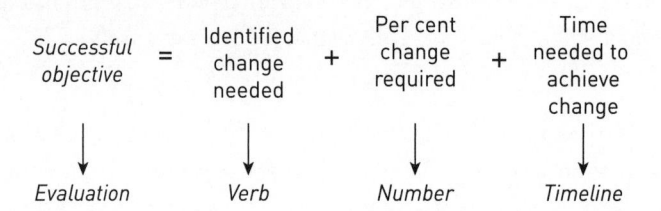

Successful objective = Identified change needed + Per cent change required + Time needed to achieve change

↓ Evaluation   ↓ Verb   ↓ Number   ↓ Timeline

Let's use the formula to write some objectives. Remember, objectives are steps towards achieving a broad goal. Earlier in this chapter we saw that a broad communication goal might be *to enhance our organisation's reputation* and that three objectives to achieve this would deal with:

+ building *awareness* of our corporate social responsibility activities
+ generating *understanding* of the importance of those activities to local communities
+ convincing target publics to take *action* by supporting those activities.

Using the formula in Figure 4.1, those objectives would be written this way:

+ **Objective 1:** Build *awareness* of our corporate social responsibility activities among 75 per cent of our primary target publics in local communities within nine months of the campaign start.
+ **Objective 2:** Generate *understanding* of the importance of our corporate social responsibility activities to local communities among 60 per cent of all target publics within a year.
+ **Objective 3:** Convince 80 per cent of target publics to support our corporate social responsibility activities by the end of the campaign.

Each has identified a change needed among specific target publics; each sets out the specific percentage change needed; each sets a time deadline for the change to be achieved. In this example, Objective 1 deals with a specific target public group; the other two objectives deal with all target publics. The definitions in the next section on target publics illustrates why this is important.

TARGET PUBLICS

Target publics are people. They are the people we want to inform about our organisation, its products or services, or its views on public policy issues. Organisations share issues with target publics, sometimes from an opposing point of view. When a practitioner knows precisely who target publics are, and what they know and believe about an issue, the easier it is to write a strategy to engage them in a discussion about the issue. A company wants its target publics to support it by, for example, buying its new lipstick; charities want target publics to donate money to support their good works; not-for-profit organisations want people to support their views on public policy issues by, say, writing letters to local politicians. Target publics are the people whose views determine an organisation's reputation, and with whom it builds relationships once it has made them aware of, and understand, what it does. Target publics are important and specific to the situation the organisation faces.

Once target publics have been segmented to define exactly who we want to receive messages, we can develop more effective communication pathways and tools for reaching them. That is because we will also know how they prefer to receive information and in what format. For example, it is likely that parents prefer to receive information about a university in a different way from their kids. Mums and dads may want to have discussions with academics and administrators about costs, accommodation options, alternative courses and entry scores, while their kids might find this out by going to the website. Everyone would get the same messages, but it would be delivered in different ways. And that is why it is vital to be clear about who target publics are and what roles they have in a public relations plan.

Most public relations plans identify three kinds of target publics, each for a specific reason:

+ *Primary* target publics are the people directly affected by the situation and are the people who should receive messages. In the university example above, the primary target public is intending students.
+ *Secondary* target publics are the people who are indirectly affected by the situation but who may be an information source for, or influence on, the primary public. In the university example, the secondary target publics would be parents, and school teachers who can provide information or influence intending students.
+ *Tertiary* (or *intervening*) target publics are not directly or indirectly affected by the situation but are people who can influence primary and secondary publics—for example, journalists. In the university example, journalists might report on an institution's national or international ranking, information that might influence intending students—and their parents and school teachers in the advice they give. By writing about current issues, journalists might not convince people to accept a particular point of view, but by choosing what they write about, they set an agenda that influences what people might think about. For this reason, practitioners provide journalists with information as one of their public relations *tools*. Journalists are, then, rarely a primary or secondary target public. They are a medium by which messages can be delivered to publics. See the discussion below about journalists as target publics.

A THOUGHT ON THEORY: IDENTIFYING RELEVANT TARGET PUBLICS

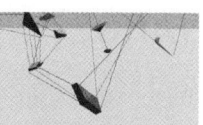

WHO

Identifying target publics for a strategic public relations plan means working out which people are important to an organisation. Some, like employees or shareholders, are easily identified. Others will become apparent from research when a practitioner is addressing a specific issue, or situation, facing an organisation.

WHY

It is important to identify what a target public already knows about the organisation and whether they have positive or negative opinions about it. Research should also uncover what they expect from the organisation, how they obtain information about it and the best, most cost-effective ways of contacting it. This information is important because it helps practitioners to write messages that target publics will understand, and to select communication pathways and tools that will reach them.

WHAT

The demographic, psychographic and geographic characteristics of target publics are important. Demographic variables like age, gender, education, cultural background, marital status and socio-economic background determine what we might say and how it might be delivered. Psychographic variables like opinions, values, perceptions and concerns determine the tone of messages. Geographic variables, like whether people live in a city or in a rural area, or whether a campaign is to be national or limited to one state, are important for working out how messages will be delivered.

The scholar Kirk Hallahan (2000) argues that because many public relations programs involve building positive relationships, differences between organisations and their publics might be minimal—or might not even exist. His view is based on research that shows that a person's behaviour towards an organisation (or issue) is determined by what they know about it as well as their involvement in it. Hallahan suggests that people are selective about the issues that they think are important and that because of this, some people simply have low levels of knowledge about an organisation and low levels of involvement in its operations. He calls these people 'inactive publics' and he argues that they are the 'forgotten publics' in public relations.

Hallahan has proposed five classifications of target publics based on their level of knowledge about an organisation or issue. Table 4.2 sets out Hallahan's five-public model based on knowledge and involvement, and includes their potential characteristics.

Table 4.2 Hallahan's five classifications of target publics

Knowledge	Involvement		
	Low	High	None
High	**Aware publics** Potentially vocal and aggressive	**Active publics** Potentially influential	
Low	**Inactive publics** Potentially volatile	**Aroused publics** Potentially inert	
None			**Non-publics** Potentially aggressive

Adapted from Hallahan (2000)

WHY 'GENERAL PUBLIC' DOESN'T WORK

Many public relations programs include the 'general public'—that is, everyone living in the nation—as a target public. That's a huge range of ages, socio-economic backgrounds, interests, education levels, regions and cultures, and connections with our organisation. It is difficult to identify one public relations program that could reasonably expect to deliver informative or persuasive messages to every single person living in the nation. An effective message about the dangers of recreational drugs for people aged 15–25 years living in a regional town would require different language and delivery techniques from those needed to reach married couples aged over fifty-five years and living in townhouses in a state capital. The 'general public' is not even appropriate for perhaps the two largest target public groups in every nation, taxpayers and voters, each of which is specifically defined: people who pay tax and people on electoral lists. If you want to reach a large group, for example 'householders', then say so and work out what you need to do to deliver a message to each household in a region or the nation.

So, the 'general public' just doesn't work as an effective target public. It is too broad and it is a lazy way of defining a target public, even if a client says they want to reach the 'general public'. That means practitioners should think more precisely about who they want to hear messages, what they need to do to reach them, which communication pathways and public relations tools will actually work, and what the costs of doing all this will be.

Utilising Hallahan's model is one way of doing this. For example, with some formative desk research you could define exactly who Ideal Widgets' *active* and *inactive* publics are. It is in Ideal's interests to identify who its *non-publics* are and to design a public relations program to reach them because they represent a potential source of support. Target publics can be further segmented to make them relevant to an organisation's public relations effort. As James Grunig and Fred Repper (1992) point out, the basic idea of segmentation is simple: divide a population into groups whose members are more like each other than members of other segments of the population. To do that, practitioners utilise demographic, psychographic and geographic variables and theories that explain how people think, behave and communicate.

JOURNALISTS AND THE NEWS MEDIA AS TARGET PUBLICS

Using terms like 'the media' or 'journalists' as target publics is, like using the general public, too broad and inappropriate. What is meant by 'the media'? Which journalists? We probably never really mean 'the media' when selecting target publics because it is a collection of TV shows, publications, radio broadcasts and websites and blogs. What we really mean is the people who produce the information that is published on those platforms. Journalists in other words. Journalists are people like every other target public. They are people who write news stories, select stories for TV and radio news bulletins, and who blog, tweet and email. In planning public relations pathways and tools that will involve journalists, practitioners need to recognise there is a wide range of journalism specialisations and things these people actually do. For example, when 'the media' are listed as a target public, does the practitioner mean the daily metropolitan press? radio or television? trade magazines? community newspapers? internet news and current affairs? blogs? Does the practitioner mean the journalists who specialise in finance reporting and analysis, the environment, politics, sport or fashion? For television, is the practitioner seeking a story on a nightly newscast or an extended interview with the Chief Executive Officer of Ideal Widgets on a current affairs program? Each program employs a different style of journalism.

reporter: a journalist who reports the news.

Journalists specialise in reporting different aspects of our lives, especially those who work on the major daily newspapers, both hard copy and online. Traditionally, these specialisations have been called 'rounds' because specialist **reporters** ring around, or visit, experts in the specialist area they are covering for news leads and comment. News outlets have reporters who specialise in covering technology, or sport (in all its variety), or politics, or cases in the law courts, or what's happening in transport, motoring, finance and business, the environment, holiday travel or education. This range of specialisations means that it is unlikely that the economics reporter will write a story about an increase in inner-city crime, but the reporter who covers the police 'round' would be ideal for the story. In planning journalists as target publics, be specific by segmenting them in the same way as you segment other target publics. It is relatively easy to identify the individual journalists to whom you need to provide information. To see how easily you can do this, peruse your capital city's daily newspaper to identify how many activities are covered by specialist reporters. In your strategic plan you could list them in the target public section by name, or by the broader specialisation, that is, for example 'environment reporters on metropolitan newspapers and television news'.

We'll look at writing messages and working with journalists in more detail later, but it is important to recognise that public relations uses reporters to reach other target publics in a quite strategic way. As we saw earlier, rarely are individual journalists the 'target' for our information: we are attempting to use them as a vehicle (an uncontrolled media communication pathway) to deliver that material to more meaningful target publics who we want to be aware of our organisation, accept its views on issues, buy its products, or take action to support it. That's why it is vital to be specific about which journalists in which media you want to reach, and why.

SUMMARY

This chapter has examined how strategic public relations plans pursue an organisation's corporate communication goals and objectives. It also discussed how to:

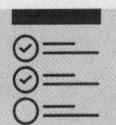

+ write effective public relations goals and objectives
+ identify clear, specific and meaningful target publics.

In the following chapters, we'll explore the principles for writing messages, identifying communication pathways and appropriate public relations tools, and writing for practical contexts.

REFLECTION

Reflect on this chapter by identifying a common interest among your immediate family and friends. Perhaps you all enjoy bushwalking. Maybe you are all interested in music—but do the older people in your family listen to the same music as you and your friends?

Would a common interest in bushwalking make it relatively straightforward for a public relations practitioner to write a strategy to promote a new, lightweight wind- and waterproof anorak to your family and friends? Why? Would that task be easier than writing a strategy to attract the same group of people to a new music shop in your town? If so, why?

ACTIVITIES

1. Public Relations Consultants

Go to the website of your national public relations professional institute or society (these organisations are identified in Chapter 1) and click on the 'Find a firm' or 'Find a consultancy' link. Limit your search to your state or province and click on five of the consultancies that are listed. Make a list of all the services offered by the firms you read about. What are the common services? How many firms offer services that could help clients to (a) manage issues, (b) help in a crisis and (c) communicate with various levels of government?

Some of the institute websites will list consultancies by area of expertise, or by geographic location. If you have trouble finding your national public relations institute, go to <http://apps.prsa.org/Network/FindAFirm> for this exercise.

2. Try Writing a Public Relations Goal

You can do this exercise even if you do not live in Australia. Assume you have just been elected the public relations officer for your local Clean Up Australia team. Write two 25-word sentences that explain what you want people in your community to know about this year's local Clean Up Australia Day. Using the information in the two sentences, write a broad goal for the public relations plan you are preparing for your team. Decide whether yours will be a reputation goal, a relationship goal or a task goal. Do whatever research you need to do to understand what Clean Up Australia is about. Your first stop should be <www.cleanup.org.au>.

3. Identify an Objective

Scan your local daily newspaper (or TV station's website) for a story about a new product. Critically analyse the story to determine whether the information on which it is based was designed to raise *awareness* of the product, build *acceptance* or persuade people to take *action*. Was the information *informative* or *motivational*?

4. Write a Measurable Objective

Assume you work in Ideal Widgets' public relations team and that you have been asked to prepare a plan that addresses the low level of knowledge that young women have about widgets. Use the formula in Figure 4.1 to write one measurable objective for your plan.

5. Identify Some Target Publics

Assume you work for the dynamic (but fictitious) Hong Kong-based public relations consultancy Pearl Communicators. Pearl has a team of young practitioners who are renowned for their creative public relations solutions, especially in dealing with issues. The consultancy has won a competitive pitch to work on a campaign (also fictitious) for the operators of the Mass Transit Railway (MTR) system, who are concerned about the increasing cost of keeping the train carriages clean. This is an important issue for the MTR's operators because the growing cleaning costs may need to be covered by increasing fares, a step they are reluctant to take. The MTR has found that most of the litter removed each day, mainly newspapers and cardboard coffee cups, is from trains that run between 6.30 a.m. and 9.30 a.m., and 5.00 p.m. and 8.00 p.m.—the daily commuter and student travel peak hours. The

CHAPTER 4: PUBLIC RELATIONS GOALS AND OBJECTIVES

> MTR wants a campaign to convince commuters to keep the carriages clean by taking their litter with them and leaving it in the big bins on MTR stations. They have been proud of the traditionally clean trains, which are used by the Hong Kong Tourism Board in international visitor-attraction campaigns.
>
> Your task in planning the campaign is to identify target publics. Do this by identifying:
>
> - three *primary* publics
> - two *secondary* publics
> - two *tertiary* publics.

Practice task

Review the work you did for Ima Chanteuse's first album at the end of Chapter 3. Remember, you are a public relations officer for Cool Musik, a new national record company that is releasing its first album, featuring the 18-year-old singer Ima. You have been asked to prepare a public relations plan for the launch of Ima's album and her national tour.

Using the information that you identified from your desk research, and any other data you can locate from additional research, write:

1. one broad communication goal for your public relations program
2. two objectives that illustrate how your objective will be achieved
3. one message that could be included in your media release about Ima's album.

TIP SHEET: HOW THEORIES CAN INFORM PRACTICE

Exploring theoretical concepts that help explain how people and organisations communicate is a major part of public relations education. Most theories used to explain what public relations is, and how it works, are adapted from psychology, philosophy, political science, management, sociology and the physical sciences. Others, like J. Grunig's Excellence and Situational Theories, and Hallahan's Typology of Publics, are developed from scholars' research into aspects of public relations practice. The works of internationally renowned scholars like Abraham Maslow and his 'hierarchy of needs', the writings of the German philosopher and sociologist Jürgen Habermas on the theory of communicative rationality, and the French social theorist Michel Foucault who wrote about power and knowledge, have all been used to help explain how professional communication works.

Most public relations textbooks include a chapter on these and other significant theories. Academic journals, from which you will probably have several readings for your classes, publish scholars' research that uses these theoretical concepts to explain research results and what they might mean for professional practice.

This tip sheet lists some theories that can help public relations writers to produce and deliver the most effective messages. You should use the library to search for academic journals and books that include detailed discussions of these and other theories.

CHAPTER 4: PUBLIC RELATIONS GOALS AND OBJECTIVES

Theoretical concept	Practical applications
Basic communication model Way back in the late 1940s Claude Shannon, an electrical engineer, and Warren Weaver, a mathematician, who both worked for the Bell Laboratories in the United States proposed a simple model to explain how radio and telephone communication worked. They argued that messages were coded by senders, transmitted via a channel (the telephone, for example) and received and decoded by receivers. In this process, there was likely to be some static, or noise, that could potentially interfere with the message transmission and impact on how receivers understood messages. This model has been adopted by communication scholars as a simple example that explains how public relations messages are transmitted and understood.	While this is a basic concept for public relations, it can help in the design and distribution of messages. For example, how a receiver (a member of a target public group) decodes a message and understands it, depends on a range of factors, including their education, world beliefs, other demographics and socio-economic status, and so on. Their ability to decode and understand the message can also be affected by 'noise', or other things going on in their world. For example, their ability to understand a message might be affected by the thousands of other competing messages they receive each day. So, while the Shannon–Weaver model is a simple way to view communication, it does suggest that practitioners need to work out as best they can what channels, or pathways, and message formats, or tools, they need to use to reach target publics and how they might reduce competing 'noise'. An understanding of the other theories in this tip sheet can also help practitioners to work these things out.
Situational theory of publics Posited by James Grunig (see Grunig & Hunt, 1984) as a way of understanding how publics will react in a given situation. A situation can be an issue or a problem that an organisation and its publics face. The theory holds that publics can be identified and classified by their awareness of a problem or issue, and whether they do something about it. Publics are thus described as *latent, aware* or *active*. A public's decision to do something about a situation depends on three key factors, or independent variables. These factors are + *problem recognition*, or the extent to which a public recognises a problem facing them and believes something needs to be done about it. + *constraint recognition*, or, briefly, whether a public believes it can do something about the situation. + *level of involvement*, or how relevant the situation is to a public. The theory suggests a public will be more involved in a problem or issue the more they understand messages.	This is a key theory that should guide practitioners' thinking about what they need to do to establish and maintain communication with target publics. Situational theory gives practitioners a framework for thinking about an issue or problem facing an organisation, and how publics might react to the organisation's communication. For example, a latent public that is not aware of an issue or a problem is unlikely to respond to an organisation's communication. However, an aware public might become highly involved in the situation if they believe an issue or a problem is relevant to them. A public that is aware but does not believe the situation is relevant to them is likely to have only low involvement. Situational theory can help to identify messages, pathways, and tools. For example, what messages need to reach a latent public, by what communication pathways and public relations tools, for them to recognise the issue (awareness) and to become involved in a debate about it (action).

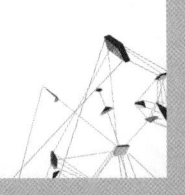

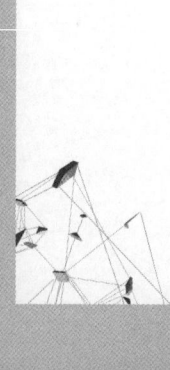

Theoretical concept	Practical applications
Hallahan's typology of publics Kirk Hallahan (2000) extended Grunig's situational theory by developing a typology—or classification—of target publics based on their high, low or no knowledge about, and high, low or no involvement in, an issue (see Table 4.2 in the Thought on Theory: Identifying relevant target publics, on p. 75). The theory holds that + *active publics* have high levels of knowledge about, and involvement in, an issue and are therefore potentially influential. + *aware publics* have high knowledge but low involvement in an issue but are potentially vocal and aggressive if they become more involved. + *aroused publics* have low knowledge about an issue but high involvement. Aroused publics are potentially inert. + *Inactive publics* have both low knowledge and involvement but if their level of knowledge increases they are potentially volatile. + *Non-publics* have no knowledge of an issue and no involvement but are potentially aggressive if their level of knowledge increases.	Hallahan's typology of publics can guide decisions about which publics an organisation needs to engage in communication and at what level that engagement should be. It can also help to work out messages and how they should be delivered. Hallahan was of course exploring inactive publics who he described as 'the forgotten publics in public relations' (see his article by this title in *Public Relations Review* 26(4), Winter 2000 at pp. 499–515.) Later, Hallahan (2001) argued that strategies for dealing with publics should vary in line with their existing level of knowledge and involvement in an issue. Using the typology as a guide, a practitioner can assess a public's likely involvement in an issue and how they might be engaged (Mahoney, 2017). This helps to work out whether publics should have *primary*, *secondary*, or *tertiary* (or *intervening*) status. That leads to decisions about effective messages for the different classifications of publics and the selection of communication pathways and tools. For example, a charity raising funds for research into a cure for a childhood cancer will have established primary, secondary and tertiary publics but there will be some who also fit the Hallahan (2001) classifications—and people who are non-publics. The task of the charity's public relations team will be to match the information needs of its publics with their potential to donate (their likely involvement). Thinking about publics in this way can determine the amount of information an aroused public, for example, will need to become active and donate to the charity. Given Hallahan's (2001) suggestions about the potential actions publics in the typology might take, messages, communication pathways and tools should be carefully crafted to reach them in ways that generate support and avoid negative reactions.

CHAPTER 4: PUBLIC RELATIONS GOALS AND OBJECTIVES

Theoretical concept	Practical applications
Media effects theory The concept behind this theory is that mass media have a powerful direct influence on people's awareness and understanding of an issue and that people change their behaviour as a result of exposure to messages delivered via this communication pathway. **Agenda setting theory** is the idea, proposed in 1963 by the American political scientist Bernard Cohen, that the news media is not always successful in telling people what to think, but it is stunningly successful in telling its readers what to think about. Cohen was expanding on Walter Lippmann's argument in his 1922 book *Public Opinion* (Harcourt, New York) that the mass news media is the main connection between events in our local, national and international communities and how we view those events. That is, people view an event or an issue as salient, or important, to them if it is covered prominently and frequently by the news media. Agenda setting theory was formally developed by Max McCombs and Donald Shaw as part of their study that compared local and national news media coverage of issues that were important to residents of Chapel Hill, North Carolina, during the 1968 American presidential election. They reported their study in a 1972 *Public Opinion Quarterly* article arguing they were able to determine the degree to which the mass news media determines public opinion. **Framing theory** This theory suggests that the mass news media focuses on certain events, issues, views and organisations and reports them within a field of meaning. The theory holds that by reporting, or presenting, news in these 'frames' the media influences how readers and viewers process news. For example, journalists and their editors decide on a 'frame' in which news will be reported. The discussion in Chapter 6 deals with some of the basic news frames of timeliness, conflict, relevance, significance, rarity and so on. Framing also includes the prominence and newspaper space, or radio and television air time, editors give to specific news stories or commentaries. This theory, of course, links to agenda setting because the selection of news frames influences how readers and viewers perceive the news they receive.	**Media effects, agenda setting** and **framing** theories explain why public relations people distribute media releases to the mass news media. That is, if the mass news media has a powerful influence on what people understand about a company, a charity, a government agency, a local council, or an issue, then it would be a good idea to try to build awareness and understanding of an organisation and its products, services or views in that media. Maybe if readers and viewers, our target publics, better understand an organisation they will change their behaviour towards it. That might mean supporting its views in a public debate about an issue, or buying its fair-trade products, or being aware of the local council's need to build a new road to give parents better access to a school. And, if the mass news media is successful in telling people what to think about, because of the choices editors make about what to publish and how that news is reported, at what length, and how prominently, then maybe skilful public relations work can set an agenda for its clients as well. This would be done by selecting information that is salient to target publics and that frames information in ways that journalists will recognise as news worth reporting. Such news framing means making sure what you write and distribute via a media release is actually news and important to a lot of people. A similar rationale applies to social media tools when they are used in public relations. Social media tools can provide specific target publics with important news about the organisation, tweets, website and Facebook posts, and pictorial information. The concepts in media effects, agenda setting and framing theories apply to social media use, especially if these tools are applied to reach journalists as tertiary, or intervening, publics. Social media tools, of course, can deliver messages directly to target publics without them being mediated by journalists, and this is a vital consideration when deciding what public relations tools to use. The ability of social media to directly reach target publics is behind the increasingly sophisticated use of these tools in political campaigning and fund raising. It is important to remember that public relations' attempts to influence media effects, agenda setting and framing are only successful if the information you distribute on behalf of clients is picked up and reported by the mass news media. And the vital key to that is your ability to write clear, concise and accurate material that journalists recognise as real news.

Theoretical concept	Practical applications
Contingency theory This theory attempts to explain how internal and external factors, or independent variables, influence organisations' abilities to do what they do (the dependent variable). This management theory suggests there is no best way to set up and manage an organisation and that leaders adapt to the external and internal situations their organisations face. The theory is often used by scholars to explore and explain the factors that influence communication.	Contingency theory can help practitioners understand the factors that influence a situation facing an organisation (see 'Situational theory' above). For example, if a charity that supports childhood cancer research needs to raise funds (a dependent variable), research will identify the factors that influence its ability to raise funds (independent variables). The charity will become aware of several factors; some will be positive influences; others negative influences. A positive independent variable might be the willingness of people to donate to causes that help prevent or cure childhood diseases; a negative independent variable could be donor 'fatigue' created by the large number of charities competing for donations from the community. The task of a practitioner faced with these variables would be to, for example, minimise the effect of donor fatigue on the charity by producing material that illustrates why its work is so important.
Complexity theory Complexity theory, developed from systems theory, a concept in the physical sciences, is the idea that natural and human systems are continually changing. Briefly, the theory holds that large and small changes in these systems affect the total system. That is, these systems adapt as changes in and around them impact on them. The theory is used by some scholars to research and explain interactions and relationships in organisations, most commonly in management and organisational studies, but it is also a valuable theoretical concept in communication research and practice.	An illustration of complexity theory in action is how mobile phone manufacturers continually adapt to new technology and competition. Digital keypads, larger screens, better graphics, and new operating systems are examples of this. Another example is how sporting competitions adapt their schedules (and sometimes the number of teams) to changes in their television, radio and online broadcast deals. One of the starkest examples of complexity theory is the vast changes in staffing levels and work practices that computer technology brought to office work. The impact of technology on office work meant that hard copy letters produced on typewriters could be more efficiently written with word-processing software on computers, without using typing staff—then the technological advance that email brought changed office practice even more. A complexity theory consequence of this is the serious drop in revenue that national postal services receive because fewer business and personal letters are snail-mailed. So, complexity theory can help public relations practitioners understand how organisations can adapt to large and small external and internal changes.

Theoretical concept	Practical applications
Two-factor theory In 1987, the US psychologist Frederick Herzberg proposed that people's workplace satisfaction, or dissatisfaction, were caused by separate factors, which acted independently of each other. That is, factors like a sense of achievement, recognition, responsibility and the nature of their work improves people's work satisfaction. Organisational policy and administration, supervision, relationships with bosses, and work conditions are factors that can make workers dissatisfied. Herzberg also found that low wages can lead to dissatisfaction, but higher wages didn't necessarily improve their satisfaction level.	This theory can inform how effective internal organisational communication programs can be designed. Knowing the general parameters of what makes people satisfied in their workplace, or cranky about it, can help managers to better do their jobs—and public relations practitioners to, say, work out what messages are needed to keep staff informed about the organisation's directions. Two-factor theory suggests useful areas for practitioners to include in surveys when they ask workers about their organisational experiences. For example, surveys could include questions about how workers regard their supervisors, or workplace safety, or the policies that make it harder for them to do their jobs, or whether they have enough personal responsibility to work effectively, or whether they feel recognised for their contributions.
Acquired needs theory Psychologist David McClelland and his colleagues studied people's personal needs. In the 1940s, they identified three 'needs' themes. The first was the need for achievement, or to do things better, or solve problems, or undertake complex tasks. The second was a need for affiliation, or a desire to have good relationships. The third theme was the need for power, or a desire to control people, or influence people, or to be responsible for others. The theory holds that different people are motivated by different needs which can be acquired over time and can be linked to different roles and preferences at work. It is an important concept for managers to understand as it suggests a way of working out the kinds of jobs people are best suited to.	While McClelland's theory deals with motivating and empowering people in organisations, it suggests concepts for public relations practice. By understanding that people need to achieve, belong, and have some power, practitioners can design messages, especially in internal communication, that reinforce these needs. For example, in an organisational change communication program messages could reinforce just how everyone belongs to one organisation and can help implement the changes, or that managers at all levels have the power to make change, or that the organisation values the work people do. Just as Herzberg's theory can be used in organisational research, McClelland's concept can help inform internal research to find out more about what staff members feel about the organisation and their role in it. McClelland's theory could also be helpful in broader communication because research that enables a practitioner to understand external target publics' needs could help in the selection of messages, communication pathways and public relations tools.

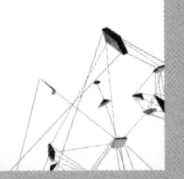

Theoretical concept	Practical applications
Expectancy theory Victor Vroom was interested in what motivates people to do work that contributes to the success of their organisation and their own individual work unit. In his 1964 book *Work and Motivation*, Vroom proposed that people are motivated to do their jobs because of their personal expectations about whether they can achieve tasks, the rewards they will get, and the personal value they give to their work outcomes. Vroom called these three variables, + *Expectancy*, or the probability that their efforts will achieve their tasks. + *Instrumentality*, or the probability that task performance will be rewarding to them personally. + *Valence*, or the value people give to rewards for the work they do. The theory proposes that these variables are related to one another and proposed a formula for measuring work motivation based on high or low expectancy, instrumentality and valence.	Vroom's theory is another approach to management that can inform professional communication practice, most directly in internal communication. In an external context, knowing what motivates a target public to do things, perhaps sign up for a new mobile phone plan, by working out the expectancy, instrumentality, and valence variables, provides rich data for developing strategic plans. Similarly, understanding these variables for a target public engaged in an issues debate can help to work out how a client might participate in that debate.

DEVELOPING AND WRITING MESSAGES

5

In this chapter, we'll cover the importance of messages and how to write them. We'll look at:

+ developing and writing informative and persuasive messages
+ matching messages to target publics, goals and objectives
+ choosing appropriate communication pathways to deliver messages to target publics
+ identifying effective public relations tools to carry messages.

THE IMPORTANCE OF MESSAGES

Messages are the information that organisations want target publics to know about a situation or issue. They are written to inform, build understanding, or persuade people to act. The ability to write clear and effective messages is one of the most important skills a public relations practitioner needs because the points they make are used in almost every aspect of a communication campaign. Messages, or the themes they cover, need to be consistently applied across all the organisation's communication platforms. So, the messages posted to an organisation's website, or used on its social media applications, are the same as those used in speeches by executives, in media releases, infographics and brochures. Organisational representatives use them in personal meetings with target publics, and they are included in sales material displays and all other public relations tools. An organisation would not communicate effectively with its target publics if messages from the chief executive differed from those given by other managers, or those published in the tools produced by the public relations team.

A public relations strategy includes the messages an organisation wants its target publics to know, so it answers the 'why', 'what', 'who', 'how', 'with' and 'when' questions about delivering them in the following ways:

+ situation analysis (Why do we need a public relations plan?)
+ goals and objectives (What do we want to achieve?)
+ target publics (With whom do we want to communicate?)
+ communication pathways (How will we reach target publics?)
+ public relations tools (What are the most effective communication tools for our target publics?)

+ implementation (When will we deliver messages?)
+ evaluation (Were our messages received by the target publics? Did people understand them, or act after reading or hearing them?).

Messages are at the heart of a public relations strategy because the other elements of a strategy explain why messages are needed or how they will be transmitted to target publics using the most effective communication pathways and public relations tools. Effectiveness also means clear writing that expresses messages concisely in a way that people who receive them can understand. Doing that includes using simple words and brief sentences, applying correct spelling, grammar and punctuation, avoiding jargon and clichés, resisting the temptation to include unnecessary adjectives, and not making unjustifiable claims about products or services.

The public relations consultancy Media Masters Training in St Louis, USA, stresses the importance of messages when it notes in the introduction to its website, 'The media has to win by getting the story. You have to win by getting your message across.' (<**http://www.mediamasterstraining.com/**>) There's certainly a message in that for public relations practitioners.

In a public relations plan, messages are expressed as the key points that an organisation wants its publics to know. These key points become the themes that guide the content of public relations tools. Sometimes they are expressed briefly, say in a tweet, or in a media release; at other times, they are expanded and supported by additional material to write an important speech or an extended website post. Messages can also be used as summary briefing notes for people from the organisation when they are interviewed by journalists or when they represent the organisation at meetings.

Messages need to be relevant

Messages must be relevant to target publics. They must be written in a way that target publics understand. If they are not written clearly, and are not relevant to the situation you are addressing, the information your organisation wants its publics to know is likely to be misunderstood or, worse, ignored. David Guth and Charles Marsh (2006) say that successful messages must respect publics' needs and preferences by addressing their values and interests. Messages must also be transmitted to target publics using the most appropriate pathways and tools. It is vital that clear, concise and relevant messages can be adapted from the key points set out in a strategy to write a web post, an email message, a media release, a speech and the organisation's annual report.

Let's say we work for Easy Living Homes, a developer proposing a new complex of single-storey townhouses. Easy Living Homes needs to inform the local community about the project, including the benefits it will bring to the community, and to provide reasons why any potential negative aspects can be overcome. As public relations practitioners at Easy Living Homes, we would need to make sure messages on these points are expressed in language that specific publics in the community who are concerned about the complex will understand. This is another reason why practitioners should be careful about defining their target publics and segmenting them into primary, secondary and tertiary publics. It is not the 'general public' but potential townhouse buyers, the local council that decides on building rules, neighbours of our site, local environmental groups, transport services, real estate agents and local reporters who write about property who are specifically interested in the development and the issues its construction will raise. When practitioners precisely identify the target publics they want to reach, they can select appropriate communication pathways and public relations tools to make sure messages reach their designated publics.

The Almond Board of Australia has the brief line 'The seriously healthy handful' on its home page (australianalmonds.com.au). That brief sentence sends a lot of information about almonds to target publics in a concise message.

A caution about messages

Some scholars are critical of public relations people who seem to focus their professional practice on message design and delivery. They argue that this sometimes happens because of the practitioners' background in mass communication or journalism and suggest that this approach to public relations is simply press agentry. Robert Heath (2001), one of the world's leading public relations scholars, says that focusing on messaging limits the vision of public relations as a discipline to an interest in message design and delivery to achieve awareness, to inform, to persuade or even to manipulate target publics. Anne Gregory (2009b, p. 186) says one limitation of messages is that they indicate one-way communication, and that preparing for participation in a dialogue requires a more complex approach. These points remind us that public relations practice is not only about issuing media releases to state a point of view, or to generate publicity for a new brand of lipstick. Writing and issuing media releases are regular and important tasks for practitioners, but effective public relations practice is much more than trying to give clients (perhaps even ourselves) a nice warm feeling because their messages appeared in the mass news media, or on someone's Twitter feed. The alchemy of public relations is that by using a range of pathways and tools in tandem, a practitioner can create effective two-way communication, that is a dialogue, with target publics to build and maintain relationships.

This chapter does focus on message design and delivery as an *element of strategic planning*. All organisations, whether they are large corporations, political parties, town councils, welfare agencies or local community and environmental groups, need to plan exactly what to tell their target publics about their views, achievements and concerns, and to contribute to any debates about issues relevant to them. Those messages can be applied at all levels of public relations practice from a simple phone call to a journalist, alerting them to an event, to a major community consultation project. A public relations plan is the place to identify key messages, to link them to target publics, strategic goals and objectives, and to explain how and when they will be delivered. Planning messages means that an organisation can work out what it needs to say to address a situation or an issue, and to establish a dialogue, even if that dialogue results in the organisation changing its views.

And there's something else to bear in mind: if messages are not properly thought through, and are delivered poorly, the communication you are trying to encourage will not work. Gregory provides four hints for developing effective messages (2009b, p. 187):

1. Take existing articulated perceptions that encapsulate the issue or problem you need to address.
2. Define what realistic shifts can be made in those perceptions.

3. Identify realistic elements of persuasion.
4. Ensure messages are credible and can be delivered through public relations activity rather than advertising or direct mail.

> **PRACTICE POINT**
>
> Public relations people deal with a lot of issues, some of them negative ones that could lead to crises. Most public relations tasks, though, involve good news, and that is an excellent frame in which to write effective messages: be positive; recognise negatives and deal with them; write clearly and unambiguously.

Messages, communication pathways and tools

Imagine that you have been promoted to Public Relations Manager for Easy Living Homes. You know the company's proposal will be welcomed by some people in the local community, but opposed by others. Your strategic public relations plan recognises Easy Living's strengths and weaknesses, and has been written to explain the project to residents, the mayor and councillors, the local newspaper's real estate writer, shop owners and other businesspeople, and members of community service clubs. You have written messages that (a) explain the project and (b) are designed to convince people that it will bring jobs and investment to the community. You have linked the *messages* to the *communication pathways* you'll use to deliver them (details about how you will reach the target publics) and set out the *tools* (the things you and your team will produce) you will use to follow the pathways.

The following sections describe how you can write effective messages for target publics and link them to pathways and tools to achieve communication goals and objectives.

How many messages?

Most public relations plans include more than one message. Some messages give information, others attempt to persuade publics to take some action. A public relations plan can include both types of messages. Your analysis of the formative research you do for a situation analysis will help you to decide how many messages you need, and what kind they should be: *informative* or *persuasive*. Research that identifies what target publics already know, or don't know, about your topic will also help you to decide the kinds of messages you need to write. The qualitative comments in this research may suggest ideas for messages. Often your client will tell you what they want to say in the material you produce, and this will help you to define the key messages. Sometimes you may have one main message for your plan—the most important point you need to express. The senior Australian practitioner Kim Harrison describes this as a 'reference point' for all communication because other messages will support and expand on it.

One way of working out what messages you need to write is to use a 'message map', a planning tool that uses a hub-and-spokes framework to help write simple, concise key messages about a topic. A message map works like a mind map to visually link ideas. A message map produces a visual representation of key messages that make the interrelationships between them easily understood and remembered. You can find examples of message maps and mind maps (which are useful when you are analysing research findings for a situation analysis) with your web search engine.

Another tool that identifies potential messages is an analysis of the organisation's communication **strengths**, **weaknesses**, **opportunities** and **threats** (a SWOT analysis). This allows you to find out what people already know and feel about the organisation. That analysis will help you to write messages that reinforce positive beliefs about the organisation or address negative attitudes. It will also help you to identify opportunities you can use to deliver messages.

> **PRACTICE POINT**
>
> Some practitioners use a message map to plan what they need to include in public relations material. Similarly, they use a SWOT analysis and mind maps to help in planning. Some computer software provides these tools.

Informative messages

Writing informative messages is often an uncomplicated task. That is because clients often already know what they want to say, or research has identified a lack of knowledge among target publics that can be fixed by providing straightforward information. For example, when the Australian government decided to pay $25 000 compensation to those Australians who were held captive by Germany, Italy or their allies during the Second World War, the Department of Veterans' Affairs needed to tell potential recipients about it. The department's primary informative message was that compensation was available. Other informative messages the department sent to former Australian prisoners of war told them:

+ who was eligible for compensation
+ that compensation was non-taxable and exempt from income support tests for pensions
+ how people could apply
+ where they could find out more information.

If you go to the homepage of the World Wildlife Fund (<**http://www.worldwildlife.org**>), click on 'Our Work' then follow the link 'Fresh Water', you'll find that the overview section has some simple, informative messages combined to create a narrative. Almost every sentence in that passage gives information, or explains something, in clear and concise language. Further down that page, you can find a 'Why it matters' section that explains the need for fresh water in a range of circumstances from how it helps to maintain healthy communities, to its role in supporting 125 000 species, and in agriculture. These, too, are informative messages designed to help build readers' awareness and understanding of the importance of fresh water to the global community.

---

strengths: in the context of a SWOT analysis, characteristics of an organisation that can help to achieve its goals.

weaknesses: in the context of a SWOT analysis, the characteristics of an organisation that might harm its ability to achieve its goals.

opportunities: in the context of a SWOT analysis, the external conditions that will assist an organisation to achieve its goals.

threats: in the context of a SWOT analysis, external conditions that could prevent an organisation from achieving its goals.

> **PRACTICE POINT**
>
> To write informative messages for a public relations plan:
>
> 1. decide exactly what you want target publics to know
> 2. summarise that information into a simple, brief sentence
> 3. limit each message to one information point.
>
> Remember that informative messages included in a public relations plan will be used to guide material written for a range of tools. Among other things, they'll form the key points for speeches; be used as headings for displays; be explained in more detail in brochures; and be used as a set of reminders when the chief executive is interviewed on television.

Let's return to our previous example in which you are the Public Relations Manager for the developer of a new housing project. Among the informative messages in your public relations plan, you might include:

+ All townhouses have solar power and solar hot water.
+ Some townhouses have been designed to cater for the needs of elderly people.
+ The public areas of the project will be monitored by 24-hour security cameras.
+ The construction phase of the project will generate fifty local jobs.

Notice how the information is straightforward.

Persuasive messages

Writing persuasive messages is a more challenging task than writing informative messages. That is because we are trying to convince publics to accept a point of view or to take some action. Persuasive messages try to convince publics to change their behaviour or attitudes, and that is always a hard job. To write persuasive messages, practitioners need to know about the ways in which people process information, and how they make decisions. And that's why studying public relations involves examining theories about communication.

Steve Mackey (2009), an Australian scholar, says that to think theoretically is to use a set of assumptions about how the world works so that we can predict what happens. That's an important point, because when we are planning a public relations program we need to work out how our messages might persuade a public to take action. If we know about a communication theory that suggests how a specific public is likely to react to information or a point of view, we can plan messages to generate that reaction. As discussed in Chapter 2, Joep Cornelissen makes the point that practitioners need to inform their work with theory so that they have a better chance of being successful than if they only relied on intuition. Similarly, Dan Lattimore and colleagues (2004) suggest that we should build a set of theories to help our professional practice. Some of these theories are covered in various sections of this book.

> ### PRACTICE NOTE FACING UP TO ETHICAL DILEMMAS
>
> When you are planning to implement a public relations program designed to convince people to take some action, you need to carefully consider the ethical implications of what you will do. This is a special consideration for practitioners who work for large organisations that have relationships with publics who do not have equal economic or political power. One way of resolving a potential ethical dilemma is to ask questions like: Is the information we are using factual? Are we asking people to do something that is against the law? Might our plan harm people in some way? Am I involved in something that goes against my personal and professional ethical standards?
>
> The code of ethics for your professional association can help you to answer these and other questions. So, too, can the code of practice that your employer might have to guide the way you and your colleagues interact with each other at work and with clients. Several laws govern how businesses operate, including those that cover **libel** and **defamation**, copyright, contracts, and the ownership and protection of ideas. If in doubt about your legal position, ask your supervisor or get legal advice.

libel: a published, unjustified statement about a person that harms their reputation.

defamation: an act, usually written or spoken words, that attacks a person's good reputation.

Persuasive messages use language that is designed to motivate people to take some kind of action. Depending on the target public, they might be written as *emotional* appeals or *rational* appeals. Political campaigns provide useful examples to help us understand what is meant by persuasive messaging. The simplest election message is a call to action that explains why someone should vote for the candidate: 'Vote for me because I will work for a new hospital for our town'. Such a call to action is implicit in campaign themes like the classic Australian Labor Party (ALP) slogan in 1972, 'It's Time'. That slogan summarised the more detailed message to voters that after twenty-three years of federal government by the conservative parties, it was time for a change. 'It's Time' was supported by other messages that argued that the ALP's policies were reasons for a change. All were designed to persuade voters to elect an ALP government—which they subsequently did. For the 2012 US presidential election, President Barack Obama used the campaign slogan 'Forward'. Only one word, but a word that epitomised what a re-elected President Obama would focus on: the future. In 2016, President Trump used 'Make America great again', which was an appeal to those who believed the USA was in some way no longer the nation it used to be. His opponent in 2016, Hillary Clinton, used 'Stronger together', an appeal to her supporters that if they stayed united they would be successful. Explore any of these US campaigns by searching for their websites to see how the ideas the slogans represent were woven into speeches and other comments during the elections. You could do the same for political party campaigns in your country, state or province.

> **PRACTICE POINT**
>
> Most public relations practitioners object to criticism that characterises their persuasive activities as propaganda. The term *propaganda*, which has its roots in Latin, was once simply used to describe information. Since the seventeenth century, the Roman Catholic Church, for example, has used the word in the name of the group responsible for propagating, or disseminating, the faith. In modern times, though, the word has had a bad rap: it is used to describe persuasive practices, especially in support of an ideology or in politics, that intentionally set out to mislead publics, and that are deceitful, false, duplicitous or based on lies. When you do the activities starting on p. 103, think about whether this kind of public relations is ethical.

To write persuasive messages, practitioners need to decide what action they want publics to take. Mostly, that will mean changing something: behaviour, attitudes, purchasing habits or voting intentions. Figure 5.1 sets out another formula that might help you to write a persuasive message:

Figure 5.1 Formula for writing a persuasive message

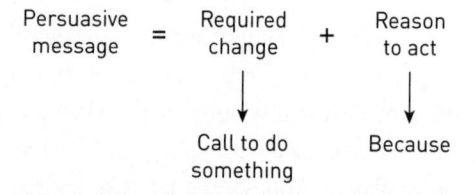

$$\text{Persuasive message} = \text{Required change} + \text{Reason to act}$$

$$\downarrow \qquad\qquad \downarrow$$

$$\text{Call to do something} \qquad \text{Because}$$

Some examples of simple persuasive messages written in this way are:

+ Vote for our local candidate Fred Southdown because he understands woolgrowers' concerns.
+ Sign up for Universal's new broadband service to experience downloads that are twice as fast as those anyone else offers. We guarantee it.
+ Our national widget manufacturers urge the government to provide more tax relief for investing in new equipment so that they can make a greater contribution to export growth.

To write a persuasive message:

1. identify the change your client seeks. You should know from your situation analysis research whether publics have all the information they need to make their decision
2. provide a reason for the desired change
3. summarise this information into a simple, brief sentence. Sometimes you might need to write two or more sentences
4. limit each persuasive message to one call for change.

For an example of this, re-visit the homepage of the World Wildlife Fund (<**http://www.worldwildlife.org**>), click on 'Species', then 'Giant Pandas'. Scroll through the panda page and write down messages that call for action, or say why it is important to protect pandas. Match these persuasive messages to informative messages about pandas to see how they work to build knowledge, awareness, understanding and generate action. This pattern of blending informative messages with persuasive messages applies all through the WWF site.

Matching messages to goals and objectives

In previous chapters, we have looked at the importance of goals and objectives. Goals are broad statements about what we want to achieve; objectives are precise and measurable statements about how goals will be achieved.

It would make sense, then, to write messages that match the change sought by an objective. A practical and successful example of how messages can be linked to objectives is the *pro bono* media liaison campaign developed after the Australian engineer Douglas Wood (who worked for a US company in Iraq) was kidnapped in Baghdad in 2005. On 10 June 2005, the Al Jazeera television network in the Middle East announced that Douglas Wood was being held by unknown people in an unknown place in Iraq. Images of a dishevelled Wood with guns to his head appeared in the world's media. Wood's captors demanded the withdrawal of Australian troops from Iraq; the kidnappers threatened to kill Wood if the troops were not withdrawn. In Australia, his family was besieged by reporters and decided to launch its own publicity campaign to support Australian officials who were seeking to negotiate Wood's release.

Neil Smail, an Australian practitioner, developed and managed a campaign (which won a Public Relations Institute of Australia Golden Target Award) to help Douglas Wood's family in their efforts to get him released. The campaign had this goal and these objectives:

GOAL

There was one goal for the family's media and communication activities: to free Douglas.

OBJECTIVES

1. To use the Iraqi media to portray Douglas in a manner that might influence his captors to free him unharmed.
2. To use the Australian and other media to present a positive message about Douglas Wood and his family to put further pressure on the captors.
3. To maintain good relations with the Australian media by providing ready access to factual information to reduce the likelihood of reporters seeking other Wood stories that might move the focus away from the key objectives. In particular, this objective sought to divert media from Douglas's wife and daughter in the USA, who were particularly concerned about maintaining their privacy.

Each of the objectives was measurable, but the timing depended on when the crisis was resolved.

Simple messages—based on a strategy to appeal to the captors' sense of humanity by portraying the kind of man Douglas Wood was—were linked to the objectives. These messages presented him as a man who:

+ had a family who loved him
+ was just doing his job to help rebuild Iraq for the Iraqi people
+ liked and respected Iraqis
+ had no political involvement
+ had health problems requiring constant medication and care.

The messages also maintained that:

+ there was no point in holding him as it would not affect the Australian government's position
+ he should be released unharmed.

These *informative* and *persuasive* messages were consistently used in all interactions with the international and Australian news media, which included press, radio and television news coverage, and interviews with Douglas Wood's brothers and, sometimes, with Smail. The simple messages provided the reference points for expanded information in interviews; they were used to persuade the kidnappers, through Iraqi and international media channels like Al Jazeera, to free Douglas Wood. Iraqi troops found Wood alive and relatively unharmed. He was returned safely to Australia.

To link messages to objectives, use information that supports what you are trying to do. If your task is to support sales efforts to achieve a market position for a new smart wrist watch, write messages that tell people about:

1. the new product and how it measures exercise activity (increase awareness)
2. how it differs from other brands (increase understanding)
3. where they can get it, how much it costs, and the benefits of using it (persuade them to buy it).

Are messages relevant to selected target publics?

In the smart watch example, the target publics for your plan to support the company's sales efforts should be relevant to what you are trying to do and the messages you need to disseminate. So who are the people who buy this kind of smart watch? When are they likely to buy them? Who are the people who influence these target publics? Do the messages you have written provide relevant information to target publics?

A THOUGHT ON THEORY: RELATIONSHIPS

Many of the theoretical paradigms that are used to explain what public relations is—or how people communicate, form attitudes or behave—are derived from other disciplines. These include psychology, sociology, philosophy, management studies and the physical sciences. For example, *complexity theory* suggests that all systems, natural and human-made, are, well, complex, and are continually changing, often in small ways. The theory comes from the physical sciences. Some scholars use complexity theory to study interactions and relationships in organisations. That has implications for organisation communication. In the tip sheet 'How theories can inform practice' on pages 80–86, we saw some examples of a set of theories that could help our professional practice (Lattimore et al, 2004).

When James Grunig and Todd Hunt (1984) proposed four models to explain public relations practice (press agentry, public information, asymmetrical communication and two-way symmetrical communication) they used *systems theory*, which is a way of thinking about relationships. It is an important approach for public relations because the theory regards organisations as systems that adapt to their environment; changes in the economic, social or political environments in which an organisation operates impact on that organisation and change the way it does things. Grunig and Hunt use this concept to suggest that ethical and effective public relations practice means building relationships in which an organisation interacts equally, or symmetrically, with its publics. The implication is that organisations change their policies and behaviours as a result of this symmetrical interaction. Their three other models of practice are simply one-way communication of information from the organisation to its target publics. The four Grunig and Hunt models are important for deciding how messages might be delivered, as long as we remember that what they propose might not be culturally suitable in all countries.

Organisations with 'open' systems allow information about what they do, and what is happening in the world around them, to flow freely to and from their internal and external environments. Those with 'closed' systems don't take this 'open' approach, so find it difficult to build relationships with publics inside and outside the organisation.

As we saw in the tip sheet 'How theories can inform practice' (in Chapter 4), the *situational theory* of public relations, also proposed by Grunig and his colleagues, can be used to predict when publics will actively seek information and how they will process it. The theory suggests that publics can be identified by the context in which they are aware of a problem and the extent to which they do something about the problem. The theory resonates with another from the physical sciences—*contingency theory*, which is also used in management studies to explain the factors that drive organisational change. Contingency theory suggests that factors (known as independent variables) outside a system (a dependent variable) can influence how the system works. Situational theory for public relations suggests there are three independent variables that impact on how target publics become aware of a problem and do something about it, and two dependent variables. The independent variables are:

+ *problem recognition* (the extent to which people recognise the problem)
+ *constraint recognition* (the extent to which they recognise factors beyond their control that limit their behaviour)
+ *level of involvement* (the personal and emotional relevance of a problem for an individual).

> The dependent variables are *information seeking* (when active publics seek information about a situation) and *information processing* (when a passive or inactive public does not seek information but processes it when it comes to them randomly).
>
> Situational theory, then, deals with context to help to explain why some people become activists on an issue while others do not and may even be apathetic towards the issue.
>
> *Social exchange theory* suggests that people make a kind of 'What's in it for me?' economic judgment on the benefits and costs of them behaving in a certain way. They want to maximise the benefit of what they are being asked to do but keep the costs of doing it low. *Diffusion theory* proposes that people go through a five-step process before they adopt an idea or buy a product. The steps are: awareness (they know about the idea); interest (they are aroused by the idea); evaluation (they decide whether the idea is useful to them personally); trial (they try the idea out on friends or family); and adoption (they accept the idea and take it up or act on it).
>
> These concepts can help you decide what kind of messages you need for your campaign.
>
> Pick one of the theories in this section and use the library's databases to find an academic journal article that discusses how it is applied in a practical public relations situation. That's one way of building an understanding of the theory. Or you could search for a scholarly article that criticises the use of the theory in public relations (there are many of these in journals that report public relations academic research).

Establishing appropriate communication pathways

Now that you have identified and written messages, matched them to objectives and decided which target publics ought to receive them, there are two more decisions you need to make. They are: How will messages reach publics? And what communication tools can best do that? Let's look first at the 'how' question: communication pathways.

Communication pathways indicate how target publics can be reached. This includes delivering messages:

+ in a way that you can *control*, or
+ by an *uncontrolled* method, or
+ through *interpersonal* communication

Choosing the best communication pathways for your situation and target publics depends on who you need to reach and what you want to achieve. Most public relations plans use a combination of communication pathways. For example, if you need to send a persuasive message about the need to save water directly to local residents, you would use a controlled pathway. This means messages cannot be changed or filtered—that is, mediated—by anyone else: you control the message, the way it is sent to target publics, and the timing at which this happens. No-one else mediates the message, a journalist does not give it an angle—it goes directly to target publics as you wrote it, by a method you choose and when you decide to send it. For an example of a controlled pathway and the tools that would implement it, see the Cashmere Green case later in this chapter.

Controlled communication means that the organisation decides on the content, tone, presentation and timing of messages, and the way they are distributed. No one outside the organisation has an opportunity to intervene in this process. Examples of controlled communication are company newsletters, videos, websites, personally addressed letters, brochures, community service announcements, email, annual reports sent directly to shareholders, either in the post or via the website, and information for employees. In each of these examples, the organisation decides what messages are given directly to target publics; no one else can adapt or amend the messages before they reach target publics. This is a potentially expensive strategy because it reaches only a selection of target public groups.

Uncontrolled communication means that someone outside the organisation can determine how messages are given to target publics. Examples of uncontrolled communication are media releases, interviews with journalists, and news conferences. When an uncontrolled communication pathway is used, we lose control of how and when a message is delivered. Someone else, mostly journalists, can interpret, or mediate, messages, put a different emphasis on what we are saying (journalists call this the 'angle' for a story, that is, their view of what is news), cut information out, control the timing of when the messages are published (or maybe not even published or broadcast) or delivered, or decide on the format in which uncontrolled communication is delivered. No matter how much information the chief executive of Easy Living Homes gives the real estate reporter from the local newspaper during an hour-long interview, it will be the reporter who decides how much will be reported in the article. The reporter will also decide the 'angle'—the news lead—of the story and what quotes from the CEO will be included. The news editor or the chief sub-editor will decide whether the story will appear in the newspaper, how big the heading will be, what page the story will be on and how many words will be used. A sub-editor will review, correct and perhaps shorten what the reporter has written, and also write the headline. That's a lot of gatekeeping before Easy Living's target public gets to read the company's messages. This is a potentially inexpensive strategy because it relies, generally, on the mass news or specialist media for delivery, but its downside is that there is no guarantee target publics will receive a message as it was originally written. Because almost every public relations program relies on uncontrolled communication in some way, usually via the mass news media, it is enormously important that you learn to write in a way that journalists recognise as news. You must learn to understand what news is and how journalists report it so that you can produce news and persuasive messages for your organisation or clients; there are no short-cuts to doing this the correct way, even though formats might change depending on the communication tools you'll use. Chapter 6 will help you to understand this.

Interpersonal communication means talking to people, and this approach to public relations is the most persuasive of all the approaches we can take and the most effective in building relationships. Examples of interpersonal communication are telephone calls, meetings, special events, displays that are staffed by people from the organisation, speeches and conferences. In all these instances, and many more you could think of, the organisation has opportunities to talk directly

controlled communication: a communication pathway that uses tools such as an organisation's own publications or other material that cannot be changed or filtered by others.

uncontrolled communication: a communication pathway that involves tools such as media releases or other material that can be changed by others.

interpersonal communication: a communication pathway that involves communicating directly with people—for example, in a face-to-face meeting.

with its publics, who then have an opportunity to ask questions, discuss points and debate issues. An effective interpersonal exchange of information, ideas and views takes place as part of the dialogue, or two-way communication, that this pathway enables. Interpersonal communication works best in small groups or in one-on-one conversations. For that reason, interpersonal communication is the most effective communication pathway, but it is expensive because it involves reaching only a relatively small number of people at one time.

Other communication pathways include:

+ *interactive (or social) media*, in which all those exciting, and potentially powerful, social media platforms and applications can be applied to reach target publics—provided there is a good reason for using them
+ *special events*, when an organisation participates in, or organises, a specific event to reach target publics
+ *sponsorship*, when an organisation provides financial or other support to a charity, good cause, sports team or event
+ *alliances*, in which an organisation builds a partnership with a like-minded group to promote common interests and jointly reach target publics.

A public relations plan should use a combination of communication pathways. The important thing is to decide which pathways best meet the needs of your goals and objectives, and are the most effective ways of delivering messages to your target publics. (For a detailed discussion of communication pathways, see Mahoney, 2017, ch. 9.)

Identifying effective tools to deliver messages to target publics

When you have selected communication pathways, you'll need to decide what tools are the best 'packages' for your messages. Communication tools are the public relations 'things' target publics see, use, or experience, like displays, blog posts, publications, websites, meetings, media releases, special events and tweets. Tools are a bit like envelopes that carry letters (messages) in the postal service's snail mail system (a pathway).

Tools relate directly to, and implement, communication pathways. That means it is possible to plan a campaign that will deliver messages in a variety of ways. The following example illustrates how all that we have been examining in this chapter can be brought together in a strategic public relations plan.

The example is part of a hypothetical plan, but it is written for a real situation. Some years ago the Cashmere Green Council in New Zealand received a proposal from a group of parents for a playground in a park opposite their children's pre-school. What follows is what the council might have done to let the Cashmere Green community (a discrete target public that can be further segmented) know about the proposed playground in preparation for a local referendum on whether it should be built. (You can find a case study that examines this example and contrasts what actually happened with another council's approach to a similar issue in Comrie, 2000.)

Goal
To gain community support at a referendum for a children's playground on Cashmere Green.

Objectives
1. To increase awareness among target publics of the request for a playground on Cashmere Green by 50 per cent in three months.
2. To convince 75 per cent of Cashmere Green residents and shopkeepers to support the playground over the next five months.
3. To generate a 60 per cent vote in favour of the playground at a referendum in six months.

Messages
1. Council has received a request for a new playground in the park opposite the Cashmere Green pre-school.
2. The request meets council's requirements and safety and environmental standards.
3. The playground will cause minimal disruption to Cashmere Green residents and shopkeepers. It may lead to extra business for shops.
4. We are seeking your views on the proposal.
5. The council will hold a referendum on whether the playground should proceed.

Target publics
1. Residents of Cashmere Green
2. Shopkeepers in Cashmere Green
3. Pre-school parents
4. Pre-school teachers
5. Environmental groups
6. Council members
7. Local newspaper editor and columnists

Pathways and tools
Target public
Residents and shopkeepers of Cashmere Green

Pathway
To use controlled media to advise residents and shopkeepers of the request to build a playground.

Tools

- Letter from council's CEO to advise on proposal and invite feedback
- Information booklet including arguments for and against, and a sketch of the playground
- A playground display in the major shopping centre in the city

Target public

Residents and shopkeepers of Cashmere Green

Pathway

To use interpersonal communication to hear residents' views about the proposal

Tool

Hold two town meetings to hear residents' feedback

Target public

The local newspaper's editor and city reporter

Pathway

To use uncontrolled media to generate news coverage of the proposal

Tools

- Media release and information booklet
- Media release announcing town meetings
- **Media conference** to announce council's decision

media conference: an event at which journalists have the opportunity to ask a representative of the organisation questions about an issue or a media release.

SUMMARY

In this chapter we have looked at matching messages to target publics and deciding on appropriate pathways and public relations tools to deliver messages. In particular, we have looked at how to:
+ develop and write informative and persuasive messages
+ match messages to target publics, goals and objectives
+ decide appropriate communication pathways
+ identify effective public relations tools.

In the next chapter, we'll work on writing and distributing media releases, one of the most basic but widely used tactics in public relations practice.

ACTIVITIES

1. Messages About the Importance of Quality Child Care

This is a practical exercise to illustrate the importance of effective messages.

Find out the messages that the community-based organisation Child Care South Africa uses to promote its programs to provide quality care for children. To do this, visit the organisation's website (<www.childcaresa.org.za>) and explore as much of it as you need to so you can answer these questions:
- What is the context in which this organisation works?
- What are four key messages, and their sub-messages, that are *informative*?
- What are the themes of the messages?
- Are there any messages in the map that *persuade* people to take some action? What are they?
- What are the differences between the language used for the *informative* messages and that used for the *persuasive* messages?
- What are the differences in the way the two kinds of messages are written?
- Do the messages you have identified reflect the context, or situation, in which the organisation works?

2. Let's Write Three Informative Messages

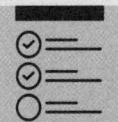

Find out through some basic research, perhaps using the internet, what Rotary International's Youth Exchange program does. Assume that you are writing a strategic public relations plan for a campaign to promote the opening of applications for the next intake of young people to participate in the exchange program. Using that information, write three *informative* messages that will be used in the campaign. Which of the messages would be directed at potential applicants? Which would be directed at the parents of potential applicants? What kind of target public would parents be in this program?

3. Why Is Ethical Practice Important?

Examples of codes of ethics for various public relations professional organisations can be found in Chapter 1 on p.16. Read the Global Alliance's code of ethics and those for two of the other organisations listed. What do they have in common? Where do they differ? What are the most significant issues they all deal with? Write 500 words discussing why ethical practice is important for public relations. It would be interesting to have a class discussion on this to find out what others believe about ethical practice.

4. Let's Write Some Persuasive Messages

Perth Modern School opened in 1911 and was the first senior public secondary school in the state of Western Australia. It provides a modern education to scholarship students with strong academic abilities. The school claims an outstanding reputation because of the success of its students academically and the contributions they have made to the community. Its graduates include a former Australian prime minister, a governor-general of Australia, Rhodes Scholars and a member of the International Court of Justice. In 2007, Perth Modern School returned to a policy of academically selective schooling and is dedicated to the promotion of excellence.

The Western Australian Department of Education and Training won a PRIA Golden Target Award for a campaign that had the following goal and objective:
- *Goal:* to educate and inform the parents of gifted and talented students of the benefits of selective schooling and the capacity of the public education system to deliver it.
- *Objective:* to achieve 400 applications from students to sit the selection examination with an expectation that 160 of them will be of the calibre to be eligible to be offered a place.

Your tasks are to:
- identify two target publics for this campaign
- use the formula in Figure 5.1 to write two persuasive messages that meet the goal and objective of the campaign for *each target public*.

5. A Situation, What Affects It and an Appropriate Persuasive Message

Let's stick with the World Wildlife Fund (<http://www.worldwildlife.org>) and pandas.

If you worked for the WWF as a public relations practitioner you would know a lot about its goals and objectives and the programs it has set in place to achieve them. If you go back to the WWF homepage, you will be able to read quite a lot about the Fund and what it does. Using this information and what you have already found out about its panda protection activities, search the site for details about the Panda Ambassador program.

When you have done this, write about 1.5 pages setting out the situation (see the Thought on Theory, above) that the Panda Ambassador program is designed to deal with to meet one or more of the WWF's goals. Then, using what you know about contingency theory, write four or five, in dot point form, independent variables that can affect the dependent variable, the Panda Ambassador program. Once that's done, you should be well-prepared to write three strong persuasive messages about why people should support the Panda Ambassador program.

- Have you addressed the situation?
- Does your work analyse the independent variables that could change the situation?
- Did you work out whether potential target publics recognise the problem you need to deal with, and what their level of involvement might be?
- Are there inactive publics who might be persuaded to become aware of your issues and get actively involved in the Panda Ambassador program?
- Can you use media effects, agenda setting, and framing theories to guide how you write your persuasive messages?
- Have you written clear, concise and persuasive messages?

Share your ideas with others in a class discussion—as you would if you were working in the WWF's public relations team.

REFLECTION

Think back to the Perth Modern School exercise in which you were asked to (1) identify two target publics for the campaign and then (2) write two persuasive messages that meet the goal and objective of the campaign for each target public. Now that you have finished the chapter, were the target publics you selected appropriate for the goal and objective the school identified for its campaign? Why or why not? Would your persuasive messages do the job you wrote them for? How would you change your messages to make them more effective?

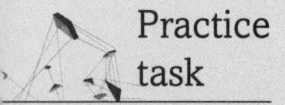

Practice task

Identify an issue in your state or province that has been publicised recently and that you are interested in. It could be a political issue, something that is happening in the local community, or an issue related to climate change, education or health. Do some basic research on the issue and decide what persuasive messages you would use if you were a supporter of that issue to convince others to support it. What goals and objectives would you write? Identify some friends who perhaps do not know anything about the issue because they are an 'inactive public'. What would be the best communication pathway for delivering your messages to your friends? What public relations tools would you use? Write all this down in the format used for the Cashmere Green case. Analyse what you have written. Are the messages relevant to your friends' values and interests? Do the tools you identified deliver the messages in the way intended by your pathway? Did you write your messages in a way that your friends would understand?

WRITING AND PLACING A MEDIA RELEASE

6

Writing material for the news media is an important skill for public relations practitioners. This chapter examines how practitioners use this material as a public relations *tool* to implement an *uncontrolled communication* pathway. At the end of this chapter, you should understand:

+ why it is important to be clear about what you mean by the term *media*
+ what media tools are, and how they are used
+ the news process
+ how to identify 'news'
+ how to write and distribute a media release.

ABOUT JOURNALISTS

Journalists have tough jobs. They are busy professionals who work long hours, often to incredibly tight deadlines, see the good and the bad parts of society, and have their personal and collective work published, broadcast, tweeted or posted on websites, to the whole world. They use social media platforms to source and publish news and to comment on current events. Their products—newspapers and online publications, radio and television news bulletins, current affairs programs, and magazines—change every edition, sometimes hourly. Two Australian writers described the process of gathering and publishing news and commentary as 'the daily miracle' (Conley & Lamble, 2006). Publishing our daily news is a planned process, based on time-honoured techniques. That this can be done so regularly and consistently, and sometimes so instantly, with so few errors, is indeed a miracle. The mistakes journalists make are obvious to people reading, watching or listening. Journalists are criticised for what they write or don't write, for alleged political bias, and for their cynicism. They regularly rate near the bottom of lists of which professions people say they trust most. Journalists can be pushy, arrogant, rude and grumpy. But most are highly skilled at what they do, and we need to work with them as part of our professional practice. To do that effectively, a strong awareness of what they do (not all journalists are reporters, for example), and how and when they do it, is important. All this means that most journalists have a sceptical (some would argue, cynical) view of society and how it works. Most have 'seen it all before'—many times. Journalists get grumpy at public relations people who try to convince them to publish non-news, or continually phone them at busy times of the day to check they received a media release, or who can't write in a news format, spell poorly and use dodgy grammar.

> ### PRACTICE POINT
> The data vary from country to country, but up to 75 per cent of journalists use public relations sources for their stories.

THE FOURTH ESTATE

Whatever view we take of its role in society, journalism is an honourable profession that is as old as democracy (Conley & Lamble, 2006). In the eighteenth century, the philosopher Edmund Burke described the reporters who covered the English Parliament as the 'Fourth Estate'. This idea expanded on the medieval view that society comprised three groups of people, or *estates*: the church, the nobility and the commoners (or the rest of the people). All three estates were represented in the English Parliament: the nobility and the church in the House of Lords; commoners in the House of Commons. In one debate, Burke, speaking in the Commons, looked up at the press gallery, where reporters covering the House still sit, and said, 'Yonder sits the Fourth Estate, and they are more important than them all'. This was an observation on the role journalists play in a democratic society. That role is encapsulated by the phrase 'freedom of the press', an acceptance that in a democracy, journalists can report on the events of the day without censorship by anyone, especially the government. In the United States, freedom of the press is guaranteed by the Constitution.

In the twenty-first century, Burke's observation about the role of the media is reflected in the work of scholars who study how the media work and how what they report affects the community. As we saw earlier, people who study *agenda-setting theory* sometimes say that the mass media don't tell us what to think, but that the choices **editors** make each day about what they'll publish mean that the media tell the public what to think about. For example, in Australia, the focus of politics on any given day is often determined by the stories that ABC Radio's morning current affairs program *AM* covers. Of course, there are some journalists who do try to tell us what to think. These journalists write columns that adopt a particular political, social or economic view. Some newspapers, television programs and websites ground their coverage of the world's news and politics in right or left wing political frames. In nearly all newspapers, editors' 'leaders' or 'editorials' published under a newspaper's name on the editorial page, give an opinion about current issues. Radio and television *news* journalists rarely offer opinions, except when they are explaining why something happened, although radio current affairs program presenters, some of whom are known as 'shock jocks', do.

editor: the executive in charge of a news organisation; the head of a section of a news organisation (e.g. the finance editor); the person who prepares written material for publication.

JOURNALISTS AS TARGET PUBLICS

In a world dominated by all forms of media and the personal devices that make it possible to access almost anything anywhere at any time, many students and beginning practitioners (and some senior ones as well) assume that giving information to 'the media' as a target public is all that is necessary for public relations success. Journalists are rarely primary or secondary target publics, and *the media* is too broad a term to convey any meaningful understanding of just who in the Fourth Estate needs to be considered in a public relations project. Both terms beg the questions: Which journalists? What media? Here's why:

+ Journalists specialise. Some are reporters; some write features; some write columns or commentaries; others work as sub-editors processing copy for publication. That is, they aren't all reporters covering the day's news. Those who do report specialise in what are known as 'rounds': 'general' news, sport, finance, business, the environment, motoring, politics, science, technology, foreign affairs, travel and many more categories. These areas are called 'rounds' because journalists regularly phone around the people working in their specialisation looking for news. That's called 'doing the rounds'. This happens whether the newspaper is published in hard copy or online, whether a news program is on television or a website. Which specialist reporters do you mean, then, when you write 'journalists' as a target public? Send your media release to the journalists who cover your 'round'.

+ The mass news media take many forms. Television, radio, news websites and blogs, special interest newsletters, magazines, technical publications, and newspapers are all part of the mass news media. Most of the large ones employ specialist journalists to cover rounds. Which particular news platforms do you mean when you write 'the media'? For example, would you send a media release about a new high-tech tennis racquet produced by your client to, say, the political, defence, foreign affairs, health, transport or environmental reporters in your state? Wouldn't you send it to the people who cover tennis—and maybe finance reporters if your client's plan is for the new racquet to soon dominate the market?

This might seem trite, but effective media relations activity depends on working with the correct journalists and media platforms when you distribute your organisation's news and opinions. And it means you need to identify which journalists cover the areas your clients work in, get to know them, provide them with appropriate information.

Most of the time, journalists, however segmented, will be tertiary, or intervening, publics in a PR project. That is, they are publics who have no direct interest in an issue or situation, but who can influence those who do (primary and secondary publics) by reporting on it. Regarding journalists as a tertiary public is a pragmatic approach that recognises they have the capacity to write about your news, and that if it is published or broadcast, it can potentially reach intended primary and secondary publics. There is no guarantee that your news will reach your target publics, though, or be read, understood, accepted or acted upon. There is also no guarantee that your news will even be reported as you intended, for at every stage of the news process, a journalist of some kind mediates what you have written. First, the reporter you sent it to must write the story, but is likely to add comments from other people and will perhaps have another view of what the news actually is; a sub-editor is likely to amend it, or even choose a different news lead; another specialist editor will decide where the story will be placed in the newspaper or on the radio or television news—even whether it will be included.

This is why practitioners need to be acutely aware of what news really is, who is interested in it and which reporter might write about it, as well as highly competent at writing material that will interest those tough journalists.

Sometimes, however, journalists who write or broadcast as commentators could be regarded as secondary, or even primary, publics. In the former case, it might be in your organisation's interests to make sure that on an important issue, say an export company's road access to a shipping port, the transport reporters in the local press and on television understand your point of view. This is because they can influence others by what they comment on. You might also develop an ongoing program to keep specialist reporters and commentators up-to-date on your organisation without necessarily expecting them to publish anything. In this example, they would be the primary target public for your program.

> ### PRACTICE NOTE WRITING LIKE A JOURNALIST
>
> Writing like a journalist means adopting the style and language that journalists use. This is vital to the success of your release because it is an approach that busy journalists recognise. If journalists can easily identify what you have produced as news, the chances of your release being reported on tonight's television news, on radio, in tomorrow's newspaper and on the linked media website increase significantly.
>
> When they write news, journalists call one sentence a paragraph. They write short paragraphs of usually no more than about twenty-five words. They use simple words and they do not waste words. They deal with facts and avoid using adjectives, clichés, and overblown language. They use both direct quotes and indirect quotes. They use the active voice when they write; some of their copy is in the past tense (usually indirect quotes), some in the present tense (usually direct quotes).
>
> Make sure the information you distribute is accurate. That means you are using facts, your grammar is accurate, you have apostrophes and other punctuation marks in the right place, and your spelling is correct. Use a dictionary to make sure you know the correct spelling and definitions of words, and a thesaurus to find synonyms so that you use the simplest words.

What happens to your media release after you've distributed it?

The process varies from media platform to media platform. In radio and television newsrooms and on news websites, it is complicated by the need for sound and vision.

However, the basic process is as follows:

- When your release arrives in the newsroom, the chief of staff (who normally allocates jobs to reporters) decides whether your material should be 'covered' and tasks a journalist to write a story. The journalist will read your release and follow it up by getting extra information from you, or by seeking comments from other people with an interest in your topic, perhaps people who oppose your organisation's views. If you have emailed the release directly to a specific journalist, perhaps the specialist writer who normally covers your industry, the process will be the same.
- Once the journalist has written the story, it will be sent to the chief sub-editor, who will ask one of their team to 'sub' the story. That involves making sure it is written in the correct style for the newspaper, or for radio or television news, and that spelling and punctuation are correct. The sub-editor will be given specific instructions on how long the 'subbed' story should be—and that means that it might be shortened. In newspapers, sub-editors also write the headline for the story and make sure that it appears in the correct typeface. In radio and television, the copy for the newsreader will include instructions on what sound and vision will be used. In newspapers, the sub-editor will know whether the story will be accompanied by photographs.
- The chief sub-editor will decide exactly where the story will appear in the newspaper. In the electronic media, the producer will decide where in each bulletin the story will be placed. These decisions are based on the importance of a story. (See 'The daily choice', below.)
- Most newspapers and radio and television stations have online news sites, which include blogs, Twitter feeds, other social media applications and video. The growing use of online news and the greater links between newspapers and broadcast media mean that journalists increasingly focus on a 'multimedia' approach to reporting and commentary. Online news sites are updated regularly by the specialist teams that produce them.

Agenda setting by the media is sometimes deliberate. It happens when the editor of a newspaper, news website, or radio or television program decides to pursue a story, or to concentrate on an aspect of a story—the 'angle' in journalism terms. Mostly, however, media agenda setting happens as a result of the choices editors have to make about how much of the daily news they can cover and how important a story is.

Competition for news space

Each day, newsrooms are deluged by information, some factual, some opinion, all of it in some way dressed up as 'news'. News happens all the time, from car accidents, bushfires, sporting events and new airline services, to politics, international affairs, wars, celebrity behaviour, product launches, court hearings, and changes to old age pensions. There is so much news that special television channels like Al Jazeera, Sky News, CNN, BBC World News and Fox News provide continuous 24-hour coverage of the world. When these channels first hear about a news item, they promote it as 'breaking news'. Each day, there is enough news left out of a newspaper to fill another edition.

> **PRACTICE POINT**
> There are more words in a full-page column of text in a broadsheet newspaper than are spoken in the whole of a half-hour television news bulletin.

The daily choice

There is a physical limit to how much 'news' can be reported in radio and television news bulletins, on websites (despite the use of links to other sources) and in the newspapers. Most television news bulletins last for half an hour, and on commercial stations that time includes breaks for advertisements. Radio news bulletins are far briefer, sometimes only a few minutes. The number of pages in each daily newspaper is decided not by the editor but by how much advertising that edition has attracted. Websites provide greater flexibility for relaying news, but this increasingly popular and important medium has its own space limitations.

Time and space limitations mean that editors make hourly choices about what they'll publish or broadcast, how much of a reporter's story they'll run, and where they'll place their choices in newspapers, bulletins, or on the webpage. These news value choices mean that editors have to decide what is the most important news. Is it news from a war, the latest political opinion poll or a report about bushfires, the snow season, transport chaos, the performance of the stock market, a murder, a court case, poverty in Africa, climate change or the latest findings about research on the solar system? An editor's decision about what the most important stories are for this day means that they will be the first covered in the bulletin, or will appear on page one of the newspaper.

That's the competition public relations practitioners face when they attempt to have their client's 'news' covered by the media. It is not easy to have a media release reported, and yours is likely to be ignored if it is not judged by journalists to be news, or is poorly written, loaded with hyperbole, or littered with spelling mistakes.

WHAT IS A MEDIA RELEASE?

A media release is information, usually in written form, about an organisation, person, product, event or issue that is given to journalists in the hope that they will publish it. Media releases are written like a news story; they are approved by the organisation, or individual, in whose name they appear, and are widely distributed. The idea is that news is 'released' to several journalists at the same time. Media releases are the most basic tools used by public relations practitioners.

The American journalist Ivy Lee, one of the founders of public relations, is believed to have issued the first 'press' release. He did this in 1906 when he convinced the US railway company that employed him to give written information about a tragic accident to journalists so that they would have accurate information about what had happened. Lee also invited reporters and photographers to visit the site of the accident. Of course, when Lee issued his first release, it went to newspapers, or the press, hence the term *press release*. Television didn't exist, radio was experimental, and there was no internet. Since then, websites and television have become the primary sources of news for most people, and radio is almost as important as a source of news. Increasingly, people first find out about the news from websites or social media applications on their tablet computers or smartphones. All this means that *press* is no longer an appropriate term: *media* or *news release* are the more common, perhaps acceptable, terms in the twenty-first century.

When you issue a media release, journalists will treat it as an official statement from your organisation that they can quote in news reports.

Sometimes students worry about writing words to be used as quotes in a media release that are attributed to someone else, usually the boss, especially if the person did not actually say those words in a speech, or a talk. It is perfectly ethical for a practitioner to write words for someone else that will be used as both direct and indirect quotes in a media release *provided* the person approves them before the release is issued.

> ### PRACTICE NOTE ABOUT MEDIA RELEASES
>
> Media releases:
>
> + pursue an organisation's objectives
> + use the adoption model—people make decisions after their awareness is raised
> + are the basis of a lot of radio, press, web and television news
> + save time for you and reporters
> + help reporters to get the facts
> + inform a number of reporters at the same time
> + may be quoted word for word
> + force you to think about what you say
> + must be approved by the organisations on whose behalf they are distributed.
>
> An associated public relations tool is a **'media alert'** or 'media advisory'. These are short releases that advise the appropriate media of an event, perhaps a news conference, usually a day or so before it occurs. Media alerts give details of what is happening, when and where it will happen, and who will be involved. The idea behind a media alert is to make sure journalists know about your event ahead of time by getting your details in the news diary, or list of events, that might be covered by the local television or radio station or the newspaper.

media alert (or advisory): a short media release to advise the media of an event, usually a day or so before it occurs.

> ### PRACTICE POINT
>
> A media release or a media alert must include information about who issued it and the date it was issued, and have phone and email details for someone a journalist can contact to follow it up. We'll look at how all this fits together later in the chapter.

What is a media kit?

A **media kit** is a package of material given to journalists when they are writing a story about an organisation, person, product, event or issue. What goes in a media kit depends on what it is being used for. Typically media kits include a media release, a backgrounder that gives more detailed information about the topic, the organisation's latest annual report, several fact sheets, a leaflet that gives some product information, perhaps a **question and answer (QnA) sheet**, and the practitioner's business card. Media kits are enclosed in a folder, often printed in the corporate design. Sometimes these folders have basic information about the organisation—like its mission statement or corporate goals—or photographs of production facilities or staff doing things printed on them.

Many organisations also publish electronic media kits on the 'newsroom' sections of their websites. This is a flexible and efficient way of compiling and distributing information, and it means there is often no need to compile material in one 'kit' for one event.

media kit: a pack of material about an organisation, usually in hard copy but often published on a website.

question and answer (QnA) sheet: a set of questions and answers about an organisation, product, event or issue written by a public relations practitioner for the media and other target publics, and usually produced in hard-copy form. The questions are usually those that the practitioner thinks journalists might ask. These questions are sometimes also described as 'frequently asked questions'.

Table 6.1 Definitions of some public relations tools for the news media

Tool	Definition
Media release	Information, usually in written form, about an organisation, person, product, event or issue that is given to journalists in the hope that they will publish it. Media releases are written like a news story and can contain direct and indirect quotes. Media releases can be supported by other tools.
Media alert or advisory	Short media releases that advise the media of an event, perhaps a news conference, usually a day or so before it occurs. Media alerts give basic details of what is happening, when and where it will happen, and who will be involved.
Media kit	A hard-copy package of material given to journalists when they are writing a story about an organisation, person, product, event or issue.
Backgrounder	Detailed information about an organisation, person, product, event or issue that is not necessarily news. Backgrounders are usually written about one topic and expand on a media release by giving, for example, technical details, or the history of an issue, or the context in which an event will take place. They are not written like a media release but in a normal prose style. Information in a backgrounder can be arranged under a series of headings. They are usually more than one page of text, and copies are kept for future needs.

Tool	Definition
Fact sheet	A set of factual data about an organisation, person, product, event or issue that is not necessarily news. For example, a fact sheet from Ideal Widgets Pty Ltd could provide information about how widgets are made and how they are used. Another might include data about Ideal Widgets' company structure, and a third might have information about export markets for widgets.
Question and answer (QnA) sheet	Answers to questions that an organisation thinks its publics might have in relation to it. These most usually take the form of responses to a list of 'frequently asked questions' in the one document. For example: What are widgets? Who makes widgets? What are the biggest export markets for widgets? Why are widgets safer than other products? How many widgets are produced in New Zealand every year? Where can I buy widgets?
Response sheet	A tool often used to answer a single question. For example, a question is posed and followed by a detailed response. This can be a handy tool if a practitioner is involved in managing a public issue or crisis, or in a political campaign.
Profile	A profile of a senior person in the organisation for distribution to the media and other target publics at appropriate times. A profile would be written after interviewing the person. For example, when a new chief executive is appointed, a profile would be a good supplement to a media release announcing the appointment. Profiles can include the person's curriculum vitae. A profile can be an important resource if a senior person in your organisation dies and the media want background material for an obituary.

response sheet: a communication tool for giving a detailed answer to a single question, usually in the context of managing an issue or crisis.

Understanding news

Once, most people who practised public relations were former journalists, and they knew what 'news' was. They were highly skilled at identifying and writing news stories. This was an important skill at a time when public relations practice concentrated on the approach that is now widely accepted as the *press agentry* model. Former journalists could not only identify organisational news, but also knew in detail how the media worked. They could write media releases in an appropriate news style and issue them in a timely way.

In the twenty-first century public relations practice is far more strategic and involves activities beyond issuing media releases. Practitioners manage organisational relationships, organise issue and crisis communication, counsel the dominant coalition on a wide range of matters, plan and conduct events, manage sponsorships, and run websites. Practitioners come from a variety of backgrounds and academic disciplines. Practitioners do not always start out in the news media, as did previous generations of public relations specialists. Many of those in previous practitioner generations did not have a university degree, let alone one in public relations. Nevertheless, writing and issuing media releases, and working with the media, are still important in professional practice, and we need to know how to write a release that will attract a journalist's attention.

Finding news: What news frames will make my release work?

It seems almost too obvious to say it, but journalists are interested in news. Practitioners must understand that journalists have a keen sense of what is news and that they waste no time in throwing out media releases that do not meet their news test. Experienced practitioners use the same test when they seek out stories they can use in their organisation's strategic public relations. To pass the news test, your information must meet at least one of the following criteria, or news frames, which journalists themselves use.

Timeliness

timeliness: a factor in deciding whether your information is newsworthy. Is it literally 'new', and are you releasing it at an appropriate time?

Your information must literally be 'new' or current. That means using the **timeliness** news frame by releasing information at a relevant time so that journalists will treat it as news. For example, a university might have the findings of a medical research project, or the local council might need to announce the route of a new road that will reduce traffic congestion around the railway station. Sometimes, as autumn begins, health authorities announce that it is now *time* for people to have flu shots. Airlines advise people to get to the airport early if they are travelling at peak times like Easter and Christmas. If you want people to know about an event, you should announce the details so that they have plenty of notice.

Relevance

relevance: a factor in deciding whether your information is newsworthy. How does your information affect people's lives, incomes, health, relationships and entertainment choices? Does it pass the 'Who cares?' test?

People like to know how information directly affects them. Journalists ask themselves what the information in a media release means for their readers. If they cannot find some **relevance** to people's lives, incomes, health, relationships or entertainment choices, the release is likely to miss out. So, for example, increases in the cost of bread, milk, petrol or telephone calls will get a journalist's attention. Of course, not all practitioners are involved with these products, but the point is that they need to find a way of showing the relevance of their information to people.

Proximity

Using this criterion to work out whether your release will interest journalists can be a lot of fun because it allows practitioners to localise their releases. That means using the 'local angle' (or **proximity**) in the first paragraph of the release to attract attention, since the local media like to report stories that deal with local people, issues or events. For example, universities often announce the winners of scholarships in a general media release giving details of the total number of scholarships and the areas the holders come from. The first paragraph of a general release about this might be: 'The top twenty-five high school students in Australia in 2020 have been awarded prestigious $15 000 National Undergraduate Scholarships at the University of Inconsequential Studies.' Then they write tailored releases for the media in the cities or towns where the students went to school. A tailored release written like this might have as its first paragraph: 'Mulwaree High School students have won four of the twenty-five prestigious National Undergraduate Scholarships awarded by the University of Inconsequential Studies this year.'

proximity: a factor in deciding whether your information is newsworthy. Can you 'localise' your information by linking it to a particular community?

Prominence

Relating your news to the experiences of a well-known person is a useful approach. Charities often use celebrities to help them promote their causes because celebrities are well known, perhaps more than the chief executive of the charity. In a similar way, when organisations give awards to **prominent** people, their presentation events are more likely to be covered by the media. Some celebrities will have a personal interest in a particular cause. Many sportspeople, for instance, have been willing to promote the work of the Asthma Foundation because they suffer from the illness.

prominence: a factor in deciding whether your information is newsworthy. Can you relate your information to a well-known person?

Significance

This criterion relates to whether your news affects a substantial number of people. The examples under 'relevance' also apply here. An example of a hypothetical release using '**significance**' as a news criterion is: 'More than three million working mothers will benefit from lower income tax rates announced in the federal budget tonight.' Another example: 'An increase in the seating capacity of the Star Arena will enable more fans to attend rock concerts in Toronto.'

significance: a factor in deciding whether your information is newsworthy. Does your information affect a significant number of people? Why and how?

Rarity

Rarity means something is not commonplace or routine, and people are interested in things that are rare. For example, when the Wollemi pine was discovered in Australia by chance in 1994, it was big news because it had previously only been known from the fossil record. Here was an ancient and rare tree, alive and healthy in a remote location (still secret) in a regularly visited forest. And almost every year the Wollemi pine creates a new story as the nursery that is propagating trees from its seeds issues new stock for people to buy for their homes. Practitioners need to be careful, however, when they claim rarity or uniqueness. If they overstate these claims, they will be found out by journalists.

rarity: a factor in deciding whether your information is newsworthy. Does your information relate to something that is not commonplace? Is it the biggest, smallest, fastest, slowest, cleanest, dirtiest, oldest, youngest?

> **PRACTICE POINT**
>
> Go to <www.abc.net.au/gardening> and click on 'Fact Sheets' to see examples of one way to write and publish fact sheets. Now visit <www.abc.net.au/gardening/stories/s1471653.htm> to see a fact sheet about the ancient Wollemi pine, a living, 200-million-year-old relic of the dinosaur age; the discovery of that ancient tree was news in both the rarity and significance frames.

Trendiness

trendiness: a factor in deciding whether your information is newsworthy. Can you relate your information to the latest trend, fashion or food craze, or to popular entertainment?

This is a problematic criterion because not everyone follows the latest trends. Nevertheless, the media often reflect the latest fashion **trends**, or popular entertainment, or food craze, or our fascination with new gadgets like smart watches and fitness trackers and it may be possible to link your organisation's news with these. Media releases about new uses for old products, new models of cars or mobile phones, or new products, ideas and research outcomes also fit this criterion. It is important, however, to be careful in the way you use the term *new*. If your release claims something is 'new' when it is not, you'll be found out.

Human interest

human interest: a factor in deciding whether your information is newsworthy. Does your information relate to interesting personal stories? Can people relate to it at a human level?

People love stories about other people, whether they are rich and famous or ordinary people overcoming huge odds. Often the media will report on one very poor family in covering the issue of unemployment. Practitioners can use **human interest** as a criterion for publicising an organisation by, say, using the oldest employee to talk about updated equipment installed in a factory: when Fred first started working here, everything was done manually and it took ten hours to do this job; fifty years later, the factory is entirely computerised and Fred's ten-hour job is done in ten minutes. Fund-raising charities use this frame—the Kids' Cancer Project in Australia (<**http://www.thekidscancerproject.org.au**>) is an example.

Conflict

conflict: a factor in deciding whether your information is newsworthy. Is your information about a controversial subject? Does your organisation have a different view of an issue from others? Have your researchers discovered something that challenges accepted, current knowledge?

Differences and arguments and wars make news. The media will report on opinions that differ from a commonly held view because journalists are trained to seek the alternative argument. This means that controversies often 'run' longer in the media than they would otherwise as different opinions are reported each day. Some people see this as the media fuelling a controversy. Practitioners working for industry associations can use the media's interest in **conflict** to draw attention to their organisation's view on a public policy issue. Other practitioners use this criterion when they use their organisation's experts on particular subjects to provide commentary. An example is the use of the chief economist of a bank to comment on the possibility of a change in official interest rates and how that might impact on home mortgages. Academics are regularly sought out by the media for their opinions on subjects ranging from the impact of climate change on the environment to the reasons terrorists use suicide bombers.

PRACTICE NOTE FINDING NEWS USING INTERNAL AND EXTERNAL SOURCES

Mostly the topics covered by media releases are part of a strategic public relations plan. That is, the **implementation** section of the plan includes details of when releases on certain topics will be written and released. That means the release announcing your company's new soft drink flavour will be written into the plan to support the start of the advertising campaign and the in-store sales promotion efforts.

However, there are always opportunities for practitioners to take an initiative and to research and write releases about people, equipment, plans, achievements and events. Also, organisations often need to respond to an unexpected issue or opportunity.

A lot of the time, people in the organisation will tell practitioners about things they believe should be promoted. That's a major reason why practitioners should regularly talk to people at all levels of the organisation about what those people are doing and planning. That is part of internal environmental scanning: keeping up with what is happening inside the organisation. Keeping up to date with what is happening inside your organisation can help you to identify good opportunities for media releases and other public relations activity. Look for people, events, plans, jobs and equipment that meet one or more of the news frames discussed above. Extend the frames by thinking about whether something is the first, last, biggest or smallest (in the context of your company).

THE WORLD AROUND US

Practitioners who keep abreast of what is happening in the world outside the organisation—its external environment—are well placed to follow up an opportunity to have their chief executive contribute to the debate about an issue that affects the organisation. They also make links between what is happening in the world outside the organisation and what it produces, or plans to build, or has expert knowledge about. In many ways, understanding the context in which the organisation operates in this external environment, and producing appropriate public relations action to address issues it faces, is at the heart of the profession. (See Mahoney, 2017, ch. 5 for a detailed discussion about identifying and analysing external issues.)

Practitioner teams often brainstorm ideas for creating news or for activities that can be included in their public relations planning. You can create news by planning and staging events. This is a common way of launching a new product. Events like this are often called 'media stunts' because they are planned to attract media coverage. It is probably better to describe them simply as launches or events.

implementation: the phase of a public relations plan that describes how and when communication tools will be implemented.

> ### INTERNAL SOURCES OF NEWS
>
> Look for news ideas inside your organisation:
>
> + in employee newsletters and websites
> + in speeches and presentations given by senior people
> + in media clipping files
> + in policy and discussion papers
> + in sales material
> + by keeping your eyes wide open and listening to people.
>
> ### EXTERNAL SOURCES OF NEWS
>
> Find news ideas by linking what is happening in your organisation to public events and issues. Ask yourself how you can link what your organisation is doing to the ideas you pick up from:
>
> + a speech you heard
> + a radio or television interview or program
> + a newspaper feature article
> + opinion polls and other surveys
> + census reports
> + government and parliamentary reports (there is a difference between the two)
> + financial analysis published in the mainstream media
> + professional periodicals
> + the latest trend
> + a major issue
> + keeping your eyes wide open and listening to people.
>
> Many organisations also generate media attention by linking what they are doing with the news of the day. They might also announce a competition or a new award or the results of an election for committee members, or when an employee is given an honour. The appointment of a new chief executive is an opportunity to generate news (what does the new CEO have in mind for the organisation's future? What are their views on issues of the day?), as are inspection tours of manufacturing facilities, and presentations by people from the organisation to government inquiries.

Writing a media release

The technique for writing a media release is similar to that used by journalists when they write a news story. After all, that's the approach Ivy Lee adopted in 1906 and there's really been no reason to change in all this time. What has changed is the technical way in which a media release is delivered and how people access news. That's now almost entirely by electronic means using email and social media applications. But the basic principles for writing a release have not changed and won't ever change.

The approach to writing a media release used in this book is based on the classic style derived from journalism practice. It is an approach that stresses the primacy of news as the focus of a release. As you explore the myriad releases you can access on the internet, you'll notice that there are almost as many ways of writing and presenting a release as there are topics. Some are written in news format, some appear to be straightforward statements with no attempt to focus on news at all, others are produced as marketing tools that promote products. Some adopt a traditional hard-copy format; others are 'social media releases' with active links to other information or online sites. The organisation for which you work will have its own writing and formatting style and you will need to familiarise yourself with this.

Before you start writing, you first need to think through what you are going to say in the release. Second, a media release must meet one or more of the criteria for deciding whether it is news. Third, a release needs to be written in clear, concise and accurate language that will be recognised by a journalist as news writing. Fourth, the organisation must be identified. Fifth, you need to include the name and telephone and email details of someone who can be contacted if reporters want more information, and the date on which the release is issued.

There are some cues that can help practitioners to work on these requirements.

Using a template and 'Five Ws and H'

The 'Public Relations Toolkit' section at the start of this book has a worksheet that you can use to plan your media release. This will help you to think through what you need to include in your media release. The template is based on the six basic, one-word questions that have always underpinned journalists' approaches to reporting. They are the '**Five Ws and H**' (or 5Ws and H as they are commonly written): What? When? Where? Why? Who? and How?

Thus, for example:

+ *What* happened?
+ *When* did it happen?
+ *Where* did it happen?
+ *How* did it happen?
+ *Who* is involved?
+ *Why* did it happen?

When you use the media release **planning worksheet**, ask and answer questions like:

+ What is the key message that the organisation wants to put in this release? Why is it 'new'?
+ What is the primary target public? The answer is not necessarily the media (see the earlier discussion of this point). Deciding exactly who your target public is will help you to decide whether you should issue a media release to all news organisations, or just to those that

Five Ws and H: the what, when, where, who, why and how questions that help to determine what needs to be included in a media release.

planning worksheet: a planning tool that helps to identify what information needs to be included in a media release, a speech or other material. For a media release, a planning worksheet includes identifying the news lead, or main point, of the release.

are most used by your public. For example, ask yourself whether a release about a new superannuation scheme for retirees would interest the news team at the local youth radio station. If your answer is no, would you then expect the station to run the story?
+ What does the target public gain from the product, service or topic you are focusing on in your media release?
+ What public relations objective does the release serve?

> **PRACTICE POINT**
>
> When you write a media release, think and write like a journalist—but answer the 5Ws and H from a public relations perspective.
>
> This could be the most important point you take from this chapter, because unless you work like this, no journalist will be interested in your 'news', irrespective of whether it is sent in hard copy or via a tweet.

THE INVERTED PYRAMID

The structure of a media release should follow the rule of the 'inverted pyramid' (see Figure 6.1). This figure is based on the rule for reporting news that the most important facts come first, followed by other information that supports, backs up or expands on the first point, in descending order of importance. This approach means that if it is necessary to cut a story to fit the available newspaper space or radio or TV broadcast time, a **sub-editor** or reporter can cut from the bottom of the story without having to rewrite the important points at the start. And that is another reason why it is good to use short sentences that deal with one point.

sub-editor: a journalist who assists the editor to prepare material for publication.

Figure 6.1 The inverted pyramid

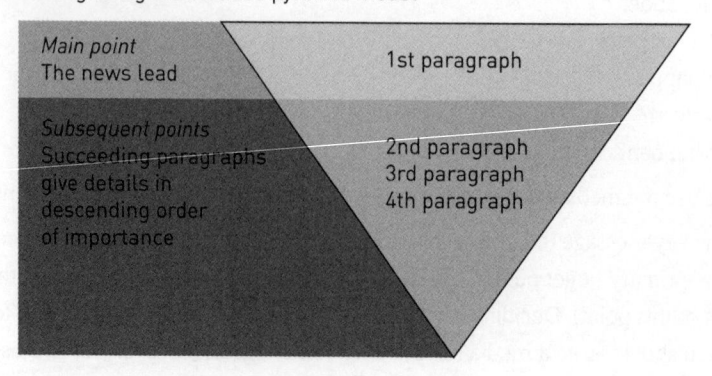

Writing using the inverted pyramid model

Main point The news lead	1st paragraph
Subsequent points Succeeding paragraphs give details in descending order of importance	2nd paragraph 3rd paragraph 4th paragraph

> **PRACTICE POINT**
>
> Buy hard copies, or use online versions, of an Oxford dictionary and thesaurus that deal with English as it is written in your country and keep them by your desk, or bookmarked. Don't ever be afraid to use them, rather than your word-processing program's spellchecker, to check spelling, word meanings, synonyms and antonyms. The Australian *Style Manual for Authors, Editors and Printers* (2002) would also be a useful addition to your professional library wherever you work in the world because it will help you to check grammar, and it has other important information about writing and production. For Australian students, this book is the accepted standard for Australian English usage in professional practice.

The news lead

People reading the first paragraph of your media release should be able to grasp your main point instantly. Write it in the active voice and use the past tense to answer one of the 5Ws and H. Remember that you are writing news, which is usually about something that is happening now.

Writing in this way means structuring your first paragraph so that the information you want to get across is immediately obvious. Don't obscure it with redundant information. For example, avoid writing a first paragraph like:

> On 4 July this year, the local Mayor, Sue Nguyen, officially opened a new access road that will reduce the volume of traffic in Main Street.

Instead, write like this:

> A new access road that will reduce traffic in Main Street was opened by the Mayor, Sue Nguyen, today.

In this case, the second version gets to the point, uses fewer words (nineteen instead of twenty-six), and is in the news style that a reporter would use. It is about something that happened today. That is, it is news.

Here are the first five paragraphs of a media release from Caltech in the United States that announced the findings of research into how ocean tides affect glacial movement in Antarctica (you can read the full release at <**http://www.caltech.edu/news/satellites-observe-traffic-jams-antarctic-ice-stream-caused-tides-53322**>):

> ### Satellites Observe 'Traffic Jams' in Antarctic Ice Stream Caused by Tides
>
> For the first time, researchers have closely observed how the ocean's tides can speed up or slow down the speed of glacial movement in Antarctica. The new data will help modelers better predict how glaciers will respond to rising sea levels.
>
> Caltech's Brent Minchew (PhD '16) and Mark Simons, along with their collaborators and in cooperation with the Italian Space Agency (ASI), exploited four COSMO-SkyMed radar-imaging satellites on the Rutford Ice Stream in Antarctica. The satellites gathered near-continuous data for nearly nine months from a variety of angles.
>
> The Rutford Ice Stream is a fast-moving river of ice, approximately 300 kilometers long and 25 kilometers wide, in West Antarctica. It connects glaciers in the Ellsworth Mountains to the Filchner-Ronne Ice Shelf, a floating chunk of ice roughly the size of California. Driven by its own weight, the stream of solid ice flows downhill toward the sea at a rate of about one meter per day, though that speed varies by as much as 20 percent with the tides.
>
> The variability is driven by the ice's interactions with the ocean. At low tide, the floating ice sinks far enough to ground out on the sea floor like a foundering ship, causing an ice traffic jam that can be detected up to 100 kilometers upstream. When the tide rises again, the ice lifts off of the sea floor and flows freely once more.
>
> 'A rising tide lifts all ships, and it also lifts all ice,' says Minchew, a PhD student at Caltech while conducting the research and now a postdoctoral researcher the British Antarctic Survey. Minchew is the lead author of a paper about the study that was published by the *Journal of Geophysical Research* on November 22.

Note how:

+ the research findings are summarised in the first paragraph, which uses the active voice and present perfect tense: *have observed*. In this case, the second sentence uses the simple future tense: *will help*. That's because the findings will continue to be relevant in more research. This paragraph answers 'What?'
+ the second paragraph answers 'Who?', identifying the researchers who conducted the study and their positions. It also explains how they conducted the research in the past tense: <u>*exploited*</u> *four ... satellites*, <u>*gathered*</u> *near-continuous data*.
+ the third and fourth paragraphs are written in the past tense, and they explain the news that was summarised in the first paragraph.
+ the fifth paragraph uses an active voice, and a direct quote from another of the researchers to start an explanation of why the research is important. It also identifies his position and his role in the academic article on which the release is based.

Subsequent points—or the 'body' of the release

The next section of the release expands on the news lead and explains why the research is important and how it expands on previous work.

> The ice stream was so sensitive to the change in tides that Simons and Minchew could detect the individual influences of solar and lunar tides.
>
> The planet's solar and lunar tides are caused by the tug of the sun and the moon, respectively, on the earth. High tide occurs simultaneously on the sides of the earth facing toward and away from the sun and the moon because their gravitational pulls create a bulge, or high tide, in the planet.
>
> The lunar and solar tides are not perfectly in sync: the lunar tide cycles from high to low every 12-and-a-half hours, while the solar tide cycles every 12 hours. When those two cycles align perfectly, the sea experiences its strongest tides. When they are most misaligned, the sea experiences its weakest tides.
>
> Previous efforts to explore the effect of the tide on glacial movement relied on placing a GPS device directly on the ice. This technique, however, provides information for only one point of movement.
>
> The Caltech team instead collected pairs of images taken from the same location in space but at different times, thus showing movement not just of a single point but continuous tracking of every single square inch of the surface of the ice streams. (Ice does not move as one solid fixed mass, but rather it flows like an incredibly viscous syrup—its motion is often likened to that of cold honey. As such, the movement of one point provides only the most basic information about the entire glacier.) Further, the variety of viewing angles provided by the constellation of satellites offered three-dimensional information about the ice's movement and revealed, for example, that the floating ice shelf moved more quickly, thus showing that the grounding effect was indeed responsible for changes in the ice's speed.
>
> Studies on glacial movement could yield important data for scientists looking to model how glaciers will respond to the effects of climate change.
>
> 'The response of ice flow to changes in sea level and ocean temperature has a direct impact on contemporary sea-level rise,' says Simons, professor of geophysics at Caltech. 'Quantifying this is critical for understanding how Antarctica will evolve over the next decades and centuries as the climate warms and the marine-terminating glaciers are exposed to warmer ocean water.'
>
> With warmer water and high sea levels, glaciers will flow faster into the sea, melting more quickly once they reach the water.
>
> Already, the study has yielded surprising information about the strength of ice and its ability to resist deforming due to glacial stress. As it turns out, ice is weaker along

> the margins of flowing glacial streams than previously suspected. The same technology and technique could be used to study the motion of glaciers worldwide, Minchew says.
>
> Simons and Minchew collaborated with Caltech alumnus Bryan Riel (PhD '14) and Pietro Milillo of the University of Basilicata in Italy, both of whom are now affiliated with JPL. Their paper is titled 'Tidally induced variations in vertical and horizontal motion on Rutford Ice Stream, West Antarctica, inferred from remotely sensed observations.' This research was funded by NASA, the National Science Foundation, the Albert Parvin Foundation, and the Achievement Rewards for College Scientists (ARCS) Foundation.

There are some other important points to note about this release. They are important because they illustrate the correct way to deal with information in a media release.

- It uses direct quotes. Journalists know that they can use these quotes and attribute them to the person making them in the release.
- Note how the direct quotes are correctly enclosed by quotation marks. A quotation mark opens the direct quote and closes it.
- Scientific research findings are obviously news, and this release is timely: it has been issued as soon as possible after a paper about it was published in scientific journal. It also has a rarity news frame—no-one else has found these research results.
- The release has enough information for a reporter to base a news story.
- The heading about Antarctic traffic jams is designed to catch attention.
- The language is clear and explains complex science in a simple way.
- What the research means, and why it is important, are explained.

This release includes another important point. It acknowledges the author, Robert Perkins, and his contact details at Caltech. In publishing the release in this way, the PR team at Caltech is using this section of the university's website as an online newspaper.

If you include a direct quote of more than one paragraph, write the first the way it has been done in the release above. Set each subsequent paragraph of the quote out as a new paragraph—and start each with a quotation mark. Do not close the quotation marks at the end of each paragraph. Use a closed quotation mark only at the end of the last paragraph of the direct quote. This approach is in any case correct grammatical usage.

PRACTICE POINT

Some ways to help your media release get attention from journalists include the following.

Do:

- use a planning worksheet
- write succinct headlines that summarise your information

- tell the news—it won't be reported if you don't
- write simple, accurate, grammatical sentences
- target your writing and make it clear how the release is important to media consumers
- be aware of the deadlines that the newspapers and radio and television stations have for receiving information before each edition, and make sure your media release is sent well before those deadlines
- critique your own writing and apply the 'Does anyone care about this?' test before you press the 'print' key on your computer.

Don't:
- use a direct quote as your lead paragraph
- overdo your writing; it isn't poetry, so flowery stuff is not needed
- exaggerate or use words like *world-class*—you'll be found out if it is not
- expect every word to be used in a news story
- highlight the name of your company in the headline if it is not well known.

Formatting a release

Most organisations have their own format for media releases, which is usually based on their corporate letterhead, adapted to indicate that it is a media release. This instantly identifies the organisation, which is important if the release is to be hand delivered, posted to a website, emailed or sent by 'snail mail'. This is called using the corporate style. There are some general principles for an effective format, and again they apply whether the release is to be distributed electronically or in hard copy.

Make sure that the letterhead you use does not overwhelm your message. It is not necessary, for example, to print the words 'Media release' in any more than 24-point bold type. Some organisations use large graphic elements to highlight the fact that something is a media release. This is not necessary, but that is a decision your organisation will make.

A media release should have the date on which it is issued prominently displayed. Some organisations put the date at the top right-hand side of the release, others at the bottom. Again, this is your (or your organisation's) choice, as long as the date is clear. Some practitioners working for organisations also like to number releases, usually for each year. For example, the eleventh release in 2020 would have the number 11/20. These numbers often appear just above the heading, set to one side of the page.

Set your page up with a reasonably wide left-hand margin. It is not necessary to justify the right-hand margin of your text.

Type in a standard, legible typeface like Times New Roman or Arial in an 11- or 12-point font. However, many people find *serif* typefaces like Times New Roman easier to read than *sans-serif* typefaces. Fancy, creative and complicated typefaces are hard to read. Keep it simple and clear.

Once it was important to set out your text in 1.5 or double (line) spacing so that journalists could write on the hard copy. Now that electronic distribution of media releases via email or direct downloading from a website is the accepted, and easier, way of distributing a release, single (line) spacing is fine.

Write a brief heading that summarises the news you are releasing. The heading on the release we have been examining in this section does just that. Type the heading in bold text. It does not have to be all in capital letters; it is actually easier to read if it is not all in capital letters. The heading can be larger than the text, and it is common for a heading to be in 18- or 20-point type. Your organisation or consultancy will probably have a style for headings, which you should follow. Sometimes organisations use a different typeface for headings from the one they use for text. This can create a useful contrast, but you should use one of the regular, simple fonts because fancy typefaces like many of those offered in word processing software are hard to read.

Always include the names of one or more people who can be contacted for further information by adding something like the following at the end of the release (alternatively, you could put the date just above the heading):

> For further information contact:
> Phyllida Murphy
> National Public Relations Manager
> W: 04 7891 0987
> M: 0802 456 123
> Email: phyllida@ourorg.com
> Issued: 15 March 2020

Remember, the person who is listed as the contact for further information must be available. Practitioners and others who offer themselves as contacts to provide further information and who are not available, or who won't answer follow-up questions, soon do themselves and their organisation serious damage with journalists.

Which journalists will be interested in your release?

As we have seen earlier in this chapter, not every journalist will be interested in your media release. That is because journalists specialise in topics. Some cover court cases; others specialise in transport matters; others concentrate on defence and foreign affairs; others on crime reporting, science, medical news, politics, rural news, entertainment, sports, food and wine, cars, finance, the environment, security, industrial matters, or religion.

PRACTICE NOTE MAKING MEDIA RELEASES WORK

A survey of Asia-Pacific journalists by the global *PR NEWSWIRE* in 2016 found that media releases were still important to journalists' work in this age of social media. Respondents ranked organisations' official media releases ahead of social media like Facebook and Twitter as trusted sources of news (<http://www.medianet.com.au/blog-dont-take-word-journalists-say-press-releases>). In its own feedback from journalists, Medianet found Australian and New Zealand journalists view media releases as:

+ Starting points for the news-gathering process
+ Essential for putting journalists and news sources in touch with each other and thus a good way to build contacts
+ Providing extra information for a story
+ Sources for stories—but are cautious about only using a release by taking it at face value, or publishing them as free advertising.

And journalists say they want short releases with good direct quotes, not wordy releases in which the important information is hidden.

Medianet advised practitioners who use its distribution service that a media release headline is the 'key part of the release that you want to get right' because it is the first thing that meets the eye of the person who will decide whether to use it (<http://www.medianet.com.au/blog-crafting-effective-press-releases-headlines-first>). So, Medianet says:

+ Don't treat the headline as an afterthought; review the headline when the release is finished to make sure it is relevant
+ Align the headline as much as possible with the first paragraph of the release
+ Don't make the headline too obscure or complicated—keep them short, simple and direct
+ Strive to make headlines compelling, and keep it to the genuine news that is in the release.

The daily international newsletter *PR NEWS* publishes tips for practitioners on the whole range of professional activity. One set of tips dealt with four outdated media release practices. Writing in *PR NEWS* (December, 2016), Catherine Spicer, manager of customer content services at *PR NEWSWIRE*, said that the following 'diehard' practices were not necessary in modern 'high-octane' releases:

+ Using the statement 'For Immediate Release'. The argument for not using this: when a release goes online, it is assumed to be ready for immediate release.
+ Embargoing media releases. Spicer argued that once a release was on an editor's desk, it was 'fair game to publish'. Embargoes were often used to

> enable journalists to work on a story in advance of something happening. An example was the use of embargoes on releases from universities advising of research to be published in an academic journal. Many experienced senior practitioners have been caught out by journalists breaking these embargoes. Besides, in the modern digital world, embargoes are not necessary because information can be distributed so quickly.
> + Using hashtags or other symbols to indicate the end of a release. (These symbols are a throw-back to what journalists used to do at the end of a story in the days before computer typesetting.) Spicer says it is far better to end a release with a compelling closing paragraph.
> + Not including the year in the dateline. Spicer says including the year in the dateline helps people to work out how old a release is, even in an era when web archives and search engines enable a release to be discoverable indefinitely.
>
> <http://www.prdaily.com/Main/Articles/19953.aspx??utm_source=salesforce&utm_medium=email&utm_campaign=PRD_1227>

Barriers to getting your media release published

From the information in this chapter, it is not hard to identify reasons why media releases might not be reported. The major reasons many releases fail to pass the news test are that:

+ they are not news
+ they fail to meet news deadlines
+ they are too long
+ they are full of hyperbole
+ they contain errors
+ there are no contact details for follow-up questions
+ practitioners ring journalists to pressure them to run stories.

SUMMARY

In this chapter you have learnt why writing material for the media is an important skill for public relations practitioners. This chapter has examined how media releases are used as public relations tools that implement an uncontrolled communication pathway (see Chapter 5). You should now have an understanding of:

+ what public relations media tools are, and how they are used
+ the news process
+ how to identify 'news'
+ how to write and distribute a media release.

REFLECTION

Reread what you wrote for the activity in which you identified news stories in the first four pages of your daily newspaper. Reflect on the information you have read in this chapter, then analyse the way the journalists have written the stories you identified. How many words are in the first paragraph of each story? What tense is used in the first paragraph of each story? Does the tense change when the reporter uses direct quotes? How does the reporter attribute the direct quotes?

ACTIVITIES

1. **Which Journalists Do You Mean?**

    Find out how many specialist journalists your city's daily newspaper employs. Buy a copy of the paper, or explore its website, to identify the names and positions of specialist journalists. These will appear on stories in the form of a by-line, listing the name of the journalist who wrote the story and his or her title—for example, Sally Jones, Science Reporter. Sometimes this information appears at the end of the story. It is important to know who these journalists are, and what their jobs involve, if you want to be successful. Updating your organisation's media database with this information is often a primary—sometimes boring—task for public relations interns, but it is essential that databases like this are kept up to date.

2. **Comparing Media Coverage**

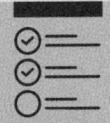

    Read your daily newspaper, and tune in to the nightly news bulletin on the television station you most regularly watch. Make a list of the stories that were covered in the first four pages of the newspaper, noting where they appeared on the page and on what page they appeared. Also make a list of the stories that the television news bulletin included, in the order in which they appeared. Compare the two lists. How similar are your two lists? How do they differ? Are the main stories (page one in the newspaper; the first two or three stories in the bulletin) about the same topics? Choose one of the stories on page one of the newspaper. What were the three main points that it reported?

3. Examine Some Media Releases

It is interesting to see how organisations write media releases. Fortunately, the web allows us to do that quite easily because it is one of the most effective ways of distributing a release—as long as you let journalists know the URL, either by an email or a phone call. We can even see the media releases issued by presidents, prime ministers and popes. These are often written in a different style from the one we have discussed here. Visit the website of your state governor or premier, or of the national head of government, to see how their media releases are written. For a format different from the one in this book, explore how the Vatican publishes media releases through its searchable *Daily Bulletin* at <http://press.vatican.va/content/salastampa/en/bollettino.html>.

Governments issue media releases to explain elements of their annual budgets, and they normally quote the relevant minister as the source of a release on budget initiatives for specific portfolios. For example, the Minister for Defence would issue a release proclaiming the importance of an increase in soldiers' salaries announced in the budget. You can check these by exploring the websites of particular ministers.

Search the website of companies and other organisations that you know to see how they write media releases.

It is a useful professional practice to look, from time to time, at how other public relations people write releases and to work out how you might improve your writing technique.

Practice task

One of the most famous speeches ever given was US President Abraham Lincoln's two-minute address at Gettysburg on 19 November 1863. The Gettysburg Address—delivered at the dedication of a military cemetery during the American Civil War (1861–65)—is reprinted at the end of this task.

CHAPTER 6: WRITING AND PLACING A MEDIA RELEASE

Assume that you are Lincoln's press secretary (his personal public relations officer—although, of course, he didn't have one). You have been asked to write a media release based on the Gettysburg Address. Before you start to write, use the worksheet in the Public Relations Toolkit to plan the media release. Write the media release in the style and format outlined in this chapter using direct quotes from President Lincoln.

The Gettysburg Address

Fourscore and seven years ago our fathers brought forth on this continent a new nation, conceived in liberty, and dedicated to the proposition that all men are created equal. Now we are engaged in a great civil war, testing whether that nation, or any nation so conceived and so dedicated, can long endure. We are met on a great battlefield of that war. We have come to dedicate a portion of that field, as a final resting place for those who here gave their lives that that nation might live. It is altogether fitting and proper that we should do this. But, in a larger sense, we cannot dedicate—we cannot consecrate—we cannot hallow this ground. The brave men, living and dead, who struggled here, have consecrated it, far above our poor power to add or detract. The world will little note, nor long remember, what we say here but it can never forget what they did here. It is for us the living, rather, to be dedicated here to the unfinished work which they who fought here have thus far so nobly advanced. It is rather for us to be here dedicated to the great task remaining before us—that from these honored dead we take increased devotion to that cause for which they gave the last full measure of devotion—that we here highly resolve that these dead shall not have died in vain—that this nation, under God, shall have a new birth of freedom—that government of the people, by the people, for the people, shall not perish from the earth.

Abraham Lincoln
19 November 1863

TIP SHEET: WRITING A MEDIA RELEASE

The ability to write an effective media release is one of the most important professional skills a beginning practitioner needs. As we saw earlier in this chapter, these skills are built on well-established principles: choosing relevant news frames; using the inverted pyramid approach; telling the story through the 5Ws and H that journalists use to report the news; writing clearly, concisely and accurately with correct grammar and spelling; using your organisation's official style and letterhead; and ensuring that there are contact details for reporters to follow up the release.

Start planning your release by using the media release planning worksheet in the toolkit.

THE IMPORTANCE OF FOLLOWING THE PRINCIPLES

Unless practitioners follow established principles for writing a release, and use correct grammar and spelling, they simply won't 'get a run'.

In their book *PR Today: The Authoritative Guide to Public Relations*, Trevor Morris and Simon Goldsworthy, English academics, note that most media releases never get used, often because they don't tell a clear story, but also because they are poorly written and badly structured (Morris & Goldworthy, 2012, p. 255). They, too, stress the need to plan a release, to be specific, to use simple English, to use quotes (which are reported speech) and to punctuate correctly. They also describe punctuation in written English as mimicking the pauses people take when they speak. Lucy Davison, the experienced copy editor who worked on a previous edition of this book, points out that punctuation also plays an important role in the mechanics of syntax, often serving to clarify the sense of a sentence and to help written English hang together in a meaningful way.

A PRACTICAL EXAMPLE

When Third Year public relations student Rosalie Iannelli wrote a media release about a real university research project for an assignment, her release followed all the principles discussed in this book. (As this release was not distributed, it is undated, but the issue date would appear either at the top, before the heading, or at the end with the other essential details.) Rosalie's release, annotated to show where the principles have been applied, follows.

CHAPTER 6: WRITING AND PLACING A MEDIA RELEASE

UNIVERSITY OF CANBERRA

MEDIA RELEASE

RESEARCH FINDS LOCAL FARMERS' MARKET IS BRINGING FOOD BACK TO BASICS

A new study has found that Canberrans can ensure their food is as fresh and wholesome as it can get by buying from the Capital Region Farmers' Market.

Research from the University of Canberra has found that the compliance of the market's committee members is so great they can guarantee you will always know where your food is coming from.

Dr Joanna Henryks, assistant professor in advertising and marketing communication, and Dr Cathy Hope, assistant professor in journalism and communication studies at the university, have been studying the local market as part of a new research project.

Brought together by their interest in not-for-profit organisations and organic and sustainable foods, Drs Henryks and Hope have conducted the first primary research on the farmers' market that has become the biggest in Australia.

By interviewing the people key to the market's success across its history the pair found that the organisers wanted to ensure the products were local and came primarily from the farmer to the customer. When a farmer wants to sell their produce at the market the organisers want to know exactly where it is coming from.

'They will even go as far as visiting the farms to investigate their claims,' Dr Hope said. 'This means they can guarantee, as much as possible, the customer will get what they expect.'

Dr Hope said those involved in the creation of the markets were retirees with powerful backgrounds including ex defence personnel, ex federal police, business owners and farmers.

'Their skill sets, experience, knowledge and hard-working, compliant attitudes made the perfect combination to ensure the market worked,' Dr Hope said.

The research also found that Canberra is an ideal place for a market of this kind due to its large percentage of well-educated public sector people. Canberrans are more likely to support local farmers and invest in quality fresh, wholesome food.

'The success of the market is a great example of where our culture is at in terms of its relationship with food and wanting local fresh produce,' Dr Hope said.

The Capital Region Farmers' Market runs every Saturday, excluding Christmas, Canberra show and Summernats from 5 am to 11 am at Exhibition Park in Canberra.

For more information contact:
Rosalie Iannelli
Media Manager
M: 0087 400 527
Email: rosaliei@genericemail.com

Annotations:
- Indicates what this is, using the official letterhead.
- A bold heading summarising the news in the release.
- First paragraph reflects the inverted pyramid approach: the main point first. The news frame is 'timeliness.' This is 'What' in 5Ws and H. Note the correct tenses in the release.
- News frame: 'significance.'
- This is 'Where' in 5Ws and H.
- This news frame of 'significance', perhaps 'rarity', reflects the correct use of the inverted pyramid approach: this is important, but not as important as the news in the first paragraph.
- This is 'How' in 5Ws and H.
- Always close the first direct quote in a media release with a comma, a closing quotation mark and by identifying who made it. Note the past tense because you are reporting what someone said. Start the next part of the direct quote with an opening quotation mark.
- Always start a direct quote with an opening quotation mark.
- When you have finished a direct quote, end with a full stop and a closing quotation mark.
- The first sentence of indirect speech following a direct quote should begin in this way. Indirect quotes are normally written in past tense.
- Another example of organising the release using the inverted pyramid approach.
- Essential details are here so that interested reporters can ask follow-up questions.

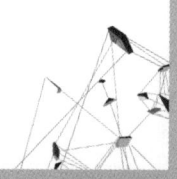

TIP SHEET: WORKING WITH THE NEWS MEDIA

The public relations specialisation that concentrates on working with the news media is known as 'media relations'. Many organisations, especially government agencies, have someone who specialises in this as the organisation's official spokesperson. So, too, do government ministers whose specialists are known as Press Secretaries, or Media Advisers. In the United States, the President's Press Secretary and the media spokespeople for the Departments of State and Defence have highly visible jobs, are formally quoted in news stories, and appear on television, often nightly. But not every organisation or client can afford to have a media relations specialist, so that task becomes one of the myriad jobs practitioners do. Managing media relations for an organisation is not as daunting as it first seems once a practitioner understands how it works; many people have a knack for, and enjoy doing, this job.

Building and maintaining good relationships with the journalists who report on your organisation, or clients, is an important aspect of media relations and, generally, professional practice. Academic research studies have shown that up to 75 per cent of news stories in the mainstream media come from public relations sources—either via releases or tips to reporters, or briefings. Perhaps this is because in the modern mass news media business model, journalists are overstretched and under-resourced in their workloads. That means that journalists rely heavily on practitioners for news but expect real news, not blatant advertising. Maybe that is one reason why the relationships between practitioners and journalists become testy at times. Ana Tkalac Verčič and Violeta Colić (2016) described this relationship as difficult, interdependent and complex. Their research found that public relations specialists underestimate journalists' opinion of the communication profession and seem to believe the relationship as more adversarial than it really is. Johnston (2007) also described media relations as complex but also as specialised and extremely demanding. Pittman (2017) tells us that media relations is more than just pitching a news story but about building valuable relationships with journalists.

In real-world public relations practice, difficulties in the relationship arise partly because different journalists seek organisations' comments at different times and on different issues, making it tough to know every reporter you are likely to deal with. More importantly, there is trouble when practitioners (sorry, but young practitioners especially) do not understand what news is, nor how the news process works, nor who the reporters are that cover their organisations, nor simple things like individual media outlets' deadlines, or send releases to journalists who do not cover the topic. This leads to 'non-news' media releases, incessant phone calls, or email and SMS, to check whether a reporter needs more information or to ask whether the release will be run—or even whether they got the release. To read how infuriating this can be for journalists, see Macnamara's (2014) article on journalism–PR relations, especially the comments he reports from senior consultants (at p. 745–6).

In this tense and adversarial relationship, reporters accuse us of pushing non-news, not understanding how their jobs work, and poor writing skills; we accuse them of errors in their reporting, using biased news frames, or pushing competitors' views ahead of ours. This is at its starkest in politics, where the term 'spin doctor' originated. US President Trump's Press Secretary, Sean Spicer, found out early in that Administration just how tough the relationship can be as he struggled to justify his boss's claims about almost everything the government did: the media reported on his missteps, factual errors (the Administration called what Spicer said 'alternative facts'), attitude towards them, and attempts to justify Mr Trump's claims about the media publishing 'fake news'.

Practice task

Use your search engine to find the story by Glenn Thrush and Michael M. Grynbaum, 'Trump Ruled the Tabloid Media. Washington Is a Different Story.', published in *The New York Times*, 25 February 2017. Note how this story uses Mr Trump's previous media relations history as a 'source' to report on, and contrast, his complaints about news leaks from his Administration, and how tough it is to work with the media in Washington.

But it need not be like this in professional practice outside politics if both practitioners and reporters understand what Dr Caroline Fisher, a journalism lecturer at the University of Canberra, describes as the 'rules of engagement'. Fisher, who has worked as a reporter, a press secretary and an academic, says public relations practitioners and reporters should treat their relationships with trust and respect and regard them as reciprocal. Media releases and verbal information given to journalists should be credible, well-researched, involve proper news, and hopefully be related to something else in the news cycle.

Fisher researched the journey reporters take when they become political media advisers and later return to journalism. Her 10-point typology of 'subtle' approaches to truth telling by journalists who become political media advisers is instructive for public relations practitioners' broader media relations work (see Fisher, 2016). Three of her points—never tell a lie, put the best foot forward; accentuate the positive, but don't 'spin', and use 'I don't know' when you truly do not know the answer—should always be observed in media relations.

In addition to these three points, the following is a guide to making media relations work.

Doing media relations
Know the reporters who cover your industry

Why: Finding out who these reporters are is relatively simple—they are often identified in the newspaper in by-lines (e.g., By Bill Jones, Transport Reporter), or in TV/radio broadcasts, and in media directories. Getting to know these reporters means the job targeting media releases and pitches is easier. You should compile a database that includes their names, email, telephone numbers, Twitter details, and, if you are good at this, notes about when and for what reason they contact you. Make sure their contact details are in your phone address book. Revise these entries regularly to make sure they are always up to date. Once the reporters on your round know who you are, they'll likely contact you when they need a news story. Help them out.

Do your research

Why: This includes knowing what news outlets should be interested in your stories and identifying the appropriate reporters. You won't make the mistake of sending a release, or trying a telephone pitch, to a journalist who simply isn't interested. You'll know the right reporter for the right story. Similarly, a health industry magazine is highly unlikely to be interested in your agricultural lobby group's story about international wheat sales. Doing this research also means you have done the work needed to fully understand the topic you are promoting, why a reporter should cover it, and how and why it can be linked to something else in the news cycle, if that is appropriate. This helps when you 'pitch' a story to a reporter because you'll know the topics they are interested in.

Write and promote news

Why: Reporters rightfully get annoyed when a PR person tries to 'sell' them a non-news story, or when they receive a media release that is poorly written and about nothing much at all.

Remember the competition for news space and time

Why: In almost every hour of the day, the news changes. Much more happens around the world, in your country, your state, your city than the news media can cover. Open one of the major news websites, like the BBC or CNN, and check it every hour to see how the contents change over a few hours, and how 'breaking news' evolves. Look at a hard copy of your capital city's major daily newspaper and work out how much of what it contains are news stories; most of the paper's space will carry advertising. This means that there is more material to publish in a newspaper, or broadcast, or post to a news website, than there is space or time available for it. Even news websites are finite. Sometimes your clients will believe that their 'news' is the most important information of the day and push you to issue a release about it. A new lipstick colour is probably important to your client's marketing director, but it won't make it into the daily news coverage.

Know the news cycle

Why: It is a cliché that the news cycle works '24/7'. That is probably true of radio, television and news websites, but once today's edition of the newspaper is published, it is difficult to bring out a special edition for 'breaking news' unless that news is hugely significant—probably a major natural disaster. Make sure you know how the normal news cycle works—hourly, daily or weekly—or for trade publications, monthly or quarterly. Find out what the submission deadlines are for radio, television and newspapers and news websites (which are more flexible)—and distribute media releases well before these deadlines. In the news media, deadline means the time at which all copy must be submitted—unless it is highly important, nothing submitted after that time will be considered for publication. US technology journalist Damon Beres advises (in Pittman, 2017) practitioners to avoid news pitches late on Friday afternoons as there is no chance he'll respond, and not ask if reporters got their email because 'We got it. If we don't respond, it implies we're not interested'. And Beres says journalists don't mind being followed on social media, but don't want to be pitched publicly there.

Understand the news process

Why: When you understand the steps in the news gathering and selection process, and the barriers to getting your story published (see Chapter 6), your life as a media relations specialist will be easier. It will help you to understand why writing news is important, why a reporter might reject your release, how the lead you have produced might be changed, who has the final say on what, and how much, is published, and the limitations of space and time facing the news outlets you have contacted. Knowing all that means you will be realistic about what is likely to be published, and you will be in a stronger position to use this information to help clients understand that their story is not real news.

Prove your value

Why: For you to be successful at media relations, reporters need to trust that everything you give them is real news, or comment that is relevant to the story they are writing, not 'self-serving content that brings no value to their readers' (Carlisle, 2017). Once you have that trust you will be regarded as a credible source who understands how the news media works, knows what is newsworthy and what is not, helps reporters to improve their stories, and can point out how your material relates to the publication's audiences. Carlisle (2017) points out that this is important because journalists pride themselves on adhering to their code of ethics and that their integrity depends on them reporting 'factual, unique and pertinent news'. Pittman (2017) notes Beres' view that the focus on 'fake news' that occurred after President Trump's 2016 election means there is a need for public relations practitioners to be more transparent because reporters will be more suspicious of company articles, pitches of news stories, website and blog posts and tweets.

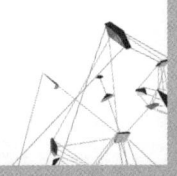

Practical steps

1. Make sure your media release, or the information you'll pass on in a phone call or email, is actually news.
2. When you issue a media release, let all the relevant reporters know about it at the same time. Don't play favourites.
3. Use the up-to-date list of reporters' email addresses from your database.
4. Double check your release has the correct contact details so that reporters can follow-up if they need to.
5. If a reporter calls you with follow-up questions, take their call immediately and answer all the questions.
6. If you do not know the answer to a question, say so and that you will get it for the reporter and call back as soon as possible.
7. *Always* call back well before a reporter's deadline, even if you can't answer the question—your reputation as a helpful contact is on the line.
8. *Never lie.* You'll be caught.
9. Mostly, reporters will want to talk directly to the person (the 'talent') quoted in your release. Check with that person before the release is issued to make sure they are prepared to take follow-up questions, and what their availability for this is. They need to know that they'll need to make this time available on the day the release is issued.
10. Media conferences are a good way of giving interested reporters equal access to your talent. Don't overdo media conferences—use them to reinforce the special importance of your announcement. When you set up a formal media conference, make sure the 'talent' is aware that reporters, especially those from radio and television, will usually want to do one-on-one interviews with your talent and that they need to be available for this.
11. Sometimes, it is not possible to do one-on-one interviews, so make sure reporters know this and why. The door-stop interviews that politicians do almost every morning are examples of how you could manage an announcement where your talent can't stay for one-on-one interviews.
12. Identify appropriate venues and backgrounds for media conferences and one-on-one television interviews. Most organisations have a room available for this, where you can place a corporate back-drop behind where your talent will sit.
13. Choose outside venues carefully (wind plays havoc with hair!) and avoid areas where there is ambient noise like heavy traffic or building works. Check that outside venues don't have inappropriate backgrounds, or that signage won't intrude on television images (for example, there's nothing worse than an 'Exit' sign beside or above a person being interviewed during a crisis).
14. Tell reporters and camera crews where they can park close to the venue for a media conference or interview—and reserve space (cost free) for them.

15. Arrange media training for all the people in your organisation who are likely to be interviewed by reporters.
16. When you pitch a story to a reporter by phone or email, do it professionally. Don't use over-blown language, especially about a product, or make promises you cannot keep. When you know the reporters who cover your round, making pitches is easier.
17. Don't expect to be successful every time you pitch a story to an individual reporter or distribute a media release—the decision on whether your idea is news will be made by the reporter, but you'll enhance your chances of success if you apply the news frames in Chapter 6.
18. If you are successful in getting a reporter to interview your boss, sit in on the interview. Don't interrupt or comment unless asked to do so.
19. If you want reporters to cover a speech made by someone in your organisation, give them copies of the speech beforehand, but tell them to check it against delivery; sometimes people change what they say in a speech—but reporters will treat the copy you give them as the official text.
20. Take great care in giving reporters information 'off the record' and always make it clear at the start of a conversation whether it is on or off the record. Make sure your 'talent' knows and uses this rule.
21. Avoid using an embargo on a media release—that is, setting a time at which the information in the release can be used. Some journalists simply won't observe them. In an age of instant electronic communication in public relations, there is no need for embargoes.
22. Always reflect on what you did when you issued a release, how a media conference went, and what media coverage you got. Critically assess your efforts so that you can improve next time.

■ PRACTICE NOTE MEDIA RELEASE CHECKLIST

This practice note will help you to check that your media releases are written in a way that attracts the attention of reporters. Remember that there is so much competition for news 'space' that there is no guarantee that a story based on your release will be published. Applying news frames based on real news written in the appropriate news style will give your release the best chance of being published.

Don't start to write a media release until you have worked through the planning worksheet in the Toolkit (see page xxviii). Then, when you have written the first draft of the release, use this checklist to make sure you have covered the essential features of a release. The advice here will work no matter what public relations tools you use to distribute your release. Chapter 7 deals specifically with writing for social media.

Essential	What to do	Check
Planning worksheet See the Toolkit	Start with an outline plan of what needs to be in your release.	
	Talk to the source of, or authority for, the release to find out as much as you can about what they want to say.	
A news lead and news frames	Use one or more news frames (see Chapter 6).	
	Decide which frame or frames best suit your news.	
	Write like a journalist: lead with the news.	
	Use active voice, past tense when not directly quoting someone.	
The inverted pyramid See Chapter 6	Make the most important point the 1st paragraph—the news lead.	
	Use the subsequent paragraphs to support the 1st paragraph.	
	Include the name and title of the source of the news in the 2nd or 3rd paragraph.	
Writing style	Write simple, concise and brief sentences.	
	Don't start with a direct quote.	
	Avoid clichés, jargon, and unnecessary, overblown adjectives.	
	Use your organisation's style guide for spelling, numbers and dates.	
	Simplify technical and scientific words.	
	Don't make claims that cannot be justified.	
Quotes See Chapter 6	Use a mix of direct and indirect quotes from the source of, or authority for, the release. Introduce what the source or authority wants to say with an indirect quote.	
	Make sure direct quotes are meaningful.	
	Give an authority for direct quotes, e.g., 'quotation,' Ms Jones said.	
	After you have stopped directly quoting someone, start the following indirect quote with the name of the person being quoted, e.g.: Ms Jones said …	
	Make sure any second 'voice' in your release is correctly identified—name and position etc. Introduce them with an indirect quote. See the Caltech example in Chapter 6.	

CHAPTER 6: WRITING AND PLACING A MEDIA RELEASE

Essential	What to do	Check
Avoid barriers	Check against these barriers to make sure your release has the best chance of being reported—your release won't be published if it • is not news • fails to meet news deadlines • is too long • is full of hyperbole • contains errors • has no contact details for follow-up questions.	
Spelling	Use the spellchecker—set your word-processing program to your language, or a dictionary.	
Punctuation	Make sure quotation marks and other punctuation tools are used correctly.	
Grammar	Write grammatically correct sentences.	
Format	Follow the format your organisation uses for media releases.	
	Avoid using 'For immediate release' before the heading. It is unnecessary.	
	Include relevant website links.	
	Use a simple, recognisable typeface in Roman style only: Times or Arial are suitable.	
	Don't use the bold and italics type in the text of your release—although bold is fine for headings and sub-headings.	
Length	Remember, there is no standard length for a media release.	
	A brief (about one A4 page) release is preferred to a long one.	
	However, write to a length appropriate to your topic.	
	Add links to fact sheets, backgrounders, reports or other sources to provide further information.	
	Use your professional knowledge to convince those who want a long release about the appropriate length.	
Release heading	Write a heading that is relevant to the information in the release.	
	Be creative—but don't overdo this.	
	Don't make the heading so big it dominates the release.	

Essential	What to do	Check
Date	Make sure the release includes the date it is issued.	
	Consider using a release number/year issued (eg,15/2020) reference.	
	Don't use a dateline (e.g., Humbleburg, January 26) to start the first sentence.	
Contact details	Include the name, title, phone and email contact details for the person who will provide further information.	
	Ensure that person will be available for follow-up calls from reporters.	
Pictures, video, graphs, charts	Give details of website links where reporters can get visual material related to your release if these are not included.	
Proofread	Proofread every draft of your release.	
	Have someone else proofread the final draft before it is issued.	
	Fact check the release.	
Approval	Ensure that the person you are quoting in the release approves the text before it is issued.	
	Follow your organisation's approval process. E.g., your boss may want to read the release before it is issued.	
Which 'media'?	Use your organisation's media contact list to build a distribution list of relevant and appropriate journalists for your release.	
	Avoid a general distribution of your release to reporters who simply won't be interested in it, e.g., political reporters getting a release about a new dental treatment. Not every reporter in every news outlet needs to get your release.	

A MEDIA RELEASE WRITING AND FORMATTING REFERENCE (PUBLISHED WITH THE PERMISSION OF THE UNIVERSITY OF LEICESTER)

An excellent reference for writing and formatting a media release (that uses the same approach followed in this book) is the University of Leicester (UK) Press Office's tip page for academics and other staff. It includes a template that makes it easy for people to write and format a release. The links on this page, <**http://www2.le.ac.uk/offices/cap/press/publicising**>, provide advice on these topics

CHAPTER 6: WRITING AND PLACING A MEDIA RELEASE

- Why work with the media?
- What to send to the Press Office
- How to write a press release
- How to use social media
- Resources

The site is also a good example of an organisational newsroom. Explore it to see how this public relations tool can work effectively for internal and external publics.

7 WRITING FOR SOCIAL MEDIA AND THE WEB

This chapter discusses writing for public relations tools that use social media and internet applications. At the end of this chapter, you should understand

+ how to adapt your writing to the needs of social media
+ the importance of public relations tools that use web and social media applications.

Use this chapter in conjunction with the tip sheet on 'Social media usage' that follows it.

FLEXIBLE TOOLS

Public relations practice in the twenty-first century relies on the myriad applications for research, writing and message delivery provided by the internet. There is almost no aspect of public relations practice that does not use the internet in some way. Research data can be accessed via the net; the chief executive can use it to communicate directly with each employee; a company's detailed annual report can be published on its website; and organisations can seek customer feedback via internet applications. Practitioners issue media releases electronically, publish staff newsletters on the internet, and post their public relations material to easily accessible websites. Blogging, tweeting and posting news, comments, images and videos to other social media applications such as Facebook, Instagram, Snapchat, and YouTube are standard practice. People in all professions sign up to LinkedIn to build worldwide contacts and to publish information about what they are doing, their interests, and their comments about issues.

Social media has become so much part of our daily lives because of its capacity to connect people (Wills, 2016). It is successful in doing this because people who use it can organise their information by the content they want to publish and/or those they want to reach (Wills, 2016). This ability to publish information generally or limit it to specific groups (Wills, 2016) is what makes social media such an important and useful public relations tool.

So effective are these now mainstream communication tools that online media have brought new tools to political campaigning. In the 2016 US presidential election, the winner, Donald Trump, used Twitter several times a day to promote his views, often tweeting in the early hours of the morning. In the period between election day and Mr Trump's inauguration, many commentators expressed concern at what appeared to be his free-wheeling use of Twitter to promote what they regarded as often exaggerated views. His Press Secretary, Sean Spicer, addressed this concern by saying Mr Trump was not randomly tweeting but understood the strategic value of using social media to achieve a goal (The Fix, *The Washington Post*, 5 January 2017). Spicer noted that he checked Mr Trump's Twitter feed as soon as he woke in the morning because 'whatever he tweets is going to drive the news'. Spicer's view was supported by one journalist who tweeted that Trump set the news agenda every morning and 'then we all write about [his views], letting him own the day'.

Mr Trump was not the first US politician to use social media to great effect. His predecessor, former President Barack Obama, used internet sites and social media in his 2007 and 2012 election campaigns and for fund-raising. Earlier, in the 2004 US presidential primary elections to select party nominees, one candidate raised most of his campaign funds via internet-based applications, the first time social media had been seriously used in this way. Obama's later success with social media as a campaign tool established a pattern now followed in elections in most countries. For example, for the 2007 Australian federal election, both major political leaders used interactive public websites to release election policies. The Opposition campaign also used a website, on which voters could not only buy T-shirts, but also blog their views. The activist group GetUp! used the internet to sign up 211 000 members in the two years leading to the election and raised $250 000 in seventy-two hours for a television advertising campaign about voting for the Senate (*TIME*, 19 November 2007). Social media use during what became known as the 'Arab Spring' enabled activists in Libya, Egypt, Tunisia and Syria to organise and coordinate rallies against incumbent governments. In 2016, social media sites were used to encourage people to vote in Britain's Brexit referendum. In Australia's 2016 federal election for both the Senate and the House of Representatives, extensive social media use on all platforms was not only an important political campaigning tool, but also a vehicle for online official advertising by the electoral commission to publish important electoral information for voters (voting is compulsory in Australia). Also in 2016, the Australian Bureau of Statistics for the first time enabled people to submit their Census details via a website.

Corporations, not-for-profit organisations, government departments and activist groups use online resources to enhance their communication efforts. One researcher who examined the use of blogs as a corporate communication tool, argues that web logs will not make traditional tools obsolete. Charles Catalano (2007) argues that the continuing use of traditional forms of communication simply reinforces the importance of content, or messages, as opposed to the technology or medium.

> ## PRACTICE POINT
>
> Applying social media applications to organise your life, keep in contact with family and friends, pay bills, listen to music, and engage in many other activities, means you already know the technical stuff about them and how versatile they are. This chapter is not so much concerned with the technical 'how to use' aspects of social media, but the contexts in which they can be applied in public relations practice. This is different from using them for personal social activities. Whatever social media tools you use in your professional work, you must write clearly, concisely, accurately, responsibly and ethically.

An important value-added aspect of using social media is that it creates almost instant communication. People can make friends, establish new professional contacts, transmit information, and begin a dialogue using social media far faster than has ever been possible before. This means that we can also find out quickly who agrees or disagrees with us—as anyone who has participated in a Facebook discussion about a controversial issue will know. This speed in social media communication is a vital asset for public relations practice because all reactions and comments to a post can help practitioners to identify support for an issue, product or service, and identify the different voices who contribute to a discussion.

In her book *Understanding New Media*, Eugenia Siapera argues that all these technologies and applications, commonly known as 'new media', 'aren't so new any more' (2012, p. 19) but that the term illustrates the dynamic and evolving features they deliver, rather than the technology on which they are based. So strongly do Brian Sollis and Deirdre Breakenridge (2009) believe in the importance of social media to professional practice that they called their book *Putting the Public Back in Public Relations: How Social Media Is Reinventing the Aging Business of PR*. They write that social media are rewriting the media landscape because blogs, social networks, online forums and other forms of social media have changed the dynamics of influence. Traditional influence flowed from the work of news- or information-gatherers like journalists; in the social media landscape, information is readily shared among peers. In our terms, that means no one mediates conversations or information.

Social media applications have been normalised as communication tools because of their ease of use and potential reach. Social media's pervasive presence in public relations practice means it is crucial that practitioners think about why they might use specific applications—and that they can justify their use to clients. Remember that using social media in professional practice is a more serious undertaking than using it with friends and family because the conversations, or dialogues, you want to create and contribute to are about your clients' business, not your personal social interaction. Maybe in its business use this communication technology should be called something else other than 'social'. Do members of a dominant coalition regard using these tools as 'social' or 'business' activity? Perhaps 'digital media' would more appropriately reflect its business use. So, like all public relations tools, social media needs to have a reason for its use, be linked to a strategy, and be planned as a way of delivering messages to identified target publics. In the context of public relations practice, treat social media applications as tools that deliver information to identified publics via an interpersonal communication pathway.

Writing on the *Blog Herald* website on 9 January 2017, Meagan Freeman noted that 'The thing is … any business or organisation should aim for getting the right Fans instead of just aiming for more Fans' on its Facebook page (see <**http://www.blogherald.com/2017/01/09/7-questions-you-must-answer-to-get-the-right-kind-of-facebook-fans**>). And that's an important message. Freeman was writing in a marketing context and suggested seven questions that need to be asked to get the right Facebook fans for a business:

1. What are the goals of your business?
2. Who is your target market (we'd say 'public')?
3. What is the online behaviour of your target market?

4. What pain does your target market have and how can you solve it?
5. What language does your ideal customer use? By 'language' Freeman means the way in which they talk about their business, social media and marketing.
6. What benefits do you offer customers that they can't get elsewhere?
7. What can you offer customers for free to attract them?

These questions are important for the social media context in which Freeman was writing, but they are the kind of questions public relations people should ask when they investigate all the communications tools needed to implement a strategy.

Social media applications are important, helpful and influential tools but an excessive use of social media risks, as Robert Heath (2001) argued about messages, limiting public relations to message design and delivery. Social media certainly delivers messages but it is not the only way of 'doing' public relations and needs to be focused on relevant publics and to work in tandem with other communication pathways and public relations tools (see the tip sheet 'Matching theory to pathways and public relations tools' and Chapter 3; for more information on public relations tools and communication pathways, see Mahoney, 2017, chs 9 and 10).

PRACTICE NOTE SOCIAL MEDIA CAPABILITIES

As public relations tools, social media provide a powerful capacity for practitioners to reach people. In an article posted on her blog, April Niemela, an academic at Michigan State University, explains just how social media does that. She writes that social media 'embraces and facilitates' people's abilities to be part of a vast array of professional and personal online communities and to 'immediately access, inform, influence, and/or create knowledge' (Niemela, 2012). Social media enable all that because of their 'affordances'—that is, the things that you can do with them. Yet we all know that not all social media applications are suitable for every task. It is important, then, that practitioners make appropriate choices about which applications they use, and when and why they select them, because willy-nilly social media use may simply waste time and resources.

Allan Cho has listed some points on his blog (<www.allancho.com/2009/09/social-media-affordance.html>) from the Learning-Affordances Wiki (<http://learning-affordances.wikispaces.com>) that can help in deciding whether the capabilities (or affordances) of specific social media applications are appropriate to the context in which their use is planned. You could use these points as a test of the suitability of specific social media to implement a communication pathway to reach your target public, and to pursue your program's goals and objectives:

1. **Positive and Negative:** Affordances can be useful or a hindrance.
2. **Fit for Context:** Affordances have to be fit for purpose—be aware that it may not work everywhere.

> 3. **Changing Contexts:** Because affordances do not transfer to each context, the learner must create and develop new affordances, to develop the ability to match a particular affordance to the context.
> 4. **Ontologies:** Affordance is relational, *an adaptation*—it's part of a complex adaptive ecology.
> 5. **Perception:** Affordances are inseparable from perception. We perceive affordances rather than objects.
> 6. **Ethics and Power:** Because affordances [are] also a way of taking up a position, they also endorse, challenge, undermine, confirm particular discourses—it means taking up a position within (or against) a social ecology.
> 7. **Mastery:** As a professional, there must be an ability to discriminate between contexts, which means being embedded in one's micro-culture and community as well as one's individual identity (adapted from Learning-Affordances, 2008).

USING THE INTERNET

The website <**www.internetworldstats.com**>, which regularly surveys internet use, reported that the world had more than 3675 million internet users (50.1% of the world's population) at 30 June 2016, an increase of 918.3 per cent since 2000. Internet World Stats showed that at 1846 million users in 2016, Asia had more internet users than any other geographic region of the world—a growth of 1,515.2% from 2000. Europe and North America were the next biggest geographic regions of internet users. See the statistics for your region at <**www.internetworldstats.com/stats.htm**>.

READING MATERIAL PUBLISHED ON THE INTERNET

It might seem a bit odd to look at how people read material on the internet before dealing with how to write for the internet, but knowing how people will deal with your finished online product helps to plan and write it.

Two general points about all written information are important. First, readers expect material to be presented in a logical way. That is, it should flow from one point to another easily and in a way that makes sense to the reader. Second, because people make sense of what they read on the basis of its context (what comes before and after it, for example), simple language and common examples help them to understand the points you are making.

Many people find reading information on a computer screen difficult, even though most of us are comfortable with reading in this format in our jobs, study and leisure time. Some studies have found that reading onscreen is about 25 per cent slower than reading from paper. It is not surprising, then, that researchers have been interested in how people read on the internet and how websites can be designed to make them accessible and useful as communication tools. Some researchers have found that people don't read internet pages but scan them, picking out specific words and sentences.

So it is important to remember that because people treat internet-based material differently from print material, writing for the internet needs a different approach.

> **PRACTICE POINT**
>
> Writing for the internet does not mean that correct spelling and grammar are unnecessary. Stick to the principles that apply to all forms of public relations writing: use simple, clear and accurate language, and don't waste words, as briefer is usually better for electronic applications. To write in any other way would be unprofessional.
>
> Writing professionally includes being considered and polite in the comments we make. Jonathan Green, an Australian Broadcasting Corporation radio presenter, addressed this point on the ABC's *Drum* website, writing that in using social media '[m]aybe we need to cultivate a new self-discipline, restore the old sense of politeness and civility to a new world that has stripped away the barriers between thought and loudly spoke[n] globally transmitted word'. He argues that these courtesies have been stripped away by the ease of using social media and the anonymity accepted by the internet (Green, 2012).

STANDING OUT

Most practitioners have technical design assistance when they produce a website. That's because specialist designers know what makes a website work. A professionally designed site is critical: researchers in Canada found that internet users can take as little as one-twentieth of a second to decide whether they like the look of a website. One of the researchers commented that it is remarkable that people make up their minds about a site this quickly and that their initial impression holds up in later judgments. Nielson (2011) has found that users often leave a website in 10–20 seconds.

A special task as practitioners is to manage the production of the site and write much of the information that appears on it. They need to make sure that their site stands out from those of their competitors, so good content written correctly is essential if those who use the site are, first, to read the information on it and, second, to find it useful.

WRITING TO AN OBJECTIVE

Even though using the internet is mainstream public relations, and it is rare to find an organisation without a website, using a website as a *tool* should always be linked to an *objective* and a *communication pathway*. Remember that there is always a planned reason for doing something in public relations. Websites are no different, and those that are successful are carefully planned. A website is a *tool* that implements a *communication pathway* to achieve an *objective*.

This means that you must write your internet content for a reason. Make sure that you know why you are writing and what your organisation wants to achieve. You'll be writing for a site that represents an organisation—the first impression that outsiders will have of that organisation. Knowing why you are writing and what you need to say will help you to represent the organisation effectively.

> ### ■ PRACTICE NOTE BENEFITS OF SOCIAL MEDIA
>
> For most of us, the internet and social media have become an essential part of our business and private lives. We work with web-based applications every day, for personal business such as paying bills, booking last-minute hotels, buying concert tickets and checking bank statements, and we find websites that amuse and entertain us. People use social media to tell their personal stories—and find out about others, and share photographs of themselves, friends, family and events—and they use mass media websites to get the latest news. The internet has become a serious tool for research in universities, and there are specialist sites for almost every profession to help people learn more, undertake additional training and communicate with colleagues. For example, lawyers can access sites that help them research previous cases; doctors use online services to help with diagnoses, and to provide patients with information about diseases and medicines. In some countries, people can join a government website on which they can store their personal medical records so that if they need to visit a doctor while travelling, their whole medical history, including information about medications, is available. Young people cannot imagine a world without the internet, their laptops, tablet computers, smart mobile phones and portable music players, and the myriad social media applications that go with this technology.
>
> Among the benefits of social media and other internet-based technologies for public relations practitioners are the following:
>
> + They enable us to interact with publics in a way that gives new meaning to the notion of two-way communication. Websites can be used to seek and receive feedback, which allows an organisation to change or adapt its messages easily and quickly if necessary. They enable people to discuss issues, and exchange opinions.
> + They are accessible twenty-four hours a day (except when technical glitches interfere).
> + They provide flexibility, enabling, for example, hard-copy material to be replaced or supported by web-published versions. Many organisations give shareholders a choice of receiving annual reports electronically rather than in a printed and posted (and more expensive) hard-copy format.
> + They help control the distribution of information and campaign messages. There are no gatekeepers like reporters and sub-editors to filter or edit what you want to say to target publics.

> + You can measure how many people visit your site, and identify the specific pages that interest them, how long they stay reading your material and their usage patterns. This important data will provide some output measures when you evaluate the site.
> + They mean direct access to publics via email and other applications.
> + They give us the ability to provide digital still and video images to the media.
> + They have the storage capacity to enable people to access information about your organisation quickly and efficiently. For example, most organisations only issue media releases via their websites, or email or Twitter, and most provide journalists with access to historical information via archives accessible through online 'newsrooms'.

REMEMBER YOUR READERS

Plan your material in a logical sequence so that your readers are able to follow it and can easily find what they are after. People use the internet to find information that is important to them … and to save time. They scan what you have published more than they actually read it. They have likely found your site through a search engine, and they want to find what you have to offer quickly and efficiently before they move on to the next reference.

Shaun Crowley (2007), a UK-based marketing and communications expert, reflects an essential PR practice when he writes that you should build a picture of your social media readers (target publics) so that you can assess whether they are likely to be regular internet users and whether they are familiar with your product (or perhaps even in regular communication with the organisation); in this way, you can personalise what you write.

Answer these questions as a planning checklist for what you are writing for the internet:

+ Who are my readers?
+ Why are they visiting this website?
+ What do they want to know?
+ What do I need to tell them?
+ How can I make it easy for them to read the information on this site?

CONCISE, ACCURATE COPY

The most consistent recommendation made in all the literature about writing for the internet is to be concise. The Australian media relations expert Richard Stanton argues that writing for 'online' purposes is governed by the same rules that apply to writing media releases. Writing about the 'Living Web'—those sites that change regularly, like news sites—Mark Bernstein (2002), a computer scientist, says that if words on a website are dull, no one will read them, and nobody will come back to the site: 'If the words are wrong, people will be misled, disappointed, infuriated. If the words aren't there, people will shake their heads and lament your untimely demise.' That's a good warning for all public relations writing, but especially for the internet. Bernstein says that we should omit unnecessary words, read and revise what we write and, if possible, choose a better word that is clearer, richer, more precise (Bernstein, 2002).

Nielsen (2011) urges internet authors to write no more than 50 per cent of the text they would have used in a hard-copy publication. If you are writing for teenagers, remember that text should be ultra-concise, because many young people have poor reading skills and often don't spend a lot of time searching for information.

Your internet writing should be to the point and use:

+ simple language
+ brief sentences
+ short paragraphs
+ subheadings, bold text and italicised text to break up the information and to make it more accessible to readers.

Headings

Headings and subheadings help you to display material in a logical way.

Your information will have a major heading that, like those on a news website or in a hard-copy newspaper, tells the reader what it is about. The heading suggests why this information is important to readers.

As a planning device, you can start by compiling a succinct list of the points you need to cover in your material and then adapt them so that they become the subheadings for your material. (You might, of course, need to edit the points in your list to make them useful as subheadings.) Using this planning approach will help to organise your information logically and to set it out in a hierarchy, much like the inverted pyramid used in previous chapters. Subheadings have the added advantages of breaking the text into more accessible parts and providing new entry points to information. Remember that most people scan websites; they don't read them. A succinct, meaningful subheading can invite readers into your material.

Link material to other sources

Linking your material to other sources is an essential part of writing for the internet. It also adds credibility to what you are writing because people know that you have researched your topic.

You can add hyperlinks to sources that provide new information, or expand on points you are making. Hyperlinks to your organisation's previous media releases on your current topic, or to an online **profile** of the managing director you are quoting, or to a fact sheet about your product, help not only to make material relevant, but also help you to be more concise. Your website designer can assist you to control how hyperlinks appear to your readers.

profile: a narrative article about a senior person, their role in the organisation, biography and achievements, sometimes based on an interview with the person.

Use these links in a logical way. That means you should not overuse links, especially when you might be able to include the information, concisely, in your text.

Remember also that other organisations might be inserting links to your site in their online material—and that increases your need to be accurate.

Using lists

Lists can be more effective in online information than in hard-copy material. You can use more of them (but don't overdo it) on an internet page, and they can be a useful way of breaking up the text. If you need to publish information in a hierarchy of importance, use a numbered list; bullet point lists are fine for information that does not need to be published in order of importance. If you use lists, make sure that they are written concisely and accurately. Lists should not be long. They should cover no more than nine or ten points.

Using graphics, podcasts and videos

Including graphics (charts, logos, emblems) and pictures in online material makes information more readable. Highfield and Leaver (2016) described the use of visual material in social media as 'a critical part of online communication' (p. 49). Graphics, diagrams, charts and pictures should be relevant and explained with captions unless it is so obvious a caption is not necessary. If you do write a caption, make sure it is unique to the graphic, diagram, chart or picture with which it deals. Seek your web designer's advice about using graphics and pictures, especially the size at which they should appear, to make sure what you do is an appropriate way of publishing them.

You can enhance your site by including facilities for people to download podcasts related to your organisation. Some think tanks and universities provide links to important speeches given at events they organise. The creative use of this tool is important in public relations, especially in an environment where almost everyone uses a smartphone that can play podcasts. Using podcasts as a public relations tool would be a way of implementing a controlled interpersonal communication pathway.

Many organisations also provide links to videotaped information via their internet sites—another example of a tool implementing a controlled communication pathway.

Stick to the template

If you are applying an internet design template from the computer software your organisation uses for its day-to-day operations, make sure you stick within the template's design parameters. The template will have been produced using all the latest internet design principles to ensure that it creates an effective internet page. That means it will have pre-set sizes for the typeface you use for headings, subheadings and text, as well as for the correct line and paragraph spacing and internet page layout.

PUBLIC RELATIONS AND BLOGS

The growth of the internet and developments in technology and computer software generated the phenomenon of 'blogging', which allows anyone with a computer, and the inclination and the time, to publish their own personal website. (Use a search engine to investigate the term *blog*.) Blogging began as a way of publishing personal online diaries, but it has developed into a massive internet-based activity that enables people to publish information about anything from animals and sport to politics, local news and hobbies.

Blogs are essentially personal endeavours, but they are also mainstream media as they report news and are used by politicians and businesses as communication tools. Most public relations practitioners will not need to publish blogs because they'll have their organisation's official website as a communication tool. Nevertheless, there may be times when practitioners need to respond to material about their organisation published on blogs or when publishing a blog of their own might be a strategic campaign move. In both cases, writing needs to be in the style used for websites, but it can be much more personal. If you go to <**http://www.blogherald.com/category/blog-tips-2**> you will find tips on how to produce and write for blogs.

> **PRACTICE POINT**
>
> Writing comments on your organisation's blog, or on someone else's, is part of public relations practice. We need to be skilled at it because we are representing clients and employers. For advice on how to construct blog comments, see the seven guidelines on the *Blog Herald* website at <**www.blogherald.com/2012/10/08/how-to-write-comments**>.

It is virtually impossible to identify, keep track of and regularly monitor the blogs that touch on your organisation's interests. However, you will soon become aware of the blogs that regularly criticise your organisation—people will tell you about them—and you can set up a mechanism for monitoring these.

Sometimes creating a blog might help your organisation respond to a crisis. But before you create one, make sure you actually need it, because publishing a blog might take up precious time, and it might create confusion when clarity is needed. If you do publish a blog during a crisis, make sure you follow two of the major principles of crisis communication: use only one author for message consistency, and stick to the facts. In a crisis, your goals are to maintain a positive image for your organisation, to provide timely, accurate and appropriate information, and to be accessible. Writing material for a specific crisis blog means using clear, concise and factual information.

THE POWER OF EMAIL

Where would we be without email? In a busy world, email has become the fastest, most efficient way of communicating for personal and business purposes, apart from a personal telephone conversation. Email hasn't entirely replaced formal hard-copy letters for business correspondence, but it is perhaps only a matter of time before it does. Using email has become so natural for most of us that we forget that millions circle the globe every day—including that annoying spam, some of which always seems to bypass the detection software, even when we are hooked up to a large system. We all receive so much email that deciding which messages we'll read and which we'll trash can often be a split-second decision based on who is sending it and what the subject line tells us. One study found that about half of most employees' work days are spent dealing with email, not all of it productive work (Rubin, 2011).

For public relations practitioners, writing email messages to provide clients, colleagues, suppliers and target publics, including journalists, with information is the normal and most effective communication approach.

When you write emails to your friends and family, you can be informal in your language and tone, and perhaps even use the short forms that are common for mobile phone text messages.

However, writing email messages for business purposes requires a more formal and professional approach, especially if you want recipients to treat what you have to say seriously. If email messages are not clear and accurate, the information you want people to read will be lost among the spelling and grammatical errors and the general chaos that sometimes pervades the way messages are constructed. There are some common approaches that help us to write effective messages.

Will I or won't I?

Think before you start to tap the computer keyboard. Each email message you send is like a personal reference: it sends a message about you that goes beyond the words you write. People will judge you by the way you write, your accuracy and language, and by whether you use email as an effective tool or just because you can. Ask whether you really need to send the message before you start to write it. For example, if you have emailed a media release to journalists, will you do your chances of getting it published any good if you follow up with an email asking whether the journalists received the release? Or would the second message just annoy a reporter?

Think about your recipients as target publics. Why are you writing to them? What is the message you need to deliver? Is it appropriate for these recipients? Do you know the person to whom this email message is directed? Working through questions like these will help you to decide whether email is an appropriate way to communicate a message, or whether a telephone call might be a better option.

Choosing the right tone

Write in a businesslike way. Most of us tend to be more casual when writing emails than we would be when we write a formal, hard-copy letter. Yet we should still take a professional approach to business email correspondence. We all have our own writing 'voice', or tone, and sometimes this can lead to miscommunication in emails. Kathy Gentile (2005), an expert on writing email messages, explains this point by noting that most people want to write an email message as fast as possible and to send it out just as quickly. That means they often don't choose an appropriate writing style for the message. Choose the right style by deciding whether you are writing for a formal reason or for a semi-formal reason, and adapt your language accordingly.

Precision and clarity always work

Clear and concise writing is as important in email messages as it is for a media release and all other public relations tools. Plan what you need to say and edit your text to ensure it is as simple, professional and concise as you can make it. Be courteous and avoid humour and inappropriate language, especially racist and sexist language. Leave your texting language, short forms and emojis for your Hangouts, Instagram, Facebook and all the other forms of social media you use to contact friends and family.

Use standard sentence and paragraph structures, capitalisations and punctuation. Avoid typing your text in all capitals (it's really hard to read and can be misinterpreted as 'shouting'), and stick to a standard typeface.

Treat recipients with respect

Remember that being professional means recognising recipients also have a professional approach to their correspondence. Approach your email message writing seriously, and understand that those to whom you are writing may not know as much about a subject as you do. If you think you need to give more detail in a business email to explain a point, then you have probably made the right assumption. Start with a polite salutation ('Dear Sally' works) and sign off similarly ('Kind regards, Fred' also works). Don't be over-familiar with people you do not know. 'Dear Sally' is fine if you know her; if you don't, and you are emailing Sally for the first time, 'Dear Ms Adams' is a polite salutation. Set up your email account with a signature block containing your name, title, organisation, and contact details. That way people know exactly who is writing to them. Respond to email messages as quickly as possible.

How important am I?

What seems urgent and important to you may not be so for your recipient, so don't assume that if you click the message priority icon to 'High Importance' your email will be so treated by the recipient. It is best to use this feature sparingly and only when it really is important. Make sure that the subject line of your email has a meaningful message. People scan subject lines to decide whether they'll open their messages now or leave them till this afternoon's coffee when they'll have a bit more time. So make your subject line message informative: what is the message about?

Attachments

Often we cannot avoid sending attachments by email, especially in our own organisations when drafts are circulated for comment. Attachments for external recipients can cause problems.

Sometimes they carry computer viruses, so many networks have firewalls to bock them. Other attachment problems include the time they take to download, the space they'll occupy on your recipient's computer, and problems with translation from one system to another (although this is less problematic now that one word-processing program is dominating computer markets, including on hand-held equipment).

If you are sending a media release, include it in the body of your message. Better still, use email messages to alert journalists to the URL for the media release on your organisation's website, where they can not only download the text but also access any accompanying graphics.

Proofread

Hitting the 'send' button as soon as you finish writing an email message can be a trap. Most of us have done this only to discover later that the message is littered with typographical and grammatical errors. That's embarrassing in a formal business message. Proofread carefully before you send messages, and check that the words you have used are in context. For example, did you mean *two*, *too* or *to*? Remember to set your word-processing language default to the appropriate English usage for your country.

Privacy

There are two aspects to email privacy. First, don't assume that what you write in an email message will stay private. Your email messages can be intercepted. In most organisations, computer network administrators can access individuals' email accounts; the police can do it; malicious hackers can do it. In public relations practice, people often deal with confidential material, so it is best to assume when writing email messages that someone might intercept what you have written. Remember, too, that email messages are formal correspondence and are part of your organisation's official files.

Second, laws ensure people's privacy rights, and that includes the right not to receive unwanted messages. Make sure you are aware of the laws governing spam and what practitioners can and can't distribute by email. Read your organisation's policy and guidelines on privacy, email etiquette, and use of business computers for private purposes.

The use of mobile phones, social media and computer technology like tablet computers for targeted communication also brings privacy considerations. For example, responding to someone's SMS might mean that you have breached their right to privacy, even though they have, for example, participated in your organisation's competition.

DID SOCIAL MEDIA KILL PR?

Back in 2010, the PR blogger Andy Beaupre (<**http://www.beaupre.com/blog/index.cfm/High-tech-PR**>) wrote,

> Strategically practiced, PR takes on a wide-ranging role, focused on earning a trusted reputation by acting in the best interests of these publics—*not* the organisation's own myopic agenda.

> Social media is the latest expression of relationship building (a two-way model that's far more inclusive and participative); other exciting new iterations will follow.

But Beaupre noted that towards the end of the first decade of the twenty-first century, people wondered whether social media would kill traditional PR. 'Companies and organisations,' he wrote, 'could now go direct, building their own conversations, communities and visibility. Specialized social media experts … understandably trumpeted this view, leveraging the opportunity to directly or indirectly de-position PR agencies and professionals. Similarly, some journalists said PR's traditional media relations centricity was a model for extinction.' Beaupre listed six reasons social media hadn't killed public relations. They are worth repeating here because they illustrate how social media has provided a range of public relations tools that don't replace, but significantly add to, mainstream practice. Beaupre listed:

- **History repeated itself**—The www tornado caught many off-guard in the mid 1990s. The communications industry was flat-footed. Web experts sprung to life—including specialised digital agency properties. For a period of time, specialists ruled—as they typically do in moments of change—to fill the knowledge vacuum.
- **Agencies got religion**—What occurred with the Web repeated itself with social media. Facing loss of relevance and revenue, many agencies, firms and communications professionals invested the time to question, listen and learn. They got smarter, broadened service offerings, aligned with experts and integrated across disciplines. Priorities and practices were re-shaped.
- **It went from niche to mainstream**—As time passed, organisations and companies also became more comfortable with social media. Ideas and initiatives that didn't work (or make sense) were discarded; promising approaches were encouraged. As corporate and not-for-profit sectors got smarter, they ramped-up their own internal talent.
- **Walls broke down**—As the PR industry shifted from wide-eyed to eagle-eyed and as clients, companies and not-for-profits became more at ease, the early days of social media panic and pointing largely dissipated. Former adversaries let down their guards and began cooperating.
- **Opportunity begat revenue**—As social media transformed from emerging to embedded—and as knowledge increased—the revenue followed. [S]ocial media [helped] the public relations sector not just survive, *but thrive*.
- **True public relations practices remained strong**—The people who sounded the PR death knell were largely equating public relations with media relations. In that narrow zone, they were right. Traditional, one-way publicity *is* an old model that's no longer relevant in an age of social-media-driven two-way conversations, communities and grassroots empowerment.

SUMMARY

This chapter looked at writing for the internet and email. You should now understand how to adapt your writing skills for public relations tools that use web and social media applications.

You should also be aware of ways in which social media, the internet and email assist public relations practitioners in their daily tasks. Like all public relations writing, preparing material for electronic distribution relies on simplicity, clarity and accuracy.

In the next chapter, we'll focus on interpersonal communication strategies that involve speechwriting presentations.

REFLECTION

The very nature of the internet means that organisations need to be transparent about what they believe and say about themselves if they create a website. People can investigate organisations in a way never imagined just a couple of decades ago. That transparency imposes an obligation on practitioners to approach their writing tasks for websites and other online applications in an ethical way to ensure that while they are positive about their organisations and their achievements, they are also accurate.

On the other hand, working with email—even with the risk that someone might intercept what a practitioner has written—is a much more private, direct interpersonal communication pathway. Consider how you can make sure that your own approach to writing email messages remains grounded in your personal and professional ethical standards. How might you avoid message approaches and language that would breach your personal and professional code of ethics? Is observing personal and professional standards when writing for the internet easier than when writing emails? Should it be easier? Why?

ACTIVITIES

1. **How Many ISP Subscribers in Your Country? Who Uses Which Applications?**

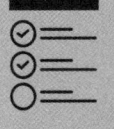

   To illustrate the importance of the internet for reaching target publics, go to the website of your country's national statistician, or the library of the national parliament or congress. Search for data that might tell you about the growth of internet subscribers in the last five years; how many households and businesses have internet access; how business income from the internet may have grown in the same period; and the reasons people give for using the net. Do people use their home computer for 'personal or private' purposes, business reasons or educational purposes? What age groups use the net and social media, and for what purposes? Has there been growth in this usage in the last five years? Where has that growth occurred? This search should uncover important planning data for a public relations campaign that would use social media. This data, especially the demographic details, will help you to determine which social media and other internet applications are appropriate for your campaign.

This snapshot illustrates the importance of the internet as a tool of modern life and business. All this technology, linked to the internet, provides public relations practitioners with valuable tools for accessing information and transmitting messages. The internet and the technologies associated with it mean that practitioners can communicate directly with individuals in their target public groups when they implement public relations tools. Yet practitioners need to work out whether the internet and the social media applications they choose are appropriate for their selected target publics. The point is that no matter how regularly and effectively you and your friends use social media and wider net applications, not everyone in your potential target publics mirrors your practice. For example, not everyone uses Twitter, nor do they regularly use Facebook to keep in touch with friends and family and to chat about entertainment, sports and what they like or don't like. While most organisations have social media accounts, most of the detailed information that publics want about them is published on their main websites. That raises questions about the reasons for having organisational social media accounts. Is it to generate dialogue? (And will it be real two-way communication?) Or is it to alert people to new information on the main site? to sell products? or just because everyone else has them? The answers to these questions require a deep understanding of why these applications are necessary, who will use them and why.

2. Research Mobile Phone Usage

Undertake an internet search for data about mobile (or cell) phone use in your country. Don't limit yourself to just one search tool; use as many sources as you can. Write a brief report (say 500 words) on what the results of your search tell you about mobile phone use. What is the most popular use of mobile phones for people aged 15–21 years? Is there a difference between the way young people use mobiles and the way people aged over fifty years use them? Suggest one idea about how a public relations practitioner might use mobile phone technology to reach target publics.

3. Planning a Website

Assume you are the public relations director of a hypothetical new charity, Our Health, which has just been formed to build awareness among 16–30-year-old women about health risks that might lead to breast cancer. Our Health also has a goal of raising money to fund research into breast cancer at the Walter and Eliza Hall Institute of Medical Research in Melbourne. The Walter and Eliza Hall Institute (<www.wehi.edu.au>) is one of Australia's most famous and respected medical research institutions. Use the internet to research the disease and its possible causes, as well as other topics that you think would be useful for Our Health's awareness-building and fund-raising goals.

Make a list of the things you think ought to be included on Our Health's new website home page. What links to Our Health's and other resources should the home page include? Write two sentences of no more than sixty words in total that summarise the importance of medical research into the causes of breast cancer and that could be published on Our Health's home page. Rewrite the two sentences by reducing the number of words to a total of no more than forty. Did you use the checklist above before you wrote the two sentences?

4. The Internet as a Public Relations Tool

While websites are designed for a wide range of reasons, some, like that for the Massachusetts Institute of Technology (MIT) in the United States, play an important role in the organisation's public communication. Visit the MIT site (<www.mit.edu>) and explore how it is designed and how it presents information. Click first on 'about the spotlight' (the link is in the menu at the foot of the home page) to see how MIT changes this feature every day to showcase a research, teaching or university initiative. Visit the 'news' section and examine how that is structured. Click on the 'community' button and explore how one US university links its staff and students to the local community.

Another US higher education site worth exploring for how it is used in public relations is that for the University of Southern California in Los Angeles: <http://www.usc.edu>. Click on the 'community' button in the menu bar at the top of the page to see how USC staff and students work in the local community. Go to the 'Press Room', accessed from the 'For Journalists' link in the 'Explore USC' menu and examine how this resource for the news media works.

Compare these sites with a university website that is familiar to you. Are there similarities? What are the main differences? Are those differences matters of design, navigation or content? Which site provides the most accessible, easy-to-read information? Why? What kind of communication pathway do these sites illustrate?

5. Writing for a Website

Search the Walter and Eliza Hall Institute of Medical Research (WEHI) website (<www.wehi.edu.au>). Assume you are a public relations consultant engaged by the University of Melbourne to write an entry about WEHI for a proposed (and, of course, hypothetical) 'Scientific Links' section of its internet page. Your task is to write a 500-word article for the site based on WEHI's history, and its links and current research collaboration with the university. Plan and structure the article as though it will be published on the internet. What are the main points you need to make? What are the main heading and subheadings? Do you have room for images? Can you cover all the information you need to in 500 words? Edit your sentences if necessary.

Practice task

This chapter looked at writing for the electronic delivery of messages. We know that journalists use the net in much the same way as public relations practitioners: they research, write and publish using the internet and its associated applications. They use email, Twitter, Facebook and Instagram for correspondence and to receive information for inclusion in stories.

For this task, assume that you are the public relations officer of Hockey Australia, the national body for field hockey in Australia. (You might choose the national field hockey association in your country.) HA has just established two new national competitions for 18-year-old men and women, which foster young talent and prepare players for possible elevation to the national teams. You need to write an article to be published on Hockey Australia's website. The two competitions will each have eight teams: one from each state and territory. They will be played on a round-robin basis over two weekends in June each year, with the venue rotating between capital cities. The first will be next year in Adelaide. Hockey Australia has a $1 million annual grant from the Australian Sports Commission to stage the two competitions, and another $1 million annually from Qantas, a major sponsor.

Write a short article of about 200 words announcing the new competitions for the Hockey Australia website. Suggest any images that should go with the article, and include any hyperlinks that will extend the information you have researched for your article. Hockey Australia wants the media to cover the announcement of the competitions. Write an email message that you would send to reporters to draw their attention to the website article. Use the internet to research the names of journalists who will receive your email message.

TIP SHEET: SOCIAL MEDIA USAGE

Using a search engine, you'll be able to find websites, books and other references full of advice on how to write for social media. In professional practice, your social media contributions will be focused on your client's, or organisation's, business, and you'll be posting using their writing and spelling styles—for example, is it *wagon* or *waggon*? *-ise* or *-ize*? *USA* or *United States*? You'll also need to adapt your writing tone to the accepted style for each platform. For instance, tweets are less formal, and briefer, than posts to a blog or material for a corporate website.

As you will be communicating on behalf of a client, or employer, all those points about PR writing still apply: write grammatically, with correct spelling, and in a clear, concise and accurate way. Abbreviations such as *LOL* and *OMG*, and emoticons are not always appropriate in a professional communication context.

CONQUERING SOCIAL MEDIA

Practitioners who are serious about effective communication will worry about whether their social media efforts are working or are even appropriate. Writing in *PR Daily's* free *News Feed* (5 December 2016) Clare Lane reported some ideas for making sure social media use is effective. While the ideas Lane reported were about marketing, they are equally appropriate for public relations. Here's a summary of what Lane reported:

Stop reaching

Many social media efforts are focused on reach, or casting an extremely wide net with the hope of catching some big fish, or influential users. More important is engaging with publics through content that authentically resonates with an audience.

Customisation—not content—will be king

The range of social media channels makes it tough to keep target publics engaged. Lane reported that Lithium's vice president of marketing, Dayle Hall, suggests that

> it's important to first understand where your audience is and not just gravitate to the newest, shiniest network on the scene. Because each network's audience deserves content that's been optimized for the channel, a good first step is sitting down with your marketing team to plan for campaigns that can easily be tweaked and customized for each.

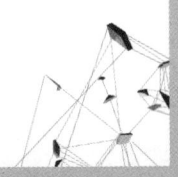

[Other advice was not to 'gate' content, that is, require users to provide personal information in exchange for access to the content. People will just turn you off.]

Adopt an interaction etiquette.

Material posted to social media will exist forever. So, always avoid becoming involved in a Twitter skirmish; remember that customers want to be involved so interact with them, forget your ego, and be aware that on social media anyone can be an influencer.

You can read Lane's full story at <**www.prdaily.com/Main/Articles/21867.aspx??utm_source=salesforce&utm_medium=email&utm_campaign=Ragan+PR+Daily+News+-+Final+-+July+29**>.

BUT WHICH SOCIAL MEDIA PLATFORMS?

You will have to write for a variety of platforms, although practitioners around the world clearly have some favourites. At the 2012 Global Alliance World Public Relations Forum in Melbourne, Australia, academics Prue Robson and Karen Sutherland (2012) reported research by international scholars that showed that

+ the most popular social media platforms among public relations practitioners are blogs, social networks and micro-blogging
+ in the United States, blogging was the most used platform
+ Twitter featured 50 per cent of the time in award-winning campaigns
+ video- and photo-sharing were commonly used in the United States
+ LinkedIn, Facebook and YouTube were the most popular sites in the Asia-Pacific Region.

(To access this paper, and others from the forum's research colloquium, go to <**http://www.globalalliancepr.org/new-page-4**> and click on the link 'here' in the last line of text on the page.)

Yet according to Robson and Sutherland (2012), practitioners face challenges in applying social media to professional practice, including in relation to generating dialogue, measuring its impact, controlling message delivery and managing governance issues. They are important issues that go to the heart of why an organisation would use social media platforms as part of its tactical implementation of a public relations strategy. These issues can't be ignored if an organisation is to ensure that content remains relevant, accurate and appropriate. This is why it is important to consider the capabilities of each social media platform. Successful communication does not come from incessant tweeting, endless Facebook posts, and publishing meaningless images on Instagram. It comes from informed decisions based on proper communication planning that lead to social media platform choices that are appropriate to the situation your client faces, the target publics you need to reach and the messages you need to send.

WITH WHOM DO WE NEED TO COMMUNICATE?

Just as we need a good reason to utilise other public relations tools, we also need a reason to use social media. That reason will be reflected in one or more objectives that pursue a broad goal. Once the organisation decides to use an interactive communication pathway to build a dialogic relationship with target publics using one or two social media platforms as tools, it has to decide which specific publics it wants to engage. Deciding on specific target publics for social media is important, even though the use of these applications is widespread. Making that decision should involve consideration of all the factors that apply to other target public identification or segmentation approaches, and it should be based on research on how people prefer to receive information. Vatican advisers thought about this when the former pope began tweeting (under his official Latin title @pontifex). Just a week after Benedict XVI started on Twitter, he had more than a million followers, 650 000 of them via his main account in English.

USING TWITTER, SMS AND MMS IN PUBLIC RELATIONS

Twitter has given public relations practitioners a versatile and valuable tool. In professional practice, target publics will follow both your organisation's Twitter account and your personal account if you set one up for business purposes. They will do this because they'll be interested in what your organisation, or you, say. Once reporters know your Twitter handle, those that are interested in your business and its issues, like customers, reporters covering your industry, and other target publics, will follow you. They'll be checking what you post regularly. You can attach media releases, pictures, YouTube video, graphics and spreadsheets to Twitter. A snappy and meaningful headline for a media release can be used as the text in a tweet to journalists to catch their attention ... with the full release attached. Equally important is the ability Twitter gives you to follow others, like people in your industry, your customers, or reporters covering your 'round'. You'll need to separate your professional use of Twitter from your personal use.

The Short Message Service (SMS) and Multimedia Messaging Service (MMS) are also handy tools for directly reaching target publics, like journalists, whose mobile phone numbers you have. They can be used to deliver information and graphics, as media alerts, and to distribute releases. Communicating with SMS is another way of creating a dialogue with target publics.

ABOUT WEBSITES

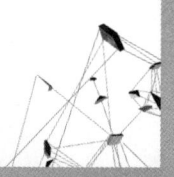

A website should be the primary communications face of an organisation and all the material published on it should reflect the goals and objectives of the business strategy and the public relations strategy that supports it. Stakeholders, including customers, shareholders, regulators, competitors and journalists regularly access websites for information. By regularly updating information on your site, especially the news room, search engines are more likely to deliver more visitors. But the public relations team won't always have control over all aspects of the website—this may be the responsibility of the IT department, or marketing team, or, if yours is an international organisation, a group at the overseas head office. In those cases the PR team needs to find ways of working with whoever has ultimate responsibility for the site to ensure that the material published on it is relevant, readable and accessible.

WHY WRITING FOR SOCIAL MEDIA PLATFORMS IS DIFFERENT

Nick Usborne (<**www.webcontentcafe.com/2010/10/10-ways-in-which-social-media-writing-is-different-from-traditional-web-writing**>) urges social media writers to remember that:

+ you're writing to individuals
+ it's about engaging attention with a variety of short-form entries
+ social media is really a conversation—engage in a one-on-one conversation
+ social media is written to be shared
+ have empathy for unhappy customers. That is, you'll interact with unhappy people, one-on-one
+ To get more Likes and Comments, ask questions—and respond to the answers you get. That's a conversation.

Usborne makes the valid point that '[w]riting for the social web is different from writing for the web. Just as writing for the web is different from writing for offline media.'

Among the tips that Matt Petronzio offers writers using social media (mashable.com/2012/02/02/social-media-writers) is to remember that part of using social media successfully is to actually be sociable, so we should interact and engage enthusiastically. He also advises social media writers to minimise self-promotion, to make valuable connections, and to not obsess about the number of followers they might have.

BE AWARE OF OTHER VOICES

It is important to be a listener on social media and to be aware of the other voices that participate in discussions and debates. Not everyone will agree with you, share your values, or be interested in what is important to your organisation. Many will use social media to challenge and question your organisation and what it stands for and what it says in public forums, or to complain about its products and service ethic. Be respectful and professional when you interact on social media and try to find out why people are concerned about, or are protesting, your organisation and its views. That approach helps to build dialogue

APPLYING SOCIAL MEDIA TO PUBLIC RELATIONS SITUATIONS

So, how might the myriad social media applications available to practitioners be applied in situations they are likely to face? The following table suggests some public relations uses for social media tools. Many of them are used for marketing and advertising, but they apply equally to public relations. Remember, the ideas in the table are for professional work not for your personal social network.

Social media tools	Public relations use
Website	A website is your client's primary online communication tool. Remember, the website is usually where people go first to find out about your organisation—and it is where people get their first impression of an organisation. Make sure the site is well designed from a communication perspective and that navigating through it is simple. Publish corporate information and news here. Include a feedback mechanism to help people to comment—and even make complaints—about the organisation. That helps to build dialogue. Create a dynamic newsroom that is regularly updated and provides your media releases, tip sheets, fact sheets, backgrounders, images and videos. Include contact names and their phone and email details. (Some organisations use anonymous templates for this, but they frustrate enquirers and in media relations personal contact is best.) Your newsroom, like the one Leicester University in Britain has set up (see Chapter 6), could include a template for writing a media release and hints for staff members to contact and work with the media. Convince the site's management team to include brief news stories (about a paragraph) and links on the homepage. Update these regularly. As a minimum, your site should have a link to your online newsroom. Some sites, like universities where lots of research is conducted, have news links that change daily. See, for example, <www.mit.edu> or <www.stanford.edu> or <http://www.ox.ac.uk> or <www.anu.edu.au>. Publish video clips of important organisational events and speeches on your site. Publish the staff newsletter on the website—and alert staff to new editions through an all-staff email. A website can be an important, efficient and easily updated public relations tool for reaching out to target publics during an organisational crisis. Not only can you publish the latest crisis news there, but also adapt elements of the site like the feedback section so that people can ask questions and receive answers.

Social media tools	Public relations use
Facebook	Most organisations link their Facebook icon, along with those of other social media applications, to their website's home page. As an organisational communication tool Facebook is less formal than the main website. It enables direct dialogue and chat sessions with customers and other target publics about products and issues. It is a good platform for posting infographics (see below) and links to video clips. Using Facebook pages for specific groups, for example, with people interested in cooking or a sport, is one way of identifying target publics. This is an important concept if you work for a charity, an industry association or a voluntary service organisation because it is easier to contact those who share your issues, and to organise events. Facebook groups are also a better way of sharing comments than bulletin boards. Together with LinkedIn, Facebook provides a mechanism for establishing and building your professional profile. If you use these two tools for your professional profile, make sure you post responsibly because potential employers will search for your pages. Before you start looking for a job in PR, you might consider closing your personal Facebook page, especially if it has posts or visuals that some might regard as less than professional. Facebook is widely used in marketing communication for targeted advertising.
Email	About 2.5 billion people use email, which is the most popular and direct form of business correspondence. Hard-copy letters are still widely used for formal correspondence, but email has become the norm for 'writing' to people inside and outside organisations. The business world operates far quicker than it did when snail mail was the only way of writing to people; decisions can be made faster; far more information can be distributed to individuals or groups by using attachments and url links. Using email for correspondence does not mean ignoring the principles of polite correspondence in favour of chatty text messaging. Most organisational email systems are part of word-processing and electronic diary software making information sharing and management highly efficient. Make sure you set up an effective filing system on your work email software—and that you regularly file important messages and attachments. In most organisations, all-staff emails are used to inform people about news and issues at work unit level as well as the whole staff. All-staff emails are important tools in a crisis so that everyone can be kept up to date on developments. Some organisations allow separate email groups that can be used for non-work-specific information like staff offering apartments for rent or sale, comments on the latest menu in the canteen, work events, and even, in winter, who left their car headlights on when they parked.

Social media tools	Public relations use
Messaging	Messaging applications like SMS, Twitter, and Messenger on Facebook, can be effective public relations tools. Use them to distribute information to target publics. SMS enables a longer dialogue with target publics than Twitter, which, of course, has a character limit—but you need to know phone numbers for those you want to contact. It is a useful tool for directly contacting reporters who cover your round. Technology specialist Edmund Ingham wrote (*Forbes*, 2015) that Twitter was 'head and shoulders above the rest [of social media platforms] in terms of time efficiency, reach, engagement and transparency.' Ingham wrote, 'The 140 characters limit is a gift for anybody creative, and of course there are visuals, links and hashtags. It is almost unbelievable how quickly you can give people an idea of what you stand for and what business you are in on Twitter. There is no hiding place.' Ingham's five tips for using this platform and his (edited) reasons were: 1. Who you follow is more important than who follows you; if you want to conduct market research, or create a newsfeed that you can constantly monitor to ensure you remain at 'the bleeding edge' of your chosen industry. 2. If you don't know what to tweet, retweet! ... [You can] very quickly create a profile that is honest and shows others that your brand is neither introspective nor self-obsessed. What you ... post helps others to understand what you and your brand are about. Passing on news and research by tweeting about it is never a bad idea, and means that when people begin to follow you it is because they are interested in the same things that you are. 3. Tweeting at people is participating in the debate; ... first you need to build up a picture of who the most influential people in your business area are. Twitter's algorithms are tremendously good at finding relevant people for you to follow, and there is no exclusivity. 4. Schedule your output for consistency; scheduling tools are commonplace (HootSuite or Twuffer) are good examples, and invaluable ... If you're consistently putting out strong, informative content that is relevant to your brand, nobody will object, and you stand to gain a reputation as a subject matter expert. 5. Image: the more you debate, experiment, and share, the more people will like and follow you.

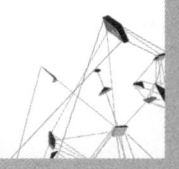

Social media tools	Public relations use
Visuals	Providing appropriate photographs, videos and other graphic material to enhance what you write is vital for successful public relations. Social media applications like Instagram, YouTube and a vast range of others give practitioners the ability to efficiently produce and distribute relevant visual material. The range of social media applications to produce visual material, either for free or for sale, grows almost weekly. Many apps include ways of linking what you produce across a range of platforms and to other applications. One site that illustrates this range is <**http://www.appappeal.com/apps/social-networking**>. It is important in business that the graphics and other visual material you distribute is of a high quality. Many social media applications enable you to produce high quality material, but if you are not a good photographer or designer, seek assistance from someone on staff who is, or from a design agency. Poorly produced graphics do not help sustain an organisation's image.
Infographics	Old timers in public relations once used hard-copy printed posters to provide text and pictorial and graphic information about their clients' products, or to explain issues. Perhaps the two most famous ever were the 'Hope' poster featuring former US president Obama, and the World War 1 British army recruitment poster featuring General Kitchener pointing with the message 'Your country needs you'. Sometimes practitioners included hard-copy charts and graphs with media releases. Posters are still useful for some public relations projects (for example, in campaigns involving public health issues where hard-copy posters can be placed in bus shelters, or in public bathrooms, or school notice boards). Newspapers and television have been adept at enhancing and explaining news stories and feature articles with graphics. You can see this at work in finance reports on the nightly television news, or in sports telecasts where commentators use graphics to explain team and individual player statistics. For modern public relations, doing that has become more efficient because social media applications have enabled complex information to be produced in electronic formats that can be easily—and cheaply—distributed to target publics. These 'infographics' present information and data in a clear visual way. They are light on text in favour of using graphics and other images to explain topics. This site, <**https://designschool.canva.com/blog/best-infographics**>, shows how infographics were used to explain forty complex topics, including one important to public relations: typography. Information about the history of infographics and how you can make them, is at <**http://www.webpagefx.com/what-is-an-infographic.html**>.

Social media tools	Public relations use
Software tools	Easily accessible software, some of it free, can enhance and manage your social media profile and accounts, and, importantly, evaluate your success using these public relations tools. This site gives details of some of this software: <**http://www.capterra.com/social-media-marketing-software**>.

A FINAL THOUGHT

Using social media platforms has become a necessity in marketing communication because, as Andreas Kaplan and Michael Haenlein (2010) point out, they allow timely and direct customer contact at relatively low cost and with greater efficiency than do traditional communication tools. They say these advantages make these platforms relevant for large and small companies, government agencies and not-for-profit organisations. But they also argue that using social media is not easy and may require new ways of thinking; the potential gains, though, are far from negligible.

That brings us back to where we started: when you use social media public relations tools for your client or employer, use them for a reason. That means using social media tools to achieve public relations objectives in ways that are appropriate for the situation you are dealing with, are relevant to your target publics, and will deliver messages effectively.

TIP SHEET: WRITING A VIDEO SCRIPT

One of the most creative and enjoyable tasks you can have in a career as a public relations practitioner is to write a script for a corporate video. A corporate video is a public relations tool that implements a controlled communication pathway (see Chapter 5) and helps to achieve a strategic goal and objective. They are called 'corporate' videos as a shorthand description for films distributed to target publics about what organisations do and believe. Corporate videos are often used by organisations to help senior managers give information to employees about business progress, structural change, and issues. Many organisations have internal video channels for this. One of the most famous—it had more than 1.7 million views in 2013—featured then Chief of the Australian Army, Lieutenant General David Morrison's tough warning to soldiers about inappropriate behaviour towards women in which he told people to 'get out' of the Army if they could not observe its inclusive values (see it at: <**www.youtube.com/watch?v=QaqpoeVgr8U**>).

Most likely you've already produced several YouTube video clips using one of your electronic devices. You probably planned in some way what would be in them and what video and other images you'd use. That experience will help you to understand a bit about the process, but high-quality video production needs more detailed planning and involves directors, script writers, camera operators, film editors, and graphic designers. Universities offer degrees in video production. If you can, it would be useful for you to do some of the subjects in these degrees so that you build a better understanding of the production process.

Organisations normally hire an expert production firm to produce their corporate videos, which, of course, will be recorded digitally. Some large organisations have their own video production facilities. The PR team's role in producing corporate videos will probably be to propose the idea for one and to write a brief. As a practitioner, you might be asked to write a script for the video setting out what scenes and other images should be shown and what the narrator or presenter should say.

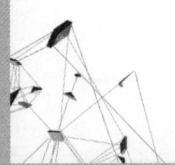

CHAPTER 7: WRITING FOR SOCIAL MEDIA AND THE WEB

Shannon Johnson, who writes for the blog hubsport.com (<**blog.hubspot.com/marketing/how-to-write-a-video-script-ht#sm.0000hi8ioopjfds2paz14yyzm6eaq**>), stresses that the brief for a corporate video should include details of its goal, the reason for making it, its precise topic, who it is being made for, and what they should 'take away' from it. Johnson says the script should be written in plain, conversational English, and indicate how you want the 'talent' to speak. It will need information about the set, scene changes and actions people will take. The script should be thorough enough that someone else can shoot the video.

So, a script has a lot of details that will help the production team shoot it. It will have the actual words those in the video will use and give as much detail as possible about the title, scenes, camera directions, graphics and other visuals and the words that should appear on the screen (known as 'supers' (short for superimpositions)) over the pictures at various places. The script should also include questions a presenter might ask of, say, a senior manager being interviewed for the video and indicate where the responses will be heard. (Use your web browser to search for video production jargon.)

Ultraglaze is a company that refurbishes bathtubs for bathroom renovations. Ultraglaze has been operating for a long time and has relied mostly on word-of-mouth among professional tilers and plumbers for its business. It has decided to promote its services to do-it-yourself home renovators and your public relations consultancy has been hired to promote the company. The public relations strategy has been approved and includes efforts to promote awareness among target publics of the firm's services through its website. Your special task is to write the script for a 10-minute corporate video explaining the refurbishing process that will appear on the website. You visit the firm's website, <**www.ultraglaze.com.au**>, for research before you start on your task.

Using the template in the Toolkit, write the script with directions for visuals.

An example of the first part of a video script follows.

Practice task

Video script template

Video title: Writing a video script
Writer: Henry Patterson
Date: 12 January 2020

VIDEO	AUDIO
CLOSE UP of fingers tapping quickly across a computer keyboard.	Theme music (10 seconds)
As the camera pulls back to a medium shot, we see the keyboard on a computer table littered with open books, pages of handwritten notes, a mobile phone and a half-empty coffee cup.	Theme music fades.
Camera slowly pans up to the computer screen to show words appearing in the audio section of a video script as the hands type.	
The screen fades to black and the video title appears in white text as the presenter starts to talk.	NARRATOR, FRIENDLY VOICE, INFORMATIVE TONE:
SUPER: Writing a video script	Today's instructional video deals with writing a video script. This can be a fun and creative job for public relations people.
Screen shows an over-the-shoulder view of young practitioner staring at the screen as they type, pausing now and then to scratch their head and sip from the coffee cup. Words keep appearing on the script.	Before you start to write a script, and plan the visuals you use, make sure you have a detailed brief for the video. This should set out the reason you are making the video, what it is about, and who the target publics are and what they should learn from the video.
Cut to a computer screen showing the cover of a document with the heading 'Corporate Video Proposal Brief'	A detailed brief will help everyone involved in the video to understand why it is being produced.
SUPER (BOTTOM OF SCREEN, CENTRED): Write a detailed brief	And once the brief is approved, and money has been allocated, you can move on to writing the script and selecting the visuals you want to illustrate it with.
Screen cuts to full frame action of our young practitioner, now smiling and giving the thumbs up sign.	YOUNG PRACTITIONER CALLS OUT: Yippee!
FADE to narrator sitting in a director's chair under a set of studio lights	NARRATOR: Now is the time for our young practitioner to show how creative they can be.

And so on until you've written the words needed to explain the topic and given details of the video footage and other visuals you want to use. Once you've written your script, you'll see how it can give the video director a lot of information about how you think it should be produced. But remember that the director and camera operator are professionals too, and they will have ideas about how it can be improved and how filming can be easier, and sometimes cheaper. So, too, will the editor who has the job of making sure the video works smoothly. Trust the experts.

Enjoy script writing.

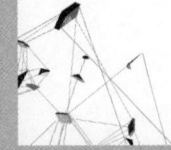

INTERPERSONAL COMMUNICATION

8

Previous chapters looked at some of the basic principles on which public relations practice is based and at those that help us to develop effective messages. We've also looked at some public relations tools that practitioners use to deliver those messages. In this chapter, the focus is on two specific tools that implement an interpersonal communication pathway: speechwriting and presentations. After working through this chapter, you'll understand:

+ the basic principles of writing a speech
+ the roles of informative and persuasive communication in interpersonal communication
+ how presentations are used to advance clients' messages.

BLAME THE ANCIENTS

More than likely, humans have been debating and arguing ever since they began to speak. Just imagine the row that a hunting party of cavemen may have had when one decided that that night's dinner was actually grazing in the opposite direction from the one they were taking, and the others insisted he was wrong. Perhaps when they finished arguing, missed out on catching dinner and returned to their cave empty-handed, they endured a tirade of opinions from their hungry families about how hopeless they were as hunters and what they needed to do to improve.

Maybe our civilisation's tradition of debating issues really did begin back then, but that kind of argument is more about blame and accusation than rational debate. It is the ancient Greeks who are generally credited with initiating this business of persuading people through speech-making. They regarded this as part of life in their democratic society. After all, the Greek philosophers (including Aristotle, Plato and Socrates among many others) wrote a lot about rhetoric and what that meant for civilised debate—not that they always agreed. They based their arguments on information, logic, reason and persuasion. So, we can blame the ancient Greek philosophers for setting us on a path that has led to the challenging public relations task of writing speeches.

PRACTICE POINT

Rhetoric comes from the Greek word *rhetor*, meaning 'orator' or 'teacher'. Most of us understand rhetoric to be the art of using oral, visual or written language for persuasion. Philosophers and others who study rhetoric debate what it actually means in the modern world. Scholars are divided between the classical definition of rhetoric, which views it as the art of persuasion, and contemporary practices of rhetoric, which include the analysis of written and visual texts. Public relations scholars like Robert Heath in the United States argue that public relations practice is essentially about rhetoric (see Chapter 2).

SPEECHES AS A PUBLIC RELATIONS TOOL

Speech-making—whether in parliament, at the opening of the local school fete, at a conference of business leaders or in the famous Oxford Union debates in England—is an exercise in rhetoric. That is, speakers are always trying to inform their listeners, to persuade them to take some action or to agree with a point of view, or simply to **entertain** them. Speechwriting requires different skills from writing a media release because a speech is not generally a short, concise outline of the organisation's latest profit result, new product or service. A speech may include that information, though, and can include detailed explanations that are not always possible with other tools. And preparing a speech requires a lot of research about the topic, the speaker, the venue, the audience, and the organisation that has invited the person who will give the speech.

entertain: in a speech, to amuse an audience.

PRACTICE NOTE KINDS OF SPEECHES

Public relations practitioners use speeches as a tool that, like social media, implements an interpersonal communication pathway. Speeches have three basic purposes—and sometimes each can be reflected in the one speech. Speeches are used to:

+ inform: to clarify, instruct, or demonstrate a point. An example of an informative speech is one given to parliament when a new Bill is introduced. That speech outlines what the Bill proposes and how it will work. Sometimes, of course, ministers also use these speeches to make a political point
+ persuade: to convince or influence target publics to a point of view, or to take some action. An example of a persuasive speech is one that an environmental scientist might give to convince us to take greater care to protect native flora and fauna

+ entertain: to, well, entertain or amuse us. Examples of entertaining speeches are those given at celebrations like birthdays and weddings, some after-dinner speeches (especially at sporting functions), and many eulogies at funerals.

When you are asked to write a speech (or to give one), you'll know from the setting in which it is to be delivered what kind of speech is required. Most organisations will tell you whether the speech is to be a light-hearted, entertaining after-dinner speech, and you'll know from the briefing you get from your boss, or client, whether you should write an informative or persuasive speech. If in doubt about the purpose, check.

Former Australian Test cricketer, the late Max Walker, who became an author and motivational speaker when he retired from active sport, used the following points for preparing a good speech (Walker & McColl Jones, 1999):

+ Know your audience or do not speak.
+ Know your subject matter.
+ Ask 'Why will the audience want to listen to me?'
+ Before actually constructing a speech:
  - think about it for several days
  - research, research and research
  - ask questions—material you will not find in textbooks.
+ What kind of speech am I going to deliver:
  - educational/informative?
  - to persuade (a point of view)?
  - inspirational/uplifting/motivational?
  - special occasion—toast?
  - after-dinner speech?
+ Brainstorm the main facts that apply to each step.
+ Cull irrelevant facts.
+ Spend time creating a good opening and closing sentence.

Tips published with the permission of the late Max Walker

Generally, speechwriting is the task of public relations teams. Some organisations employ a specialist speechwriter or regularly give the task to the practitioner on their team who has an interest in speechwriting and a talent for it. Speechwriting can be fun and highly creative. Practitioners also play a role in helping the person for whom they have written a speech to present it. That involves preparing any illustrative material that might be needed, and coaching the speaker in delivery techniques. Most senior executives who regularly give speeches have been trained in this art and are comfortable without staff support at the **venue**, but there are times when a practitioner might accompany the speaker to make sure that equipment like microphones and

venue: the place where an event is held.

data projectors work, and, if necessary, to hand out hard copies of speeches to the news media or the audience.

It is a good idea to read speeches written by other people to compare how they deal with their topics, the styles in which they write, and how they use words to craft sentences to make their points. By doing this, you can work out a speechwriting style that suits you and your clients. You can find examples of speeches by using your search engine, or visiting the websites of large organisations (they are usually in the newsroom), or the parliamentary record (which, of course, is full of them, some serious, some funny and a lot official and boring), or the websites of senior politicians. It is often useful to read the first speeches of new members of parliament, and the final speeches of those who retire, because at these times politicians are often quite personal and less worried about party politics.

PLANNING A SPEECH

Speechwriting is a collaborative process in which you work with the speaker to craft something that meets specific objectives. The noted Australian speechwriter Don Watson says speechwriting is about putting words into someone else's mouth. Like writing a media release, that's not unethical practice because the 'someone else' has briefed you on what they want the speech to be about and the points they want to make. It is your job to put these thoughts into a logical and coherent speech. By delivering a speech you have written, the speaker is accepting the words you have crafted on their behalf. That is the same process practitioners follow with media releases and other material they write for internal or external clients.

It is important that you also know the person you are writing for, their style and pattern of speaking, the tone of voice they like to use (serious, light-hearted) and sometimes how they use body language to make a point. In most organisations, this is not difficult as you'll know most of the people you'll write for. However, if you work for a public relations consultancy, you will not necessarily have this detailed knowledge of people in your client organisations.

You'll need to make sure you have plenty of time to research the speech topic, and write an outline and drafts, and get the appropriate approvals of the text, so that you are not rushed. Block out this time in your personal workload schedule.

To plan a speech, you need to know the main points that the speaker wants to cover and whether you need to be informative, persuasive or entertaining—or to write a speech that blends all three. It is important that you know how long the speech should be so that you can write it to that length. You can find that out by discussing the approach, content and tone of a speech with the person for whom you are writing. Use the speech planning worksheet in the Public Relations Toolkit section at the start of this book to help you work through your first meeting and to set down the approach you should take.

PRACTICE POINT

Remember that people 'listen' to speeches, so we are writing them more to be heard than to be read on paper or the computer screen. Use simple language and sentences; don't use lots of numbers if you can avoid it; be specific and certain that what you write is factual; use humour carefully, because what you think is funny may not be for others, and may be offensive. Most people remember only a small part of what they hear, so it is a good idea to read out loud what you have written to make sure that it flows as the spoken word should and, if you know your client well, that it matches the way they use words and speak.

In the days before televised parliamentary debates, former Australian politicians Sir James Killen (Liberal) and Fred Daly (Labor) used humour to make devastating political points in speeches they delivered in the House of Representatives. Sir James almost never used a prepared speech, or cue cards, because he didn't believe debate in parliament should be the set-piece and structured events they have become. Mr Daly kept files of newspaper clippings about politicians and events, and quoted from these to crack jokes and make his political points.

In this planning stage, make sure that you:

+ discuss the objectives, approach, points of emphasis, and facts to be included with the person for whom you are writing the speech.
+ are clear on your objective: What is the speech supposed to achieve? What information, attitude or opinion should the audience take from?
+ research the audience. Ask questions like:
  - Who? When? Where? How many people?
  - What time of the day will the speech be delivered (at a morning meeting, a luncheon or a mid-afternoon conference session, or after dinner)?
  - What is the meeting or function about, and what's the purpose of the speech?
  - How long should the speech be?
  - Will other people also be speaking? What about? For how long will they speak?
  - Who will introduce your speaker?
  - Are there important people at the function who should be acknowledged by your speaker in the opening to the speech?
  - Will the chair of the function acknowledge the traditional owners of the land, and would it be appropriate for your speaker to also make this acknowledgment?
  - Is the speech being delivered in an open forum, or is it a private meeting? If it is being given in an open forum, will media be there? If the media haven't been invited, is it OK for you to release the speech to them anyway?

If your speaker is unable to answer these questions, the organisers of the function will. Call or email the person to find out.

+ research the speaker. If you don't work with the speaker, you'll need to find out:
  - how that person likes to give speeches: Do they read the text or just use cue cards based on what you write? Do they speak without any notes? Do they like to use PowerPoint—and will there be facilities for this if they do?
  - how their mind works: Do they prefer to be serious or light-hearted? Do they work best by analysing things? Do they like to use complicated words and sentences—and can you convince them to simplify what they want to say?
  - what words and phrases they use a lot.

PRACTICE POINT

Remember that if your speaker likes to talk with cue cards, or without notes, the full text of the delivered speech can still be available to the audience and to appropriate news media as if it were delivered as written. The full text of a speech should be published on your website and it can be sent to reporters via social media applications. It is a good idea to make a note on the front page of the speech that it should be checked against delivery, especially if you give hard copies to the news media at the event before it is delivered.

Preparing a speech outline

The first step in planning a speech, after you have been briefed by your client, is to prepare an outline. Use the worksheet in the toolkit to plan points that you can use to write:

+ *an opening*. You'll need to work on a few sentences that will:
  - catch the audience's attention. Sometimes, if it is appropriate, a speaker might include a joke to catch people's attention, but be careful with humour because what is funny to you may be offensive to others. Some speakers like to make self-deprecating jokes at the start of a speech.
  - tell the audience what the topic is, why it is important, and the direction the speech will take
  - suggest what the conclusion to the speech might be
+ *the body*, or the main part of the speech that presents all the evidence needed to draw the conclusion. This should include:
  - an outline of all the main points. Explain each in detail (but remember the time limit)
  - the arguments that back up the theme and the points the speaker will make

- examples, statistics and quotes from experts that drive the points being made in the speech. Remember not to use so many statistics that the audience's eyes will glaze over
+ *a closing section.* This is where you'll bring all the information and arguments presented in the speech to the conclusion that you pointed to in the opening section. This final section will:
  - summarise the evidence the speech has presented
  - point out what the evidence means.

It is best practice to submit your outline to your client to make sure you are taking the approach that is needed. This gives you an opportunity to revise the direction before you start to write a draft.

A THOUGHT ON THEORY: PERSUASION

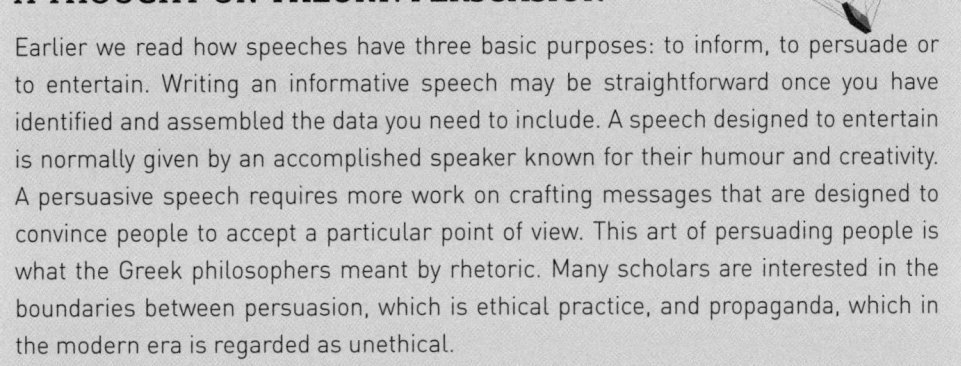

Earlier we read how speeches have three basic purposes: to inform, to persuade or to entertain. Writing an informative speech may be straightforward once you have identified and assembled the data you need to include. A speech designed to entertain is normally given by an accomplished speaker known for their humour and creativity. A persuasive speech requires more work on crafting messages that are designed to convince people to accept a particular point of view. This art of persuading people is what the Greek philosophers meant by rhetoric. Many scholars are interested in the boundaries between persuasion, which is ethical practice, and propaganda, which in the modern era is regarded as unethical.

We are better able to write persuasive messages if we have some understanding of how people process the information they hear.

One theory that helps us to understand this is Richard Petty and John Cacioppo's elaboration likelihood model (see Gabbot & Clulow, 1999). The theorists use their model as a way of explaining how people process, or elaborate, persuasive messages. In the context of the model, elaboration refers to the thinking activities an individual uses to add to or embellish a message. The model suggests that people elaborate messages in one of two ways. The first is 'central route processing'. People use this route when they carefully consider the merits of information and reach an evaluated conclusion. That is, a person who uses the central route to process information is more likely to be persuaded if they are able to elaborate on a message extensively. If the message is delivered in a way that motivates them to think about it, they are likely to be persuaded by it. An example of central route processing would be someone who is considering buying a new car and thinks about how increasing interest rates on car loans might affect their ability to pay. The second way in which people elaborate is via a 'peripheral route'. That is, the person relies on peripheral cues, or cues that have them reacting emotionally to a message. This occurs when the person's motivation to elaborate on a persuasive message is low. Someone who doesn't think about a message extensively may still be persuaded to accept a message by cues that have nothing do with the actual content of the message but that are positive, familiar factors they would associate with the message. An example of this is the person who bases their decision to buy a new car on the emotional appeal of a particular brand.

Two other theorists, Mark Gabbot and Val Clulow (1999), argue that the two most important task-related variables affecting motivation to elaborate are the personal relevance of a message and the perceived responsibility for evaluating the message's recommendation. They argue that the key point about the elaboration likelihood model is that it is about persuading people to a new attitudinal position that may conflict with an opinion they already hold.

There are other theories that also help us to understand how people deal with and act on messages. The tip sheet 'How theories can inform practice' between chapters 4 and 5 is a good place to start. Steve Mackey's (2009) outline of theoretical perspectives for public relations practice discusses theory in detail as do Jim Macnamara (2012, especially ch. 4)) and Marianne Sison (2012, pp. 56–87) in Chia and Synnott (2012). Cornelissen (2000, pp. 315–26), Gabbott and Clulow (1999, pp. 172–88) and Wood et al. (2004, pp. 140–61) are other good resources. You might also like to explore what Aristotle had to say about ethos, logos and pathos to find out more about the credibility of speakers, the nature of messages, and attitudes that audiences might hold. Another research task you could do is to find out why the term propaganda has such bad connotations.

Writing a speech draft

Now that you've completed the planning phase and prepared an outline, and had it approved by your speaker, you need to start writing. You may need to do some more research after discussing the outline with the speaker. That's normal because people's ideas change.

Your next step is to write a draft for the speaker to edit. This is where you can apply your writing skills and your creative talents. Stick to your approved outline and the style the speaker wants to use, but treat the words you use with respect and convey their correct meanings. In his book *Death Sentence: The Decay of Public Language* (2003), Don Watson makes the point that while pictures rule in communication, 'words define, explain, express, direct, hold together our thoughts and what we know. They lead us into new ideas and back to older ones' (p. 65). That's a useful observation for all aspects of public relations writing, but it is a particularly instructive message for speechwriters. So, too, is his remark that Australian speechwriters are typically asked to add jokes and sporting analogies, and to include thoughts about mateship or the Anzac legend in speeches. He is, of course, complaining about stereotyping and the lack of originality in speechmaking, and that's also a point we should bear in mind. Dare to be different.

PRACTICE POINT

Understanding the power of words and how to use them is stock-in-trade for public relations writers. The Australian biographer, author of popular history, and newspaper columnist, Peter FitzSimons, reported the following as examples of how we use words.

Order of magnitude

A single paragraph by the English writer Mark Forsyth, in his book *The Elements of Eloquence* went viral on the internet this week. Tell us, again, Mark, while we lean in close.

'Adjectives in English absolutely have to be in this order: opinion-size-age-shape-colour-origin-material-purpose noun. So you can have a lovely little old rectangular green French silver whittling knife. But if you mess with that word order in the slightest you'll sound like a maniac. It's an odd thing that every English speaker uses that list, but almost none of us could write it out.'

In a follow-up piece, for the BBC, Forsyth noted there are a couple of small exceptions to the rule. 'Little Red Riding Hood may be perfectly ordered, but ... Big Bad Wolf seems to be breaking all the laws of linguistics. Why does Bad Big Wolf sound so very, very wrong? What happened to the rules?'

Well, occasionally, the rule above is trumped by another rule we know.

'The rule of ablaut reduplication. You've been using it all your life. It's just that you've never heard of it. But if somebody said the words zag-zig, or cross-criss you would know, deep down in your loins, that they were breaking a sacred rule of language. You just wouldn't know which one ... We always, always say clip-clop, never clop-clip. Every second your watch (or the grandfather clock in the hall makes the same sound) but we say tick-tock, never tock-tick. You will never eat a Kat Kit bar. The bells in Frère Jaques [SIC] will forever chime 'ding dang dong'.

'Reduplication in linguistics is when you repeat a word, sometimes with an altered consonant (lovey-dovey, fuddy-duddy, nitty-gritty), and sometimes with an altered vowel: bish-bash-bosh, ding-dang-dong. If there are three words then the order has to go I, A, O. If there are two words then the first is I and the second is either A or O. Mish-mash, chit-chat, dilly-dally, shilly-shally, tip top, hip-hop, flip-flop, tic tac, sing song, ding dong, King Kong, ping pong.'

Fabulous, innit?

Published with the kind permission of Peter FitzSimons from *The Sun-Herald*, 17 September 2016, p. 24

ON CREATIVITY

Taking a creative approach to speechwriting by doing something different can be rewarding and interesting for audiences. For example, university graduation ceremonies almost always include a speech by someone who is well-known or an expert in a special field; the speeches are supposed to be short, and a way of inspiring graduates as they begin careers. Some graduation speakers take a humorous line (Australian broadcaster Phillip Adams used the Ten Commandments in this way), others make political points, some bemoan the state of their work discipline, and others ignore everyone at the ceremony except the graduates and offer wise advice on life based on their own experiences.

In the 2016 US presidential election, one cartoonist illustrated creativity when he published this:

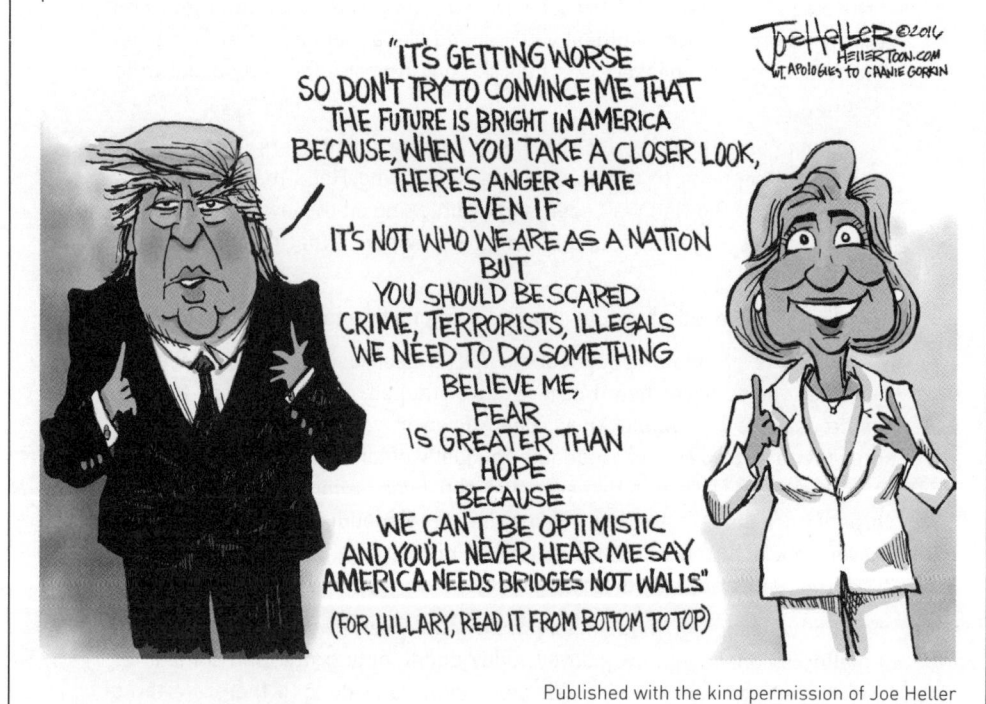

Published with the kind permission of Joe Heller

Your draft might be accepted immediately, but you might also have to make substantial changes. That's normal, too. The ideal process for writing a speech is for it to go through several drafts. Sometimes, you might write two or more drafts before you submit it to your speaker for approval.

Preparing your speaker

Mostly, people for whom you have written a speech will be quite comfortable to deliver it without any further help. Others will ask you to help them prepare to deliver it. Coaching your speaker can involve:

+ a rehearsal. Stay with the speaker while they read the speech out loud, perhaps in a setting that approximates the one in which they will actually be speaking—without the audience, of course.
+ working with the speaker to get the tone of voice right, to know which words or phrases to emphasise, and to work on the speed of delivery so that they don't rush or speak too slowly. Remember that it takes about two minutes to read a double-spaced page of text. That means a 20-minute speech will be about 2500 words.

Some speakers will ask you to underline the words or phrases that need to be emphasised, or to write them in bold type. It is also possible for you to add some directions to your text to suggest where the speaker should look at this point, or what gestures they should make.

After the speech

It would be a good idea for you to review with the speaker how the audience received the speech. When you do that, you can identify approaches that worked well and areas that need improvement.

PRESENTATIONS

A regular task for most public relations teams is planning and delivering presentations on aspects of the organisation's activities. Presentations are adaptations of speeches that include demonstrations or displays of materials or information. To present something means to introduce, offer or exhibit it for public attention *(Australian Concise Oxford Dictionary)*. That is precisely how they are used in public relations practice: they are a **communication, or public relations, tool** that implements a **communication pathway**. Like other public relations tools, presentations pursue strategic objectives to build awareness or understanding, or to generate action among target publics.

Presentations are almost always accompanied by graphics: the regular electronic slides produced on your laptop computer and projected to a screen; video material; flip charts; and static displays.

A presentation can be given at, for example, a conference, a production facility or a town meeting. If Practical Widgets Pty Ltd in Hong Kong has introduced a new production technique, an expert from the company might be invited to give a presentation on this to the annual conference of the World Widget Manufacturers' Association in Toronto, Canada. The public relations team will most likely work with the technical and production people at Ideal to plan and prepare the presentation.

Sometimes practitioners formally present a new strategic public relations plan to an organisation's board. Marketing teams will use a presentation to report on annual sales outcomes, and the personnel section will use the same technique to outline, for example, new occupational health and safety rules to the board and to staff.

communication, or public relations, tool: the physical things and activities that target publics see or hear or experience. Examples are websites, blogs, tweets, displays, media releases, meetings, publications, speeches and events. (Sometimes known as a public relations tactic, or as collateral.)

communication pathway: a communication method to reach target publics. (Sometimes known as a message delivery strategy.)

Practitioners working in public relations consultancies use presentations to pitch for business in competition with other consultancies. These presentations respond to a potential client's brief on what they'd like external consultants to do for the organisation. The consultancy will use a presentation to outline the strategic plan it proposes and to give details of its own expertise. Presentations like this support the consultancy's written response to the organisation's brief. Your consultancy will have its own style for these presentations, and requirements about what needs to be included, as well as the formatted slide template you should use.

Planning and writing a presentation

Planning and writing a presentation should follow the same disciplined approach that practitioners use for writing speeches and media releases, and for using social media and other tools. The writing needs to be clear, concise and accurate. You can adapt the Speech Planning Worksheet in the toolkit for a presentation—but remember that you need to consider the graphic elements that you'll use.

If you use electronic slides, make sure that you don't try to tell the whole story in one slide. Electronic slides should support and illustrate what you are saying by summarising the key points of that section of the presentation's text. Electronic slides can be effective communication supports, but they have become so common that many people simply loathe them. Make sure you don't use them just for the sake of it. Question whether you, or your presenter, needs them, and investigate alternatives.

> **PRACTICE POINT**
>
> Practitioners don't always have the skills, or the time, to produce every part of a presentation, especially the graphic elements. If you have the budget, use a graphic designer to produce your slides, static displays or flip charts. Involve the graphic designer in planning the presentation so that they understand the objective of what you are doing, and what is required as the end-product.

exhibition: a large event at which organisations from a range of industries display their products.

trade show: a special event at which groups or organisations representing a particular industry, or trade, display their products.

EXHIBITIONS AND TRADE SHOWS

Exhibitions and **trade shows** provide opportunities for organisations to make presentations. Your organisation may have its own annual event, or a trade show that it sponsors, to generate opportunities for interpersonal communication with target publics.

SUMMARY

The purpose of this chapter was to consider the role of speeches and presentations—public relations activities that all practitioners use—as tools that implement an interpersonal communication pathway. You should now understand:

+ the roles of informative and persuasive communication in interpersonal communication
+ how to plan, write and structure a speech
+ how presentations advance clients' messages.

The next chapter discusses writing for other public relations tools like brochures, annual reports, backgrounders, fact sheets, feature articles for newspapers, and community service announcements.

REFLECTION

When you reflect on this chapter, try to make connections with the information in the previous chapters. The common theme is the need for clearly written messages that implement measurable objectives in a planned, strategic approach to public relations. The tools we have discussed so far are different, but complementary, ways of delivering messages. Each tool is an opportunity to convey your organisation's messages in another format: a media release performs a special task; a website or other social media posting performs another; and a speech or presentation performs a third. In a strategic sense, practitioners should use as many tools as possible in a coordinated way to promote messages to relevant target publics. That coordination comes from choosing appropriate communication pathways and public relations tools that link goals, objectives, messages and target publics. For example, the communication pathway you would use to tell business people about your organisation would be different from the pathway you would use for high school leavers. So, too, would the tools. The main messages will be the same, but they'll be refined to suit the information needs of the identified target public and probably use different tools. A speech, for example, is an opportunity to expand on your message in greater detail than you would be able to do in a media release. As you read the next chapter and explore other tools that expand our public relations toolkit, keep these strategic links in mind.

ACTIVITY

Read and Compare These Speeches

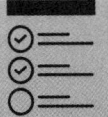

Read the extract from the late Max Walker's speech below. Use the speech planning worksheet in the Public Relations Toolkit to work out what Walker and Mike McColl Jones might have written if they'd used one. How would you plan this speech? Does this speech work? Would you lose interest, or would you keep listening?

'A Fear of Public Speaking'

The beads of perspiration were as large as 20-cent pieces, multiplying rapidly until eventually a trickle began to run down his rather prominent nose.

His throat became parched, as dry as the Nullarbor. His heart was trying to leap through his rib-cage. His eyes were open, but not seeing, and he was almost choking in a failed attempt to breathe normally.

The audience totally understood the speaker's predicament (they always do).

He was using the lectern as a crutch, still yet to utter those familiar opening words, 'Ladies and Gentlemen'. A mild sort of panic set in. His head was spinning from the reams of foolscap jottings he agonised over until 3 am. The words are on the sheets of paper stacked neatly on the lectern, yet he cannot see them, and even worse, he can't say them! The paralysis of fear had set in.

This unfortunately is such a common occurrence, a man or woman, boy or girl forced into the terrifying role of standing up and attempting to speak to a crowded room. Even the description above does not convey adequately the sheer terror involved for some people confronting a jury-like gathering of people.

To a great majority of the western world, the examination is looked upon as a fate worse than death. For his part, he was only twelve years of age when he was cajoled into experiencing that very same fear. 'It all began with my best mate's dad reckoning I was gutless; and he was right! I'd refused to enter the school lecturette competition.'

In delivering in excess of 4000 presentations world wide, Max was the ultimate professional.

His vast life experiences enabled him to shape individual presentations to suit any audience.

One of Max's great pluses was his user-friendliness. Another reason why Max Walker was one of Australia's most sought-after speakers.

> *Max placed importance on verbal, tonal, visual and body language to portray an interesting, unpredictable identity. His natural enthusiasm engaged the audience leaving them well entertained, informed and uplifted.*
>
> Adapted from Walker and McColl Jones (1999). Published with the permission of the late Max Walker.
>
> Now go to <www.youtube.com> and search for 'Paul Keating's Redfern Address' to view a famous speech delivered by a former Australian prime minister. Watch the speech. Compare the style with Walker and McColl's speech above. How do the styles differ? Why?

Practice task

Every year, thousands of people living in coastal areas are entranced by the antics of whales as they cruise the coast, moving from their summer feeding waters off Antarctica to warmer ocean water to the north. But whale-watching from boats can be dangerous to the whales and to the watchers. National parks authorities annually advise people about safe whale-watching.

Assume that you live in a state that has an ocean coastline and that you are the speech-writer for the national parks and wildlife service. Your chief executive has been invited to speak about whale-watching at the annual conference of the Society for the Prevention of Cruelty to Animals at a seaside venue near your capital city. You've been tasked to write the CEO's speech. You've had your first meeting with the CEO, who has told you that a persuasive speech that argues the case for tighter controls on people using boats to watch the annual whale migration is what is needed. You know that the news media and some specialist environmental reporters will be covering the speech.

To do this practice task, you will need to:
- find out as much as you can about the whales that frequent the coastline of your state, including their migratory and breeding habits
- use the speech planning worksheet to set out how you would plan this speech
- write a 150-word introductory section for the CEO's speech
- write a 300-word conclusion for the speech
- write the first four paragraphs of a media release based on the speech that will be issued to the media at the conference, with a full copy of the speech, as the CEO arrives to speak.

9 BEYOND THE MASS NEWS MEDIA

Public relations practitioners produce a lot of materials that inform target publics about their clients' organisations. This chapter deals with writing these important public relations tools, which include brochures, backgrounders, fact sheets, question and answer sheets, feature articles, op-ed newspaper articles and annual reports. Having got this far into the book, you should have picked up the basic and vital point that you need to write clearly and accurately. The public relations tools this chapter covers give practitioners opportunities to be more creative, and expansive, in their writing because they will not be constrained by the need to be concise like they are when they write media releases. Think about the tools in this chapter as ways to provide more information to back up media releases, or interviews, or to answer target public questions.

After reading this chapter, you should:

+ recognise the breadth of material that public relations writers produce
+ understand the need to adapt your writing style to different formats
+ appreciate how public relations tools are linked together to implement communication pathways.

BUILDING A MATRIX OF PR TOOLS

Once you get past the inconvenience of them, construction sites for office blocks are fascinating places. Gradually, open pits are filled with concrete foundations; pillars follow, and then over time the building's shape becomes clear as floor after floor is added. Finally, the outer shell of windows goes up, the interior partitioning is finished, and the scaffolding that has protected workers during construction is taken down. All of this follows schedules set out in a matrix of plans prepared by architects and engineers to make sure that the office block is built to safety standards, on time and within budget.

Public relations plans are a bit like that because tools work together in a matrix to produce an integrated strategic approach to delivering organisational messages to target publics. Each of the tools examined in this chapter implements a specific communication pathway in a strategic plan, sometimes in combination with others, sometimes on their own. The messages they contain should be consistent with those used in other tools in the plan, but each may be directed at different target publics. For example, the Ideal Widgets' annual report to shareholders will provide detailed information about the company's 'triple bottom line' performance. Fact sheets for the media and other publics about Ideal Widgets' financial, environmental and community service outcomes will not be so detailed but will support media releases, interviews, and so on, and perhaps be used as briefing materials for community leaders, politicians and bureaucrats.

DECIDING WHAT TOOLS FOR WHICH TASK

The tools discussed in this chapter are almost always on websites, but most public relations offices keep hard-copy sets of **brochures**, fact sheets, backgrounders, and question and answer sheets (see Table 6.1 on p. 114 for definitions) that explain aspects of their organisations or their views on important issues. These can be included in media kits (on the web or in hard copy) and be used to answer individual enquiries about the organisation and its products. They are published on an organisation's website, and they back up media releases with detailed information, or by extending the points made in the release. A good way to think about how this 'collateral' can be used in a coordinated way would be to pick a large organisation in your state and find out the sorts of issues that it is dealing with. From the public relations tools it has on its website, make a list of which could be included in separate media kits for each issue that could be published on the website. Some of these tools would be in each kit, but most kits would have issue-specific tools.

brochure: printed material about a particular topic in booklet form. The term is often used more broadly to mean a leaflet, pamphlet or booklet.

Corporate and other brochures written by public relations staff, often in conjunction with the sales and marketing team, provide hard-copy information that can be supported by colour photographs and other graphics, diagrams and charts for publication on the organisation's website, and in hard copy.

> ### PRACTICE POINT
>
> Go to <www.elections.org.nz> and click on 'Voting system' and then 'Resources and learning' to see how one New Zealand agency uses tools like these to provide information about enrolling to vote and how elections are conducted. Then, on the same site, click on the other navigation buttons to find examples of how information brochures can be published on a website. Finally, click on 'Information in different languages' for variations of the same brochures in different languages, which demonstrate inclusive and culturally aware public relations practice.

But which of these tools would you choose for what role? The answer is that it depends on what your task is. Your strategic public relations plan should include information about which tools will be used for each communication pathway. For example, backgrounders, fact sheets, and question and answer sheets are flexible tools that can be easily amended, changed or even deleted. They can be produced for all the topics your organisation deals with but for which information rarely changes, with perhaps an annual review of the text to make sure it is still relevant to communication goals and objectives.

If your organisation is dealing with an emerging or current issue, or facing a crisis, these flexible tools provide convenient formats for releasing information specific to those events. Stocks of a full-colour, illustrated brochure outlining, say, the production facilities, export markets, research program and staff achievements of Ideal Widgets can usually be kept for at least a year before a major reprint is needed. Always make sure that when the copy on the website is updated, hard-copy versions are also revised.

> **PRACTICE NOTE** SHORTENING SENTENCES
>
> The last paragraph in the text before this practice note is eighty-one words long. The paragraph could be edited to make it briefer (sixty-three words), and hopefully clearer, yet still provide the same information:
>
>> These flexible tools are a convenient way of releasing information about an emerging or current issue, or in a crisis. Keep stocks of a full-colour, illustrated brochure outlining, say, the production facilities, export markets, research program and staff achievements of Ideal Widgets for at least a year before a major reprint. Make sure online and hard-copy tools are updated at the same time.
>
> With practice, everyone should be able to revise what they write to make the language simpler, clearer and more concise. The idea is to reduce redundant words by finding a shorter way of saying something but not changing the meaning. Writing in this way is as important for the tools discussed in this chapter as it is for writing a media release. Read the paragraph again and try to reduce the number of words still further while retaining the meaning.
>
> Tip: You won't write in news style, or for other PR tools, effectively unless you practise. Often. Your journalism colleagues at university practise writing in news style from almost their first day of study—and they continue right through till their final assessment. Senior practitioners often say they give PR jobs to journalism graduates because they can write. That's a lesson for PR students.

ABOUT ANNUAL REPORTS

Annual reports to shareholders are required by law and, for companies, must also be filed with government agencies responsible for the legislation that sets out how companies must operate. The public relations staff usually write and produce the annual report, although the financial information is compiled by the accounting team and the auditors, who will know the legal deadlines for producing and distributing them. This means that 'doing the annual report' is programmed into the organisation's publication schedule so that it can be written, designed, approved, printed and distributed by the legal deadline. Sometimes organisations engage external public relations consultants who specialise in producing annual reports to write the text and manage the production.

Preparing an annual report requires attention to detail; consultation and collaboration with other areas of the organisation; a good working relationship with outside contractors like designers, photographers, printers, and mailing houses; effective management skills; and an ability to write well. Most annual reports are produced in both hard-copy format and on the organisation's website. Increasingly shareholders are being given the option of receiving an electronic version of the report to save the costs of printing and mailing hard copies.

Writing an annual report is serious business, but the copy does not need to be boring. The writing style is more formal than that used for media releases, but it must still be clear and accurate.

PLANNING AND WRITING BROCHURES

Most organisations publish a series of brochures that explain aspects of their operations or products. In Chapter 11, we'll look at production processes for producing brochures, but here we'll discuss their role as public relations tools.

> ### PRACTICE POINT
>
> The *Australian Concise Oxford Dictionary* notes that *brochure* comes from French and means, literally, 'a stitched work'. That is an interesting derivation for a word that is nowadays liberally, but perhaps incorrectly, used as a cover-all description for the range of leaflets, pamphlets, booklets—and brochures—published to distribute information about organisations, products or causes. A 'stitched work' means one in which the pages are held together with stitching (like a hard-cover book) or staples. A good example of a brochure is the printed material new car salespeople give you when you are investigating a particular model. For this chapter, though, *brochure* will include leaflets, pamphlets and booklets.

Writing and producing a brochure—whether it is a glossy, full-colour corporate document or a leaflet designed as a single sheet of A4, printed on both sides and folded to DL size to fit a standard envelope—requires planning. First, the brochure will have been included in a public relations strategy as one tool to be distributed via a controlled communication pathway. The public relations team will have worked out why they need to produce it—perhaps after a communication audit that showed there was a gap in the material they have available to promote the organisation.

Perhaps there is a need for an impressive, full-colour brochure to convince shareholders to invest in a new stock offering for the company, or as a corporate-level explanation of the organisation for important visitors. At other times, there might be a need for an inexpensive series of leaflets that explain aspects of the services offered by the organisation. Examples of this latter approach are the leaflets universities produce about each of their degree courses, or those that deal with services offered by the local government, or those you can find at your local bank branch that explain different investment products and accounts.

Mostly, brochures are produced so that the organisation has a stock of material that can be used to answer questions, included in media kits, or used to promote the organisation's view on issues. Often, decisions about what brochures are needed reflect sales and marketing communication action to promote a particular product or service. In not-for-profit organisations, decisions about brochures reflect their need to raise funds, to report to donors about how money is spent, or to promote a new focus. Many industry associations prepare information brochures about the general products and services of their members (the uses of coal, for example) or as explanations of policy positions they take on current issues (the widget industry's view on foreign investment).

When you plan a brochure, you need to:

+ know the target public. Who is it being written for and why? And what do they need to know about this topic?
+ identify an objective that the brochure will help to achieve
+ decide on the approach you need to take. Will this be:
    - an informative or persuasive brochure? Do you simply want to provide some facts about the rules of, say, a university loans scheme, or do you need to argue a case to persuade young people to enrol and to vote?
    - written as a technical explanation of a product?
    - a sales promotion or marketing communication tool?
    - a general description of your organisation's business?
+ decide on the format. How long should it be? What should the physical format—such as page size and use of colour and graphics—be? A graphic design team can help you to produce the brochure, but you will need to work out which format will be most appropriate for what you need to do. Will the target public accept a brochure that is:
    - text only, or that includes photographs and other illustrations?
    - a small, single-colour DL-size format?
    - a 16-page, A4-size brochure with a striking design, colour photographs and other graphics?
    - printed and held as stock? Or do you need it for a particular event, like a trade show or a major exhibition?
    - for the organisation's website only?
+ research the topic and identify people in the organisation who can help you
+ use a planning checklist, or a Gantt chart (there's a template in the Public Relations Toolkit), to set out the detailed steps and timeline you need to follow to:
    - research
    - write

- design (use a graphic designer, but include the time involved in their work in your checklist or chart)
- seek approvals of the text, design and graphics
- revise the text
- print the brochure
- distribute the brochure.

Your decisions about the target public, the brochure's objective and the approach will determine the style in which you write. Your organisation might have its own style for writing a brochure, and you'll need to follow that. The organisation might also have a template that determines the word length, format, corporate image parameters, use of colour and graphics, and perhaps even the use of your brochure. You'll need to check whether there is a template for what you are doing and follow it. The template is vital for ensuring the corporate design style is always followed and for an attractive and easily accessible product on the organisation's website.

Whichever approach you take, your writing needs to be clear and accurate.

Writing a backgrounder

Backgrounders are one of the most useful public relations tools. They allow you to give the background to an event, a product, an issue or your organisation. The format lets you:

+ focus on the news in your media release
+ treat your material in depth.

Backgrounders almost always accompany a media release and are normally included in a media kit, but they don't always have to be about a current topic. For example, you might be asked to write a backgrounder that explains the history of your organisation, which will be posted on the website and kept in stock in hard-copy format to always be included in media kits. When your team is announcing an event to raise funds for cancer research, you might need to write a backgrounder about your organisation's community support program to also go in a media kit and on the website. Your PR team will always have an up-to-date backgrounder on the organisation and what it does, perhaps with some history and some data about financial performance. This should always be in any hard copy media kit, even if you have also included the latest annual report. Include a link to this backgrounder (and other relevant material) in the electronic versions of your media releases.

A backgrounder is a good way of expanding on whatever your organisation has announced in a release. They should be written as a narrative and so can be much longer than a media release, sometimes 'running' to three or four pages of text. You do not need to write them in a news style like a media release, but it is a good idea to use the '5Ws and H' to help you work out what you need to say. That approach means that you:

+ open with an introductory statement about your subject
+ write about the history of the subject
+ present implications for the future
+ provide a summary of your information or argument.

backgrounder: a narrative usually written about one topic that extends the information published in a media release.

Writing a backgrounder allows you to be comprehensive in your treatment of a subject, yet still use clear and concise language. A backgrounder has a heading that indicates what it is about and is usually produced on an organisation's letterhead with 'Backgrounder' on it in the same way that 'Media release' appears.

The text can be broken up with subheadings, and with graphs and charts that might not be suitable for a media release (because they would take up valuable space). Referring readers to sources of more information, like another backgrounder or a fact sheet, is good technique. Include the relevant URLs to take people to the additional sources.

Mostly you'll need to use internal and external sources to research widely for the content of a backgrounder. This is important because your internal research will provide the details about the product, or the background to the organisation's view on an issue. External research will help you to find the broader context for the issue you are dealing with. Sometimes you'll find the information you need from existing material (the organisation's library, brochures, speeches, annual report or other files, for instance) that you can adapt for your backgrounder. Talking to senior people and other experts in the organisation is also a good way of doing 'desk research'.

Backgrounders can also be used to publish an interview with your chief executive on an important issue, or as a way of providing that person's biography.

Adapt the media release planning worksheet in the Public Relations Toolkit to plan and write a backgrounder.

Writing fact sheets

fact sheet: a set of factual data about an organisation's product, person, event or issue, usually in hard-copy form.

Fact sheets are also common public relations tools and, like backgrounders, do not have to be time sensitive. That is, you can also keep hard copies of fact sheets in stock to 'hand out' when people ask questions about your organisation, its products or services. They are also vital inclusions in the information provided in an online newsroom. As the name suggests, fact sheets set out basic, but important, facts about one topic, an organisation, a product or service. Fact sheets are not a narrative (but they might have a sentence or two as an introduction) but give facts in lists, or tables or charts. They:

+ extend media releases
+ are an opportunity to give information in an uncluttered, easy-to-read format. Bullet points are acceptable for a fact sheet
+ can be kept as reference guides to an organisation
+ sometimes generate a news story.

Your PR team might produce fact sheets giving factual data about

+ your organisation, its history, important dates, production statistics, number of employees, location of factories, and so on
+ each of its products, giving statistical data about the number of units produced, where they are sold, how many are exported
+ the services the organisation offers

- how much the organisation pays annually in federal, state and local taxes, for electricity and water supply, the number of local jobs that rely on its operations (this is known as the multiplier effect).

Fact sheets, whether written specifically to provide more information about the news you are releasing or taken from your stock, are also generally included in media kits.

Writing talking points

If you work in a government agency, one of your jobs might be to write **talking points**. These are usually short summaries of important points about an issue that the minister can use to answer parliamentary questions, in media interviews, or at public or private functions. Your team selects the issues for talking point topics from its environmental scanning and uses existing policy to explain the department's position on those issues. Each department has a format for writing talking points. Public relations practitioners in private industry and consultancies sometimes write talking points for their clients to help them to participate in public discourse about issues that affect their organisations. Mostly talking points are for internal use only, but sometimes if they are relevant, talking points can be sent to journalists as part of the information in a media kit, or separately as another way of promoting the organisation's views.

talking points: a short summary of important points about an issue that help executives in interviews with journalists or in giving speeches.

Question and answer (QnA) sheets

These are a subset of fact sheets and are sometimes called 'frequently asked questions'. The concept is to propose questions and to answer them in your own terms. This approach enables you to pre-empt questions that journalists might ask and is a useful way of releasing information when you are managing an issue or dealing with a crisis. When you are dealing with an issue and need to give a more detailed explanation of your organisation's position than can be included in a media release, a QnA sheet can be adapted so that you pose one question and provide a lengthy answer. In this case, you could call the result a 'response sheet'. This is a tactical use of a public relations tool in which a practitioner poses an important question in detail. QnA and response sheets are valuable public relations tools in dealing with issues debates and in crises. They are easily updated and should have a page in your online newsroom.

It is important to adapt the '5Ws and H' concept when preparing QnA sheets to plan out what you need to say. Ask yourself:

- Why talk about this subject?
- Why is it important?
- What questions might reporters ask?

When you answer these questions, and others you might think of, you'll be able to better understand the importance of your subject and explain it to those who read the QnA sheet. Give examples to support your answers.

It is a good idea to apply the 'So what?' test to the questions and answers you plan to include. What does this topic mean to those who will read it? Is the subject really important? How is it relevant?

COMPILING A MEDIA KIT

Now that you have written some basic resources, you can consider building a media kit to give to journalists when they arrive for your media conference. We had a brief look at media kits in Chapter 6.

Media kits are sometimes called 'press kits', reflecting the era when newspaper journalists—'the press'—were the only reporters seriously interested in news. The growth of radio, television and online news, both as sources of information and in importance, has made 'the press' an inappropriate term. Journalists also describe media kits and media releases as 'handouts' because, well, we hand them out.

Media kits are a common public relations tool for giving journalists information, and they can be adapted for other purposes: as a promotional pack for a shopping centre display or at a trade fair or major exhibition, and to answer enquiries about your organisation from school kids. Your online newsroom can publish 'virtual media kits' for every topic you need to deal with. Media kits:

+ are helpful when used properly
+ are a flexible way of compiling a number of relevant public relations tools for a specific issue, product launch, event (the opening of a new university building for example), or to accompany the distribution of the CEO's latest major speech to the media
+ should provide enough information to meet the needs of your target public—keep this point in mind when you are compiling one, even if the kit is for that major tertiary public, journalists
+ may contain:
  - a media release
  - backgrounders, fact sheets, QnA sheets
  - a copy of the organisation's annual report and other relevant organisational publications
  - relevant photographs and other graphic images that support your topic
  - a copy of the speech the chief executive will make—and on which your media release is based
  - biographies of important people who are relevant to the news you are releasing
  - giveaways, if these are appropriate for the occasion—and at most times they are not
  - corporate information printed on the kit's folder
+ should display your contact details (landline, mobile number, email address, and website, as well as, just in case, your fax number), both on the media release and on the cover of the kit. Attaching your business card to the kit is a good way of doing this.

Media kits are highly visual and physical representations of your organisation, which is one reason many companies use high-quality graphics for this section of their online newsrooms and produce well-designed folders for their hard-copy kits. You must also publish accurate, thorough, credible and not too commercial information and you do not lie in the material you use to compile a media kit.

PRACTICE POINT

Publishing backgrounders, fact sheets, talking points, QnA sheets, photographs and a chronological set of media releases on your website means you can build a dynamic online 'newsroom' as a useful resource for journalists and other publics interested in your organisation and the industry in which it works.

Your online newsroom should be kept up to date, because the journalists on the round that covers your organisation will go to it regularly for information. Make it easy to find from the home page and for people to navigate. One of the best online newsrooms is managed by the Press Office at the Massachusetts Institute of Technology, a world-leading university. The newsroom is constantly updated, and the 'about the Spotlight' on the MIT home page is updated regularly as a way of promoting the university's research. Go to the home page at <**www.mit.edu**> and click on the 'MIT News Press Center' link (under 'news' on the home page) to see how its focus is on providing information for the mass news media, including news tips, and MIT's versions of the public relations tools discussed in this chapter. Note, too, how at the top of each page in this newsroom, MIT gives links to the social media applications it uses. Click on some of these links to see how they are used for public relations, not personal social, purposes. You find the same information published in the appropriate format for each social media application.

A THOUGHT ON THEORY: USING THE MEDIA TO RELAY MESSAGES

Ivy Lee was pretty clever when he recognised that he could help journalists with their daily tasks by writing news copy about his clients and distributing it in a timely way. These 'press releases' became the basic tool of our profession, and the technique was one of the reasons so many journalists became public relations people. James Grunig and his colleagues have, of course, argued that this most basic of public relations tools ('press agentry' in their four models of practice) is not always acceptable in a time when public relations is about building and maintaining relationships through ethical, two-way communication. Yet it is vital that practitioners use the mainstream news media (an uncontrolled communication pathway) as a way of relaying client messages to target publics. Media releases—whether distributed, for example, totally electronically via social media or some other use of the net or in hard copy as handouts at a news conference—remain basic public relations tools.

The reason for this is partly the continuing convenience and efficiency of distributing the same information rapidly to several journalists at once (back to Ivy Lee) in the hope that news stories will be written and published. This uncontrolled communication pathway has the potential to reach a lot of people. However, there is a risk that your news will be mediated by a reporter and by the rest of the news production cycle. That means there are no guarantees that your material will make it into the news media in the format you released it, or at all. Also clients often demand that you produce a media release about their product, event or views. In politics, media releases are distributed relentlessly, and they are often about nothing more than one politician trying to score a cheap political point. Check any political party leader's or minister's website to see how many releases one individual can publish in a single day.

So despite slightly raised eyebrows from Grunig and colleagues about this aspect of practice, there's little chance we'll stop writing and issuing media releases or using other tools to get our messages on a news website, on a popular blog, in the mainstream newspapers, on radio or in a television news program. That means it is useful to think a bit about why 'media' are so important to practitioners.

First, as we discussed in Chapter 1, it is important to be aware of what is happening in the world around us. In the 1920s the great practitioner Edward Bernays put this another way. He reckoned that as well as knowing something about how people form attitudes through their cultural and sociological backgrounds and experiences, practitioners ought to be aware of how people develop a view of the world as a result of the media they use. Bernays would no doubt be surprised at what 'the media' means in the modern era, but his point applies equally to television, websites, podcasts and all the other elements of the electronic and social media that did not exist in the 1920s. Bernays also argued that practitioners need to know something about how people process information because that knowledge would help them to decide on tools that had a better chance of working with specific target publics. That advice resonates a bit with the elaboration likelihood model discussed in Chapter 8.

A number of 'media effects' theories attempt to explain the impact that the mass media have on the way people view their world, and how messages are received by publics. The tip sheet 'How theories can inform practice' covers some of these as do various 'Thoughts on Theory' throughout this book.

It is possible to build broad profiles of target publics based on the media they use (Millennials as heavy social media users, for example) and from publicly available demographic data about who watches, listens to or reads television, radio, websites, blogs and newspapers. Once a practitioner has this information, a profile would be important for writing appropriate messages and developing strategies to deliver them. You could use research data on internet usage in your country to work out a profile of those who regularly surf for news and other information, to determine what sites they are most likely to use, and to plan strategies and messages accordingly. Similarly, the profile of people who read the financial media regularly is different from those who get their daily news from a popular music radio station.

> The 'two-step flow' theory explains how opinion leaders can be used to communicate messages: if someone influences the way in which others form their opinions, it would be useful to enlist them to your cause. The concept of 'uses and gratifications' attempts to explain the perhaps obvious point that people use different media for different purposes.

NEWSPAPER FEATURES

Newspapers do more than report the day's events. They have a unique role in reflecting the wide range of views that make up public discourses about social, environmental, political, sporting, technological and economic issues. They do this by providing time and space for expert commentators to offer opinions about the news and current or emerging issues. These commentaries cover, for example, what a rise or fall in the stock market would mean for the economy, why politicians have made certain decisions, the reason behind an increase in welfare payments, why environmental protection for a water catchment area is vital, or how and why professional sports bodies take a tough stand on performance-enhancing and recreational drug use. This kind of informed commentary is published in weekday editions of the major newspapers, and most of the major dailies also have special weekend 'review' sections that contain in-depth commentaries about the events of the week. The contents of some online and hard-copy publications, like *The Saturday Paper* in Australia, *The Spectator* and *New Statesman* magazines in Britain, and *The Atlantic* in the United States, are almost exclusively opinion and comment. Articles like these implement the concept of '5Ws and H' to explain what is behind the news.

In the daily newspapers, these 'feature' articles, or 'think pieces', are sometimes called 'op-ed' articles because they appear 'opposite the editorial page'—the page on which the newspaper publishes its editor's opinions (the editorial, or 'leader') and letters to the editor. Most are written by staff journalists who are either regular columnists or reporters specialising in areas like politics, sport, finance, foreign affairs and so on. Sometimes external experts and academics are invited to write these commentaries. Major Australian capital city newspapers regularly publish commentaries on developments in the Middle East written by Professor Amin Saikal of the Australian National University, who studies the politics of the region. Not all op-ed articles are about such serious subjects, but they all deal with the background to the news. It is possible to propose op-ed articles by, say, your CEO.

If you are asked to write an op-ed piece for someone in your organisation, research how the publication in which it will feature treats these articles, check their spelling styles (wagon or waggon?), and whether they accept creative material or stick with serious discussion.

PRACTICE POINT

Almost always, the definite article, *The*, is an official part of the name of a newspaper, as in *The South China Morning Post* or *The Guardian* or *The Washington Post*. It is, then, correct style to include *The* in the title of a newspaper when you refer to it.

SUMMARY

This chapter dealt with public relations tools that build the range of information sources available to practitioners. It looked at why and how practitioners write annual reports, brochures, backgrounders, fact sheets, question and answer sheets, feature articles and op-ed newspaper articles. After reading this chapter, you should:

+ recognise the breadth of material that public relations writers produce and how these tools can be adapted for publication in hard-copy and web-based formats
+ understand the need to adapt your writing style to different formats
+ appreciate how public relations tools work together to reinforce messages
+ recognise the importance of planning to ensure that public relations tools meet clearly defined objectives and can be delivered via appropriate communication pathways.

In the next chapter we'll look at ways in which organisations communicate with their employees and the role of public relations writing in that process.

REFLECTION

The underlying themes for all the material we've covered in this book so far have been the importance of planning and writing public relations tools that meet strategic *goals* and *objectives*, and the need for clear, concise and accurate writing. Those themes are based on the premise that no public relations activity should be pursued unless there is a reason for it. No client wants to spend money on an activity that does not have an *outcome*, even though at times in professional practice it will seem that you have just been asked to do something for the sake of it. Now might be the time for you to think back over the activities and practical tasks that you've completed as you've read the book. Is it possible for you to adapt some of the tools in this chapter, for example, to serve the strategic goals and objectives you wrote for Ima Chanteuse in Chapter 4 based on the research you did in Chapter 3? What communication pathways might be used for Ima that would help you choose one of the tools discussed in this chapter? Might it be better to promote Ima's new album using web-based tools? Think about how the topics discussed in each chapter link up to show how clear and concise writing helps to explain to your client first what your strategy aims to achieve and, second, how your tools deliver the client's messages.

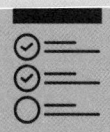

ACTIVITIES

1. Find Corporate Information on Websites

Visit gmsustainability.com/index.html to find out how one international car manufacturer uses its website to publish corporate information.

Companies understand the powerful role of their corporate websites in presenting the media with relevant information. They know that many journalists will search a website to confirm facts or gain background information before contacting the company. Grant Common advises that if your industry attracts a lot of media attention, your organisation's home page should have navigation buttons called 'Media' or 'News' and 'About Us' that, once clicked, include links to:

- 'Latest news'
- 'Press releases'
- 'Fast facts'
- 'Financial information'
- 'Executive biographies'
- 'Media kit'
- 'Image gallery'
- 'Contact' (meaning who to contact in your organisation for more information).

For an example of how this works, explore the home page menu links at <www.bhpbilliton.com>.

2. Write an Annual Report

To see how one company makes information available to target publics (customers and potential customers), go to <www.amp.com.au> and, in the 'Personal' view, click on the 'News and education' tab. Then click on 'News & insights' for examples of a range of public relations tools. Back on the home page, select the 'Business' view to see a similar approach for business target publics. Use the search function on the home page to find the company's latest annual report or shareholder review (no need to download them). Notice how these talk about serious matters in a formal but relaxed style. All information is written in a way that explains the company's performance in the last year, and its prospects for future years. The style changes when information is provided with the financial tables, but that is because of the special requirements of the companies legislation.

Assume that you are a member of the local tennis club and, because you work in public relations, you've been asked to help out with the annual report. The club has increased its membership from fifty to 250 in the past year, has $20 000 in the bank (up from $5000 last year) as a result of the increase in members and sponsorship of $15 000 from local businesses, and has won the A-, B- and C-grade competitions for men and women this year—for the first time in the club's 25-year history. The club's successful year means it can now look at buying new nets for the three courts, painting the clubhouse and buying a new gas barbecue for after-match refreshments. Using this background, write a one-page informative 'Chair's report' that would be the first section of the annual report to members.

3. On the Website

If you go to <www.hsbc.com.hk> and explore the 'Personal' section of the home page (click on 'Personal' at the top left hand side), you'll see electronic versions of information brochures and leaflets that will be available in hard copy in the bank's shopfronts.

4. Write a Backgrounder

It is interesting to visit online 'newsrooms' and to explore how different organisations present public relations tools. Delivering messages via tools published on websites has meant that public relations teams have greater flexibility in the way they present material. Visit <www.mit.edu> and <www.humanservices.gov.au> to see how these two organisations, one American and one Australian, present their news and information online. You'll need to use the site menus for this task.

Choose a topic that interests you. It might be about a sport that you play, an issue that you are concerned about or the organisation where you work. Research the topic to find out as much information as you can. Look for information that will help you to set the topic in a broader context, perhaps the details of the teams in your sport that play in international competitions. Adapt the media release planning worksheet in the toolkit to plan a two-page backgrounder.

Write a two-page backgrounder about your topic. Explain the topic, outline the history of the sport or issue, demonstrate any future implications, and write a summary. Use subheadings to break up the text.

5. A PR Tool in Web Format

At <www.un.org/en/faq/index.shtml> you can see how the United Nations uses a traditional public relations tool, a question and answer sheet, or frequently asked questions, in a web format.

6. Find Out about Op-ed

If you go to *The New York Times*' home page (<www.nytimes.com>), and click on the 'Opinion' link, you'll be taken to 'The Opinion Pages', where you'll find a specific reference to op-ed in the menu at the side of the page. Click on this link to find current and archived op-ed pieces.

It is possible for an expert from your organisation to contribute an op-ed piece on a relevant current issue. If an op-ed editor is aware that someone in your organisation is an expert on a particular subject that is in the news, that editor may invite them to contribute. At other times, you might take the initiative and phone or email the editor to propose that one of your experts contribute a feature article. That's called 'making a pitch'. If you do that, you need to ensure that your expert understands that the article needs to be written (in simple language!) and submitted by the newspaper's deadline—and mostly it will be needed within hours rather than days. Sometimes you will be asked to write the feature.

Some important rules apply to writing an op-ed or feature article for a newspaper:
- The editor will set a word limit. For the op-ed page, this may be about 800 words; for a weekend review piece, the length may be greater. It is important that you do not write more than the word limit you have been given.
- The topic must be current and about something that is in the news or about an important issue.
- Generally, write in the third person. Sometimes, especially when dealing with a topic that has a personal impact, it is possible to write in the first person.
- Research the topic and make sure when you use facts that you quote them accurately.
- Meet the deadline the editor has given you.

The main reason experts are invited to contribute op-ed articles is that editors are constantly looking for material that explains important news and events. That means that it is acceptable for your expert to express personal opinions that they have formed from their knowledge of the subject and their experience. Sometimes, especially on contentious subjects, editors use two or more experts with different views to discuss an issue.

Remember that you can also suggest your organisation's experts as interview guests for radio and television current affairs programs. This approach is akin to op-ed articles, because electronic news producers use interviews with experts to explain or comment on the news and current issues. The format is, of course, vastly different, though, and it is a public relations practitioner's role to make sure that the experts in their organisation have some training in electronic media interview techniques.

7. Compare Newspaper Editions

Read your capital city's major daily newspaper on a day during the working week and on the Saturday of the same week. Make a list of the articles published on the op-ed page on the weekday and compare this with the news reported elsewhere in the paper. How many op-ed articles comment on that day's news? How many comment on an issue that has been running earlier in the week?

Read the articles in the Saturday review section (*not* the lift-out, colour lifestyle magazine). Do the commentaries in the Saturday edition differ from your weekday edition (a) in length and (b) in the way they treat their topics? Using both editions, compare the authors' backgrounds (most articles end with a sentence that explains who the author is). How many appear to be staff journalists? How many are external experts or commentators?

When you read the news stories and the op-ed articles, compare the different writing styles. Does each in some way deal with the '5Ws and H'?

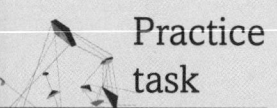

Practice task

Select a current issue in which you are interested. Perhaps there is a political debate in your state about increased car registration, or driver's licence fees or your local council has planned a new road across some parkland, or you would like an explanation of why young people run the risk of damaging their ears by having the volume on their smartphone earphones too high.

Research the topic you have chosen as widely as possible, then select one of the following two tasks (or both if you wish):

1. Assume you are the public relations officer for an organisation that has an interest in your issue. Write 300 words, with a main heading and subheadings, for a response sheet that your organisation will produce for its website newsroom to explain its position on the issue. Decide whether this will be an informative or persuasive leaflet before you start to write.
2. After your research, assume you are an expert on the issue and you have been invited by the editor of your capital city's daily newspaper to contribute an op-ed article expressing your opinion. Write 800 words to do this.

10 COMMUNICATION WITHIN ORGANISATIONS

It sounds almost like a cliché, but employees are an organisation's most important asset. Keeping employees informed about the business and, sometimes, social life of an organisation is an important task and one that is most often the responsibility of the public relations team. This chapter will discuss the principles of employee communication. In this chapter, you will:

+ be introduced to how communication pathways are used in employee communication
+ discover the public relations tools used to communicate with employees.

PRINCIPLES OF EMPLOYEE COMMUNICATION

People who work for organisations often know more about how their company, not-for-profit or government agency goes about its business than do senior managers. It is not hard to work out why: the staff must make management's policies and systems work. While the board of directors and senior management set directions, look after financial and corporate governance issues and find markets, it is the employees who make and sell the widgets, and interact with customers and other target publics.

When managers ask their staff for suggestions on how things might be done faster, better and perhaps cheaper, they'll get answers, because employees know how things work, and about the barriers that prevent them from doing their jobs more effectively. Richard Pascale and Jerry Sternin (2005), two US researchers who study management, have written about the role of 'innovators' in organisations, people who are not normally in the management hierarchy but whose approach to work enables them to find solutions to problems that others can't find. The researchers describe these people as 'secret change agents' and 'positive deviants', and suggest that most organisations have employees like this who should be asked for their views about how things are done, or could be changed. One chief executive of a major Australian government agency took this approach when he told senior managers to ask their staff how things ought to be changed in the organisation. The managers, the CEO said, would be surprised by the answers. They were, because the staff had valuable suggestions about how things could be improved.

> **PRACTICE POINT**
>
> Employee communication is the process by which management builds team spirit by disseminating information to employees about the organisation's goals and performance and by generating feedback.

Senior managers who make sure that their employees know the strategic directions of the organisation, and who keep them up to date on progress in achieving goals, are more likely to have a motivated staff. That means employees will be more productive and the organisation can operate at its most effective level.

In the 1980s, two American researchers, Tom Peters and Robert Waterman (1984, pp. 280–1), examined why some companies performed better than others. They found that the companies they described as 'excellent' were better at communicating with employees than were those who did not perform as well. They described these excellent companies as large networks of informal and open communication in which people at all levels were encouraged to talk about the company and how it was operating. Later, James Grunig and his colleagues examined the role of excellence in public relations management, including employee communication. Grunig (1992, p. 569) wrote that internal communication was the catalyst, even the key, to organisational excellence and effectiveness. Grunig noted that symmetrical internal communication could help employees to make sense of how they fit into the organisation, to understand its activities in the external environment and to be able to communicate with management about plans and policies. Another US academic, Deborah Barrett (2002), describes effective communication as 'the glue that holds an organisation together'.

KNOWING THE GAME PLAN

Lee Iacocca, the former chief executive of both Ford and Chrysler in the United States, put this message about communication with employees in a more direct way. Iacocca said the best way to motivate staff was to let them know the game plan so they could be a part of it.

Knowing the game plan means employees have the information they need to do their jobs, and helps to build and maintain high staff morale. It is even more important that employees understand the game plan when an organisation is changing, if the new directions are to be successfully implemented with the support of, rather than resistance from, staff.

> **A THOUGHT ON THEORY: COMMUNICATING WITH STAFF**
>
> Many academic experts in communication, management and psychology have written about effective communication with employees. Others have looked to theories associated

with the physical sciences—like complexity theory—to explain how communication inside organisations works. The specific role that internal communication can play in organisations when structural change is being planned has been a special focus of this research because of the need to ensure that employees know about, understand and accept new directions.

A common theme runs through the writings of these scholars: the importance of employee morale in organisational success. High staff morale means that companies operate successfully. Donald Alexander (2006), an Australian public relations academic and senior practitioner, wrote about the need for chief executives to be competent communicators in order to manage the myriad interests and publics, including employees, that impact on business goals. Alexander wrote that effective employee communication programs could result in higher staff morale and increased productivity. But what is 'morale'? Theodore Caplow, in his book *How to Run any Organisation* (cited in Dakin, 1989), describes morale as:

+ **satisfaction** with the organisation. Staff in a high-morale organisation accept its goals, obey its important rules, and choose to stay working in it
+ **commitment**, which means people are willing to contribute to organisational goals even if it may mean personal discomfort.

Various theoretical perspectives help us to understand how employees can be satisfied with their work and committed to their organisations.

First, the work of Frederick Herzberg (1987) highlights the factors that might generate workplace satisfaction among employees—the things that motivate them—and those that might make them dissatisfied (see Wood et al., 2004, pp. 148–53). Herzberg's 'two-factor theory' suggests that employees are motivated by factors like personal achievement at work, recognition, work itself, the responsibility they are given, and advancement in their jobs. Among work factors that dissatisfy them are the organisation's policies and administration, supervision, their relationships with supervisors, work conditions, and their relationship with subordinates. A highly motivated staff is also likely to have high morale. Two other theories suggest why that might be so.

David McClelland's acquired needs theory (discussed in Wood et al., 2004, pp. 146–8) can help to work out the needs that motivate an individual's behaviour. This theory suggests that, at work, individuals have three basic needs: for affiliation, for achievement and for power. That suggests that employees who have a high level of affiliation with an organisation, and the ability to achieve personal work goals, are likely to have high morale. Victor Vroom's expectancy theory (also discussed in Wood et al., 2004, pp. 156–60) suggests that a person's behaviour is influenced by their cognitive processes. Vroom proposes that people calculate the benefits of behaving in certain ways, or do what they can when they want to. People place a value, or 'valence', on work outcomes after they assess the effort, or 'expectancy', involved in performing a task and the probability that performing that task, or 'instrumentality', will lead to a rewarding outcome. That suggests that employees in an organisation with high morale are likely to see a positive valence in the jobs they do because they are satisfied with their workplace and committed to the organisation.

Most employees prefer to hear news about their organisation directly from their immediate supervisor via interpersonal means as part of continuing communication action. This would be an interpersonal communication pathway, implemented with public relations tools that enable supervisors to talk directly with their teams and receive feedback about what is happening or is proposed. This approach reflects Grunig's two-way symmetrical model and helps to build honest, open and trusting relationships between management and employees (Jo & Shim, 2005).

Most organisations have sections of their websites set up for the exclusive use of their staff (see below). These sections facilitate staff access to information about the organisation's goals, structure, governance and policies. They include information about safety at work, rights and responsibilities, and individuals' pay. These sections publish news and alerts that are in addition to all-staff emails.

PREPARING AN EMPLOYEE COMMUNICATION PLAN

The public relations team is usually responsible for an organisation's employee communication plan, often working closely with personnel staff, but always with senior management. The plan will be linked to the current public relations strategic plan.

Writing an employee communication plan in this way involves using the same disciplined approach that an organisation would apply to financial planning and operational requirements. Some organisations do not do this, especially in times of change, when effective employee communication is vital (Barrett, 2002; Ströh, 2006). Yet, because employee communication informs employees about corporate goals and strategies, builds a sense of connection with the organisation and leads to better teamwork, it has a direct impact on the organisation's decision-making (Jagoe, 1987, cited in Corbett, 1989, p. 193).

Apart from formal communication through email and face-to-face meetings, employee communication also often includes:

+ the internal website, which provides information that employees need to do their jobs, helps them find out about pay and conditions, provides access to the staff telephone directory and email addresses, and can be used to deliver news and podcasts about important matters
+ the staff newsletter in electronic or hard-copy format—or both

- occasional publications produced for a specific purpose. Some organisations, for example, publish an abridged version of the annual report for staff. Often there is a need for the public relations team to produce material that advises employees of new workplace safety requirements, or about changes to the superannuation scheme, or that gives people some new company information
- award schemes that recognise long service to the organisation, outstanding work performance, service to the local community, or sporting achievements
- mechanisms that enable staff to make suggestions and provide feedback
- functions that celebrate success, or that are held to present awards or to enable the chief executive to address the entire staff
- competitions, including (if the organisation is big enough) sporting competitions
- social events like the annual Christmas party.

> **PRACTICE NOTE** ELEMENTS OF AN EMPLOYEE COMMUNICATION PROGRAM
>
> An employee communication plan should be written with the same professional approach that practitioners use in strategic public relations planning. The nature of employee communication, of course, means that there is only one target 'public'—employees—although for some pathways and tools it might be useful to identify specific groups of employees. For example, communicating with shift workers in different operational locations might require public relations tools that may not be necessary for people in head office. It would be a good idea to think this through before deciding that, for example, only the company's internal website will be used to provide information to employees.
>
> The plan will include:
>
> - *a situation analysis*. This sets out the research on which the plan is based, and the rationale for the activities that are proposed
> - *goals*. It is likely that at least one broad goal will address the need to keep staff informed about the organisation's business goals, and that another will deal with building a motivated and committed staff
> - *objectives*. What needs to be done to meet the goals, and in what time frame?
> - *target public*. Should the public be defined more broadly than 'employees'? Is it necessary to use separate communication pathways and tools for the board of directors, senior managers, production staff, maintenance teams, and company sales representatives?
> - *messages*. What are the specific messages? Should they be informative or persuasive? Do they reflect the messages in the strategic plan? Is there a need to write new messages for a specific purpose? This would be especially appropriate at a time of organisational change, when management seeks employee support for the new directions

- *communication pathways*. How will messages be delivered? Are interpersonal and controlled media pathways appropriate? Should an uncontrolled media pathway be used to reinforce messages to employees? That is, would it be a good idea to include messages to staff in a release to local media in the town where the widget production factory is located?
- *Tools*. These implement the communication pathways to achieve goals and objectives. Is a staff newsletter on the internal website sufficient? Should there be a hard-copy staff newsletter? When should an all-staff email be used? Does everyone on the Ideal Widgets' payroll have a staff email address? Would it be best to set up face-to-face meetings with groups of staff to give them important news?
- *implementation*. Is there a budget? Is there a timeline that shows when the staff newsletter will be published? or when face-to-face meetings will be held? or when an all-staff email message will be distributed? When will the Christmas party be held—and how long will it take to plan? Don't forget to book Santa for the kids!
- *evaluation*. How will success be measured? If the plan didn't work, how will that be assessed?

Staff newsletters

One of the most efficient ways of distributing information to employees is through a staff newsletter. Staff newsletters are like internal newspapers, even though they are almost always published in an online format or via email. They report news about the organisation, and about the achievements of individual employees or work teams; provide information about a new manufacturing plan; publish a regular column from the chief executive; and promote and cover social and other events and how company sporting teams have performed.

It is usually the public relations team's role to research, write, edit and publish staff newsletters. In most public relations teams, one staff member has the specific responsibility of editing the newsletter, but other members of the team write articles for it.

Traditionally staff newsletters were published in a hard-copy format. Electronic publishing has meant staff newsletters can appear on the internal website or that they can be emailed directly to each staff member. An electronic staff 'newsletter' can work like an online newsroom, providing up-to-date news and information in addition to links that help people find, for example, information about their pay, internal phone numbers, policies, and maps of the production facilities.

PRACTICE POINT

Writing and editing a staff newsletter can be a delicate task, irrespective of the online or hard copy format in which it will be published. That is because employees sometimes regard the newsletter as the mouthpiece of management. It is not unreasonable for

> management, which funds the newsletter, to want to publish its views on matters it believes staff should know about. Rarely are staff newsletter editors given free rein to report the organisation in the way the mainstream media report the daily news. The fortnightly newspaper of one Australian university, which was distributed to staff and students, the mainstream media and the wider community, had a tradition of reporting criticisms of management along with positive news about research and teaching. The vice-chancellor's only instruction to the editor was that if a criticism of management or university policy was to be published, he wanted the right to reply as soon as possible, preferably in the same edition. One of the early staff newsletters produced in Australia, by CSR Ltd, was highly respected by employees because it published letters from them that criticised management.
>
> While many organisations may not allow that kind of editorial freedom, most recognise the need for staff to value the newsletter as a way of disseminating important and factual information. After all, a staff newsletter that is not read doesn't help to build an informed, motivated staff.

The decision to produce a staff newsletter at all, and whether it should be published in an electronic or hard-copy format, depends on the size and goals of the organisation. For example, a small business that employs only four staff at one location wouldn't need a staff newsletter when the proprietor can talk individually to each staff member. On the other hand, a large employer like Qantas (which has more than 30 000 staff) needs a cost-effective way of regularly reaching its workforce, many of whom are frequently overseas or travelling throughout Australia.

An electronic staff newsletter has major advantages:

+ It is a flexible format. Content can be quickly updated, or replaced, and there is no need to distribute the whole publication to individual staff—an email alerting them to the new edition is sufficient.
+ It is cheaper and less time consuming than hard-copy publishing, for which printing and distribution time and mechanisms must be planned.
+ Information can be linked to other electronic documents, enhancing the usefulness of the information being disseminated. For example, a brief news story reporting the chief executive's speech to a business group can be hyperlinked to the full text of the speech. Similarly, in an organisation undergoing structural change, stories about what is planned can include hyperlinks to more detailed documents.
+ People can print out a hard copy if they prefer to read a newsletter that way.

Meetings with employees

Employees mostly prefer face-to-face meetings with supervisors over all other forms of communication. Staff meetings can be expensive in terms of the time involved and potential loss of productivity but they mean people can hear first-hand about what is proposed, or has just happened, or how things will change, and they can ask questions and give feedback. Staff meetings are a good example of a *tool* to implement an *interpersonal communication* pathway.

Special staff meetings to discuss a particular topic, like a new process for packaging widgets at the factory, can take time to organise (requiring you to find a venue and let people know the day and time, and how long it will take, for example), and they do take people away from actual work. Nevertheless, these meetings are effective and they give real meaning to the term *communication*.

The public relations staff, too, will have regular staff meetings to discuss the work program and other matters. Sometimes, the senior practitioner will bring people together to brainstorm how the team might develop and manage a new public relations project, or improve the existing employee communication program. These meetings provide everyone with an opportunity to contribute their ideas and specialist skills.

PRACTICE POINT

One American researcher, Angela Sinickas (2006), studied ten organisations to find out employees' top two sources of information about a range of business matters. The researcher found that the preferences of sales, manufacturing, management, and research and development staff for receiving information on different organisational topics varied. On topics like organisational strategy, financial results and competitive issues, publications were the best method of delivering information to all employees, backed up by the intranet. Meetings were the best way of delivering information about business unit goals. Sales staff preferred to hear about the organisation's financial results in large group meetings; professional staff preferred to hear information from people in high levels of management rather than from their direct supervisors.

These findings led the researcher to suggest that communication tools used in internal communication programs might be tailored to cater for the preferences of work groups for receiving information about the organisation. That is, organisations might use the internet for some people, mass meetings for others, and publications for yet other groups—and tailor these again for specific issues.

A good task for a public relations team in any organisation would be to do some internal research to find out how the different sub-groups of employees in the organisation prefer to receive information. It may be that staff forums and web-based applications are preferred by workers especially when opportunities for feedback are offered.

The staff website is a wonderful communication tool for delivering visual material to people—perhaps a YouTube recording of the CEO's latest staff forum, or a special interview with the head of Human Resources when there are changes to enterprise bargaining agreements.

Email

Providing information to staff via an email message is an effective and efficient way of keeping people up to date about the organisation. Regular (perhaps weekly or monthly) emails from the CEO or section managers, for example, also contribute to building effective communication in an organisation, especially if there is an opportunity to reply with feedback. Sometimes email messages like this work as a staff newsletter. If you recommend an 'all-staff email' as a tool for an interpersonal communication pathway, make sure that you don't just add to what is sometimes an almost never-ending flow of email to people. Write email messages that are concise and to the point.

> **PRACTICE NOTE** AWARD-WINNING EMPLOYEE COMMUNICATION PROGRAM
>
> When IBM introduced a new staff intranet for Australia and New Zealand to improve employee communication, it won a Public Relations Institute of Australia Golden Target Award for its employee communication strategy for the relaunch. What follows are elements of the strategy used for the relaunch, taken from the award-winning entry.
>
> **Situation analysis**
>
> IBM's employee communication strategy is strongly focused towards supporting managers to communicate directly with their employees and teams via face-to-face and two-way communication.
>
> With approximately 12 000 employees throughout IBM A/NZ, a culture of transformation and change, and an increasingly mobile and virtual workforce, manager communication has not always been practical. The Intranet, however, provided employees with a central source of current information and workplace tools, regardless of their location or time zone.
>
> IBM's research also revealed that employees said they received too many mass emails that were not always relevant and this was impacting productivity and even employee morale.
>
> The existing Intranet had grown substantially in the two years since it was launched and was difficult to navigate. For the Intranet to be a key communication tool it was important to direct employees to a site where information was easy to find—a challenge given there are some 4000 IBM Intranets and over four million IBM Intranet pages worldwide.
>
> Employees needed to be able to access and use the new tools, but this was difficult with the 'old' Intranet. With the relaunched Intranet the tools below are now integrated and part of daily work-life in IBM:
>
> - Virtual teaming via instant messaging (Sametime)
> - Accessing knowledge experts via employee directory profiles (BluePages/Persona profiles)
> - Online meetings and training (eMeetings and eLearning)

- Discussion forums (Jams)
- Video messaging (Jukebox)
- Online human resources functions (eHR and 'Index of How'), and more.

Many employees work outside a traditional office. A communication medium that allowed people to share experiences and stories and build a sense of community was essential.

Key to our Intranet strategy was that no matter what an employee's role in the company, they need only go to one domain to easily source any information needed, be it customer data, company and employee news or tools and training material to help them be more effective at work.

Goals and objectives

The goal of the A/NZ Intranet is to be a trusted source of relevant, timely, easy to access information, allowing employees to do their jobs better, while creating an open and informed employee climate.

The aim of the relaunched Intranet site was to enhance employee productivity, effectiveness and morale by:

- Reducing the number of 'all employee' email memos
- Addressing employee concern that it was hard to find information, because of the complexity of the organisation
- Equipping employees with tools to help them do their jobs
- Tapping into the company's collective knowledge
- Building a greater sense of community through sharing employee profiles, stories and experiences.

Once the site was redeveloped, an extensive employee communications campaign was undertaken. The goal was to ensure all employees in IBM A/NZ were aware of, and used the A/NZ Intranet as their primary workplace tool.

Research

The following research was used to plan the redevelopment and relaunch campaign:

- Review of Intranet versus email usage
- Employee surveys to identify concerns and issues
- Manager surveys to identify concerns and issues
- Intranet feedback mechanism
- Executive feedback and direction
- Employee Communications team brainstorming
- Usability testing
- Intranet Champions focus groups
- External studies and best practice examples
- IBM global/corporate direction i.e. communication strategies, web, Intranet and the 'On Demand Workplace'.

The research underpinned the redevelopment program and provided the basis for the development of key messages and communications initiatives in the relaunch campaign.

Target publics

- **IBM employees** in A/NZ (including all sales and support staff and NZ staff): For the Intranet to become an important and trusted source of information, all audiences had to be catered for. Caution had to be exercised to ensure the site wasn't too 'Australian-centric', but was inclusive of New Zealand and regional employees.
- **IBM managers**: First line managers are essential in ensuring information is communicated to employees. The Intranet had to support managers in their role as communicators.
- **IBM Executive Team and General Managers (GMs)**: GMs regularly send out cross-team emails aimed at boosting performance, communicating their own strategy messages etc. We needed to demonstrate the effectiveness of the Intranet as the preferred communication tool for their communication.
- **Technology Deployment Office**: This team was instrumental in ensuring that the technology supported the site redevelopment.
- **Philip Bullock, Country General Manager IBM Australia & New Zealand**: The Country GM's support was needed to provide a mandate for transitioning communications from email memos to Intranet headlines.
- **Employee Communications Manager and team**: As the main recipients for communication requests, this team had to be proponents of the Intranet as the primary communication channel.
- **Regional and IBM Corporate stakeholders**: The ANZ Intranet needed to comply with corporate guidelines and have buy-in from our regional and worldwide communication and Intranet teams.

Strategy

To achieve the goal—that the Intranet is a trusted source of relevant, timely, easy to access information, allowing employees to better perform their jobs while creating an open and informed employee climate—key messages were linked to the issues that had been identified during the early research phase.

The strategy also aimed to change employee behaviour from being 'spoon fed' communications via email to self-selecting information online.

Key messages

The improved Intranet:

- makes it even easier to find everything you need to do your job
- saves you time with the new navigation icon and 4 main information quadrants
- integrates all your workplace tools and information accessed via one URL
- assists you to become an open and informed employee
- is your one-stop shop, your window or portal to all other information online
- is the new era, the latest technology.

Published with the permission of the Public Relations Institute of Australia

EMPLOYEE COMMUNICATION DURING CHANGE

The Russian-born American science fiction writer Isaac Asimov's comment that the only constant in our lives 'is change, continuing change, inevitable change' is often quoted as a way of explaining, perhaps cynically, why the world, including our workplaces, always seems to be in turmoil.

Change—maybe inevitable, but not always continuing—is a significant aspect of our working lives. That is because managers are always trying to find ways to reduce the costs of producing their widgets and to make more of them by using new processes or new technologies that don't need as many people. The result is that the way an organisation's workforce is set up might change ('restructured' is the common term) to reflect the new way of doing things, because fewer people, or staff with different skills, are needed. Examples of this are often reported in the news media, especially when staff are made redundant.

> **PRACTICE POINT**
>
> It is vital during organisational change that employees know what is planned before the media are told. Consider why: how would you feel if you turned on the television news and heard that staff in your workplace were to be retrenched but you had not been told this by your managers? That is why announcements about things that affect employees should be made to staff before they are released outside the organisation.

Facilitating communication with staff when changes need to be made to the way they do things, and the way they are organised to do them, is a critical role of the public relations team, who usually write the special tools used to communicate change directions and what they mean to employees. Often, these are versions, or 'special editions', of existing communication tools; sometimes, they are new. For example, IBM used the intranet (described in the practice note above) as a communication tool for disseminating information to employees in Australia and New Zealand about organisational change. Some organisations create a special intranet site for their change program, or produce a special, regular newsletter to provide information about what is proposed, why it will happen and how staff will be consulted about the proposed changes.

Most of the time, change directions are set by the dominant coalition, and staff are consulted about what is proposed. Scholars have studied how this process works and the role of communication in the success, or otherwise, of organisational restructures. Some have found that often employees resist change because the organisation does not have a good communication program to help explain what is proposed and what it means to individuals. Others argue that continuing, effective two-way communication would help senior managers to identify, and help to resolve, employee concerns about proposals for change. Barrett (2002) argued that internal communication programs should be integrated into an organisation's overall strategy because this helps to implement change.

This reinforces the point that, like any other aspect of public relations, communication with staff during change should be simple, clear, open and consistent. This is especially important during an organisational restructure because people can be stressed about losing their jobs, about the new ways in which they will have to do their work, about losing work colleagues, or about being in a new team doing different jobs.

Report writing

Report writing sounds boring when all you want to do is get on with your creative campaign to convince young people to stop smoking. Yet we all end up writing reports about what we plan to do, how we are going with Project X, why we recommend a new strategy, what transpired in a phone conversation, or our response to the latest memo from the boss. That's part of professional business life.

Organisations have their own requirements for how reports should be written. These 'house styles' describe the way in which letters and memos should be set out, how the logo should be used on the cover of internal and external documents, the typefaces and point sizes that should be used, and the headings that need to be covered when you are writing a submission for more money or to brief the board of directors on an important issue. These styles are usually embedded in electronic templates, especially for letter and memo formats, that you can download from the staff website. Public relations consultancies have house styles for documents that respond to clients' briefs, for pitching for new business, for reporting campaign progress to clients and for recording conversations with clients or other contacts, such as journalists.

While we need to know about these process requirements to do our jobs properly, our task is to write for outcomes. That means that people who read our reports must be able to understand them if they are to take the actions we seek. For example, a submission to your boss for more money in next year's budget needs to clearly outline the reasons why you are seeking the increase, why it is important and what it is that you actually want. That requires clear, concise and persuasive language. The same principle applies to writing a report that summarises how you've implemented your new campaign after it has been running for a month. The boss will know if you are waffling, or dodging the real issue, and may reject your request if they can't understand what you have written.

The principles apply whether your report will be distributed electronically or in hard-copy format, or posted to the intranet.

Email has become the dominant medium for written communication. However, there are still times when formal hard-copy communication is necessary for internal purposes as well as for external publics. Let's look at some of those internal communication tools.

Writing a memo

memo (short for memorandum): a short written note about a specific point, usually for internal purposes.

A **memo** (*memorandum* is the unabbreviated formal noun) is a note or a record used especially in business and government to advise people about something. Memos are not usually as long as letters; nor are they generally treated as formally as letters, because they are usually internal communication tools.

Most organisations have templates for writing memos and letters. The stationery for memos usually has the word *Memorandum* (or, if the organisation takes a more relaxed approach, *Memo*) printed on it—or a space where you can type it near the top. The Australian businessman Dick Smith has an even more friendly approach: his memos are headed 'From the desk of Dick Smith'.

The format of a memo is as follows:

> **MEMO**
>
> **To:** [name of the chief executive]
>
> **From:** [name of the manager, Public Relations]
>
> **Date:** 24 February 2020
>
> **Subject:** Issue with production safety mechanisms

These headings are followed by the text of what the manager has to tell the chief executive. There is no need to end a memo with 'Yours sincerely', but it should be signed.

Writing a file note

It is good practice to record important meetings, conversations, information and events in the appropriate file. This usually is done via a '**file note**' written as soon as possible after the conversation or event, or after the information is received. For example, if you have a tense conversation with a client, it would be a good idea to record what you both said 'for the file' so that you can refer to it later. Some people write file notes after they meet someone for the first time and make similar notes after subsequent conversations. This is a convenient way of keeping track of issues that are discussed. If you build an electronic database of your organisation's news media contacts, a 'field' to record topics individual journalists enquire about each time they phone is useful. File notes are a standard way of recording information in the public service, because a series of file notes about a particular subject, along with reports, letters and other documents, builds a more complete record to be used by others. After a successful award ceremony to recognise high-achieving employees, you might write a file note so that the things that worked really well, and those that weren't quite as successful, are recorded to help those planning next year's event. Make sure that you date the file note.

Of course, it is not necessary to physically put the note in a hard-copy file unless that is a policy requirement of the organisation's auditors, or of archive legislation as is the case for most government agencies. Most organisations 'file' electronically using sophisticated electronic systems that manage storage and retrieval of information. It is important, however, to know where you filed the note on your computer's system—perhaps by setting up a 'File notes' folder.

file note: a written record of a conversation, an event or a meeting that is filed for future reference.

Writing a submission

Often you'll need to write a **submission** seeking approval to spend money or to introduce a new strategic public relations plan, or recommending how a particular issue should be addressed. Organisations have guidelines for writing submissions to the board of directors or the chief executive

submission: a detailed written argument supporting the organisation's views on an issue or proposal, usually for an external inquiry. Sometimes, submissions are required internally to support an application for a budget increase or other resources, or to seek approval for a proposed course of action.

or a senior manager. Most require people to provide information under some broad headings. The most common headings are:

- *Issue.* State the issue the submission addresses—for example, problems with the safety mechanisms in the factory
- *Background.* Provide the background to the issue. For example, what precisely is the problem? How long has it been a problem? Is it an industry-wide problem? How have other organisations solved the problem? Is there a solution? Is one likely? When? Use subheadings if appropriate
- *Discussion.* Use this section to discuss the possible solutions to the problem, or ways to address the issue. Give the arguments for and against a possible course of action. End the section with a summary of the arguments, and suggest a possible recommendation. Discuss the budget and other resource implications of the possible solutions to the problem, and suggest timelines. Summarise any information that might be provided in attachments so that the reader can access more detail. Use subheadings if appropriate
- *Recommendation.* Succinctly state your recommendation for action—for example, that Ideal Widgets replace production safety mechanisms with the advanced technology provided by Gee Whiz Solutions at a cost of $500 000.

Submissions do not need to be long. Most can be written in clear, concise prose in no more than two pages, summarising the main points. Detailed technical or financial information, research findings, reports and other documents on which the submission is based should be attached—or hyperlinked in electronic submissions. It is up to the reader to work through these (most will), but you should make reference to important points in the text of the submission—for example, 'See page 15 of attachment B for details'.

SUMMARY

This chapter looked at the important role of internal, or employee, communication in organisations and the communication tools that a public relations team can use to make this successful. The chapter has stressed the similarities between strategic public relations planning and writing and the principles used for employee communication. You should now have an understanding of:

+ how communication pathways are used in employee communication
+ the tools used to communicate with employees
+ how to approach internal report writing.

This chapter has brought us to the point where we need to consider the production aspects of public relations, and how to evaluate what we have implemented. The next two chapters deal with these topics.

REFLECTION

When reflecting on what you have read in this chapter, try to make links with the other aspects of public relations writing we've looked at so far. Ask questions such as:

+ How should an employee communication program be linked to the strategic public relations plan?
+ Why might that be important to the organisation?
+ Could you write a strategic goal for an employee communication plan that reflects the goals of the strategic plan?
+ Would you plan similar pathways and communication tools for external publics and employees? Why?
+ Could you think of a time when employees might be a primary public in a program that has been written for external publics?

Think about why organisations write strategic public relations plans, what they are trying to achieve, and how they plan to go about it. For the strategic plan to be successful, who are the important people they need to inform or persuade? What role do employees play in that? Reflect on how public relations tools need to be tailored to the way in which people prefer to receive information, and how employee communication needs similar decision making.

ACTIVITIES

1. Working with the New Managing Director

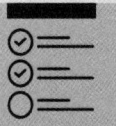

You are the Public Relations Director for Black Rubber Tyres, a major manufacturer of tyres for cars, motorcycles, trucks, buses and bicycles. The new Managing Director, Alison Sydewall, has just taken up her job and has decided that she wants to improve communication with all employees. Black Rubber Tyres has 300 employees at its factory. You have decided that an effective way of improving communication with employees (Black Rubber Tyres already has a staff newsletter that is published on the internal website once a fortnight) would be for Alison to meet the staff once every three months. You believe that about a hundred staff members should attend each meeting. Alison will use the meetings to tell employees about company developments and to answer questions on any topic they want to raise.

1. Write a memo to Alison of no more than 200 words, giving your reasons for recommending meetings with the staff.
2. Speeches can be used to inform, to persuade and to entertain. Alison has asked you to advise her about the approach she should take in the five-minute speech she wants to give at each of the meetings. Decide whether the five-minute speech should be to inform, to persuade or to entertain. Explain in *no more than fifty words* why you think the approach you recommend would be appropriate for the staff of Black Rubber Tyres.
3. What advice would you give Alison about reporting the meetings in the staff newsletter?

2. Write the Outline for a Staff Website

Assume you work in the public relations team of Raindrop, a company that produces garden tools, water hoses, tap fittings, sprinklers and in-ground watering systems. The company has 500 employees in Hong Kong, and 250 in Cape Town, South Africa, where it manufactures these products for export markets in South-East Asia, Australia, New Zealand, South Africa and North America. During a long drought in Australia, sales in Australia, traditionally strong, fell to only 10 per cent of the company's business. Now that the Australian drought has ended, and sales are recovering, Raindrop faces a new challenge: a severe drought in North America. Raindrop's board of directors does not believe that the recovering Australian market will cover the decline in sales in North America for five years. Consequently, the board has decided to retrench 150 staff in Hong Kong and twenty-five in Cape Town as part of an organisational restructure, so that the business can reduce its costs.

You've been tasked with preparing a special page on the company's staff website that will be used as the primary tool for communication with staff during the restructure. You'll be using a web designer to do all the technical and graphic work, but your job is to recommend the public relations tools to be included on the site to make sure that communication with employees is open and transparent.

Write a list of your ideas about the communication tools that should be included on the intranet site. For each communication tool, write a one-sentence explanation of why you think it should be on the page.

3. Write a Memo

You are still in the PR team at Raindrop and you've finished your previous task. Now your manager wants the report you've written setting out your ideas for the intranet site. The manager wants this to be done formally, so you have to write a memo to accompany your report.

Using the format set out earlier in the chapter, write a half-page memo to the Manager, Public Relations, submitting your report and its recommendations for her approval. Remember, this is like a covering letter, so you might want to briefly summarise the main arguments you have made in the report.

Practice task

You are still in the public relations team at Raindrop. Your recommendations on the special staff website for the company's restructure have been accepted, and now you've got to write some material to publish on it. Your boss wants a news story for the site announcing that Raindrop will retrench 150 staff from its Hong Kong workforce and another fifty in Cape Town. The boss has also asked you to write the media release announcing the retrenchments. You've been told to quote Raindrop's Managing Director, Alyse Maxwell, in the intranet story and in the media release. These two tasks have illustrated for you how external and internal public relations activities are often linked.

For this practice task, use:

1. the project checklist in the Public Relations Toolkit to plan how and when news of the retrenchments should be given to Raindrop's staff and released to the media. Consider how you would use public relations tools that implement interpersonal, controlled and uncontrolled communication pathways

2. the planning worksheet in the toolkit to set out the main points you need to include in a media release about the retrenchments. Use the information about Raindrop, and why it needs to retrench staff, set out in the activities earlier in this chapter. Research the impact of the drought on water restrictions for private homes in North America to back up your main points. Write the first three paragraphs of your media release
3. the media release planning worksheet to plan an item for your special intranet site. Write a 200-word item for the intranet site advising Raindrop's employees about the retrenchments.

GETTING THE JOB DONE

11

In this chapter you'll look at how practitioners work with other specialists to implement public relations projects. The chapter deals with basic project-management concepts, production principles and the importance of briefing other specialists on the tasks required. You should use the checklists and other material in the Public Relations Toolkit as you work through this chapter. After reading the chapter, students should understand the importance of:

+ project management
+ building their knowledge of production processes
+ writing a brief for contractors.

FLYING BY THE SEAT OF YOUR PANTS

Whenever people do something without planning their actions, or without adequate background knowledge, others say they are 'flying by the seat of their pants'. This phrase, which originated in the late 1930s, described pilots who at that time flew aircraft without using instruments or radios. In 2005, *The Sydney Morning Herald* published a series of letters to the editor about the phrase. One letter writer, Harry Rowlands, explained the term this way: 'Before aircraft had instruments, pilots had to rely on their innate sense of balance to detect changes in movements of the plane, transferred to [a pilot's] body by the contact with the seat'. In public relations, though, there is no need to fly by the seat of our pants when we implement a project; there are instruments we can use to help deliver outcomes on time and within budget. Those instruments help practitioners to plan the steps and time needed to write, design, produce and distribute the public relations tools identified in the strategic plan, to schedule an evaluation and to prepare a budget. They help in this process regardless of whether the project is delivered totally online or via traditional tools like displays, hard-copy brochures and staged events. That's because these instruments provide mechanisms for detailed planning of the steps needed to deliver a project—from brainstorming ideas through to delivery.

PROJECT MANAGEMENT

Public relations practitioners have to manage the planning and implementation of a project even if they are the only person involved. A practitioner not only contributes ideas and writes the tools that will be used, but also coordinates the efforts of the other team members and specialists working on the project. Sometimes a practitioner is part of a team; sometimes they lead the team. In both roles they must have a detailed knowledge of what needs to be done in their own job as well as what the team needs to do. A project to redesign the organisation's internet site probably includes a web designer and some technical people as well as other people in the organisation who will contribute ideas and material for the site. The practitioner coordinating the project needs to know how long each person will take to complete their part of the project and the sequence in which their output is needed before others can be involved—or which parts of the project can be written or designed at the same time as others. The project team will meet regularly to discuss progress and the next steps, and to sort out any problems. The implementation section of a strategic plan sets out the timelines for implementing and evaluating the project and the budget needed to make it happen. The crucial point is that the exciting and creative parts of a project—like a launch event, a redesigned website, running a Twitter feed or posting to the organisation's Facebook page—don't happen without detailed planning that defines why, when and how all this will be done. A creative idea for the launch of a new range of make-up won't happen unless someone has specified all the steps needed to plan it, and identified the funds needed to pay for it. You couldn't launch the make-up by flying by the seat of your pants.

PRACTICE POINT

Practitioners do not need to know how to do everything involved in a project. For example, they don't have to be web designers to manage a project to relaunch the organisation's revised website, but they do need to understand that other professionals have specialist knowledge and skills that can help. It is useful for them to have a basic knowledge of production processes so that they understand what designers, printers (yes, they are still needed), audio-visual producers, photographers and other specialists are talking about. That is the main reason most public relations offices have some version of a style manual in their professional libraries. These usually include the office's preferred English usage style, and sometimes information about design and production, typography, the use of photographs and web design. Other official (usually government) publications provide practical guidance, like orders of precedence for officials at functions and how to address people formally in correspondence or when introducing them at functions.

When in doubt about something, ask. For example, the printer you have contracted for your project will tell you how long it will take to print your 24-page, full-colour

> brochure, and the person constructing your display can tell you not only how long it will take to build, but why it will take that long, and the web designer can tell you why the totally redesigned site can't be launched a week after you brief them. As you become more experienced, you'll build your knowledge of these practical aspects of public relations, but as a beginning practitioner you'll need to read and ask questions.

Using timelines

A primary project-management task is preparing a realistic time frame in which your campaign can be planned and implemented. To write the timeline, you'll need to know how long it will take to:

+ complete any formative research that still needs to be done
+ design and produce each of the public relations tools
+ edit and publish material on the website
+ approve drafts, final copy, artwork and budgets
+ actually print materials
+ deliver material to distribution points, or to a mailing house
+ prepare for a launch event or a media conference
+ set up equipment at an event
+ evaluate the project.

Most of the time, senior managers will approve material quickly, but you need to make sure that you schedule approval steps in plenty of time to meet production deadlines and to suit the manager's own work schedule. For example, it would not be much use scheduling a particular day for a manager to approve the text of a proposed shopping centre display if that person was going to be on an overseas trip on that day. Forgetting to check the manager's schedule for an appropriate time would mean that your project could be delayed.

To prepare a timeline, write down all the steps involved in your project. Rearrange them in approximate date order, from the things that need to be done first through to the last items. For example, don't schedule the delivery of refreshments for the day after your launch. Work out how long each step will take. Identify which steps rely on others finishing their part first and how long it will take them to complete their tasks. If you are planning a launch, one of the first things you could do is to identify and book a venue that is available on the date of the event.

A Gantt chart (there's a template, and an explanation, in the Public Relations Toolkit at the start of this book) is one way of visually displaying each of the steps involved in your implementation plan. If you use a chart like that, you can see at a glance how all the steps in the implementation plan interrelate, and identify those that need to be done before others are started. You may prefer to set up a table in a word-processing document, or use a spreadsheet, for your implementation plan. A project checklist is another approach (again, there's an example and an explanation in the toolkit).

> ### PRACTICE POINT
>
> Here's a tip: not all steps in a planning process happen sequentially. That is, many steps don't need to wait until another one is completed. Often, some steps can be started while others are still under way. For example, for the launch of the new make-up mentioned previously, booking the venue and ordering any catering doesn't need to wait until the information brochure and website material have been produced or the CEO's launch speech has been written. If you use a Gantt chart, you can see how the various steps involved in planning your project overlap. When steps do need to be sequential and one part of the process absolutely depends on the completion of another, computer software can automatically plot a 'critical path' for your project. The software will re-plot the critical path if any of the due dates change. If you use your search engine's 'images' function, you'll find some examples of what a critical path looks like.

The important thing to remember is that a project manager needs to identify all the steps involved, the time it takes to do them, which tasks need to be done first, and who is responsible for doing them. Once you have this information, you will be able to manage the project to make sure you meet all the deadlines and implement the project on time.

If you are a member of an in-house public relations team, you'll be working to an annual program calendar, perhaps displayed on a large Gantt chart that sets out the dates on which individual activities will be planned and implemented. For example, the program will show the date of Ideal Widgets' factory open day and the regular dates for updating the company's newsletter on the website. If you are responsible for the open day, you'll have a more detailed planning document that shows what you need to do, and when you need to do it, to make the open day successful.

Writing a budget

budget: a list of items needed for a public relations plan that shows how much each item costs, and/or how much income will be derived from it.

Writing a **budget** is an important element of project planning because nothing can be implemented unless there is money to pay for it. Most of the time practitioners know how much money has been allocated to a public relations project. Those working in-house have annual budgets for their ongoing projects—the events and other public relations tools that are implemented every year, like a factory open day, the annual report, webpage publishing and maintenance, keeping the social media feeds up to date and relevant, media relations work—and are allocated funds for special one-off tasks, such as a community consultation meeting. Annual budgets are normally set on a financial year basis. Consultants are generally told how much money a client has for a project when they are briefed on a job. Sometimes, but rarely, clients ask consultants to recommend a budget to implement a strategic plan. Whichever way funds are allocated, it is prudent to produce a budget that shows how the money will be spent on each project.

Budgets need to cover the costs of every part of the project, including (for practitioners who work in consultancies) the fees that will be charged for the service being provided. If you work in-house, your public relations department will have an annual budget, prepared according to the requirements of the organisation's business-planning cycle and outlining funding for each part of the department's program.

> ### ■ PRACTICE NOTE A PROJECT BUDGET
>
> Budgets need to provide the detailed costs of every part of the project. The costs of items like graphic and web design, printing and mailing can be identified when you seek quotations for the work from possible contractors. It is usual to seek two or three quotations from designers, printers, mailing houses and other contractors like web designers, specialist writers, audio-visual producers or display builders. That allows you to accept the best price for what you need to do. Sometimes projects have tight deadlines and need to be completed quickly. When that happens, you'll need to make sure that the contractors, and others involved in the project, know the deadlines for their involvement so that they can give you a realistic quote and an indication of how long they'll need to do their part of the project. That will help you to select the best option both in terms of cost and the contractor's ability to meet your deadline. If you have identified a celebrity that you want as the spokesperson for a campaign, you'll need to know the fee that that person will charge for being involved. Similarly, for events, you'll need to identify the costs of hiring venues, equipment, transport and refreshments. Include an amount for a contingency in case there is an unexpected cost.
>
> Clients need to know how much tax will be charged for their project. In some countries, for example, a goods and services tax is imposed on everything associated with public relations, including consultancy fees. Some organisations are exempt from taxes of this kind, though, so it is a good idea to check with your organisation's accountants to make sure you know which public relations services attract these taxes.
>
> The more complex a project is, the more detailed the budget needs to be. For example, if you are launching a campaign to attract young people to donate blood to the Red Cross at a special event, you'll need to produce a budget that covers the costs of:
>
> + a media kit, leaflets and other tools you'll use, including social media
> + displays
> + hiring a venue for the campaign launch (including, if necessary, sound equipment)
> + any audio-visual aids and the equipment you'll need to show them

+ refreshments, if these are to be provided for guests
+ transport, perhaps to bring your campaign spokesperson from interstate.

A simple budget for a public relations consultancy to produce and mail a leaflet to 20 000 households could look like this—and of course the dollar figures are just examples:

Item	Cost ($)
Graphic design (3 days @ $600/day)	1800
Printing 20 000 copies	10 000
Mailing costs (includes mailing house fees and postage) for 20 000 copies	8500
Couriers	400
Telephone	100
Consultancy fees (6 days @ $1000/day)	6000
Services tax (10%)	2680
Contingency (15% of budget, including taxes)	4422
Total	33 902

Consultants' fees

Public relations consultants charge fees for the services they provide to clients. Consultants can manage all aspects of a project including identifying and commissioning others to help with web and other design, printing and other production aspects of a project. Consultants' fees are usually based on an hourly rate, which varies depending on the experience of the consultant involved in the project, but there is no standard schedule of fees like those charged by doctors; each consultancy has its own fee structure.

The rate charged for the work of a beginning practitioner will be lower than that for a more senior staff member. The rate may be even higher when the consultancy's chief executive works on the project. Sometimes consultancies have long-term contracts with organisations to provide continuing support and advice. When this happens, the consultancy is usually paid a set fee, or retainer, for the period of the contract. When work outside this arrangement is needed, the consultancy charges its normal project fee. Highly complex work, like managing a crisis, is sometimes charged at a higher rate than the normal fee. Most consultancies also provide free, or pro bono, services to charities or other causes in which their principals are interested, as a practical contribution to the community. Practitioners working in consultancies must keep a timesheet that records the actual hours they work on each client's business. Timesheets enable the consultancy to work out how much they need to charge clients. This means that if an experienced practitioner works on a client's project for ten hours, and their hourly rate is $100 per hour, the client is charged $1000 as a consultancy fee.

> **PRACTICE POINT**
>
> Annual salaries paid in public relations vary according to the experience of practitioners and the industry sector, and business, in which they work. There are generally no set industrial awards, so salaries paid in the private sector, public relations consultancies, not-for-profit organisations and government agencies vary. In Australia, for example, starting salaries in government agencies can be substantially higher than those for beginning practitioner jobs in private enterprise, consultancies or not-for-profits. Your country's professional public relations association or society will have some details of potential starting salaries—and those paid at the top of the profession—to guide you.
>
> Consultants are involved in a competitive business, and the salaries and other costs of the practitioners they employ are the most expensive part of running a practice. Consultants need to make enough money to:
>
> + pay their employees
> + contribute to employee superannuation
> + rent office premises
> + buy equipment
> + pay for electricity, telephone and internet services
> + pay for all the other expenses associated with operating a business.

Over a year, the fees charged for a practitioner's time need to cover not only their annual salary, but also their share of the other business costs, or overheads, as well as generate a profit for the consultancy. These overheads are usually factored into the rate the consultancy charges for a practitioner's involvement in a client's project. A practitioner needs to generate about 2.5–3.0 times their annual salary in revenue to cover these overheads and to make a profit for the business. In the corporate world and in government, these overheads are accounted for by adding 27–30 per cent of the practitioner's salary to the annual budget.

Most consultancies work out hourly charge-out rates (or billable hours) using a formula that assumes people won't be 100 per cent productive for the whole year. The formula assumes that people will take annual leave, that they may be sick for some time, and that they won't be working on public holidays. Even when they are at work, they are likely to be involved in meetings (like regular consultancy staff meetings) and other activities that are not directly related to client business. All that means that a practitioner is likely to be productive for about 80 per cent of the time, and that they are at work for just forty-six weeks of the year after accounting for holidays and sick leave. Most people work a standard 35-hour week (of course many actually work more than that), so the formula assumes a standard working week for practitioners. That means a consultancy can expect a practitioner to be productive for 80 per cent of forty-six weeks of the year, or

$$46 \text{ weeks} \times 35 \text{ hours/week} = 1610 \text{ hours} \times 0.8 = 1288 \text{ hours}$$

To work out the hourly rate for a consultant earning, say, $70 000 a year, the consultancy would apply the formula like this:

$$\$70\,000 \times 2.5 = \$175\,000 \div 1288\,\text{hours} = \$135.87\,\text{per hour}$$

Working with consultants

Some in-house public relations offices are fortunate in having access to the organisation's own graphic designers and other skilled people. The public relations team at a manufacturing company may, for example, be able to use apprentices to build a display, or organise the facilities staff to move equipment. While this happens, it is rare, and most public relations offices need to contract outside specialists to provide services they cannot source internally. Adequately briefing external contractors on what precisely is required of them is vital. Not only does a detailed brief ensure you get what you need, but it also means you will be given a more accurate quote on the costs of providing the service.

If you need to engage a public relations consultant to support a project, the brief you write needs to be structured like a strategic plan. Your brief should:

+ identify the situation your organisation faces
+ analyse the situation, summarise any research that you have, and outline other activities in the same area that might have been implemented previously
+ outline goals and objectives
+ identify target publics
+ indicate the messages you want to promote
+ provide a timeline for implementation
+ indicate the budget, including whether you are exempt from GST or other taxes and charges
+ set out how you want the consultant to respond
+ identify the person on your team with whom the consultant will most directly work
+ identify the time allowed for the consultant to respond to your brief with a proposal for how they will deal with your project
+ outline the format the consultancy should use in its response, if that is appropriate.

Of course, some of this may be the task that you want the consultant to do, but your brief should provide as much information about the situation as you can assemble.

This approach is often called a 'competitive pitch'—the process whereby two or three, sometimes more, consultancies are invited to respond to a brief with ideas for dealing with the situation outlined in the brief and the costs involved. Your team will personally brief each of the consultancies individually about what they are being asked to do, and they'll be given a few weeks to respond, again in person. After the consultancies have responded, your team will decide which proposal is best for your organisation, based on their creative solutions to your situation, the costs involved and, sometimes, how comfortable you feel working with each consultancy's team.

Often consultancies decide to pitch to potential clients without having been invited because they believe they have services and skills that will help these organisations and they hope to win some business. This kind of pitch involves a direct approach, usually by the chief executive, to the potential client requesting a meeting to explain how the consultancy can help. At the meeting, the consultancy might give an audio-visual presentation about its services, skills, specialisations, successful campaigns and other clients. It will almost certainly leave a credentials document with the prospective client setting out all this information and listing staff members. As a beginning practitioner in a consultancy, you'll most likely be involved in helping to prepare a credentials document, perhaps by revising parts of it to make it relevant to the potential client's business and industry.

> **PRACTICE POINT**
>
> Most consultancies have their own methodology and format for responding to briefs that will be based on their specialisations, strengths and perhaps the theoretical approaches they believe work best in certain situations. If you join a consultancy, you'll be briefed on the approach they take in responding to briefs. You are likely to be involved in preparing responses. Your role may be to do some additional research, to chase up quotes from web and graphic designers, printers, mailing houses, couriers and other contractors, or to prepare the electronic slides that the consultancy's chief executive will use at a meeting with a prospective client.

Once your organisation has selected a consultant following a competitive pitch, it will sign a contract that sets out what needs to be done, who will be responsible for doing it and at what cost. Normally contracts are straightforward and based on a standard format used by your organisation or the consultant.

While the consultant works with your team, you'll meet regularly for 'work-in-progress' (WIP) discussions. There's likely to be a set agenda for these WIPs, but it is important that at least the timelines and checklists you have for the project are reviewed and changed if necessary. It is also important for you to write notes about these meetings, even formal **meeting minutes** if that is appropriate.

meeting minutes: a record of the discussion at a meeting.

Briefing designers

When you work with graphic designers on print material, or web designers, you need to make sure that they know exactly what you want. They can't do the work you require, or charge you appropriately, if they do not know clearly what is expected of them. It is a good idea to provide them with a written brief and to schedule regular meetings to discuss progress.

> **PRACTICE POINT**
>
> If you use a competitive pitch to select a designer (or external consultant of any kind), it is vital that all those you invite to compete have exactly the same brief so that their proposals can be assessed equally.

When you work with any designer, treat them as professionals who are skilled in their craft. Avoid telling them how to do their job. Your task is to brief a designer in as much detail as possible so that they can use their creative skills to produce the products you are after. Your task is not to design the products. However, it is appropriate for you to suggest an approach you'd like a designer to take ('the display is for older people who visit libraries, so we'd like to take a classic approach', for example) but leave it to the professional to interpret your instructions. Take the time to discuss exactly what you want and why; the designer will propose something appropriate for your objectives, target public, messages and communication pathway. If you have a mutually respectful relationship based on a professional approach, the designer will be open to your ideas and suggestions for change after you see what they propose.

SUMMARY

This chapter has outlined the importance of project management in implementing public relations activities. It has dealt with using timelines, checklists and budgets, and how to brief external contractors. You should now have a working knowledge of how to write the implementation section of a strategic public relations plan based on your understanding of:

+ the role of project management in public relations
+ how to plan timelines and checklists
+ what needs to be included in a budget
+ how to write a brief for a consultant or a designer
+ the importance of building professional relationships with people engaged to help with your project.

REFLECTION

Ethical practice is essential in all aspects of public relations work. Clients, target publics, senior managers, colleagues, competitors, observers and the authorities expect practitioners to work and manage their businesses in accordance with the law and to ethical standards. These requirements are especially important when they involve the way in which practitioners deal with colleagues or enter contracts to work for clients or consultants. Review the code of ethics for your country's professional public relations association to identify those parts that deal with how practitioners should deal with and charge clients. What are the specific requirements of each clause? Is there a common theme to these clauses? How do the clauses work together to ensure an ethical approach? Do these clauses apply to the relationships in-house practitioners have with outside contractors? Why or why not?

ACTIVITIES

1. Plan an Event

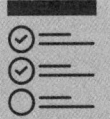

Most practitioners have to organise events, and many specialise in this because of their particular expertise or because they like this kind of work. Assume that as a member of Ideal Widgets' in-house public relations team, you have been asked to organise an end-of-year party to celebrate the success of the new safety widget launched in January. Ideal wants to invite senior staff, suppliers, the company's directors, local residents who live near the factory, the mayor and councillors, representatives of the outlets that sell the safety widgets, and journalists. You have two months to organise the party, and other members of the PR team are available to help you. Your manager wants the event to be in a local art gallery near the factory site on a Friday afternoon, starting at 5 p.m., but the venue has not been booked. You need to organise catering for the event (you have approval to order canapés and other finger food, and wine, orange juice and water). Ideal regularly uses a local caterer for events, and you have approval to hire that caterer without seeking quotes. You do not need to produce any special materials for the party, but you've decided that the small portable digital display used by the sales department, and updated with the PR team's infographics, should be set up at the gallery. Invitations will be sent to an invitation list that you have yet to prepare from the database managed by the public relations department.

Using the checklist in the toolkit, plan the steps you need to take to organise the event. Once you've worked out what needs to be done, and the time each task will take, transfer the information to a Gantt chart. If you are brave, plot a critical path.

2. Work Out Your Billable Hours

Assume you've just started work at Axiom Public Relations Counsellors in your first job as a practitioner. You have an annual salary of $50 000. Your timesheet shows that you have spent fifteen hours on your first project.

Using the formula mentioned previously, work out the fee that your consultancy will charge your client for the fifteen hours of work you've done.

Your best friend, who works in a government department's public relations team, earns $60 000 as a beginning practitioner. Her department uses a factor of 30 per cent of annual salary to account for staff overheads. How much is allocated in the department's budget for your friend's salary and overheads?

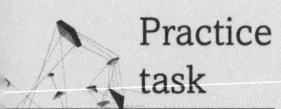

Practice task

A little girl needs your help

Thailand's Phuket Island is a popular destination for thousands of international tourists and tourism is the major contributor to the island's economy. Tourism employs hundreds of local people. A not-for-profit foundation, Phuket Has Been Good To Us, raises money to fund high-quality English language classes in government schools on the island to enhance young people's life chances and their ability to get well-paid jobs in local tourism. It also runs a sport, arts and crafts program for orphans and kids whose families are not able to look after them (see <www.phukethasbeengoodtous.org>).

CHAPTER 11: GETTING THE JOB DONE

You work as a consultant for Axiom Communication, a public relations consultancy based in your capital city. Your boss holidays every year on Phuket with his family. On his last family holiday he heard about Phuket Has Been Good To Us and became intrigued by its work. Searching for information about the foundation, your boss found a video clip, A Little Girl Needs Your Help. In the clip, four-year-old Grace B. Tiraraktummakij seeks donations of English language books for the foundation (see <**https://www.youtube.com/watch?v=LeZ7CJPR97g**>). The clip was produced by Grace's mother, a Thai businesswoman, and advertising expert, Apiradee Bunyalekha, to support the foundation's fund raising and book donations.

Back home from holidays, your boss has decided to support the foundation. He will finance a stand at the next major university student recruitment show to raise awareness of Phuket Has Been Good To Us to encourage financial and book donations as well as volunteers. Your boss believes that this will be the most cost-effective way of promoting the foundation to visiting students, parents, teachers, and university staff. He has heard that up to 10 000 people visit the three sessions of this show each year. In his view, these target publics are likely to donate money or their time as volunteers, and some students will take gap years to work for the foundation on Phuket as English tutors. He has the foundation's approval for doing this and to use material from its website. He also has approval to use Grace's video clip. The recruitment show will be held on one day, four months from when the boss briefed you on this project.

Your boss has tasked you with managing this pro bono project. You will have the help of others in the consultancy to produce the materials to be used on the stand, but you will be responsible for making this project happen on time and within budget. Axiom's website, Facebook page and Twitter account will be used to promote the stand.

You'll need to book the stand (the venue will open two days beforehand to enable exhibitors to set up—or 'bump in'—and close a day after the show to allow people to remove their stands—or 'bump out'). You'll also need to hire a designer to build the stand after seeking competitive quotes from three agencies. You'll also need to hire equipment and to set up a roster for two members of Axiom's team (different people each time) to help you at the show in each of the three periods it will be open: 9.30 a.m. till 12.30 p.m.; 1.30 p.m. till 4.30 p.m.; and 5.30 p.m. till 8.00 p.m.. They'll want food and refreshments! Your boss will attend the stand for the first two hour and for the whole evening session.

The stand's back wall will feature a large montage of photographs showing English language classes and arts, sport and craft activities. Two large free-standing banners with dot points about the foundation will be on each side of the stand. The stand will use three large television screens to show infographics about the foundation's work, and Grace's video clip. There'll be a counter on which hard copies of a promotional leaflet will be displayed, along with electronic donation forms and applications to volunteer for a six-week stint teaching English. These will be set up on tablets and linked to a database back in the office. Axiom's webpage, Twitter feed, Instagram account and Facebook page will carry reports and photographs on how the stand is going, and people who donate or volunteer will be able to use these applications to comment on why they are participating.

The boss has arranged for an airline that flies directly from your city to Bangkok to co-sponsor the initiative, so you'll need to work out how that sponsorship will feature in material at the stand.

Using templates from the Toolkit in this book, your practice task is to:
- Set out everything that needs to be done by the Axiom team from the start of the project to the end of packing the stand up and getting it to storage for future use, and returning equipment you have hired. Be realistic about the amount of time available to plan and implement each part of this project.
- Include public relations tools that are not identified earlier but which you think should be included in this project
- Identify who is responsible, and the deadlines, for each part of the project
- Prepare a budget for the exercise (just list the things you need to pay for—don't worry about the actual money).

WRITING A PUBLIC RELATIONS EVALUATION PLAN

12

Explaining how the success of a public relations plan will be measured is the essential final section of a strategic plan. This chapter discusses the importance of writing an outline of the steps you will take to evaluate public relations outcomes and outputs against agreed strategic goals and objectives. It examines questions such as:

+ Why evaluate?
+ Were goals and objectives achieved?
+ Did the messages, communication pathways and public relations tools work?
+ What can be done better next time?

WHY EVALUATE?

In professional sport, teams play their matches according to a 'game plan' worked out by the coach. Most involve the team implementing set plays in certain circumstances, or using the natural talents of individual players to respond to an opposition move. Some teams play to complicated game plans that attempt to have a solution to every situation they are likely to encounter. Others allow players to read the game and respond accordingly. Whatever approach a team takes, after every match coaches and players review how well their game plan worked and what they might need to change next time. In television coverage of basketball, football, hockey and netball, coaches are often seen pointing out plays to their teams at time outs or other breaks in the game. Mostly, planned plays work; sometimes they don't, but after a match coaches always try to find ways to help the team improve.

Evaluating public relations projects is like that. Reviewing how well the plan worked is a vital step in planning what needs to be done next time. Practitioners sometimes schedule evaluations at key points of an implementation timeline so that a project can be fine-tuned to ensure that it is still on track. In large organisations that have an overall strategy covering all segments of the regular public relations program, annual evaluations help with budgeting for the following year, and in reporting to senior management and the board on how well the strategy worked. An effective evaluation that shows what was achieved and why is a valuable way of showing how public relations contributes to realising corporate goals and objectives. That is why writing an evaluation section to show how success will be measured is an essential step in strategic public relations planning.

The evaluation section of any public relations plan should outline the processes that will:

+ demonstrate that the plan worked—or if it didn't, why
+ show how practitioners are accountable for the budgets they have been given.

> ## PRACTICE POINT
>
> Ronald Smith, an academic who writes about strategic planning, says that when evaluation is properly built into a strategy it can increase the effectiveness of public relations, an advantage that should appeal to bosses and clients, and enhance the prestige and role of the profession (Smith, 2009, p. 272). György Szondi and Rüdiger Theilmann (2009, pp. 198–221) note that evaluation is essential and should be purposeful and systematic. Jim Macnamara (2012, pp. 388–407), a world expert in evaluation research and measurement, says that evaluation is about determining the value of an activity after it has been created. That process can be via various formal and informal techniques. But Macnamara points out that public relations remains 'notorious for failing to adequately evaluate its activities in a systematic and rigorous way' (p. 388).

Most practitioners agree that evaluation is necessary even though they often struggle to show the value of their work. A.J. Bruno (2016), founder of the US blog, TrendKite, says that most senior executives don't fully understand public relations and do not see it as crucial to their businesses. Nevertheless, Bruno says, most practitioners know how to measure their activity but not its value. A major survey of Australian, South African and US practitioners in 1994 by the International Public Relations Association (IPRA) found evaluation was more talked about than practised. Since then, researchers (see especially Walker, 1994, 1997; Xavier et al., 2004; Xavier et al., 2006; Simmons & Watson, 2005; Watson, 2006; Watson & Noble, 2007) have found an increased focus on evaluation in public relations practice.

HOW IS PUBLIC RELATIONS EVALUATED?

When they examined the evaluation techniques reported in 118 PRIA Golden Target Award winners in Australia, Robina Xavier and her team at the University of Technology, Queensland found that practitioners used an average of three evaluation methods in each program (Xavier et al., 2004). However, Australian practitioners appeared to favour *output* evaluation methods over *outcome* methods. This meant that evaluations were primarily based on media monitoring, response rates (such as attendances at meetings, or call-centre feedback); few used communication audits. The most common outcome evaluation methods were surveying to confirm changes in target public opinions, and activity outcome to measure the result of a program aimed at a particular target public. Bruno (2016) listed similar metrics: number of media releases issued, quantity of earned media mentions, number of successful media relations pitches, number of interviews given, awards received, events attended. These are standard output measures that demonstrate practitioners have been busy 'but it fails to establish whether you're closer to reaching your business goals' (Bruno, 2016). Bruno says that public relations should be assessed by metrics like search rankings, website traffic, whether your views lead conversations, social media engagement, ratings and reviews, customer retention and revenue.

Peter Simmons and Tom Watson (2005) noted a 'media relations-centric focus' to evaluation in Australian public relations practice. However, they also found that practitioners in government agencies were less likely to evaluate outcomes than were those working in consultancies, commercial organisations and not-for-profit groups. Practitioners working in not-for-profit groups were more likely than others to believe in measurability of their work but, like those in government, were under less pressure to demonstrate results. Consultants were under pressure to evaluate, but they were more confident than other practitioners about the measurability of their work. Simmons and Watson reported that practitioners support evaluation but that the main barriers are time, lack of training and budget limitations. They found that practitioners would welcome:

+ cost-effective standard evaluation measures
+ an evaluation model
+ an industry-standard tool to measure evaluation of public relations campaigns.

These specific tools are not generally available, but many commercial research and monitoring firms use techniques based on sound evaluation models. Practitioners do not need to engage external consultants to evaluate their programs; they can develop their own effective evaluation tools. However, these tools should go beyond measuring simple outputs like media coverage by generating data that indicate outcomes from public relations activities. That is not to say that measuring outputs is not necessary; a complete evaluation should include this information as well.

Scholars' research on evaluation practices illustrates the point IPRA made in 1994: evaluation should be sufficient to prove that an activity is well directed, well implemented and achieving the desired result. Anne Gregory explains that our public relations activities are no different from other business functions in that it is essential to know whether they worked (2009b, p. 193).

PRACTICE NOTE MEASURING PUBLIC RELATIONS PROGRAM PERFORMANCE

Most successful public relations program evaluations should be based on four categories of measurement. These are:

1. input: the formative research and other information that was used in the initial program planning and that contributed to writing the situation analysis and identifying goals, objectives and target publics, and that helped to decide on messages that need to be included in the public relations program

2. output: a measurement of the frequency with which a program's tools were used: the number of media releases issued, telephone enquiries received, speeches given, people in an audience, visits to web pages, references to the organisation on radio or television or in newspapers, and people who visited your display at an industry exhibition. Sometimes, practitioners report media coverage of their organisation by assessing whether individual stories were positive, negative or neutral towards the organisation. Measurements like these demonstrate that the work you said you would do was done. However, measuring outputs does not say anything about whether target publics received, processed, understood, accepted or acted on the messages you have written for the program
3. **outtake**: a measurement of what a public might do with a message. In other words, people might remember a message (smoking is bad for your health) but not change their behaviour (I recall the message, but I enjoy smoking so I won't quit)
4. **outcome**: a measurement of whether a public changed its knowledge, attitudes and behaviour as a result of a public relations plan. This is the most important category because outcomes are the results we planned when we wrote goals and objectives. Measuring outcomes is also more difficult because changes in knowledge, attitude and behaviour do not generally happen in the short term. It may take weeks, months or years for a practitioner to measure these changes. It is also generally more expensive to measure outcomes because summative research can involve in-depth surveying through polling, focus groups or other survey methods.

Adapted from Szondi and Theilmann (2009), and Macnamara (2012)

outtake: measurements of what a target public does with a message. For instance, they might remember a message but take no action as a result of it.

EFFECTIVE ALTERNATIVES TO ADVERTISING VALUE EQUIVALENTS

Sometimes practitioners are asked to calculate how much a client would have to pay for the newspaper space, or TV/radio time, that a news or feature story sourced from their media release generated. This is known as the advertising value equivalent (AVE) of news coverage. This is, of course, easy to calculate by multiplying the number of column centimetres, or air time, the release was given by the column-centimetre or advertising time cost of paying for that space. Clients and managers understand that dollar value. However, it is not a useful evaluation approach and it could be unethical. Most public relations scholars and senior practitioners criticise this evaluation technique. The distinguished Australian consultant, and former PRIA president, Rob Masters says strong editorial coverage can be valuable and effective but the appearance and size of editorial measured by advertising rates bears no relationship to the effectiveness of the article. Others suggest that measuring public relations in this way is not only invalid, but also undermines the worth of public relations. First, a news article has to be relevant and written in a way that helps it to be reported (see Chapter 6 for a discussion of news frames). Then, at its best, an AVE only indicates the cost of the space in which a news item appeared, not whether the article was read and understood, or whether a target public took action as a result. Alternative valid, reliable and internationally acceptable editorial evaluation systems include measuring:

+ **share of voice** (how much of the organisation's view was included in the story)
+ **reach**, or opportunities to see (the potential readership of the newspaper, or ratings for a television news program)
+ **target-to-story ratio** (the number of stories published compared with what you planned for)
+ **message carriage** (whether the organisation's message was carried in all news stories on the topic of your media release)
+ **prominence** (where the story ran on the news blog, in the newspapers, or on a television news broadcast; whether it was the main story on the television news or the major story on page four of the newspaper, or a minor story at the end of the bulletin or on page fifteen)
+ **focus** (whether the focus of the story was the main point in your media release, or whether the reporter led with the views of your opponents or competitors)
+ **tonal analysis** (whether the news coverage was positive or negative towards your organisation, or neutral)
+ **behaviour, awareness and attitudinal analysis** (any changes in any of these as a result of news media coverage).

The data to help you make these calculations can be found by measuring the items that turn up in your organisation's daily media monitoring. Data on reach can be identified from news organisations' websites where they report readership, or from regular ratings surveys of radio and television stations and their programs.

Making an evaluation work

Knowing what to measure well before it is measured is the key to public relations evaluation. That theme was pursued way back in 1985 by Patti Nelson Andrews, an academic who used her accountancy background to research how a number of key US companies judged the effectiveness of their public relations efforts. Andrews found that most of those companies' public relations goals could be classified into three distinct categories according to whether they sought to:

+ gain and maintain credibility and legitimacy
+ facilitate timely and appropriate responses
+ have a positive financial impact.

Andrews proposed that PR evaluation should:

+ be rational, understandable and simple
+ take into account the fact that public relations directors have more responsibility than authority
+ deal explicitly with the difficulty of knowing with confidence that there is a true cause and effect between action and results
+ be flexible and recognise that the public relations time horizon can vary from a few days for a crisis to many years for an intractable issue.

Andrews' approach demonstrates the importance of writing meaningful public relations goals and objectives. To summarise:

+ Goals are broad statements; objectives are steps that help implement goals.
+ Objectives deal with reputation, relationships or tasks.
+ Clear, precise and measurable objectives are steps along the way towards meeting goals.
+ Objectives can be informative or motivational.
+ Objectives are written to achieve outcomes by building awareness, generating acceptance and persuading target publics to take action.

A task goal (for example, to generate attendance at a school's open day) is an example of an output and may have process-oriented objectives (for example, letterbox the open-day **flyer** to all residents in the school's catchment area during the next month).

flyer: usually a single sheet of printed information for wide distribution.

Goals and objectives written in this way mean that an evaluation of how a public relations plan was implemented will be rational, understandable and simple. Precise objectives can be measured, and that means you can show how these steps towards meeting the goal have been achieved.

Equally important is the link between objectives and communication pathways and public relations tools. Remember that a communication pathway is the way an organisation will deliver the important information it wants to give to its publics; public relations tools are the actual packages in which those messages will be delivered. If an objective is to increase awareness of a new way of paying unemployment benefits to young people by 10 per cent in six months, then pathways and tools will be selected for specific publics to achieve the objective. That means an evaluation also needs to assess whether communication pathways and tools were appropriate to achieving the objective. For example, if a program that used an uncontrolled media pathway to deliver the unemployment benefits message to 16–20-year-olds failed, an evaluation would have to address whether the pathway was correct.

■ PRACTICE NOTE REPORTING A CAMPAIGN EVALUATION

In 2006, Reed Weir Communications Pty Ltd won a PRIA Golden Target Award for an Australian Egg Corporation Limited campaign to announce that eggs had received the National Heart Foundation's (NHF) 'tick' of approval as a heart-healthy food.

Before the campaign, national research among consumers and general practitioners in Australia examined knowledge and understanding of the links between eggs, cholesterol, diet and heart disease. The research highlighted key areas of concern, especially in relation to the perceived effect eggs have on cholesterol levels and their contribution to heart disease. Eggs were regarded as part of the 'bad food' group, and this long-held consumer myth highlighted the massive task AECL had ahead of it: to shift public perceptions back in line with current scientific evidence. The research was repeated at the end of the campaign.

A compendium of clinical data and scientific research was presented to the NHF to show eggs have very little, if any, effect on blood cholesterol levels and heart disease risk in most people. This research eventually led the NHF to issue the tick of approval to eggs as a highly nutritious food source. This clinical research was also used to help educate health-care practitioners, and consumers, regarding the new evidence on eggs, nutrition, diet, cholesterol and heart disease.

The campaign's evaluation read:

> Objective 1: Change the understanding and acceptance of health-care professionals regarding the link between eggs and blood cholesterol.
>
> GP research at the conclusion of the program conducted by Decisions Research showed 57% of GPs were aware of the NHF Tick Program's approval for eggs, 52% of GPs said the NHF Tick Program influenced their opinion on a healthy level of egg consumption and 60% of GPs said egg intake had little or no effect on cholesterol levels.
>
> Objective 2: Generate national media coverage that widely publicises the fact that eggs now have the Heart Foundation 'Tick'.
>
> Media interest and coverage was overwhelming. Television, print, and radio news and talkback all covered the story with hundreds of interviews conducted by the various NHF, AECL and Egg Nutrition Advisory Group (ENAG) spokespeople. A minimum of 283 media mentions were recorded. Only one mention was judged as negative. Newspoll research showed a total of 38% of Australians had heard of eggs gaining the NHF Tick.
>
> Objective 3: Change consumer opinion regarding the consumption of eggs and its effect on blood cholesterol levels.
>
> Four weeks after the launch, Newspoll consumer research commissioned by AECL showed a 25% improvement in consumer attitudes towards eggs and cholesterol and an 11% improvement in understanding of the relationship between eggs and fat.
>
> AC Nielsen's Homescan data showed a significant upturn in sales following the NHF Tick Launch. During the December 2005 period, sales volume increased 14.4% and value increased 16% compared to the equivalent period the preceding year.

> Objective 4: Achieve 50% or greater inclusion of NHF Tick on on-shelf product.
>
> Within six months of launch, 59.7% of egg packaging by volume included the NHF Tick nationwide.
>
> Notice how the evaluation is a blend of outputs and outcomes.
>
> This is an edited extract of the GTA entry, published with the permission of the Public Relations Institute of Australia

Writing an evaluation plan

The evaluation plan for your strategy does not need to be long, but it does need to identify how you will analyse success. That is, an evaluation plan describes how you will measure outputs, outcomes and outtakes. In each case this will involve qualitative and quantitative methods and may include desk research (perhaps a **media analysis** of daily media clippings to generate output and outcome data) or a series of post-campaign focus groups using an external expert to determine whether there has been a change in awareness, understanding, attitude or behaviour. Measuring outtakes is a bit harder but if you revisit the definition in the practice note mentioned earlier, you can work out what kind of research you'd need for this.

The plan needs to include the tools that you will use for the evaluation. Evaluation criteria need to be established, and agreed, at the planning stage of a public relations strategy to ensure an effective link between formative research, correctly written objectives and the summative research used in an evaluation (Glenny & Singh, 2009). When you write your evaluation plan, you need to decide which of these methods, or combination of methods, is appropriate for what you need to measure. Objectives that deal with reputation, relationships and tasks may require different evaluation methods. The following practice note contains an example of how you might write an evaluation plan.

media analysis (or media content analysis): the process of analysing the contents of articles in the print and electronic media to identify how the issues they discuss might impact on the organisation, how the organisation has been reported, and what others are saying about the organisation.

> ### ■ PRACTICE NOTE WRITING AN EVALUATION PLAN
>
> Let's assume our consultancy has been engaged to help the Christchurch City Council in New Zealand generate community support for a children's playground on a lawn near a stone church on a tourist route in the elite hillside suburb of Cashmere. The playground has been proposed by parents of children at the local pre-school. We know from benchmark research that 40 per cent of ratepayers in Cashmere support the playground, 40 per cent do not, and the others are undecided. The council will conduct a referendum among ratepayers in six months to test community support for the playground before it makes a decision on whether the development should proceed. Target publics for our program include ratepayers and business people in

Cashmere, council members, environmental groups, parents, schoolteachers and, as a secondary public, the local media. We have used three communication pathways (controlled, uncontrolled media and interpersonal communication) and a range of public relations tools in our program during the last four months. The public relations program has several goals and objectives, but here we'll look at the evaluation plan for just one goal and the three objectives designed to achieve it.

An evaluation plan for Goal 1 might be set out like this:

GOAL 1

To gain community support for a children's playground on Cashmere Green.

OBJECTIVE 1

To increase awareness among target publics of the proposal for a playground in Cashmere by 50 per cent in three months.

Evaluation

1. Repeat benchmark quantitative survey of ratepayers and business people in Cashmere to determine whether awareness of the playground project has increased.
2. Conduct three focus groups with residents, ratepayers and business people in Cashmere to determine their level of knowledge of what the playground development will involve.
3. Monitor media to assess positive, negative and neutral coverage, and whether campaign messages are included.
4. Audit campaign materials to assess whether they were appropriate for target publics.

OBJECTIVE 2

To convince 75 per cent of Cashmere residents and shopkeepers to support the playground over the next five months.

Evaluation

1. Analyse content of calls to the playground hotline weekly to determine whether there is a trend for or against the development.
2. Ask respondents to the repeated benchmark survey whether they received messages about the development.

3. Ask about support or non-support for the proposal in the repeat benchmark quantitative survey.
4. Use the three focus groups to identify reasons for changes in attitude towards the playground proposal.

OBJECTIVE 3

To generate a 60 per cent vote in favour of the playground at a referendum in six months.

Evaluation

1. Referendum results will indicate success of campaign.
2. Analyse results for each voting place to determine areas of support for, or rejection of, proposal.

<small>This fictitious example is based on a case study that examined two community consultation projects in New Zealand (Comrie, 2000), and on a classroom exercise on that study devised by Dr Ron Knight.</small>

Evaluating the public relations impact on organisational credibility

A major role of public relations is to build and maintain the credibility of the organisation among target publics. This is especially important when the organisation has to respond to issues or manage a crisis. We can evaluate our success in maintaining credibility by assessing how our activities influenced target publics. Figure 12.1 suggests a framework for assessing how well we built and maintained the organisation's credibility. By using tools like qualitative and quantitative opinion surveys, in-depth interviews with publics, communication audits, attitude scaling, and variance analysis, we can test how well our public relations communication pathways and public relations tools contributed to, for example, acceptance of messages to build commitment and thus help to enhance credibility.

Figure 12.1 Evaluating organisational credibility

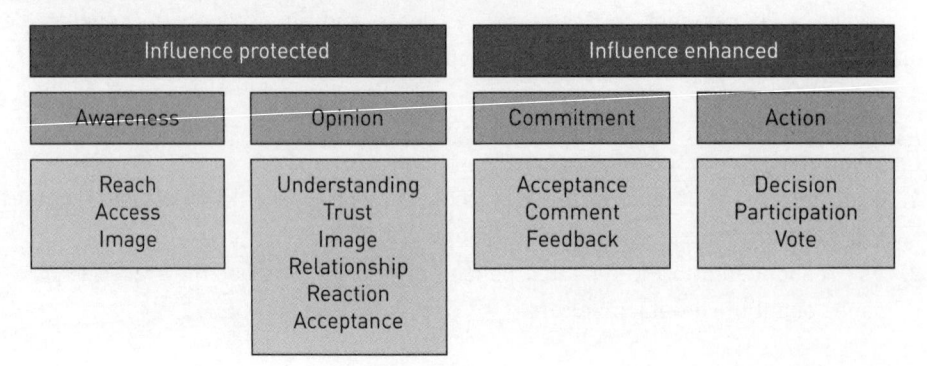

Influence protected		Influence enhanced	
Awareness	Opinion	Commitment	Action
Reach Access Image	Understanding Trust Image Relationship Reaction Acceptance	Acceptance Comment Feedback	Decision Participation Vote

Adapted from Andrews (1985)

CHAPTER 12: WRITING A PUBLIC RELATIONS EVALUATION PLAN

> **PRACTICE POINT**
>
> Qualitative feedback is important and legitimate information to include in an evaluation. For example, an evaluation report can include comments from journalists about how quickly you provided an answer to their questions, or from a client who has written to thank the team for the speed with which their request was answered. You should, however, include negative as well as positive feedback.

EVALUATING RESPONSE CAPABILITY

It is important to be able to demonstrate how well the public relations team worked with the dominant coalition to identify and manage issues. Chapter 3 looked at the importance of identifying issues as part of the strategic planning process. Doing this quickly—many organisations have a continual issues-monitoring process—enables practitioners to implement a plan to address a current or emerging issue. Practitioners can use evaluation tools like opinion surveys, scenarios, and trend analysis, and the opinions of experts, to work out how well an issue was anticipated and how their program avoided it becoming a problem. Figure 12.2 illustrates how this might be done. Our capacity to scan the external environment, gather information and analyse it in order to *anticipate* those issues we might need to address also enables us to advise (or counsel) the dominant coalition about how it should act to *avoid* the issue impacting adversely on the organisation.

Figure 12.2 Evaluating response capability

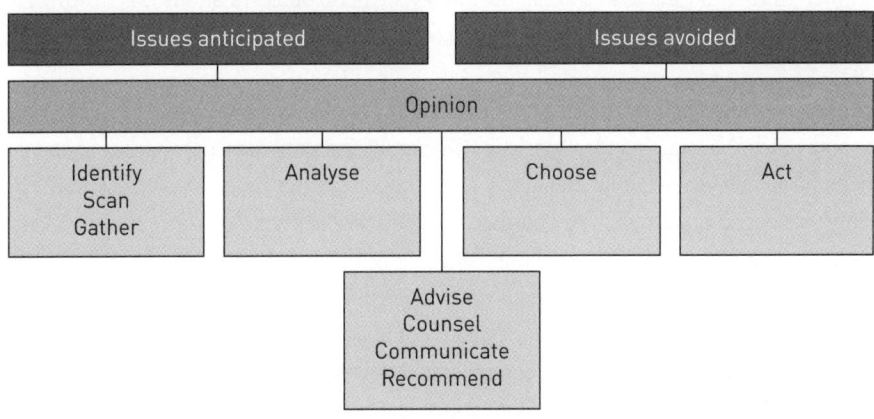

```
        Issues anticipated          Issues avoided
    ┌──────────────────────────────────────────────┐
    │                  Opinion                     │
    └──────────────────────────────────────────────┘
    ┌──────────┬──────────┬──────────┬──────────┐
    │ Identify │ Analyse  │  Choose  │   Act    │
    │   Scan   │          │          │          │
    │  Gather  │          │          │          │
    └──────────┴──────────┴──────────┴──────────┘
                    ┌──────────────┐
                    │   Advise     │
                    │   Counsel    │
                    │ Communicate  │
                    │ Recommend    │
                    └──────────────┘
```

Adapted from Andrews (1985)

MEASURING THE FINANCIAL IMPACT OF PUBLIC RELATIONS

Practitioners often find it difficult, in the hard world of business, to demonstrate that what they do has a positive financial impact. Marketing and sales people can draw a clear link between what they do and an increase in sales, especially when they launch a new product. How can you demonstrate the financial impact of a positive change in attitude towards an organisation? In many organisations, public relations is viewed as a cost item that doesn't generate revenue. However, research (Kim, 1999) has examined the so-called bottom line impact of public relations and found that:

+ increasing public relations budgets can have a positive impact on the organisation's reputation
+ improving reputation will have a positive impact on revenues.

The measures for determining this kind of return on investment in public relations would require cooperation with the accounting and finance teams of the organisation. For example, a cost–benefit, investment or variance analysis could be correlated with the findings of a qualitative survey designed to measure a change in attitudes towards the organisation as a result of public relations activity.

Another financial impact of public relations flows from good budget management. That means, first of all, preparing a realistic budget and making sure you stick to it. To do that, you need to make sure you don't waste money. Seek several quotations for work you need from external consultants; implement the tools you need for a communication pathway, not those that you might simply want; and regularly review your program, especially long-term programs, to make sure you are getting the best value for money. It is legitimate to write in an evaluation report that you implemented your project on time and within budget.

Building a program evaluation

The evaluation of each outcome or output objective links with those for other objectives to build a total picture of how successful the project has been. That, in turn, provides relevant data for clients or senior managers who want to know that the money spent on public relations was worthwhile. This is equally important for specific individual projects and for overarching corporate public relations programs.

Andrews proposes a similar approach for evaluating annual corporate public relations programs like that outlined in the strategic plan matrix in Chapter 4. She proposes that measuring the success of a major program—the 'Public Relations Department' in the chart—was best done by first evaluating each tactic or 'Activity'. You can see how this works if you look at, say, the 'Community relations' column in the chart. The combined evaluations of the activities listed under 'Community relations' determines how successful that component has been. Similarly, the combined evaluations of the 'Components' would show how successful the 'Public Relations Department' has been.

Approaching evaluation in this way demonstrates how important it is to write clear goals and measurable objectives, and to make sure that you select communication pathways and public relations tools that effectively and efficiently implement them.

SUMMARY

This chapter has examined the importance of evaluating public relations outcomes and outputs against agreed strategic goals and objectives. It has looked at how practitioners can measure the success of their public relations projects and has discussed how writing clear goals and precise, measurable objectives in the strategic planning phase leads to a meaningful evaluation. Evaluation is concerned with assessing whether:

+ goals and objectives were met
+ messages, communication pathways and public relations tools worked
+ the effectiveness of what was implemented can be improved for the next project.

A meaningful evaluation should address outcomes as well as outputs. It should use a range of tools to gather data that show how the clear, concise and measurable objectives we wrote when we planned the program were met.

REFLECTION

Go back to the two measurable objectives you wrote for the practice task at the end of Chapter 4. Think about the communication pathways you would use to pursue those objectives. Are they appropriate for the target publics you need to reach? What public relations tools might you use to deliver messages to those publics? Are there clear links between your objectives, pathways and tools? Are your objectives directed at outputs or outcomes? What outcomes are you seeking from your public relations work for Ima Chanteuse? Would you now change your objectives to reflect the outcomes you seek?

ACTIVITIES

1. Understanding Evaluation

Search the public relations academic journals available in your university library to identify one article that deals with evaluation, perhaps for social media tools. (Publications like the *Journal of Communication Management*, the *Journal of Public Relations Research*, *PRism*, an online-only journal, and *Public Relations Review* have all published many articles on research into evaluation. Briefer and non-academic articles can be found in the daily free online editions of *PR Daily Extra* and *PR Daily News Feed* which may be available through your university library.) As you read the article, make a list of points you think would help practitioners to understand how to evaluate their activities.

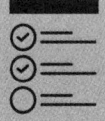

2. Measuring Outputs and Outcomes

An online research exercise can help us to understand the difference between outputs and outcomes.

First, *outputs*. Go to the media centre on a political leader's internet site and find a media release that was issued a week before you visited the site. Use your internet browser to search for references to the topic of the release in as many daily newspapers as you can in the week since it was released. Count the number of references. The result is an example of measuring an output.

Does the information you gathered so far allow you to answer questions about who read, understood or took action as a result of the media coverage? Pick two or three of the news stories you found and try to produce a summary table using the alternative measures listed in the AVE discussion on page 246 to develop a richer evaluation of media coverage. If you are able to do this, you could then write a detailed analysis. Remember, though, that while such an analysis would be helpful, it would still only be reporting on *output*.

Now *outcomes*. Again use your browser to search for examples of 'deliberative polling'. Read one of the reports you identify. Notice how the technique uses polling research before and after information is provided to participants. Was there a change in the participants' attitudes towards the topic when the final polling was reviewed? This is an example of an *outcome*.

3. Revising Your List of Evaluation Points

Now, revise the list you made in the first activity. Has it changed? How? Why would you change the list? What are the five most important points you've taken from this chapter?

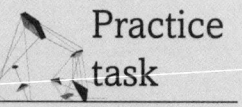

Practice task

Using the information in this book, the results of your reflection at the end of this chapter, and items in the toolkit, do this task:

Explore the website ultraglaze.com.au. Assume your public relations consultancy has been hired by Ultraglaze to promote its services more widely than has happened in the past when it has relied on word-of-mouth contact with builders and renovation specialists for most of its business. As the consultant assigned to this project, you've decided to implement a social media campaign directed at reaching people who are planning do-it-yourself renovations.

You'll also be contacting lifestyle and home improvement television programs, websites and newspaper sections, and technology reporters from the major news media. The campaign's messages include building broader awareness of the company's product, its technological strengths and ease of application. In addition to do-it-yourself renovators, target publics for the campaign are bathroom tilers and renovation specialists and builders. Then prepare an outline for a public relations strategy that includes (we'll assume there is a situation analysis):

1. a communication goal
2. two outcome objectives and one output objective
3. messages
4. three key primary target publics and one secondary target public
5. two communication pathways
6. at least three public relations tools to match each of the communication pathways
7. a Gantt chart that shows the timeline for implementing your strategy
8. an evaluation plan that suggests how you will measure your success in implementing your outcome and output objectives.

A REFLECTION

In the final essay of his volume of *Sceptical Essays*, the British philosopher Bertrand Russell took a cynical view of how the world, as he viewed it in 1935, would change. Russell, an avowed socialist, predicted that change over the following 100 years would lead to the world being organised through a central control authority. This would probably mean more democracy, more monopolies, a breakdown of the idea of 'family', and a tendency for culture to move away from art and literature towards science. Historians will tell us if Russell's predictions were realised. Some already appear to be our reality.

Russell wrote that education would teach people to do rather than to think or feel. People would know a 'good deal of mathematics, a fair amount of biology, and a great deal about how to make machines'. They'd be able to do all manner of things with great skill but would be incapable of considering rationally whether what they did was worth performing. Broadcasting would replace newspapers, and reading would be replaced by 'listening to the gramophone, or to whatever better invention takes its place'. Sadly, Russell predicted that writing would be replaced in ordinary life by the dictaphone.

For 'broadcasting', read television, YouTube, Instagram, DVDs, Bluetooth and myriad internet-based applications, especially social media; for the 'gramophone', read smartphones, iPods, tablets and computers; and for the 'dictaphone', read smartphones again, SMS messaging and email. None of this is static, and in five years we'll probably look with wonderment on new technological devices that no one even imagines today.

The focus of this book has been on the contexts in which public relations is practised and the development of the writing skills a beginning practitioner needs to work successfully in the profession. It hasn't been about the 'toys' that enable public relations tools to be disseminated, but about how to write copy for those tools and about knowing why we do it; it has demonstrated that public relations involves far more than traditional media releases and Facebook, Twitter and any other social media application, powerful mainstream tools though they are. Today's physical and social media equivalents of Russell's predicted changes are indeed the context and reality of modern public relations practice. Like generations before us, we'll adapt to the new technologies that await us, just as we have adapted to the undreamt-of services offered by smartphones and iPads; just as Ivy Lee adapted to the changes occurring in his world. Lee would probably not be surprised at how public relations has grown since he sent his first 'news release'. After all, he had a creative idea that met the needs of both his clients and his target public, and he would no doubt have been delighted at how this simple idea has evolved as part of modern professional practice. Nor would Lee be surprised that despite the technology available to practitioners in the twenty-first century to advance their clients' goals and objectives, good professional writing remains essential to success.

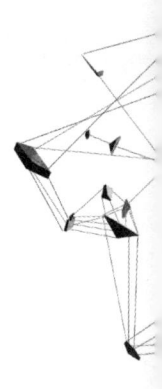

It is the ability of effective practitioners to read the times, as that other historical philosopher Machiavelli advised the Medici princes, and to understand the contexts to which their strategic skills and public relations tools are applied, that makes them successful professionals.

How many senior practitioners were at first startled by, then intensely curious about, the 2007 McKinsey study that found four new financial powerbrokers reshaping the world? McKinsey, a pre-eminent management consultancy, found that oil, Asia, hedge funds and private equity were shaping global financial markets and would do so permanently. Those practitioners who recognise the importance of context probably began to think about what this research finding would mean for the role of public relations in a new world dominated by these four financial powerbrokers. How are practitioners reacting to another new world order initiated by the election of Donald Trump as US president? And have they changed their practices to reflect overwhelming world concern about global climate change?

Yet public relations practice requires more than reading the times, applying high-level professional skills and using the latest technology effectively. It requires a commitment to ethical practice by everyone working in the profession; it requires a commitment to continuing professional development long after the pages of textbooks are closed and writing assignments are handed in; and it requires a belief that public relations makes a difference, is a force for good when ethically practised and is an honourable profession.

Getting better at writing for public relations comes with practice, from learning the style in which your client or employer wants material written, and from observing how others write speeches, media releases, brochures, newspaper stories, poetry, blogs and tweets. Read and learn; practise and improve. Practise again. Russell was right about one prediction. Education has become heavily focused on professional skills. Despite this, and the reality of modern education, effective public relations practice requires you to think, and to ask questions. Never give up on that; never stop thinking about why a situation is important, who is interested in it, what it means, what the context is and how it can be resolved. Never stop asking questions, even if they are obvious and even if—especially if—they are tough. Seek knowledge about the world around you; understand your clients' businesses and the contexts in which they operate; learn to use the wonderful technology available to you purposefully and in a considered and rational way, not just because you can.

As a philosopher and writer, Bertrand Russell observed the world and the way it worked. His writing attempted to explain what it all meant and how the world might be improved. Many of us won't agree with much of what he had to say, but he did understand context, and he could write. Russell may have predicted the end of writing as a craft, but he wasn't happy about it. Perhaps, despite our reliance on the speed of communicating via social media, tablets, media players, smartphones, SMS and email, we can keep public relations writing clear, concise and accurate. After all, that's why we've spent our time with this book. Good luck.

JSM

GLOSSARY

Analysis
A detailed examination of something. In public relations, analysis involves examining the internal and external environments that impact on the organisation, or examining research results. See *situation analysis*.

Annual report
An official publication that deals with the organisation's performance for the previous twelve months, usually the *financial year*.

Backgrounder
A narrative usually written about one topic that extends the information published in a *media release*.

Brochure
Printed material about a topic in booklet form. The term is often used more broadly to mean a *leaflet*, pamphlet or booklet.

Budget
A list of items needed for a public relations plan that shows how much each item costs, and/or how much income will be derived from it.

Business
Usually what organisations do; a series of things that an organisation, or an individual, needs to deal with.

Checklist
A planning tool that identifies the tasks that need to be undertaken to implement a project.

Communication pathway
A communication method to reach target publics. (Sometimes known as a message delivery strategy.)

Communication, or public relations, tool
The physical things and activities that target publics see or hear or experience. Examples are websites, blogs, tweets, displays, media releases, meetings, publications, speeches and events. (Sometimes known as a public relations tactic, or as collateral.)

Conflict
A factor in deciding whether your information is newsworthy. Is your information about a controversial subject? Does your organisation have a different view of an issue from others? Have your researchers discovered something that challenges accepted, current knowledge?

Consultancy
A business that provides public relations services, sometimes also known as an agency. See *consultant*.

Consultant
An external public relations practitioner engaged by the organisation to work on a specific project or to provide advice.

Context
'The circumstances relevant to something under consideration (*must be seen in context*)' so that something that is *out of context* is 'without the surrounding words or circumstances and so not fully understandable' (The *Australian Concise Oxford Dictionary*, 6th edn).

Controlled communication
A communication pathway that uses tools such as an organisation's own publications or other material that cannot be changed or filtered by others.

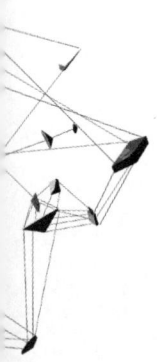

Culture
'The customs, civilisation and achievements of a particular time or people' (The *Australian Concise Oxford Dictionary*). Some people, perhaps migrants, suffer 'culture shock' when they experience an unfamiliar culture or way of life. 'Multiculturalism' means the existence of many culturally distinct groups in a society.

Defamation
An act, usually written or spoken words, that attacks a person's good reputation.

Desk research
Research that practitioners can do from existing published sources like reports, historical data, the media, official files, and websites.

Dominant coalition
The most senior group of decision-makers in an organisation. Membership of a dominant coalition can vary according to the issue being addressed, or a particular operational focus.

Editor
The executive in charge of a news organisation; the head of a section of a news organisation (e.g. the finance editor); the person who prepares written material for publication.

Entertain
In a speech, to amuse an audience.

Environmental scanning
A process of identifying, analysing and interpreting internal and external social, political and economic factors that impact on an organisation's ability to pursue its business.

Ethics
'**1** the science of morals in human conduct. **2 a** moral principles; rules of conduct. **2 b** a set of these (medical ethics)' (*The Australian Concise Oxford Dictionary*, 6th edn).

Evaluation
The process of reviewing whether a public relations plan achieved its goals and objectives.

Exhibition
A large event at which organisations from a range of industries display their products.

Fact sheet
A set of factual data about an organisation's product, person, event or issue, usually in hard-copy form.

File note
A written record of a conversation, an event or a meeting that is filed for future reference.

Financial year
The twelve months for which a company reports its annual financial performance.

Five Ws and H
The what, when, where, who, why and how questions that help to determine what needs to be included in a media release.

Flyer
Usually a single sheet of printed information for wide distribution.

Formal research
Either *qualitative* or *quantitative research* that is normally commissioned through an external commercial market research company.

Formative research
Formal or informal research that is conducted before a public relations plan is written and that is used to inform the *situation analysis*.

Goal
A broad statement of what the organisation hopes to achieve and which reflects the organisation's business strategy. Goals deal with *reputation*, *relationships* or *tasks*.

Human interest
A factor in deciding whether your information is newsworthy. Does your information relate to interesting personal stories? Can people relate to it at a human level?

Implementation
The phase of a public relations plan that describes how and when tactics will be implemented.

Inform
In a public relations context, to clarify, instruct or demonstrate a point.

Informative communication
A message delivery strategy that utilises tools that only provide information.

Input
The formative research used to write a situation analysis.

Interpersonal communication
A communication pathway that involves communicating directly with people—for example, in a face-to-face meeting

Interview
An event at which a journalist asks someone questions, usually on a one-to-one basis.

Issue
An internal or external factor that has an impact on the organisation's ability to pursue its business.

Journalist
A professional who works in the news media. Not all journalists are reporters; some are editors and sub-editors.

Launch
An event, or action, that marks the beginning of an event, a project, or the availability of a product.

Leaflet
A small publication of several pages.

Libel
A published, unjustified statement about a person that harms their reputation.

Matrix
A grid that shows in a graphic form how the parts of something—in this case, activities in a public relations plan—fit together.

Media alert (or advisory)
A short *media release* to advise the media of an event, usually a day or so before it occurs.

Media analysis (or media content analysis)
The process of analysing the contents of articles in the print and electronic media to identify how the issues they discuss might impact on the organisation, how the organisation has been reported, and what others are saying about the organisation.

Media conference
An event at which journalists have the opportunity to ask a representative of the organisation questions about an issue or a media release.

Media kit
A pack of material about an organisation, usually in hard copy but often published on a website.

Media monitoring
The regular scanning of the print and electronic media for articles of interest to the organisation. Most organisations contract a commercial media monitoring agency to do this work.

Media release
The supply of information on issues and events to the media, usually in written form (see Stanton, 2007).

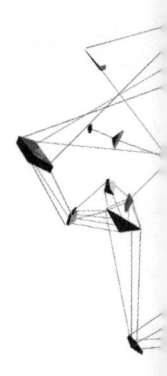

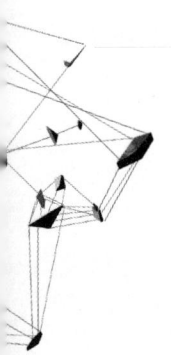

Meeting minutes
A record of the discussion at a meeting.

Memo (short for memorandum)
A short, written note about a specific point, usually for internal purposes.

Message
Information given to target publics to create awareness, or build credibility, or persuade them to take action that is favourable to the organisation. Messages can be *informative* or *persuasive*.

News release
See *media release*.

Objective
A precise and measurable statement of what the organisation needs to do in order to achieve a goal. Objectives deal with changes: raising awareness, building acceptance and convincing publics to take action that is favourable to the organisation.

Opportunities
In the context of a *SWOT analysis*, the external conditions that will assist an organisation to achieve its goals.

Outcome
A measurement that shows whether a public changed its knowledge, attitudes and behaviours as a result of a public relations campaign. Achieving outcomes is the most important part of a public relations plan.

Output
A measurement of the frequency with which a program's public relations tools were used.

Outtake
Measurements of what a target public does with a message. For instance, they might remember a message but take no action as a result of it.

Persuade
In a public relations context, to convince a target public to adopt a point of view or to take a particular action.

Persuasive communication
A message delivery strategy that uses tools designed to persuade people to a particular point of view or to take action.

Planning worksheet
A planning tool that helps to identify what information needs to be included in a media release, a speech or other material. For a media release, a planning worksheet includes identifying the news lead, or main point, of the release.

Practice
A noun that describes the professional work of public relations people.

Practise
A verb that describes the action of doing public relations work.

Practitioner
A professional who does public relations work.

Press release
See *media release*.

PRIA
Public Relations Institute of Australia.

Profile
A narrative article about a senior person, their role in the organisation, biography and achievements, sometimes based on an interview with the person.

Prominence
A factor in deciding whether your information is newsworthy. Can you relate your information to a well-known person?

Proximity
A factor in deciding whether your information is newsworthy. Can you 'localise' your information by linking it to a particular community?

Public relations
The deliberate, planned and sustained effort to establish and maintain mutual understanding between an organisation (or individual) and its (or their) publics.

Public relations strategic plan
A description of how an organisation will achieve its communication goals and objectives.

Public relations tool
See *communication tool*.

Qualitative research
Research that is concerned with finding out people's attitudes and opinions.

Quantitative research
Research that reports results as numbers.

Question and answer (QnA) sheet
A set of questions and answers about an organisation, product, event or issue written by a public relations practitioner for the media and other target publics, and usually produced in hard-copy form. The questions are usually those that the practitioner thinks journalists might ask. These questions are sometimes also described as 'frequently asked questions'.

Rarity
A factor in deciding whether your information is newsworthy. Does your information relate to something that is not commonplace? Is it the biggest, smallest, fastest, slowest, cleanest, dirtiest, oldest, youngest?

Reflection
Thinking about information you have read, or your experiences, to analyse what you have learnt.

Relationship
A connection or association between people or organisations.

Relevance
A factor in deciding whether your information is newsworthy. How does your information affect people's lives, incomes, health, relationships, and entertainment choices? Does it pass the 'Who cares?' test?

Reporter
A journalist who reports the news.

Reputation
What is said about a person (or organisation) or their behaviour; how others regard a person (or organisation).

Response sheet
A *communication tool* for giving a detailed answer to a single question, usually in the context of managing an issue or crisis.

Significance
A factor in deciding whether your information is newsworthy. Does your information affect a significant number of people? Why and how?

Situation analysis
The first part of a public relations plan in which a practitioner analyses the communication issues facing an organisation, and assesses the results of formal and informal research.

Strategy
What organisations and individuals do to achieve goals, usually over the long term. Like many terms used in business and other areas, strategy is a military term. See message delivery strategy.

Strengths
In the context of a *SWOT analysis*, characteristics of an organisation than can help to achieve its goals.

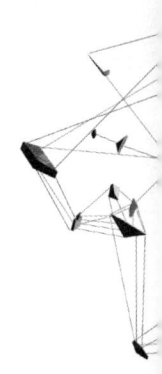

GLOSSARY

Sub-editor
A journalist who assists the editor to prepare material for publication.

Submission
A detailed written argument supporting the organisation's views on an issue or proposal, usually for an external inquiry. Sometimes submissions are required internally to support an application for a budget increase or other resources, or to seek approval for a proposed course of action.

Summative research
Formal or informal research conducted at the end of a campaign to assess effectiveness.

SWOT analysis
An analytical tool that helps to classify an organisation's strengths, weaknesses, opportunities and threats from *formative research* findings.

Talking points
A short summary of important points about an issue that help executives in interviews with journalists or in giving speeches.

Target public (or often 'public')
The people to whom public relations messages are directed.

Task
Something that needs to be done to implement a plan.

Think tank
An organisation that employs specialists to research and comment on important public issues.

Threats
In the context of a *SWOT analysis*, external conditions that could prevent an organisation from achieving its goals.

Timeline
A graphic representation or typed list of the length of time taken to complete tasks in a project.

Timeliness
A factor in deciding whether your information is newsworthy. Is it literally 'new', and are you releasing it at an appropriate time?

Trade show
A special event at which groups or organisations representing a particular industry, or trade, display their products.

Trendiness
A factor in deciding whether your information is newsworthy. Can you relate your information to the latest trend, fashion or food craze, or to popular entertainment?

Uncontrolled communication
A communication pathway that involves *communication tools* such as *media releases* or other material that can be changed by others.

Venue
The place where an event is held.

Weaknesses
In the context of a *SWOT analysis*, the characteristics of an organisation that might harm its ability to achieve its goals.

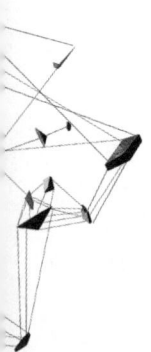

Worksheet
See *planning worksheet*.

REFERENCES

Alexander, D. (2006). 'Reframing leadership communication: Consequences for organisational leaders resulting from communication failure: An Australian case study', in J.C. Anyanwu (ed.), *Empowerment, Creativity and Innovation: Challenging Media and Communication in the 21st Century*, ANZCA and University of Adelaide: Adelaide: <www.anzca.net/past-conferences/anzca06proceedings.html>.

Andrews, P.N. (1985). 'The sticky wicket of evaluating public affairs: thoughts about a framework', *Public Affairs Review*, 6(3), pp. 94–105.

Bach, D. & Allen, D.B. (2010). 'What every CEO needs to know about *non*market strategy', *MIT Sloan Management Review*, 51(3), pp. 41–8.

Barrett, D.J. (2002). 'Change communication: using strategic employee communication to facilitate major change', *Corporate Communications: An International Journal*, 7(4), pp. 219–31.

Bernstein, M. (2002). '10 tips on writing the Living Web', *A List Apart*, issue no. 149, 16 August: <www.alistapart.com/articles/writeliving/>.

Bouzon, A. & Devillard, J. (2009). 'Changes in contemporary organisations and interculturality: From orchestrated communication to confidence', *PRism*, 6(2): <www.prismjournal.org/fileadmin/Praxis/Files/globalPR/BOUZON_DEVILLARD.pdf>.

Bruno, A.J. (2016). '2 steps to simplifying PR metrics', *PR Daily News Feed*, 16 November, 2016 (n.p.).

Carlisle, A. (2017). '3 missteps that can kill your media relations efforts', *PR Daily News Feed*, 8 February 2017 (n.p.).

Catalano, C.S. (2007). 'Megaphones to the Internet and the world: The role of blogs in corporate communications', *International Journal of Strategic Communication*, 1(4), pp. 247–62.

Chia, J. (2009). 'Trends and developments', in J. Chia & G. Synnott (eds), *An Introduction to Public Relations: From Theory to Practice*, Oxford University Press: Melbourne, pp. 31–53.

Comrie, M. (2000), 'Communication and community: Two experiences of communication', *Asia Pacific Public Relations Journal*, 2(1), pp. 21–34.

Conley, D. & Lamble, S. (2006). *The Daily Miracle: An Introduction to Journalism*, 3rd edn, Oxford University Press: Melbourne.

Corbett, W.J. (1989). 'Techniques of internal communication', in S.A. White (ed.), *Values and Communication: Selected Proceedings of the 11th Public Relations World Congress*, Melbourne, 26–29 April 1988, Longman Professional: Melbourne, pp. 193–207.

Cornelissen, J. (2000). 'Toward an understanding of the use of academic theories in public relations practice', *Public Relations Review*, 26(3), pp. 315–26.

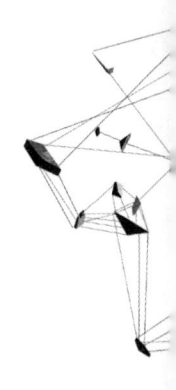

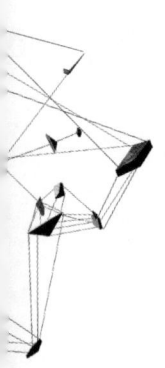

Cornelissen, J. (2005). *Corporate Communication: Theory and Practice*, SAGE: London.

Crowley, S. (2007). 'Who needs headlines?' *A List Apart*, issue no. 238, 29 May: <www.alistapart.com/articles/whoneedsheadlines>.

Cutlip, S.M., Centre, A.H. & Broom, G.M. (2006). *Effective Public Relations*, 9th edn, Pearson: Upper Saddle River, NJ.

Dakin, S. (1989). 'Research for workforce morale', in S.A. White (ed.), *Values and Communication: Selected Proceedings of the 11th Public Relations World Congress*, Melbourne, 26–29 April 1988, Longman Professional: Melbourne, pp. 234–42.

Dilenschneider, R.L. (1989). 'Keynote address: communication', in S.A. White (ed.), *Values and Communication: Selected Proceedings of the 11th Public Relations World Congress*, Melbourne, 26–29 April 1988, Longman Professional: Melbourne, pp. 17–21.

Dutta, M.J., Ban, Z. & Pal, M. (2012). 'Engaging worldviews, cultures, and structures through dialogue: The culture-centred approach to public relations', *PRism*, 9(2): <www.prismjournal.org/fileadmin/9_2/Dutta_Ban_Pal.pdf>.

Fisher, C. (2016). 'Ten shades of truth: A study of Australian journalists' shift to political PR', *Public Relations Review*, 42(4), pp. 665–72.

Gabbot, M. & Clulow, V. (1999). 'The elaboration likelihood model of persuasive communication', in P.J. Kitchen (ed.), *Marketing Communications: Principles and Practice*, Thomson: London, pp. 172–88.

Gentile, K. (2005). 'The essentials of writing effective emails', *GoogoBits.com*, 3 June: <www.googobits.com/articles/356-the-essentials-of-writing-effective-emails.html>.

Glenny, L. & Singh, R. (2009). 'Research and evaluation', in J. Johnston & C. Zawawi (eds), *Public Relations Theory and Practice*, 3rd edn, Allen & Unwin: Sydney, pp. 140–70.

Green, J. (2012), 'The truth is we're probably not very nice', *The Drum*, 4 October: <www.abc.net.au/news/2012-10-04/green-jones/4293938>.

Gregory, A. (2009a). 'Management and organisation of public relations', in R. Tench and L. Yeomans (eds), *Exploring Public Relations*, 2nd edn, Prentice Hall: London, pp. 19–34.

Gregory, A. (2009b). 'Public relations as planned communication', in R. Tench and L. Yeomans (eds), *Exploring Public Relations*, 2nd edn, Prentice Hall: London, pp. 174–97.

Grunig, J.E. (ed.) (1992). *Excellence in Public Relations and Communication Management*, Lawrence Erlbaum Associates: Hillsdale, NJ.

Grunig, J.E. (2001). 'Two-way symmetrical public relations: past, present, and future', in R.L. Heath (ed.), *Handbook of Public Relations*, SAGE: Thousand Oaks, CA, pp. 11–30.

Grunig, J.E. (2006). 'Furnishing the edifice: ongoing research on public relations as a strategic management function', *Journal of Public Relations Research*, 18(2), pp. 151–76.

Grunig, J.E. & Hunt, T (1984). *Managing Public Relations*, Holt, Rhinehart and Winston: New York.

Grunig, J.E. & Repper, F.C. (1992). 'Strategic management, publics and issues', in J.E. Grunig (ed.), *Excellence in Public Relations and Communication Management*, Lawrence Erlbaum Associates: Hillsdale, NJ, pp. 109–16.

Guth, D.W. & Marsh, C. (2006). *Public Relations: A Values-Driven Approach*, 3rd edn, Pearson: Boston.

Hallahan, K. (2000). 'Inactive publics: The forgotten publics in public relations', *Public Relations Review*, 26(4), pp. 499–515.

Harrison, K. (2011). *Strategic Public Relations: A Practical Guide to Success*, Palgrave Macmillan: Melbourne.

Heath, R.L. (2001). 'A rhetorical enactment rationale for public relations: The good organisation communicating well', in R.L. Heath (ed.), *Handbook of Public Relations*, SAGE: Thousand Oaks, CA, pp. 31–50.

Herzberg, F. (1987). 'One more time: How do you motivate employees?' *Harvard Business Review*, 65(5), September/October, pp. 109–20.

Highfield, T. & Leaver, T. (2016). 'Instagrammatics and digital methods: studying visual social media, from selfies and GIFs to memes and emoji', *Communication Research and Practice*, 2(1), pp. 47–62.

Ingham, E. (2015). 'Here Are The Reasons Why Twitter Is The Best Social Media Platform For Your Start-up Business', *Forbes*, May 31, 2015: <http://www.forbes.com/sites/edmundingham/2015/05/31/here-are-the-reasons-why-twitter-is-the-best-social-media-platform-for-your-start-up-business/#6a703aa17991>.

Jagoe, A.L. (1987). *The Winning Corporation*, Acropolis Books Ltd: Washington, DC.

Jaques, T. (2009), 'Integrating Issue Management and Strategic Planning: Unfulfilled Promise or Future Opportunity?' *International Journal of Strategic Communication*, 3(1), pp. 19–33.

Jaques, T. (2014). *Issues and Crisis Management: Exploring issues, crises, risk and reputation*, Oxford University Press: South Melbourne.

Jo, S. & Shim, S.W. (2005). 'Paradigm shift of employee communication: The effect of management communication on trusting relationships', *Public Relations Review*, 31(2), pp. 277–80.

Johnston, J. (2007). *Media Relations*, Allen & Unwin: Sydney.

Johnston, J. & Zawawi, C. (eds) (2004). *Public Relations Theory and Practice*, 2nd edn, Allen & Unwin: Sydney.

Johnston, J. & Zawawi, C. (eds) (2009). *Public Relations Theory and Practice*, 3rd edn, Allen & Unwin: Sydney.

Kaplan, A.M. & Haenlein, M. (2010). 'Users of the world, unite! The challenges and opportunities of social media', *Business Horizons*, 53, pp. 59–68.

Kim, Y.W. (1999). 'Measuring the bottom-line impact of public relations at the organisational level', paper submitted to the Institute for Public Relations for the 1998 Smart Grant, Florida.

Lattimore, D., Baskin, O., Heiman, S., Toth, E. & van Leuven, J. (2004). *Public Relations: The Profession and the Practice*, McGraw Hill: Boston.

Mackey, S. (2009). 'Public relations theory', in J. Johnston and C. Zawawi (eds), *Public Relations Theory and Practice*, 3rd edn, Allen & Unwin: Sydney, pp. 47–77.

Macnamara, J. (2012). *Public Relations: Theories, Practices, Critiques*, Pearson: Sydney.

Macnamara, J. (2014). 'Journalism–PR relations revisited: The good news, the bad news, and insights into tomorrow's news', *Public Relations Review*, 40(5), pp. 739–50.

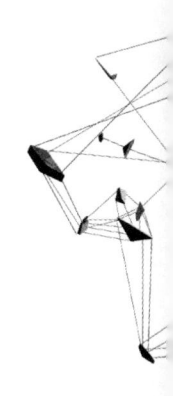

Mahoney, J.S. (2013). *Strategic Communication: Principles and Practice*, Oxford University Press: Melbourne.

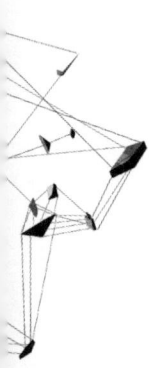

Mahoney, J.S. (2017). *Strategic Communication: Campaign Planning*, 2nd edn, Oxford University Press, Melbourne.

McCoy, L. (2009). 'Ethical practice', in J. Johnston & C. Zawawi (eds), *Public Relations Theory and Practice*, 3rd edn, Allen & Unwin: Sydney, pp. 108–35.

McDonald, L.M. & Hebbani, A.G. (2011). 'Back to the future: Is strategic management (re)emerging as public relations' dominant paradigm?', *PRism*, 8(1): <www.prismjournal.org/fileadmin/8_1/mcdonald_hebbani.pdf>.

Morris, T. & Goldsworthy, S. (2012). *PR Today: The Authoritative Guide to Public Relations*, Palgrave Macmillan: Houndmills.

Nielsen, J. (2011). 'How long do users stay on web pages?', *Jakob Nielsen's Alertbox*, 12 September: <www.nngroup.com/articles/how-long-do-users-stay-on-web-pages/>.

Niemela, A. (2012). 'The affordances of social media', <www.aprilniemela.com>, 1 June.

Pascale, R.T. & Sternin, J. (2005). 'Your company's secret change agents', *Harvard Business Review*, 83(5), pp. 72–81.

Peters, T.J. & Waterman, R.H. (1984). *In Search of Excellence: Lesson from America's Best-Run Companies*, Harper & Row: Sydney.

Pittman, B. (2017). 'Keep the love alive: 3 ways to sweeten PR pitches', *PR Daily Extra*, 8 February 2017 (n.p.).

Robson, P. & Sutherland, K.E. (2012). 'Public relations practitioners and social media: Themes in a global context', in M.D. Sison & M. Sheehan (eds), *World Public Relations Forum 2012: Research Colloquium— Conference Proceedings*, World Public Relations Forum and Public Relations Institute of Australia: Melbourne, pp. 103–7.

Rubin, C. (2011). 'Study: Employees are unproductive half the day', *Inc.*, 2 March: <www.inc.com/news/articles/201103/workers-spend-half-day-being-unproductive.html>.

Seitel, F.P. (2011). *The Practice of Public Relations*, 11th edn, Pearson: Upper Saddle River, NJ.

Siapera, E. (2012). *Understanding New Media*, SAGE: London.

Simmons, P. & Watson, T. (2005). 'Public relations evaluation in Australia: Practices and attitudes across sectors and employment status', *Asia Pacific Public Relations Journal*, 6(2), pp. 1–14.

Sinickas, A. (2006). 'Tailoring campaigns by audience', *Strategic Communication Management*, 10(1), pp. 12–13.

Sison, M.D. (2009a). 'Whose cultural values? Exploring public relations' approaches to understanding audiences', *Prism*, 6(2): <www.prismjournal.org/fileadmin/Praxis/Files/globalPR/SISON.pdf>.

Sison, M.D. (2009b). 'Theoretical contexts', in J. Chia & G. Synnott (eds), *An Introduction to Public Relations: From Theory to Practice*, Oxford University Press: Melbourne, pp. 54–89.

Sison, M.D. (2012). 'Theoretical contexts', in J. Chia & G. Synnott (eds), *An Introduction to Public Relations and Communication Management*, 2nd edn, Oxford University Press: Melbourne, pp. 56–87.

Slater, A. (2006). 'Laws that affect public relations practice', in C. Tymson, P. Lazar & R. Lazar (eds), *The New Australian and New Zealand Public Relations Manual*, Tymson Communications: Sydney, pp. 154–79.

Smith, R.D. (2009). *Strategic Planning for Public Relations*, 3rd edn, Routledge, New York.

Sollis, B. & Breakenridge, D. (2009). *Putting the Public Back in Public Relations: How Social Media Is Reinventing the Aging Business of PR*, Pearson: Upper Saddle River, NJ.

Stanton, R. (2007). *Media Relations*, Oxford University Press: Melbourne.

Ströh, U. (2006). 'The impact of organisational change communication approaches on employee relationships: An experimental study', *Asia Pacific Public Relations Journal*, 7, pp. 247–76.

Style Manual for Authors, Editors and Printers (2002). 6th edn, John Wiley & Sons: Brisbane.

Szondi, G. (2009). 'International context of public relations', in R. Tench & L. Yeomans (eds), *Exploring Public Relations*, 2nd edn, Prentice Hall: London, pp. 117–46.

Szondi, G. & Theilmann, R. (2009). 'Public relations research and evaluation', in R. Tench & L. Yeomans (eds), *Exploring Public Relations*, 2nd edn, Prentice Hall: London, pp. 198–221.

Tench, R. & Yeomans, L. (2009). *Exploring Public Relations*, 2nd edn, Prentice Hall: London.

Tkalac Verčič, A. & Colić, V. (2016) 'Journalists and public relations specialists: A coorientational analysis', *Public Relations Review*, 42(4), pp. 522–9.

Tymson, C., Lazar, P. & Lazar, R. (2006). *The New Australian and New Zealand Public Relations Manual*, 5th edn, Tymson Communications: Sydney.

Vaughn, R. & Cody, S. (2007). 'Seize the day: Dynamics that will raise the profile of public relations in 2007', *Public Relations Tactics*, January: <www.prsa.org/Intelligence/Tactics/Articles/view/6C-010701/101/Seize_the_day_Dynamics_that_will_raise_the_profile>.

Wakefield, R.I. (2010). 'Why culture is still essential in discussions about global public relations', in R.L. Heath (ed.), *The SAGE Handbook of Public Relations*, SAGE: Thousand Oaks, CA, pp. 659–70.

Walker, G. (1994). 'Communicating public relations research', *Journal of Public Relations Research*, 6(3), pp. 141–61.

Walker, G. (1997). 'Public relations practitioners' use of research, measurement and evaluation', *Australian Journal of Communication*, 24(2), pp. 97–113.

Walker, M. & McColl Jones, M. (1999). *Ladies and Gentlemen: Tales and Misadventures from the Microphone*, Allen & Unwin: Sydney.

Watson, D. (2003). *Death Sentence: The Decay of Public Language*, Vintage Books: Sydney.

Watson, D. (2005). *Watson's Dictionary of Weasel Words, Contemporary Clichés, Cant and Management Jargon*, Vintage Books: Sydney.

Watson, T. (2006). 'Editorial: Evaluation—let's get on with it', *PRism*, 4(2): <www.prismjournal.org/fileadmin/Praxis/Files/Journal_Files/Evaluation_Issue/EDITORIAL.pdf>.

Watson, T. & Noble, P. (2007). *Evaluating Public Relations: A Best Practice Guide to Public Relations Planning, Research and Evaluation*, Kogan Page: London.

Wilcox, D.L. & Cameron, G.T. (2012). *Public Relations Strategies and Tactics*, 10th edn, Pearson: Boston.

Wills, T. (2016). 'Social media as a research method', *Communication Research and Practice*, 2(1), pp. 7–19.

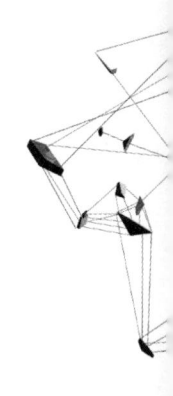

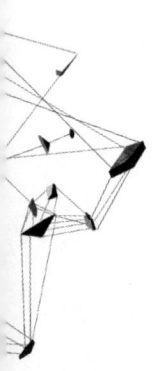

Wood, E. (2009). 'Corporate communication', in R. Tench & L. Yeomans (eds), *Exploring Public Relations*, 2nd edn, Prentice Hall: London, pp. 539–59.

Wood, J. et al. (2004). *Organisational Behaviour: A Global Perspective*, 3rd edn, Wiley: Brisbane.

Xavier, R., Mehta, A. & Gregory, A. (2006). 'Evaluation in use: The practitioner view of effective evaluation', *PRism*, 4(2): <www.prismjournal.org/fileadmin/Praxis/Files/Journal_Files/Evaluation_Issue/XAVIER_ET_AL_ARTICLE.pdf>.

Xavier, R., Patel, A. & Johnston, K. (2004). 'Are we really making a difference? The gap between outcomes and evaluation research in public relations campaigns', paper presented to the Australian and New Zealand Communication Association Annual Conference, Sydney, July 2004: <conferences.arts.usyd.edu.au/papers.php?first_letter=X&cf=3>.

INDEX

AC Nielsen 249
acquired needs theory 212
active voice, use of 124
Adams, Phillip 186
advertising value equivalents 246–7
affordances 149–50
Age, The 20
agenda setting theory 83
Al Jazeera 95–6, 111
Alexander, Donald 212
Allen, David 24
Allert, John 35
alliances 100
Almond Board of Australia 89
AM (ABC Radio) 108
analysis 14
Andrews, Patti Nelson 247–8, 254
annual reports 51–2, 61, 194–5
Apostrophe Protection Society 13
'Arab Spring' 147
Arts & Letters Daily website 20
Asimov, Isaac 221
Atlantic, The 203
attachments, use of 158–9
Australian Broadcasting Commission Standing Committee on Spoken English 9
Australian Bureau of Statistics (ABS) 51, 147
Australian Labor Party 93

Bach, David 24
backgrounders 114, 193, 197–8, 201
Barrett, Deborah 211, 221
basic communication model 81
BBC World News 111
Beaupre, Andy 159–60

behaviour, awareness and attitudinal analysis 247
Beres, Damon 139
Bernays, Edward 202
Bernstein, Mark 153–4
Blog Herald 148, 156
blogs 146–7, 156, 166, 244
boundary spanning 3, 5, 24
Bouzon, Arlette 65
Breakenridge, Deidre 148
Breit, Rhona 36–8
Brexit 147
brochures 193–7
Brookings Institution 54
Bruno, A.J. 244–5
budgets for projects 232–4
Burke, Edmund 108
business 31

Cacioppo, John 183
Cameron, Glen 72
Caplow, Theodore 212
Carlisle, A. 139
Catalano, Charles 147
census 51
Centre for Strategic Studies: New Zealand 54
charities 31
Chartered Institute of Public Relations (UK) 55
checklists 15
Chia, Joy 31, 184
chiefs of staff 111
Cho, Allan 149
Christchurch earthquake 57–8
Clinton, Hillary 93

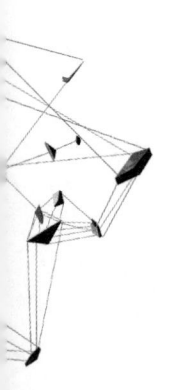

closed systems   3, 97
Clulow, Val   184
CNN   111
Cody, Steve   23, 35
Cohen, Bernard   83
Colic, Violeta   136
Common, Grant   205
Commonwealth Scientific and Industrial Research Organisation (CSIRO)   54
communication
   asymmetrical   45–6, 97
   controlled   44–6, 99
   with employees during change   221–4
   informative   10
   interactive   100
   interpersonal   99–100, 177–91, 213
   multicultural   63–5
   within organisations   210–24
   pathways   14, 34, 43–5, 49, 87, 98–100, 201–2, 215
   peer-to-peer   148
   persuasive   10, 39, 178, 183
   symmetrical   45–6, 97
   two-way symmetrical   38, 45–6, 97, 100, 160, 213
   uncontrolled   44–6, 99, 201–2
Competition and Consumer Act 2010   37
complexity theory   84, 96–7, 212
conflict as news   118
constraint recognition   81, 97
consultants   4, 68–9, 234–7
context   22–3
contingency theory   84, 97
Conversation, The (website)   54
Cornelissen, Joep   23, 28, 92, 184
Corporate Communications: Theory and Practice (Cornelissen)   28
Crowley, Shaun   153
cultural diversity   65
culture   63
Cutlip, Scot   30

Daly, Fred   181
Davison, Lucy   134
Death Sentence: The Decay of Public Language (Watson)   12, 184
defamation   93
designers, briefing   237–8
desk research   26, 50
Devillard, Joëlle   65
Dictionary of Weasel Words, Contemporary Clichés, Cant and Management Jargon (Watson)   12
diffusion theory   98
Dilenschneider, Robert   24, 34–5
dominant coalitions   8, 33
Drum website (ABC)   151
Dutta, Mohan   63

editors   20, 83, 108, 111–12, 203
efficiency   44
elaboration likelihood model   183–4, 202
Elements of Eloquence, The (Forsyth)   185
email
   direct access to publics   153
   as public relations tool   156–9, 170
   for staff communication   218
employee communication plan   213–21
environmental scanning   24, 26–7, 29–30, 50
ethics
   assessment   38
   codes of practice   6–7, 10, 37, 93
   definitions   6
   message writing   93
evaluation
   of credibility   252
   definition   49–50
   of financial impacts   253–4
   methods   244–7
   reasons for   243–4
   of response capability   253
   staff communication plan   215
   strategic plans   68–9, 88, 243–54
   successful   247–8

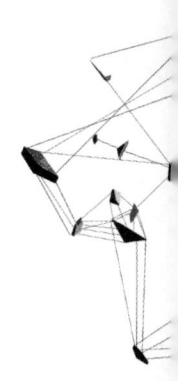

Excellence Theory (Grunig)   80
exhibitions   188
expectancy theory   86, 212–13

Facebook
    broad applications   146
    getting the right 'fans'   148–9
    monitoring   50
    popularity   166
    product launches   8
    as public relations tool   170
fact sheets   115, 118, 193, 198–9, 201
feedback
    for evaluation   244, 252–3
    Murray–Darling example   6
    to and from staff   213–14, 217–19
    via social media   152
    via website   6, 45, 146, 152, 169
file notes   223
financial years   51
Fisher, Caroline   137
FitzSimons, Peter   185
Flatman, Michael   58
flyers   248
focus   247
'For Immediate Release'   129
force-field analysis   xviii
formal research   55
formative research   49
Forsyth, Mark   185
Foucault, Michel   80
Fourth Estate   108
Fowler, H.W.   18, 20
Fowler's Modern English Usage (Oxford University Press)   18–19
Fox News   111
framing theory   83
Freeman, Meagan   148–9
futurists   24

Gabbot, Mark   184
Gantt chart   xviii, xxii, 196, 231–2
Gao Xingjian   10
'general public'   75
Gentile, Kathy   157
Gettysburg Address (Lincoln)   132–3
Global Alliance World Public Relations Forum   166
goals
    definitions   14, 48, 69–70
    evaluation and   248
    matching messages to   95–6
    matching objectives   71–2
    role in strategic plan   87
    for staff communication plan   214
Goldsworthy, Simon   134
grammar
    adjectives   185
    importance   10, 18
    see also punctuation; spelling
Green, Jonathan   151
Gregory, Anne   28, 48, 89, 245
Grunig, James   6, 24, 28, 33, 36, 44–5, 75, 80–1, 97, 201–2, 211, 213
Grynbaum, Michael M.   137
Guth, David   88

Habermas, Jürgen   80
Haenlein, Michael   173
Hall, Dayle   165
Hallahan, Kirk   74–5, 80, 82
Hallahan's typology of publics   82
Harrison, K.   37–8, 90
Heart Support-Australia   58–9
Heath, Robert   31, 36, 89, 149
Hebbani, Aparna   35
Heller, Joe   186
Herlt, Isabelle   58–9
Herzberg, Frederick   85, 212
'hierarchy of needs'   80
Highfield, T.   155

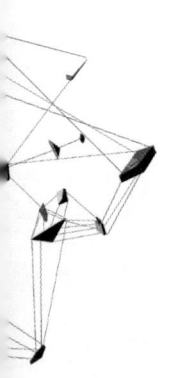

Homescan 249
honesty 137, 139–40
HootSuite 171
How to Run any Organisation (Caplow) 212
human interest 118
Hunt, Todd 6, 45, 97

Iacocca, Lee 211
Iannelli, Rosalie 134
IBM 218–21
impact xxi
implementation 49, 88, 119, 215
infographics 172
information processing 98
information seeking 98
informing 39
Ingham, Edmund 171
input 39
Instagram 146
International Public Relations Association (IPRA) 244
internet
    reading screens 150–1
    as research tool 55
    usage statistics 150, 166
    see also intranets; social media; websites
interviews
    definition 7
    outside venues 140
intranets 213, 217–20
inverted pyramid 122, 142
issues
    definition 1
    identifying and analysing 26–7
issues matrix xx, xxi

Jacques, Tony 26
jobs in public relations 3–6
Johnson, Shannon 175
Johnston, J. 136
Journal of Communication Management 255
Journal of Public Relations Research 255

journalists
    contacts 138, 140, 144
    definition 4
    frustrations with PR practitioners 136–7
    role of 107–8
    specialists 109, 128
    as target publics 73, 76, 109–10
    views of media releases 129
    views of social media 129

Kaplan, Andreas 173
Keating, Paul 12, 191
Killen, Sir James 181
Knight, Ron 252

Lane, Clare 165
Lattimore, Dan 28, 92
launches 4
Lazar, Peter 24
Lazar, Richard 25
leaflets 4
Leaver, T. 155
Lee, Ivy 112, 120, 201, 259
legal aspects 36–8
level of involvement 81, 97
libel 93
libraries 51
Lincoln, Abraham 132–3
LinkedIn 146, 166, 170
Lippmann, Walter 83
Lowy Institute 54
Lyons, Stephanie 58–9

Machiavelli, Niccolò 22, 260
Mackey, Steve 92, 184
Macnamara, J. 137, 184, 244
Mahoney, J.S. 65
market research 52–3
Marr, David 9
Marsh, Charles 88
Maslow, Abraham 80

INDEX

Massachusetts Institute of Technology 54, 163, 201
Masters, Rob 246
matrix 67–8
McCarthy, Jan 58
McClelland, David 85, 212
McColl Jones, Mike 189
McCombs, Max 83
McCoy, Lelde 37–8
McDonald, Lynette 35
McKinsey 260
Médecins Sans Frontières 32
media
    controlled 44–6, 99
    interactive 43–5, 100
    interpersonal 44, 46, 99–100
    uncontrolled 43–6, 99
media advisory 113–14
media alert 113–14
media analysis 250
media conferences 102, 140
media content analysis 250
media effects theory 83
media kits 114–15, 200
Media Masters Training 88
media monitoring 53
media relations 136–41
Media Relations (Stanton) 10
media releases
    addressing 131
    approval 144
    barriers to publication 130, 143
    body of release 124
    checklist 142–4
    contact details 126, 134, 140, 144
    dating 130, 144
    defining target public 121–2
    definition 11, 112–14
    embargoes 129–30, 141
    fonts 127
    formatting 127–8, 143
    graphics 155
    headings xxvi, 128, 135, 143, 154
    honesty 137, 139–40
    inverted pyramid 122, 142
    length 143, 154
    lists 155
    pathway after distribution 110–11
    planning worksheet xxvi, xxvii, 121, 142
    podcasts 155
    practical steps 140–1
    profiles 115, 154
    proofreading 144, 159
    quotes, use of 126, 135, 142
    social media checklist 153
    use of social media 146–73
    videos 155
    website links 144, 154–5
    'why', 'what', 'who', 'how', 'where', 'when' 121, 134–5, 203
    writing 120–30, 134–5
media stunts 119
media training for interviewees 141
Medianet 129
meeting minutes xxiv–xxvi, 237
memos 222–3
message carriage 247
messages
    communication messages 34
    consistency 87
    definitions 8, 14, 48
    importance 87–8
    informative 91–2
    'message map' 91
    persuasive 92–5
    quantity 90
    relevance 88–9, 96
    repetition 43–4
    richness 44
messaging 167, 171
Morris, Trevor 134
multicultural communication 63–5

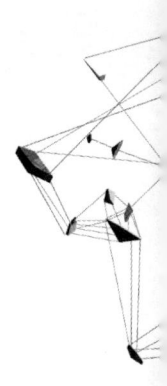

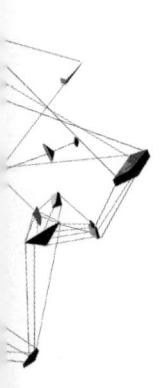

multiculturalism   64
Multimedia Messaging Service (MMS)   167
Murray–Darling River catchment   6, 27

National Heart Foundation   248–50
needs   80, 85
New Statesman   203
New York Times, The   20, 207
news
   conflict   118
   external sources   120
   frames   116, 142
   human interest   118
   internal sources   120
   news cycle   139
   news lead   123, 129, 142
   prominence   117
   proximity   117
   rarity   117
   relevance   116
   significance   117
space   111–12
   timeliness   116
   trendiness   118
   understanding   115–16
NewsBank database   59
newspaper features   203, 207–8
newsworthiness   112, 138
Nielsen, J.   151, 154
Niemela, April   149

Obama, Barack   93, 147, 172
objectives
   communication objectives   34
   definitions   14, 48, 69–70
   evaluation and   248
   matching goals   71–2
   matching messages to   95–6, 122
   role in strategic plan   87
   for staff communication plan   214
   writing   72

'off the record'   141
omnibus surveys   52
'op-ed' articles   203, 207–8
open systems   3, 97
organisations
   communication during change   221–4
   communication within   210–24
   decision making   32–3
   dominant coalitions   33
   evaluating credibility   252
   evaluating financial impacts   253–4
   evaluating response capability   253
   strategic plans   31–5
   structure   33–4
outcome evaluation methods   244–6, 256
outcomes   70
output evaluation methods   244–6, 256
outputs   15
outtake measurements   246

Pascale, Richard   210
persuading   10, 39, 178, 183
PEST analysis   xviii
Peters, Tom   211
Petronzio, Matt   168
Petty, Richard   183
Phuket Has Been Good To Us   240–1
Pittman, B.   136, 139
podcasts   155
PR Daily   165
PR Daily Extra   255
PR Daily News Feed   255
PR NEWS   129
PR NEWSWIRE   129
PR Today: The Authoritative Guide to Public Relations (Morris & Goldsworthy)   134
practice   1
practise   1
practitioners   1, 116
   pitfalls   136–7
presentations   187–8

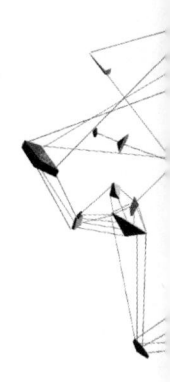

press agentry   45, 97, 115
Prince, The (Machiavelli)   22
PRism   255
privacy   159
probability   xx, xxi
problem recognition   81, 97
profiles   115, 154
project checklist   xxii, xxiii, xxiv, 231
project management   230–6
prominence   117, 247
propaganda   94
proximity   117
public information model   6, 45, 97
Public Opinion (Lippmann)   83
Public Opinion Quarterly   83
public relations
    as communications driver   25
    as corporate conscience   37
    definitions   2–3, 5
    jobs   3–6
    matrix   66–8
    organisational decision making   32–3
    organisational position   33–5
    programs   66–8
    as strategic function   22–3
    tasks   4–5, 14
    theoretical basis   28, 38–9, 80–6
Public Relations Institute of Australia   2, 37, 55
    Golden Target Awards   95, 105, 218, 248
Public Relations Institute of Australia (ACT) Student Challenge   58
Public Relations Institute of New Zealand (PRINZ)   55
Public Relations Review   255
Public Relations Society of America   2, 23, 55
publics   81
punctuation
    apostrophes   13, 18
    commas   25
    importance   35

Putting the Public Back in Public Relations (Sollis & Breakenridge)   148

qualitative research   50, 55
quantitative research   50
question and answer (QnA) sheets   114–15, 193–4, 199, 201, 207
quotes, use of   126, 135, 142

Ramsey, Alan   26
rarity   117
reach   43, 247
reduplication   185
Reed Weir Communications Pty Ltd   248
reference books   123
reflection   41, 141
relationships
    definition   14
    with management   35–6
report writing   222
Repper, Fred   75
reputation   14
research for public relations   49–55
response sheets   115
rhetoric   178
Robson, Prue   166
Rowlands, Harry   229
Russell, Bertrand   259–60

Saikal, Amin   203
salaries   235
Saturday Paper, The   203
Sceptical Essays (Russell)   259
Seitel, Fraser   10, 31
Shannon, Claude   81
Shannon–Weaver model   81
share of voice   247
Short Message Service (SMS)   167
Siapera, Eugenia   148
SIDS and Kids   60
significance   117

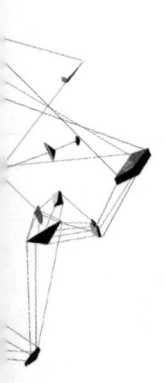

INDEX

Simmons, Peter   245
Sinickas, Angela   217
Sison, Marianne   3, 63–5, 184
situation analysis
   definitions   14, 48, 56
   for staff communication   214
   for strategic plan   87
   writing   56–9
Situational Theory (Grunig)   80–1, 97–8
Sky News   111
Slater, Anny   37
Smail, Neil   95–6
Smith, Dick   223
Smith, Ronald   70, 244
Snapchat   146
social exchange theory   98
social media
   attachments   158–9
   benefits   152–3
   broad applications   146–7, 152
   capabilities   149–50
   etiquette   151, 158, 166
   graphics   172
   journalists views of   129, 139
   media releases   121
   peer-to-peer communication   148
   political uses   146–7
   as public relations tool   43–5
   reacting to others   168
   speed of communication   148
   target publics   83, 167
   usefulness of statistics   153, 166
   videos   172
   writing for   153–9, 165–73
software tools   173
Sollis, Brian   148
South China Morning Post, The   20
Spectator, The   203
speech planning worksheet   xxvii–xxviii

speeches
   as public relations tool   178–80
   speakers   179–82, 184, 187
   written copy   141
speechwriting   177, 179–86
spelling   12–13, 19–20, 35, 142–3, 165
Spicer, Catherine   129–30
Spicer, Sean   137, 147
'spin doctors'   137
sponsorship   44, 46, 100
staff meetings   216–17
staff newsletters   213, 215–16
Stanton, Richard   10, 153
Sternin, Jerry   210
strategic plans
   corporate   30–1, 33–5
   elements   48
   evaluation   68–9, 243–54
   implementation   119
   messages   87–9
   overview   7–9, 47–9
   'why', 'what', 'who', 'how', 'with', 'when'   87–8
   writing   66–8
strengths, weaknesses, opportunities and threats (SWOT) analysis   xix, xx, 59, 91
style guides   12
Style Manual for Authors, Editors and Printers   25, 123
sub-editors   111, 122
submissions   223–4
summative research   49
Sutherland, Karen   166
Sydney Morning Herald, The   229
Synnott, G.   184
systems theory   3, 84, 97
Szondi, György   63, 244

'talent', the   140–1
talking points   199, 201

target publics
    classification   40
    definitions   5, 13, 48
    direct access via email   153
    focus of strategic plan   87
    identifying   74–5
    listening to   25
    primary   73, 121
    relationships with   36, 39
    secondary   73
    social media   167
    status of publics   82
    tertiary   73, 109
    types of   81–2
target-to-story ratio   247
terminology   13–15
Theilmann, Rüdiger   244
think tanks   54–5
Thrush, Glenn   137
time management   xix
timelines   15, 231–2
Times, The   20
tonal analysis   247
toolkit   xviii–xxix
tools, public relations   43–6, 87, 100, 193
trade shows   188
trendiness   118
TrendKite   244
Trump, Donald   93, 137, 139, 146–7
trust   139
Twitter   50, 146–7, 166–7, 171
two-factor theory   85, 212
'two-step flow' theory   203
two-way symmetrical model   38, 45–6, 97, 100, 160, 213
Twuffer   171
Tye, Ray   58
Tymson, Candy   24
Typology of Publics (Hallahan)   80

Understanding New Media (Siapera)   148
United Nations   207
universities as research resources   54
University of Leicester Press Office   144–5, 169
University of Southern California in Los Angeles   163
Usborne, Nick   168

Vatican releases   132, 167
Vaughn, Roy   23, 35
Verèiè, Ana Tkalac   136
videos   155, 172
    scriptwriting   xxix, 174–6
Volkmann, Fred   26
Vroom, Victor   86, 212

Wakefield, Robert   64
Walker, Max   179, 189–91
Walter and Eliza Hall Institute of Medical Research   163
Waterman, Robert   211
Watson, Don   12, 180, 184
Watson, Tom   245
websites
    as communication tools   151–2, 167–9
    design   151
    internal within organisations   213, 217–20
    navigation headings   205
    as online newsroom   201
    templates   155
    transparency   161
White, Patrick   9–10
Wilcox, Dennis   72
Williams, Roy   10
Wood, Douglas   95–6
Wood, Emma   31, 34
Wood, J.   184
Work and Motivation (Vroom)   86
workplace satisfaction   85–6
World Advertising Research Centre   53

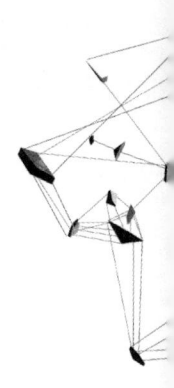

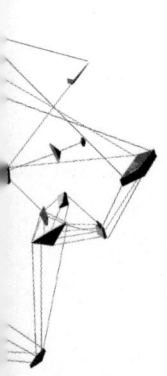

World Wildlife Fund   91, 94–5
writing
    backgrounders   197–8
    brochures   195–7
    clarity   9–13, 19, 35
    definite articles in newspaper titles   203
    emails   157–9
    evaluation plans   250–2
    fact sheets   198–9
    file notes   223
    like a journalist   110
    memos   222–3
    question and answer (QnA) sheets   199
    reference texts   18–19
    reports within organisations   222
    shortening sentences   194
    for social media   153–9, 165–73
    style   142
    style guides   12
    submissions   223–4
    synonyms   20–1
    talking points   199
    video scriptwriting   xxix, 174–6
    see also media releases

Xavier, Robina   244

YouTube   146, 166, 172, 174

Zawawi, Clara   35